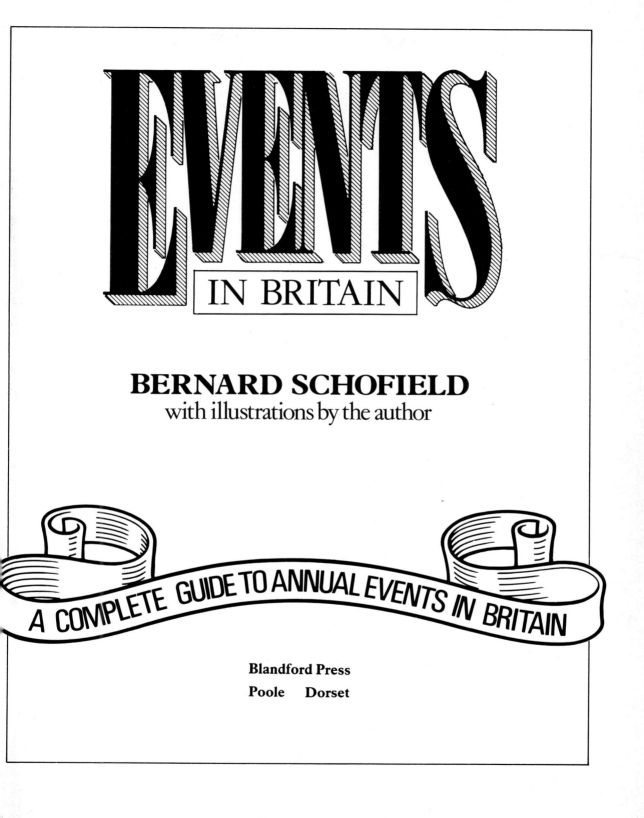

EVENTS

IN BRITAIN

BERNARD SCHOFIELD

with illustrations by the author

A COMPLETE GUIDE TO ANNUAL EVENTS IN BRITAIN

Blandford Press

Poole   Dorset

AN IMPORTANT MESSAGE FOR READERS

Every care has been taken to ensure the accuracy of the details regarding the events which appear in this book and to the best of our knowledge this information was correct at the time of preparation. We suggest that readers who intend making a special visit to see an event should double-check the date and location by contacting the nearest Tourist Information Centre (see rear of book) or Tourist Information Officer of the local Borough Council in question. We regret we cannot accept responsibility for any changes or cancellations.

ACKNOWLEDGEMENTS

Sincere thanks are given to the many contributors to this book. I particularly wish to thank Andy Pittaway and everyone at Walkaways Studio; Irene, Linda McDonnel and the Northern Ireland Tourist Board; Jane Davies, Ray Moller, Martin Cartwright.
Photo Credits:
British Tourist Authority; Home Counties Newspapers; Shuttleworth Collection; E.C. Payne; Bucks Free Press; Bucks County Press; Cambridge Evening News; Nick Lyons; Peterborough Advertiser; Cheshire Chronicle Series; Cheshire News Series; Robert Rostrow; Mr. Tremain; Cumbrian Newspapers; Derbyshire Times; Devon Express & Echo; Waverley Photographs; Harry Green; Arthur Grant; North of England Newspapers; Sunderland Echo; Bristol Evening Post; Cheltenham Festival Society; Stroud News & Journal; Hampshire Chronicle; Portsmouth & Sunderland Newspapers; Madley Festival Society; Hereford Times; Berrow Newspapers; Herts Evening Post; Folkstone Herald;
Kentish Express; Eastern News; Faversham News; Lancs Evening Post; Blackpool Gazette; Market Harborough News; Kentish Independent; P.R. Lange; Northamptonshire Newspapers; Newark Advertiser; Notts Evening Echo; Oxford Mail; Shropshire Journal; Eric Purchase; Jack Beale; Surrey Advertiser; Worthing Gazette; Crawley Advertiser; George Gregory; Salisbury Times; Wiltshire Newspapers; Whitby Gazette; Scarborough Evening News; Scottish Universal Newspapers; Jim Austland; Whyler Photographs; Glenrothes Gazette; G.M. Cowie; Bill Hill; Buchan Observer; Northern Scott; Nairnshire Telegraph; Andrew Smith; D.P. Pearce & Co.; Shetland Times; Scotsman Publications Ltd.; Oban Times; Mr. McKintyre; Viv Shaw; Norman Burnistan; Arbroath Herald; Perth Advertiser; Welsh Tourist Board; W.D. Evans; Martin Caveney; South Wales Argus; J.R. West; Larry Parkinson; Impartial Reporter, J. Sloane; Northern Ireland Tourist Board.

First published in the U.K. 1981 by Blandford Press
Link House, West Street, Poole, Dorset, BH15 1LL

Copyright © 1981 Bernard Schofield

Edited, designed and produced for Blandford Press by The Fieldway Press
Suite 3, 11/13 Broad Court, Covent Garden, London, WC2
(Part of the Countrywide Group, Banbury, Oxon.)

British Library Cataloguing in Publication Data

Schofield, Bernard
  Events in Britain.
  1. Great Britain – Recreational activities
  I. Title
  790'. 0941   GV181.2

ISBN 0 7137 1230 9

Filmset by Bookworm Typesetting, Manchester.
Printed in Hongkong by Mandarin Offset Ltd.

CONTENTS

INTRODUCTION p6

PART 1 : ENGLAND
Bedfordshire p8
Berkshire p12
Buckinghamshire p16
Cambridgeshire p18
Huntingdonshire p22
Cheshire p24
Cornwall p27
Cumberland p31
Westmorland p34
Derbyshire p36
Devon p40
Dorset p45
Durham p49
Essex p52
Gloucestershire p54
Hampshire p59
Isle of Wight p64
Herefordshire p67
Worcestershire p69
Hertfordshire p71
Kent p73
Lancashire p78
Leicestershire p84
Rutland p87
Lincolnshire p88
London p91
Middlesex p97
Norfolk p99
Northamptonshire p102
Northumberland p105
Nottinghamshire p108
Oxfordshire p111
Shropshire p115
Somerset p118
Staffordshire p123
Suffolk p126
Surrey p129
Sussex p132
Warwickshire p136
Wiltshire p140
Yorkshire p143
PART 2 : SCOTLAND
Berwickshire p150
Peebles-shire p152
Roxburghshire p154
Selkirkshire p156
Clackmannanshire p157

Stirlingshire p158
Dumfries-shire p160
Kirkcudbrightshire p161
Wigtownshire p162
Fife p163
Aberdeenshire p166
Banffshire p168
Kincardineshire p169
Morayshire p171
Caithness p173
Inverness-shire p174
Nairnshire p176
Ross & Cromarty p177
Sutherland p178
Orkney & Shetland p180
East Lothian p182
Midlothian p183
West Lothian p186
Argyllshire p188
Ayrshire p190
Buteshire p193
Dumbartonshire p194
Lanarkshire p196
Renfrewshire p198
Angus p200
Kinross-shire p202
Perthshire p203
PART 3 : WALES
Denbighshire p208
Flintshire p210
Cardiganshire p212
Carmarthenshire p213
Pembrokeshire p215
Glamorganshire p217
Monmouthshire p220
Caernarvonshire p222
Merionethshire p224
Brecknockshire p225
Montgomeryshire p228
Radnorshire p230
PART 4 : ULSTER
County Antrim p232
County Armagh p238
County Down p241
County Fermanagh p244
County Londonderry p246
County Tyrone p249

TOURIST INFORMATION CENTRES p251
ACKNOWLEDGEMENTS p256

This calendar of "Events in Britain" presents an astonishingly rich choice of annual occasions in which is mirrored virtually every facet of our national way of life. It is drawn both from the cultural traditions of the past and from those of our modern age; from such grand and auspicious affairs as London's Royal Tournament and the State Opening of Parliament to the competitive fun of local community festivals, and the simple gaiety of countless village carnivals, galas and fêtes.

In this book alone are gathered details of over 1000 festivals, 400 fairs, 200 galas, 300 old customs, 600 horticultural and agricultural shows, and 1500 sporting events. Indeed, if it had been possible to record every single annual event throughout the length and breadth of the United Kingdom, it is more than likely that this book would have been more than twice as long. However, despite the physical limitations of space which has entailed some degree of selectivity, "Events in Britain" does represent the most extensive, comprehensive and informative guide ever compiled.

Britain's long and colourful history, influenced so profoundly by successive influxes of peoples and cultures from beyond our shores, has provided us with a wealth of traditions and customs which, despite the technological advances of the modern age, still play an important role in the everyday lives of ordinary people. On the one hand they govern the working of the highest legislative assembly and are deeply rooted in the administration of the common laws and of local government, while on the other hand there are, in cities, towns and villages everywhere, a surprising number of outwardly strange and colourful annual customs which have particular associations with the religious festivals of long ago.

Of even more ancient origin, and usually deeply rooted in the paganism of long lost cultures, are those quaint customs centred round activities on the land or changes in the seasons – such as ploughing, fertility of crops, May Day, and the harvest. And these in turn have been responsible, either directly or indirectly, for an even greater variety of celebratory or leisure events such as the humble local produce show, the ploughing match, or one of the inumerable spectator sports, games or artistic occasions.

Whether carnival, festival or fête, an annual event is a special, even a great occasion. Whether as a commemoration of past glories, or as a means of marking a contemporary historical occasion, the aim is the same – to give people the opportunity to come together and celebrate the pleasures of a common interest, of a shared enthusiasm. These uniquely British events bring together hundreds of thousands of people from all walks of life every year, to renew their loyalty to that part of our national life, our heritage, which they specially cherish.

The information within the book has been laid out under the county system currently operating in Britain which was introduced during the middle seventies under a massive re-organisation scheme. The new system swept away many old counties with lovely evocative names such as Rutland and Westmorland and each with their own very individual character and cultural history, fusing them into larger impersonal areas under new collective names. Fortunately each of these lost counties still retains its identity and it is for this reason that in the book we have broken each new area down into the old county boundaries.

I therefore hope that the wealth of information within the pages of this book will be of good use to anyone who wishes to discover the pleasures of special events which are there for all to enjoy and that it may inspire others to do the same.

BERNARD SCHOFIELD

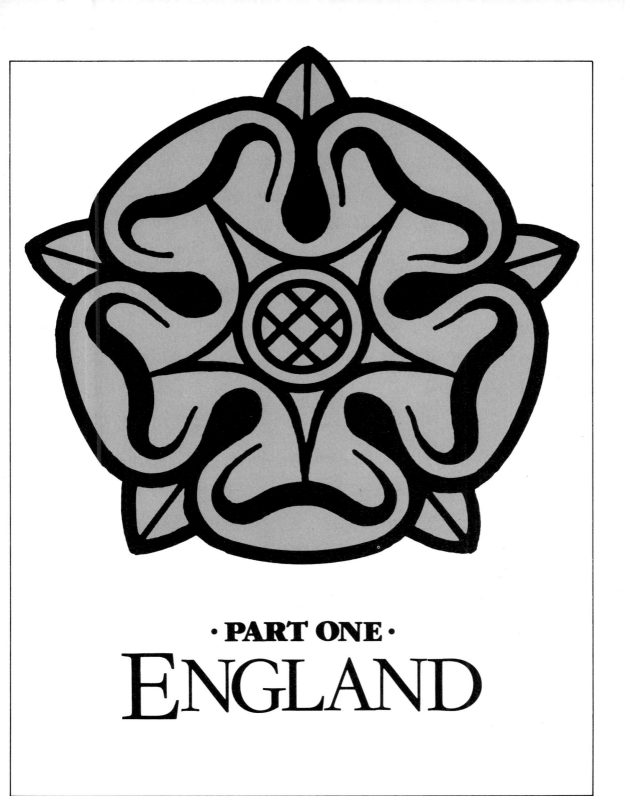

· PART ONE ·
ENGLAND

◆ *Bedfordshire* ◆

CONSTANT·BE

Arlesey, *Arlesey, naughty people*
Sold their bells to build their steeple.
BEDFORDSHIRE FOLK RHYME.

Old Customs

GOOD FRIDAY (IRREGULARLY)
Orange Rolling:
Dunstable Downs, and Pascombe Pit,
Dunstable.
A custom related to egg-rolling of the North
of England and believed to be symbolic of
the stone being rolled away from Christ's
tomb and now carried out by local children.
MAY 1
May Day Celebrations:
Elstow.
A colourful occasion celebrated with
dancing on the village green, the crowning
of the May Queen, and a procession through
the streets.
MAY
Beating the Bounds:
Leighton Buzzard.
MAY – LAST SATURDAY
Ickwell May Day Celebrations:
Ickwell Green.
This Particular May Day has been
celebrated for over four centuries and has a
permanent maypole. Apart from the usual
May Queen, Morris Dancers and other
traditional forms of the May Day
Ceremony, there are two 'Moggies' – i.e. a
man-woman figure and her husband dressed
in rags with blackened faces who take part
in the procession and make a collection.

Festivals

FEBRUARY/MARCH
Bedfordshire Competitive Music
Festival:
Details: Mrs J. Fraser. c/o W. Kreis, 56

Bromham Road, Bedford.
APRIL/MAY
Independent One-act Drama Festival:
The Library Theatre, Luton.
Details: Miss A. Whitley. Festival
Director, c/o Library Theatre, Bridge
Street, Luton.
MAY – 4TH WEEK
Bedford River Festival:
Town Stretch, Bedford.
MAY
Elstow May Festival:
Elstow.
JUNE – EARLY
Flower Festival:
Parish Church of St. Paul, Bedford.
AUGUST – 1ST WEEK
Bedfordshire Country Festival:
Holme Mills, Biggleswade.
AUGUST – 4TH WEEK
Luton Folk Festival:
Luton.
Details: Barry Goodman, 18 Alpine Way,
Sunden Park, Luton.

Fairs

HELD REGULARLY THROUGHOUT
THE YEAR
Antique and Collectors Fair:
Corn Exchange, Bedford.
MARCH 3; APRIL; OCTOBER
Luton Fair:
Luton.
APRIL 21; 22; OCTOBER 12, 13
Bedford Fair:
Bedford.
MAY – 4TH WEEK

Luton Carnival Fair:
Luton Town Centre, George Street,
Luton.
SEPTEMBER
Statty Fair:
Dunstable.

Carnivals

WHITSUN
Biggleswade Carnival:
Biggleswade.
MAY – 4TH week
Luton Carnival:
Town Centre, Luton.
MAY – LATE
Dunstable Carnival:
Dunstable.
AUGUST
Vauxhall Spectacular & Carnival:
Vauxhall Motors Recreation Ground,
Luton.

Agricultural, Horticultural & Breed Shows

JULY
Bedfordshire Agricultural Show:
Bedford,
SEPTEMBER – 1ST WEEK
Luton Show:
Stockwood Park, London Road, Luton.

◆

ICKWELL MAY DAY
The Maypole on Ickwell Green is perhaps
the most celebrated in the country. The May
Day celebrations have been in existence
some four centuries and the tradition of
crowning the May Queen, the Procession
and, of course, the Morris and Maypole
dancing, are still as popular today as ever.
See: OLD CUSTOMS.

⇧
VAUXHALL SPECTACULAR

The giant Vauxhall motor works at Luton stages an impressive line-up of entertainment each year which is primarily for the workers and their families who are employed by the company. The stunt driving shown here is one of many events which include Tug-of-War, Fancy Dress, Country Dancing, Vintage Rally, Fun Fair and Miss Vauxhall competition. See: CARNIVALS.

Motor Racing – May Day Festival of Speed:
Santa Pod Raceway, Podington.
MAY – 3RD WEEK
Beech Hill Blues Tug-of-War Club Open Competitions:
Luton Regional Sports Centre, St. Thomas Road, Stropsley, Luton.
MAY – 4TH WEEK
Luton Junior Tennis Tournament:
Putteridge Recreation Centre, Putteridge Road, Stropsley, Luton.
MAY – 4TH WEEK
Motor Racing – Spring Bank Holiday Big Go:
Santa Pod, Raceway, Podington.
MAY – 4TH WEEK
Luton Cycle Race:
Luton Town Centre, George Street, Luton.

◆
▽ SHUTTLEWORTH FLYING DAY

Interest in ancient forms of transport has increased tremendously over the years and here at the Shuttleworth Collection of Historic Aeroplanes at Biggleswade the annual Air Day attracts enthusiasts from all over the country. See: MISCELLANEOUS.

SPORTS

MARCH – 1ST WEEK
English National Cross Country Championships:
Luton Regional Sports Centre, St. Thomas Road, Stropsley, Luton.
APRIL – 2ND WEEK
Easter International Motor Racing:
Santa Pod Raceway, Podington.
MAY – 1ST WEEK

Regattas:

JUNE – 2ND WEEK
Bedford Head of the Great Ouse and Bedford Regatta:
Town Stretch, Bedford
Details: L. J. Rise, 48 Harpur Street, Bedford.

MISCELLANEOUS

APRIL/MAY
Flying Day:
Shuttleworth Collection of Historic Aeroplanes. Old Warden Aerodrome, Biggleswade.
JUNE – 4TH WEEK
Armstrong Siddeley Owners Club Rally:
Woburn Abbey, Woburn.

JULY – 4TH WEEK
Military Air Pageant Event:
Shuttleworth Collection of Historic
Aeroplanes, Old Warden Aerodrome,
Biggleswade.
AUGUST – 1ST WEEK
Radio Society of Great Britain Rally:
Woburn Abbey, Woburn.
AUGUST – 4TH WEEK
Totternhoe Steam Rally:
Totternhoe, Nr. Dunstable.
SEPTEMBER – 3RD WEEK
Roxton Park Traction Engine Rally:
Roxton Park, Nr. Bedford.
NOVEMBER – 1ST WEEK
Fireworks Fiesta:
Lower Sports Ground, Wardown Park,
New Bedford, Luton.

STATTY FAIR
*An evocative name to one of Bedfordshire's
oldest fairs which, like so many others of
ancient origin, has developed into a fun
fair. See: FAIRS.*

Berkshire ◆

O *Pangbourne is pleasant in sweet summertime,*
And Streatley and Goring are worthy of rhyme;
The sunshine in hot and the breezes are still,
The River runs swift under Baildon Hill.

FROM "THE LADY MINSTREL"
BY ASHLEY-STERRY.

——— OLD CUSTOMS ———

FEBRUARY – SHROVE TUESDAY
Pancake Races:
Newbury.
FEBRUARY – SHROVE TUESDAY
Pancake Races:
Hungerford.
MARCH
Dame Elizabeth Marvyn Charity:
Ufton Court.
From the time of her death in 1581, Dame
Elizabeth Marvyn made provision in her
will for the 'poor people of the Parish of
Steeple Langforde, Wylye and Tysburye'.
The distribution takes place from the
downstairs window in Ufton Court in the
form of a loaf of bread per head to every
home of an agricultural worker, and a loaf
to every other home in the parish. Nine old
age pensioners also receive a pair of sheets.
GOOD FRIDAY
Maidservants Charity:
Reading
Britain's oldest surviving charity takes
place in St. Mary's Church House where
three girls who have proved to have served
well in a Reading household over a period
of five years each cast lots for the sum of
twenty nobles, as decreed by John Blagrave
in his will of 1611.
EASTER SUNDAY
Clipping the Church:
Radley.
EASTER – TUESDAY FOLLOWING

Hocktide
The day when Hungerford elects its Bailiff,
Feoffes, Tutti Men, Portreeve and other
officials of the 'Hockside Court', a day
originally recognised for paying rents and
other dues. The ceremonies begin with a
bugle call on a horn dating back to 1634.
JUNE – SATURDAY NEAREST 4TH
The Glorious Fourth of June:
Eton College, Eton.
The traditional speech day at Eton, which
coincides with the birthday of George III,
one of the College's most beneficial patrons.
JUNE – 4TH WEEK
Garter Ceremony:
Windsor.
This ceremony dates back to the 14th
century and is attended by the Queen at St.
George's Chapel where a service is held for
the Order of the Garter, the highest order of
chivalry. Following the service there is a
procession of the Knights of the Order, the
Yeomen of the Guard, and the Household
Cavalry.
JULY – MID
Swan-upping:
The River Thames – Walton to Windsor;
Walton to Windsor; Windsor to Marlow;
Marlow to Sonning; Sonning to
Whitchurch; Wargrave to Cookham.
Swan-upping (correctly, 'swan-hopping')
was formerly a sport in which the birds were
captured, not without some considerable risk
to the captors. Nowadays this custom is

restricted to a census of the birds (i.e. by the
placing of distinctive markings on the beaks
of cygnets) which belong to the Queen and
two City of London Companies – the Royal
Swanhead and the Swan Wardens of the
Dyers and Vintners. A flotilla of decorated
skiffs crewed by boatmen in distinctive
costumes proceed up river from City to the
various stretches of the Thames where the
census is carried out.
NOVEMBER – SATURDAY NEAREST
30TH (ST ANDREWS DAY)
Eton Wall Game:
Eton College, Eton.
This 11-a-side game of football between the
Collegers (scholarship boys who live in the
College) and the Oppidans (those who live
outside) is played on a narrow field with the
goals being a tree and a gate. Scrimmages
are played against a high wall running
alongside the field and goals are rarely
scored.
DECEMBER – (TRIENNIAL)
Aldermaston Candle Auction:
Aldermaston.
Dating back to 1801 this particular candle
auction was used to raise money for a piece

◆

HUNGERFORD PANCAKE RACES
Along with the Shrovetide races at
Newbury this traditional event is a
well-loved local custom. The competitors
are seen here warming up for the first race.
See: OLD CUSTOMS.

HOCKTIDE
The various dignitaries, including the
Mayor, who attend the ancient 'Hocktide
Court' at the Town Hall, Hungerford, are
seen here leaving after the proceedings. See:
OLD CUSTOMS.

of ground called Church Acre, which is paid into the church fund every year for a three year period.

FESTIVALS

MARCH
Woodley Festival of Music & Arts:
Woodley.
Details: Mrs. J. Telfer & Mrs. S. Pullen, c/o 2 Nightingale Road, Woodley.
MARCH/JUNE
Tilehurst Eisteddfod:
Tilehurst.
Details: R. H. Downing, 15 Wardle Avenue, Tilehurst, Reading.
APRIL
Newbury & District Music Festival:
Newbury.
Details: Mrs. T. Morrish, Wayside Cottage, Kintbury, Newbury.
MAY – 4TH WEEK (BIENNIAL)
Details: Cookham Festival Society, The Malt Cottage, School Lane, Cookham.
MAY
Newbury Spring Festival:
Newbury.
Details: Helen Gale, 52 Evendons lane, Wokingham.
JUNE – 4TH WEEK
Berkshire Midsummer Folk Festival:
Whitehouse Farm, Spencers Wood, Nr. Reading.
JUNE
Reading Summer Festival of Arts:
The University and other venues, Reading.
JULY – 2ND WEEK
Bracknell Jazz Festival:
Bracknell.
Details: Bracknell Folk Festival, South Hill Park, Bracknell.
JULY – 2ND WEEK
Bracknell Folk Festival:
Bracknell.
Details: Bracknell Folk Festival, South Hill Park Arts Centre, Bracknell.

READING SHOW
Though once primarily an agricultural event the Reading Show has developed over the years into a family entertainment spectacular similar in content to many other town shows throughout Britain. See: SHOWS.

READING CARNIVAL
The multi-racial quality of Reading's annual carnival ensures a high standard of creativity in the costumes and floats. The event is one of the highlights of the year for residents. See: CARNIVALS.

JULY – 3RD WEEK
Bracknell Festival of English Music:
Bracknell.
Details: Bracknell Folk Festival, Douth Hill Park, Bracknell.
JULY – 4TH WEEK
Flower Festival:
Eton College Chapel, Eton.
JULY
Bracknell Beer Festival:
Bracknell.
SEPTEMBER – 3RD OR 4TH WEEK
Windsor Festival:
Windsor Castle & Eton College.
Details: Artistic Director, Windsor Festival Society Ltd., Dial House, Northcroft Road, Egham, Surrey.
OCTOBER/NOVEMBER
Maidenhead Music Festival:
Maidenhead.
Details: R. W. R. Oakes, 46 Walker Road, Maidenhead.

—————**FAIRS**—————

HOLY THURSDAY; JULY 5; SEPTEMBER 4; THURSDAY AFTER OCTOBER 11
Newbury Fair:
Newbury.
FEBRUARY 2; MAY 1; JULY 25; SEPTEMBER 21
Reading Fair:
Reading.
JUNE – 4TH WEEK
Victorian Fair:
Batchelor's Acre, Windsor.
OCTOBER (MICHAELMAS)
Newbury Michaelmas Fair:
Newbury.
OCTOBER (MICHAELMAS)
Abingdon Michaelmas Fair:
Abingdon.
NOVEMBER – MID
Cottage Industry Craft Fair:
Corn Exchange, Market Place, Newbury.

—————**CARNIVALS**—————

JUNE
Wallingford Carnival:
Wallingford.
WHITSUN
Abingdon Carnival:
Abingdon.
SUMMER
Reading Carnival:
Reading.
Details: Dr. I. Vinall, Reading Council for Community Relations, 46 Caversham Road, Reading, RG1 7AZ.

—————**GALAS**—————

JULY – 4TH WEEK
Beenham Gala:
Beenham Park, Beenham.

—————**PAGEANTS**—————

JULY –(IRREGULARLY)
Maidenhead Pageant:
Grenfell Park, Maidenhead

—————**AGRICULTURAL,**—————
& HORTICULTURAL &
—————**BREED SHOWS**—————

JUNE – 4TH WEEK
Windsor Championship Dog Show:
Home Park, Windsor Castle, Windsor.
JULY – 1ST WEEK
Royal Windsor Rose & Horticultural Show:
Home Park, Windsor Castle, Windsor.
AUGUST – 3RD WEEK
Reading Show:
Kings Meadow, Reading.
AUGUST – 4TH WEEK
Littlewick Show:
Maidenhead.
SEPTEMBER – 2ND WEEK
Richmond Championship Dog Show:
Ascot Racecourse, High Street, Ascot.
SEPTEMBER – 3RD WEEK
Newbury Agricultural Show:
Henwick Court, Newbury.

—————**SPORTS**—————

FEBRUARY – 2ND WEEK
Horse Racing – Whitbread Day:

⌂
MAIDENHEAD PAGEANT
Once a regular event, this Pageant is now sadly presented rather irregularly. It is a striking and colourful occasion which traces the history of the town from Roman times up to the modern day. See: PAGEANTS.

◆

Ascot Racecourse, Ascot.
MAY – 2ND WEEK
Royal Windsor Horse Show:
Home Park, Windsor Castle, Windsor.
JUNE – 1ST WEEK
Holyport Fair Committee Open Tug-Of-War Competitions:
Holyport Village Green, Holyport
JULY – 4TH WEEK
Horse Racing – Crown plus Two Apprentice Championships (Fri.) Diamond Day. The King George VI & The Queen Elizabeth Diamond Stakes (Sat.):
Ascot Racecourse, Ascot.
JUNE – LATE
Reading Chronicle Horse Show:
Prospect Park Bath Road, Reading.
SEPTEMBER – 2ND WEEK
World Carriage Driving Championships:
Smith's Lane, Windsor Great Park, Windsor.
SEPTEMBER –4TH WEEK
Horse Racing – Hoover Day (Thur.) Charity Day (Fri.) Cavendish Cape Day (Sat.):
Ascot Racecourse, Ascot.

◆ *Buckinghamshire* ◆

VESTIGIA NULLA RETRORSUM

Grendon Underwode
The dirtiest town that ever stode.
OLD RHYME

────── OLD CUSTOMS ──────

FEBRUARY – SHROVE TUESDAY
Pancake Day Race:
Olney.
This particular race is one of Britain's oldest and dates back to 1445.
MAY
Weighing-in Ceremony:
High Wycombe.
A curious ceremony which celebrates the appointment of the new mayor and mayoress. Outside the Guildhall the new mayor and mayoress followed by the ex-mayor and ex-mayoress, and any other officials joined to the office, are weighed and recorded by the chief Inspector of Weights & Measures. The weights are then read out by the beadle who rings his bells and cries "Oyez! Oyez! Oyez!" The custom is thought to originate from the possible censureship of corpulent councillors of ages past.
JUNE/JULY – SUNDAY NEAREST TO ST. PETER'S DAY
Hay Strewing Ceremony:
St. Peter & St. Paul Parish Church, Wingrave, Nr Aylesbury.
Hay is strewn between the aisles and pews on the Feast Day of St. Peter in a ceremony similar to many other grass, hay, and rush-bearing ceremonies throughout Britain. Their principle purpose in ancient times was to keep what were then mud floors, dry, clean and warm for worshippers.
NOVEMBER 11
Firing the Poppers:
Fenny Stratford.
The custom of firing six large and ancient guns at set intervals throughout the day first began in 1760 after the death of the Lord of the Manor, as an added attraction to the annual parish feast.

────── FESTIVALS ──────

FEBRUARY
Milton Keynes Festival of the Arts:
Milton Keynes.
Details: Festival Director, Teresa Collard, Borough of Milton Keynes, Civic Offices, 1 Saxon Gate East, Central Milton Keynes.
FEBRUARY
Milton Keynes Brass Band Festival:
Milton Keynes.
MARCH
Wycombe Arts Festival:
High Wycombe.
Details: 7 Telford Way, High Wycombe, HP13 5EB
MARCH/MAY
Chalfont St. Peter Arts Festival:
Chalfont St. Peter.
Details: Mrs. A. Colley, The Druids, 63 Copthall Lane, Chalfont St. Peter.
MAY/JULY
Wavendon Festival Season:
Wavendon.
Details: Wavendon Season Office, Old Rectory, Stockwell Lane, Wavendon, Milton Keynes, MK17 8LT.
JUNE/JULY
Willen Festival:
SSM Priory, Willen, Milton Keynes.
JULY – 4TH WEEK
Festival of Flowers:
Hartwell House, Aylesbury.
SEPTEMBER
Wooburn Festival:
Wooburn.
Details: Festival Administrative Director, 48 Wooburn Manor Park, Wooburn Green.
OCTOBER – EARLY
Little Missenden Festival of Music and the Arts:
Little Missenden, Nr. Amersham.
NOVEMBER
Buckingham & District Festival Of Music & Drama:
Buckingham.
Details: Miss H. J. Kimberley. The Vicarage, Buckingham, MK18 1BY.
NOVEMBER
Chesham Arts Festival:
Chesham.
Details: Miss P. R. Tamkin, 21 Hampden Avenue, Chesham.

────── FAIRS ──────

FRIDAY AFTER JANUARY 18; SATURDAY BEFORE PALM SUNDAY; 2ND SUNDAY IN MAY; JUNE 14; 1ST SUNDAY IN AUGUST; 4TH SUNDAY IN OCTOBER; OCTOBER 12; 2ND WEDNESDAY IN DECEMBER
Aylesbury Fair:
Aylesbury.
JUNE – EARLY
Country Fair:
The Bowl, Central Milton Keynes.
SEPTEMBER – MONDAY & TUESDAY BEFORE 29TH
High Wycombe Fair:
High Wycombe.

OLNEY PANCAKE RACES
These famous Shrovetide races attract hundreds of spectators on Pancake Day. The ancient Olney Pancake Bell heralds the start of the races which take place in the High Street and only ladies residing permanently in the town and wearing skirts, aprons and scarves are eligible to enter. See: OLD CUSTOMS.

WEIGHING-IN CEREMONY
The first ever lady Mayor of Higher Wycombe is ceremonially 'weighed-in' during this unusual custom which is said to date back to the 18th century. See: OLD CUSTOMS.

FAYRES

JUNE – EARLY
Gerard's Cross Summer Fayre:
Gerard's Cross.

FÊTES

AUGUST – 1ST WEEK
Stone United Football Club Annual Fete:
Stone F.C., Stone, Nr. Aylesbury.

AGRICULTURAL, HORTICULTURAL & BREED SHOWS

AUGUST – 3RD WEEK
Lavingdon Show
Lavingdon Recreation Ground, Lavingdon.
AUGUST – 4TH WEEK
Chalfont St. Giles Show:
Stone Meadow, Chalfont St. Giles.
SEPTEMBER – EARLY
Buckinghamshire County Show:
Hartwell Park, Aylesbury.

SPORTS

APRIL – 2ND WEEK
B.S.A.D. Swimming Gala:
Stoke Mandeville Stadium, Harvey Road, Aylesbury.
JUNE – 3RD WEEK
Long Distance Swimming Trials:
Willen Lake, Milton Keynes.
AUGUST – 2ND WEEK
Prairie Boys Tug-Of-War Club Annual Open Competition:
Temple Farm, Brill, Nr. Aylesbury.

Regattas:

JUNE – 3RD OR 4TH WEEK
Marlow Regatta:
Marlow Bridge, Marlow.
Details: G. Every, Holme Farm, Aston, Henley-on-Thames.

MISCELLANEOUS

JULY – 1ST WEEK
The Chilterns Steam Rally:
Magpie Lane, Coleshill, Nr. Amersham.
JULY – 4TH WEEK
National Street Van Association Truck-In:
Cowley Lodge, Twyford.
Details: Roger Pocock, 15 Vicarage Close, Steeple Claydon.
SEPTEMBER – 1ST WEEK
Brill Working Steam Rally:
Temple Farm, Brill, Aylesbury.

◆ Cambridgeshire ◆

SAPIENTES · SIMUS

I sing Floods muzled and the Ocean tam'd
Luxurious Rivers govern'd and reclaim'd,
Water with Banks confin'd as in a Gaol
Till kinder sluces let them go on Bail,
Streams curb'd with Dammes like Bridles, taught t'obey
And run strait, as if they saw their way.

FENLAND VERSE.

OLD CUSTOMS

FEBRUARY – SHROVE TUESDAY
Pancake Races:
High Street, Ely.
A popular event in which dignitaries and personalities from the local community often take part including the current Miss Anglia.
MAY – OR MAYDAY WEEK
Mayday Revels:
Corn Exchange and City streets, Cambridge.
JULY
Rose Fair:
St. Peter's Church & Gardens, Wisbech.
This famous event is in fact a strawberry fair and reflects the importance of strawberry cultivation in the area. The fair lasts for a week and includes a flower show, a carnival, and the traditional strawberry market and serving of strawberry teas.

FESTIVALS

MARCH/APRIL
Cambridge Competitive Festival of Music, Speech & Drama:
Cambridge.
Details: D. Buxton, Kett House, Station Road, Cambridge, CB1 2JX.
Cambridge Poetry Festival:
Cambridge.
Details: Cambridge Poetry Festival, 1 Queensway, Trumpington Road, Cambridge, CB2 2AX.
JULY
Cambridge Folk Festival:
Cherry Hinton Hal Grounds, Cherry

Hinton Road, Cambridge.
Details: Cambridge Folk Festival, Amenities & Recreation Dept., Kett House, Station Road. Cambridge, CB1 2JX.
JULY/AUGUST
Cambridge Festival:
Cambridge.
Details: Cambridge Festival Association Ltd., Kett House, Station Road, Cambridge, CB1 2JX.
SEPTEMBER –4TH WEEK
Berrycroft Flower Festival
Methodist Church, Berrycroft.
DEC 24TH – CHRISTMAS EVE
Festival of Carols:
Kings College Chapel, Cambridge.

FAIRS

JUNE 23–26; SEPTEMBER 24
Cambridge Fair:
Cambridge.
2ND THURSDAY IN MAY; JULY 25; 1ST THURSDAY IN AUGUST
Wisbech Fair:
Wisbech.
VARIOUS DATES THROUGHOUT THE YEAR
Antinque & Collectors Fair:
Ely.
MARCH
Whittlesey Spring Fair:
Ely.
APRIL – 3RD WEEK
Antiquarian Bookseller's Fair:
Guildhall, Wheeler Street, Cambridge.

FAYRES

JULY – 2ND WEEK
Victorian Fayre:
Parkers Piece, Cambridge.

CARNIVALS

JUNE – 2ND WEEK
Willingham Carnival
The New Recreation Ground, Willingham.
JULY
Aquafest River Carnival:
River Ouse, Ely.

SHOWS

JUNE – EARLY
Cambridge University Footlights Club Annual Revue:
Arts Theatre, St. Edward's Passage, Cambridge.

AGRICULTURAL, HORTICULTURAL & BREED SHOWS

JANUARY
Mill Lodge Equestrian & Leisure Centre Show:
Mill Lodge, Rectory Road, Outwell, Wisbech.
MAY
Cambridgeshire & Isle of Ely Show:
Ely.

◆

ROSE FAIR (WISBECH STRAWBERRY FAIR)
There is nothing quite so temptingly delicious in the summer as luscious ripe strawberries and at Wisbech's ancient fair prospective strawberry gluttons can indulge to the limit. Apart from the strawberry stalls the week-long event provides a varied presentation of entertainment. See: OLD CUSTOMS.

JUNE — 1ST WEEK
Cottinham Young Farmers Club Heavy Horse Show:
Willingham.
AUGUST — 4TH WEEK
Willingham Horticultural Show:
Willingham.
SEPTEMBER — 4TH WEEK
Annual Nearly New & Produce Sale:
Village Hall, Steeple Morden.
SEPTEMBER — 4TH WEEK
Horse & Dog Show & Gymkhana
Lanwades Park, Kennett, Nr. Newmarket.
SEPTEMBER
Ely Flower Show:
Ely.

SPORTS

JANUARY — 3RD WEEK
Eastern Counties Hockey Championships:
Kelsey Kerridge Sports Hall, Queen Anne Terrace, Gonville Place, Cambridge.
FEBRUARY — 3RD WEEK
Cambridgeshire Senior Open Badminton Championships:
Corn Exchange, Cambridge.
MARCH — 3RD WEEK
Stuart Surridge Hockey Tournament:
Kelsey Kerridge Sports Hall, Queene Anne Terrace, Cambridge.
MAY — 2ND WEEK & SEPTEMBER — 4TH WEEK
The George Ramsey Forty Foot Tug-Of-War Club Gala:
Ramsey Forty Foot Playing Field, Cambridge.
JUNE — 1ST WEEK

◊ RAG DAY
University Rags are well known for the ingenuity and boisterous energy students inject into the proceedings and Rag Day at Cambridge is no exception. Here a champagne breakfast is well under way on one of the city roundabouts. See: MISCELLANEOUS.

MAY DAY REVELS
Fancy dress and a carnival spirit are an integral part of the spring celebrations held in Grantchester Meadows and in the city streets of Cambridge. See: OLD CUSTOMS.

CAMBRIDGE FAIR
The fair is traditionally opened by the Mayor and Mayoress who then take rides on the various events. Free rides are given to children on opening day. See: FAIRS.

Coveney Tug-Of-War Club Annual Competition:
Coveney Playing Field, Cambridge.
AUGUST – 2ND WEEK
Mill Lodge Showjumping Show:
Equestrian Centre, Cambridge.
AUGUST – 2ND WEEK
Palmers Tug-Of-War Gala:
Wimblington Recreational Ground, Wimblington.
OCTOBER – MID
The Town Plate Women's Jockey Race:
Newmarket Race Course, Newmarket.

Regattas:

MAY – 4TH WEEK
Cambridge Regatta:
Stourbridge Common.

◆ MISCELLANEOUS ◆

FEBRUARY
Rag Week:
Cambridge University and throughout the City.
NOVEMBER – SATURDAY PRECEEDING ARMISTICE DAY
Poppy Day:
Cambridge.

◆

ELY HORTICULTURAL SHOW
An impressive array of exhibits fill the hall during a recent annual show. See: SHOWS.

AQUA-FEST RIVER FESTIVAL
For water fans this zany event is essential, either to participate in or simply to watch. Local clubs build pedal powered rafts and compete over a ½ mile stretch of the river in a Battle of the River which includes a liberal use of flour. See: CARNIVALS.

◆

GEORGE RAMSEY FORTY-FOOT TUG-OF-WAR
This premier tug-of-war event is held every year in a playing field of the same name with teams competing from all over the county. See: SPORTS.

PANCAKE RACES
It is not unusual for celebrities to take part in Ely's traditional Pancake Races and here Clement Freud M.P. is obviously in fine form as he competes with the current Miss Anglia. See: OLD CUSTOMS.

◆ Huntingdonshire ◆

UNITED · WE · ADVANCE

Glatton Round Hill,
Yaxley Stone Mill
and Whittlesey Mere
are the three wonders of Huntingdonshire.
16TH CENTURY VERSE.

OLD CUSTOMS

WHIT TUESDAY
Dicing for Bibles:
St. Ives.
In 1675, Dr. Wilde died and in his will he
left provision that the income from £50 be
spent each year on bibles which were to be
given to six girls and six boys who were "of
good report". The bibles are allocated by the
method of casting dice, at 12 o'clock noon.
JULY – SUNDAY NEAREST JULY 15TH
(ST SWITHIN'S DAY)
Rushbearing Ceremony:
St. Mary Redcliffe Church, Old Weston.
The Lord Mayor is welcomed by a fanfare
of trumpets and the church is strewn with
rushes, with a bouquet of flowers placed on
every pew.

FESTIVALS

MAY
Peterborough & District Musical
Competition Festival:
Details: Ms. C.M. Morris, 31 Audley
Gate, Peterborough, PE3 6PG.

FAIRS

JULY 18; NOVEMBER 13
Huntingdon Fair:
Huntingdon.
HOLY THURSDAY; 3RD THURSDAY
AFTER 3RD THURSDAY IN SEPTEMBER;
3RD THURSDAY AFTER OCTOBER 11
St. Neots Fair:
St. Neots.
APRIL – 4TH WEEK
National Pig Fair:
East of England Showground, Alwalton,
Nr. Peterborough.

CARNIVALS

AUGUST
St. Neots Carnival:
St. Neots.
JULY/AUGUST
Huntingdon Carnival:
Huntingdon.

FAYRES

JULY – LATE
Tilbrook Country Fayre:
Kimbolton Castle, Kimbolton.

SHOWS

MAY – 4TH WEEK
East of England Motor Show:
Lilford Hall, Lilford Park, Oundle,
Peterborough.

AGRICULTURAL, HORTICULTURAL & BREED SHOWS

MARCH – 4TH WEEK
National Heavy Horse Show:
East of England Showground, Alwalton,
Nr. Peterborough.
JULY – 3RD WEEK
East of England Agricultural Show:
East of England Showground, Alwalton,
Peterborough.
JULY
Master of Basset Hounds Association
Show:
Peterborough.
JULY
Peterborough Show:
Peterborough.
JULY
Peterborough Royal Foxhounds Show:
Peterborough.
JULY
Ponies of Britain Club Summer Show:
Peterborough.
AUGUST – 3RD WEEK
Ponies of Britain Show:
East of England, Alwalton,
Peterborough.

NATIONAL HEAVY HORSE SHOW
At one time the heavy horse featured strongly in the lives of men who worked the land and at this show, which is the biggest of its kind in the country; one can enjoy and appreciate the splendour of these majestic beasts who are now largely bred for entertainment purposes. See: SHOWS.

◆ *Cheshire* ◆

JURE · ET · DIGNITATE · GLADII

Man born of England's North
In your eyes waits the cold,
Thickening the taste, leathering the skin,
Deadening the voice, turning the face grim.
Your prime cold-shrunk, soon old.
Dance in the rhythm of the work of your life:
The going back and forth, the pride and the kick,
the sound of the clog on the cobble.
FROM "THE CLOG MORRIS" BY MARYON JEANE.

──── OLD CUSTOMS ────

MAY – 1ST WEEK
May Day Festivities:
Norton Priory, Astmoor, Runcorn.
MAY – SATURDAY FOLLOWING 1ST
Royal May Day:
Knutsford.
First began in 1864, this ceremony includes the crowning of the May Queen, a large procession and 'sand painting' in the streets – i.e. the streets are covered with arabesques and mottos traced in brightly coloured sand, a custom related to the victorious battle won by King Canute in 1017.
JUNE – 1ST THURSDAY
The local female friendly society, which was founded in 1814, walk in procession to the church for a special service, carrying white staves topped with flowers. Following the service tea is served in the nearby hall.
JULY 5TH (OLD MIDSUMMER'S DAY)
Bawming the Thorn:
Appleton Thorn.
The thorn is a living tree growing in the centre of the town. The first thorn planted on this site was said to be an offshoot of the Holy Thorn of Glastonbury, planted in Appleton by Adam de Dutton in 1125. The tree is honoured on Old Mid Summer Day (irregularly) by adorning it with garlands

and ribbons and dancing round it, which appears to have a connection with ancient worship of "guardian trees".
AUGUST – 2ND SUNDAY
Rushbearing Ceremony:
Forest Chapel, Macclesfield.
Locally gathered rushes are strewn over the church floor and during Evensong a special rushbearing hymn is sung, with the sermon preached in the churchyard.
NOVEMBER – EARLY (ALL SOULS DAY)
Souling:
The begging of Soul Cakes or 'Dole Bread' is still practised by children in some places. Long ago the cakes were collected on All Saints Day for the souls of the dead.
NOVEMBER – EARLY
Soul Caking Play:
Antrobus & Comberbach.
A once popular folk play of North Cheshire similar to mummers plays elsewhere, and includes the Hodening Horse or Wild Horse. Now only performed by one group of 'Soulers', it is believed to be a descendant of Marbury Dun.

──── FESTIVALS ────

FEBRUARY
Hazel Grove Musical Festival:
Organiser: Mrs. A. Baldwin, 10 Cedar Road, Woodsmoor, Stockport SK2 7DN.
MARCH
Ellesmere Port Music & Verse Speaking Festival:
Details: H. Smith, 278 Chester Road, Whitby, Ellesmere Port, Wirral, Merseyside.
APRIL – 2ND & 3RD WEEK
Poynton Folk Festival:
The Folk Centre, Park Lane, Poynton, Stockport.
APRIL
Heaton Mersey Music Festival:
Details: Mrs. P. M. Dresser, 10 Pleachway, Heaton Mersey, Stockport SK4 3DR.
MAY
Barthomley Festival:
Organisers: The Rectory, Audley Avenue, Barthomley, Crewe CW2 5PL.
MAY
Alderley Edge Musical Festival:
Organiser: Ms. R. H. Kendal, Norwood Cottage, Macclesfield Road, Alderley Edge.
MAY/JUNE
Cheshire Festival of Music & Drama
Details: Ms. M. Whitehead, Cheshire Community Council, Watergate House, Watergate Street, Chester CH1 2LW.
MAY/JUNE – TRIENNIAL (NEXT ONE 1984)
Macclesfield Arts Festival:
Macclesfield.
Details: 358 Park Lane, Macclesfield SK1 8JU.
JUNE – 4TH WEEK, TO JULY – 1ST WEEK
Chester Festival:
Civic Hall & various local pubs.
Details: c/o Publicity Officer, Council of the City of Chester, Town Hall, Chester CH1 2HJ.
JUNE/JULY – EVERY 5 YEARS (NEXT

BAWMING THE THORN
Children encircle the thorn tree during the ancient ceremony at Appleton Thorn. See: OLD CUSTOMS.

ROYAL MAY DAY
Sand arabesques created in the street are a fascinating part of Knutsford's local May Day celebrations. See: OLD CUSTOMS.

ONE 1982)
Chester Miracle Plays – held during the Chester Festival:
Cathedral Green, Chester.
JULY – 3RD WEEK
Crewe & Nantwich Folk Festival:
Details: Glen Casey, 15 Park Road, Haslington, Nr. Crewe CW1 1TQ.
JULY – 4TH WEEK
Chester Summer Music Festival:
Chester.
Details: Festival Committee Chairman, 6, Northway, Chester.
OCTOBER
Macclesfield Music Festival:
Macclesfield.
Details: J. Walker, 9 Baliol Close, Sutton, Macclesfield.
OCTOBER
Wallasey Art Festival
Wallasey.

FAIRS

1ST WEEK IN JANUARY; 3RD WEDNESDAY IN JANUARY; 1ST THURSDAY IN JANUARY; EVERY 4TH THURSDAY AFTER
Chester Fair:

25

Chester.
EVERY MONDAY
Crewe Fair:
Crewe.
WHIT MONDAY & TUESDAY; 1ST WEEK
IN NOVEMBER
Runcorn Fair:
Runcorn.
JANUARY 1; MARCH 4 & 25; MAY 1;
JULY 9; OCTOBER 23; FEBRUARY 1;
JULY; AUGUST; SEPTEMBER &
DECEMBER
Stockport Fair:
Stockport.
FEBRUARY
Stalybridge Fair:
Stalybridge.
MARCH – MID
Antiques Fair:
Tatton Hall, Tatton Park, Knutsford.

CARNIVALS

MAY – 4TH WEEK
Congleton Carnival:
Congleton Park, Congleton.
JUNE
Wallasey Carnival:
Wallasey.

AGRICULTURAL, HORTICULTURAL & BREED SHOWS

JUNE
Cheshire Agricultural Show:
The Showground, Pulford Drive,
Eccleston, Chester.
JUNE
Cheshire County Show:
Tatton Park, Knutsford.
JULY
Nantwich Agricultural Show
Nantwich.
JULY
North East Cheshire Agricultural Show
Hazel Grove.
AUGUST
**Betley & District Horticultural Society
Show:**
Betley, Crewe.
SEPTEMBER
Altrincham Agricultural Show:
Devisdale.
SEPTEMBER
**Middlewich & District Agricultural
Show**
Middlewich.
SEPTEMBER
Bowdon Agricultural Show:
Bowdon.
OCTOBER
Cheshire Ploughing Match:
Malpas.

⬁
CHESHIRE PLOUGHING MATCH
*Ploughing contests make for a fascinating
insight into the skills of those who work the
land especially when, as shown here, the
heavy horse and plough-share are the tools
of the trade. See: SHOWS.*

CONGLETON CARNIVAL
*Congleton puts on one of the county's most
elaborate carnivals which is always worth
seeing. The picture shows the Congleton
Queen and Princess Rosebud ceremonially
robed for the occasion. See:
CARNIVALS.*

◆ Cornwall ◆

(INCLUDING SCILLY ISLES)

ONE AND ALL

By Tre, Ros, Pol and Pen
You may well know all Cornishmen.
OLD CORNISH SAYING.

──── Old Customs ────

JANUARY 6
Wassailing:
Bodmin.
A New Year's Eve custom still prevailing in Cornwall and other parts of the country, in which a 'Wassail Bowl' of spiced ale is carried through the streets to the accompaniment of festive song and much drinking of health.
JANUARY
Guise Dancing:
Villages throughout Cornwall.
Traditional New Year celebrations of this part of the country.
FEBRUARY — MONDAY OF CANDELMAS WEEK
Shrovetide Hurling:
St. Ives.
The game commences at 10.30 a.m. where the Mayor throws the ball from the wall of the parish church. Whoever holds the ball at noon is declared the winner and receives a small prize.
FEBRUARY — SHROVE TUESDAY & 2ND SATURDAY FOLLOWING
Shrovetide Hurling:
St. Columb Major & St. Columb Minor.
Held every year on Shrove Tuesday, this custom is a relic of the various Shrovetide throwing practises which occurred in old Cornwall and elsewhere. A 'silver' ball is used here and as many as five hundred take part in the game held in the town.
MAY 1 (MAY DAY)
May Day Celebrations:

St. Mary's, Hugh Town, Isles of Scilly.
MAY 1 (MAY DAY)
Hobby Horse Festival:
Padstow.
Traditional rustic bufoonery. Wooden puppet horses are "ridden" by a party of Padstow 'mayers'. They gather by tradition outside the Golden Lion Inn, where the 'Old Oss' is stabled. Procession begins at 11.00 a.m. Originally the custom was thought to ward off invaders.
MAY 8
Furry Dance:
Helston.
This falls on the day of the Feast of the Apparition of St. Michael Archangel, who is patron saint of the Parish. It is called the Furry Day, supposedly Flora's Day, after the garlands worn for the occasion, but this spring festival dance is also thought to have pagan roots and the word "Furry" may be derived from the old Cornish word "feur" which means a fair. Organised by Flora Day Association. Four set dances and 'Hal-an-Tow' revels. Climax comes at noon as Guildhall clock strikes when 150 dancers begin main dance.
JUNE 23
Banishing the Witches:
St. Cleer, Nr. Liskeard.
Held traditionally on Mid Summer's Eve and a leftover from Cornwall's rich and fascinating witching past.
JUNE 23
St. John's Eve Mid Summer Bonfires:
Various places.

This custom is said to have been derived from the attempts in ancient times to increase the power of the sun after Mid Summer's Day and also to combat the forces of evil. Here a succession of bonfires are lit from St. Ives in the West of Cornwall through to the East of the county; the ashes being reserved to form a foundation for the following year's fire.
JULY 25
The Knill Ceremony (Knillian Games):
St. Ives.
Founded by John Mill in 1797, this custom, which occurs on the Feast of St. James the Great every five years (next one: 1986) survives through the deed of trust he drew up. This provides for children to dance at his tomb and sing the Old Hundredth.
AUGUST 10
Furry Dance:
Mousehole, Penzance.
AUGUST — MONDAY FOLLOWING 12TH
Marhamchurch Revel:
Marhamchurch.
August the twelfth is the Feast of St. Marwenne day and the village commemorates this 6th century Celtic saint who is said to have introduced Christianity to the area. A 'Father of Time' crowns the 'Queen of the Revel' and this is followed by a procession through the streets.
AUGUST 24
Blessing of the Mead:
Gulval, St. Mounts Bay.
St. Bartholomew is the patron saint of bee-keepers and honey-makers, so on his day the ceremony of Blessing the Mead (made mainly from honey) is conducted by the Almoner of the Worshipful Company of Mead Makers.

FESTIVALS

MARCH
Cornwall Music Festival:
Details: Ronald Grubb, Reen Cross Farm, Goonhavern, Truro.
MARCH
Roche Victory Hall Music Festival:
Details: Mrs. D. D. Washington, 28 Chapel Road, Roche, St. Austell.
MARCH
Wadebridge Competitive Music Festival:
Details: W. R. Hawke, 37 Glen Road, Wadebridge.
APRIL
Bugle Music Festival:
Details: Mrs. E. M. Pinch, 12 Charles Street, Bugle St. Austell.
APRIL
Penzance Porth-en-Alls Music Festival:
Details: c/o 7 Kempe Road, London, NW6.
EASTER
St. Endellion Easter Festival:
St. Endellion Church, St. Endellion, Nr. Port Isaac.
Details: Festival Organiser, 1c Morpeth Terrace, London, SW1.
MAY
East Cornwall Bach Festival:
Saltash.
Details: D. Pearson, Yeomans, 3 Hollies Road, St. Stephens, Launceston.
MAY – 4TH WEEK
Falmouth Festival:
Details: Mike Smith, Camborne Cottage, Wendron, Helston.
MAY – 4TH WEEK
Music-In-May Festival:
Bude, Stratton.
JUNE – 4TH WEEK, TO SEPTEMBER – 1ST WEEK
Minack Theatre Festival:
Details: The Manager, The Minack Theatre, Porthcurno, Penzance.
JUNE – 4TH WEEK
St. Day Feast Festival:
St. Day.
JUNE
West of England Bandsmen's Festival:
Bugle.
AUGUST – 1ST & 2ND WEEKS
St. Endellion Festival of Music and Drama:

◆

FURRY DANCE
Perhaps the most colourful and entertaining of all English customs – certainly, the most enchanting. Here dancers perform in the main dance of the day. See: OLD CUSTOMS.

St. Endellion Church, St. Endellion, Nr. Port Isaac.
AUGUST – 3RD WEEK
Linkinhorne Annual Folk, Bluegrass & Country Music Festival:
Linkinhorne, Nr. Callington.
AUGUST – LATE
New Cornwall Folk Festival:
Details: Alison Cock, 31 Bawden Road, Bodmin.
SEPTEMBER – 1ST WEEK
The Cornish Gorsedd:
The grounds of the Old Priory, Bodmin.
SEPTEMBER
St. Ives Festival:
Details: Festival Administrator, Guildhall, St. Ives.
SEPTEMBER
St. Ivel Brass Band Festival:
Penzance.

FAIRS

1ST MONDAY EVERY MONTH EXCEPT FEBRUARY MAY & JUNE
Bodmin Fair:
Bodmin.
3RD SUNDAY EACH MONTH
Falmouth Fair:
Falmouth.
EVERY TUESDAY
Launceston Fair:
Launceston.
MARCH 25; SEPTEMBER 8; 4TH THURSDAY IN NOVEMBER
Penzance Fair:
Penzance.
WEDNESDAY AFTER MID-LENT; WHIT MONDAY; NOVEMBER 19; DECEMBER 8
Truro Fair:
Truro.
JULY
Praze Fair:
Praze.
SEPTEMBER – EARLY
Helston Harvest Fair:
Lake Park & Market, Helston.
SEPTEMBER – LATE
Bude Fair:
Bude.
SEPTEMBER
Summercourt Fair:
Summercourt.

FAYRES

AUGUST – 2ND WEEK
Polgooth Fayre:
Polgooth.

FÊTES

JUNE – 1ST WEEK
Mousehole A.F.C. Fête:

The Playing Field, Paul Lane, Mousehole, Nr. Penzance.
AUGUST – 1ST WEEK
Chaplaincy Garden Fête:
The Chaplaincy, St. Mary's, Isles of Scilly.
AUGUST – 2ND WEEK
Tresco Fête:
The Abbey Green, Tresco, Isles of Scilly.

CARNIVALS

MAY – 4TH WEEK
Millbrook Carnival:
Millbrook, Torpoint.
MAY – 4TH WEEK
Newquay Carnival:
Newquay.
JUNE
Mevagissy Feast Week:
Mevagissy.
JULY – 3RD WEEK
Mousehole Carnival:
Mousehole to Penzance. Nr. Penzance.
AUGUST – 4TH WEEK
Cross Country/Fêtes/Carnival:
Castle Grounds and Lower Wharf, Bude.
AUGUST – 4TH WEEK
Isles of Scilly Carnival:
Hugh Town and Garrison, Hugh Town, Isles of Scilly.
SEPTEMBER – 1ST WEEK
Falmouth Carnival Week:
Falmouth.

AGRICULTURAL, & HORTICULTURAL & BREED SHOWS

MARCH – 3RD WEEK
West Cornwall Spring Show:
St. John's Hall, Alverton Street, Penzance.
MARCH – 3RD WEEK
Spring Flower Show:
Falmouth.
MARCH
St. Mary's Spring Flower Show:
St. Mary's Isles of Scilly.
JUNE – 2ND WEEK
Royal Cornwall Show:
Wadebridge.
JULY – 3RD WEEK
Lanivet Agricultural Association Show (Horse & Horticultural Show):
Forde Farm, Bodmin.
JULY
St. Mary's Summer Flower Show:
St. Mary's, Isles of Scilly.
AUGUST – 1ST WEEK
Falmouth Horse Show:
Falmouth.

SHROVETIDE HURLING
As many as five hundred participants congregate in the streets of St. Colomb for this famous Shrovetide game. See: OLD CUSTOMS.

ROYAL CORNWALL SHOW
The supreme champions are put through their paces in the Parade of Beasts at Cornwall's major agricultural show. See: SHOWS.

SPORTS

MARCH — 2ND WEEK
Creadow Tug-Of-War Club Match:
Playing Field, Lostwithiel.
Details: I. Giles. 32 St. Julita, Luxulyan, Bodmin.
JUNE — 1ST WEEK
Warbstow Tug-Of-War Club Annual Tournament:
Church Town Farm, Warbstow.
JUNE — 1ST WEEK
White Hart, St. Teath Annual Tug-Of-War:
St. Teath, Bodmin.
JUNE — 3RD WEEK
Surf Coast Cruisers' Summer Run:
Clowance Hotel, Praze-an-Beeble, Nr. Camborne.
JULY — 4TH WEEK
Start of Tall Ships Race to Isle of Man:
Fowey.
AUGUST — 1ST WEEK
Open Golf Tournament:
Falmouth.
AUGUST — 4TH WEEK
National Surf Life Saving Championships of Great Britain:
Praa Sands, Nr. Helston.

Regattas:

AUGUST 3RD WEEK
Falmouth Regatta Week:
Falmouth.
AUGUST — 4TH WEEK
Fowey Royal Regatta & Carnival:
Fowey.

MISCELLANEOUS

JULY — 4TH WEEK
R.N.A.S. Culdrose Air Day:
Naval Air Station, Culdrose, Helston.
AUGUST — EARLY
Donkey Derby:
Bude.
AUGUST — 3RD WEEK
R.A.F. St. Mawgan's International Air Day:
R.A.F. St. Mawgan, Nr. Newquay.

CUMBRIA
◆ *Cumberland* ◆

*Yet once again do I behold the forms
Of these huge mountains, and yet once again,
Standing beneath these elms, I hear thy voice,
Beloved Derwent, that peculiar voice
Heard in the stillness of the evening air,
Half-heard and half-created.*

FROM "THE VOICE OF THE DERWENT"
BY WILLIAM WORDSWORTH

OLD CUSTOMS

GOOD FRIDAY; EASTER TUESDAY &
THE FOLLOWING SATURDAY
Uppies and Downies:
Workington.
*A traditional football game played in the
streets between two teams – "The Uppies
and the Downies'" and very similar to other
football games such as Ashbourne's
"Up'ards and Down'ards" and
Chester-le-Street's "Up-Streeters and
Down-Streeters".*
EASTER
Egg Rolling:
Castlemoat, Penrith.
*Traditional Easter custom in which
coloured eggs are rolled down hills as a
symbolic gesture of biblical origin when the
rock was rolled away from Jesus's tomb.*
SEPTEMBER – SATURDAY NEAREST
18TH
Egremont Crabapple Fair:
Egremont.
An ancient fair dating back to 1267 and
*celebrated with many unusual and
traditional sports, which include climbing a
greasy pole to retrieve a pound note,
scrambling for pennies, pipe-smoking
contests, the best sentimental song contest,
and the World Champion Gurning
Competition in which contestants are
invited to compete with each other by
snarling and distorting their faces into weird
contortions.*

FESTIVALS

FEBRUARY
Millom Musical Festival:
Millom.
*Details: Mrs. K. Bailey, 100 Market
Street, Millom, LA18 4AJ.*
MARCH
Carlisle & District Musical Festival:
Carlisle.
*Details: J. H. Barton, 41 Victoria Road,
Carlisle, CA1 2UE.*
APRIL

Cumberland Rural Choirs Festival:
*Details: High Rigg,
Grange-in-Borrowdale, Keswick.*
MAY
Whitehaven Musical Festival:
Whitehaven.
*Details: Mrs. S. M. Smith, 21 Carlton
Drive, Whitehaven.*
MAY
Lake District Festival:
Various venues throughout the county.
JUNE
**Keswick Festival (Lake District
Festival)**
Keswick.
Details: 28 Highgate, Kendal, LA9 4TB.
JUNE – ALL MONTH
Holme Cultram Abbey Festival:
Holme Cultram Abbey, Abbeytown,
Carlisle.
AUGUST – 3RD WEEK
Brampton Village Festival:
Brampton.
NOVEMBER
Workington Muscial Festival:
Workington.
*Details: Ms. J. Baker, Carnegie Arts
Centre, Finkle Street, Workington.*

FAIRS

1ST SUNDAY IN JANUARY; 3RD
THURSDAY IN MAY; WHIT SUNDAY;
OCTOBER 11; SATURDAY AFTER
OCTOBER 20; MARTINMAS
Keswick Fair:
Keswick.

FEBRUARY 21; SHROVE TUESDAY;
APRIL 23 & 24; WHITSUN;
MARTINMAS; SEPTEMBER 26
& 27
Penrith Fair:
Penrith.
EASTER MONDAY; WHIT SUNDAY;
AUGUST 26; SEPTEMBER 19
Carlisle Fair:
Carlisle.
THURSDAY IN WHIT WEEK; THURSDAY
AFTER NOVEMBER 11
Whitehaven Fair:
Whitehaven.
AUGUST – 1ST WEEK
Lanercost Craft Fair:
Dance Hall, Lanercost.
AUGUST – 1ST WEEK
Lowther Country Fair:
Lowther Castle, Brampton, Nr. Penrith.
AUGUST – 4TH WEEK, TO SEPTEMBER
– 1ST WEEK
Carlisle Great Fair:
Carlisle.
SEPTEMBER – 4TH WEEK
**Cumbria Naturalists Trust Autumn
Fair:**
Mott Hall, Market Place, Keswick.
NOVEMBER – 4TH WEEK
Craft Fair:
Brewery Arts Centre, Kendal.

FÊTES

AUGUST – 4TH WEEK
Eskdale Village Fête:
Outward Bound Mountain School,
Eskdale Green, Holmrook

CARNIVALS

JULY – 2ND WEEK
Maryport & District Carnival Week:
Maryport.
JULY – 2ND WEEK
Millom Carnival Parade:
Millom.

GALAS

JULY – 2ND WEEK
Down-a-Gate Gala Day:
Down-a-Gate Field, Warwick Bridge,
Carlisle.

AGRICULTURAL, HORTICULTURAL & BREED SHOWS

MAY – 4TH WEEK
Fell Pony Society Stallion Show:
Lowther Castle Forecourt, Nr. Penrith.
JUNE – 3RD WEEK
Foxhounds, Beagles & Terrier Show:

Helbeck Road, Brough.
JULY
Cumberland Show:
*Details: Cumberland Agricultural Society,
9 Victoria Place, Carlisle, Cumbria.*
AUGUST – 1ST WEEK
Cockermouth Agricultural Show:
Greenlands, Cockermouth.
AUGUST – 2ND WEEK
Appleby Agricultural Show:
The Barley Field, Brackenber Golf
Course, Appleby.
AUGUST – 2ND WEEK
English National Sheep Dog Trials:
Lowther Park, Lowther.
AUGUST – 2ND WEEK
Fell Pony Society Breed Show:
Brougham Farm, off A6, Nr. Penrith.
AUGUST – 3RD WEEK
Gosforth Agricultural Show:
Gosforth.
AUGUST – 3RD WEEK
**Skelton Horticultural & Agricultural
Society Show:**
Unthank Park, Nr. Skelton, Penrith.
AUGUST – 4TH WEEK
Ennerdale Agricultural Show:
Bowness Knott, Ennerdale.
AUGUST – 4TH WEEK
**Crosby Ravensworth Horticultural &
Agricultural Show:**
Crosby Ravensworth.
AUGUST
Ullswater Sheep Dog Trials:
Penrith.
AUGUST
Penrith Agricultural Show:
Penrith.
SEPTEMBER – 1ST WEEK
Hesket-Newmarket Agricultural Show:
Lane Head Field, Hesket-Newmarket.
SEPTEMBER – 1ST WEEK
Longtown Flower Show:
Memorial Hall, English Street,
Longtown.
SEPTEMBER – 3RD WEEK
**Loweswater & Brackenthwaite
Agricultural Show:**
School Field, Loweswater.
SEPTEMBER – 4TH WEEK
Eskdale Agricultural Show:
Brotherilfield, Boot, Holmrook.
SEPTEMBER
Keswick Agricultural Show:
Keswick.
OCTOBER – 2ND WEEK
Wasdale Agricultural Show:
Wasdale, Nr. Gosforth, Whitehaven.

SPORTS

MAY – 4TH WEEK
Bassenthwaite Moto Cross:
Whittas, Bewaldeth, Nr. Bassenthwaite.

JUNE – 3RD WEEK
**Three Thousand Peaks Marathon
Walk:**
*Details: Rugby Club Baths, Tithebarn
Street, Keswick.*
JULY – 3RD WEEK
**Derwent Water Junior Long Distance
Swimming Championships:**
Derwent Water.
JULY
Keswick Sports Meeting
Keswick.
AUGUST – 1ST WEEK
Combined Driving (Horse) Events:
Lowther.
AUGUST
Bassenthwaite Sailing Week:
Keswick.
DECEMBER – LATE
**Cumbria Junior Open Badminton
Championships:**
Market Assembly Hall, Carlisle.

Regattas:

JUNE
Ullswater Regatta:
Penrith.
AUGUST – 1ST & 2ND WEEK
Bassenthwaite Week Sailing Regatta:
Dubwath, Bassenthwaite Lake.

MISCELLANEOUS

MAY – 2ND WEEK
**Annual Memorial Service & Military
Parade – The King's Own Royal
Border Regiment:**
The Castle, Carlisle.
JULY – 3RD WEEK
Cumbria Vintage Air & Family Event:
Silloth Airfield, Silloth.
JULY
Keswick Convention
The Tent, Skiddaw Street, Keswick.
OCTOBER – 4TH WEEK
Solway Stages Car Rally:
Starts from: Carlisle.
OCTOBER/NOVEMBER
Wigton Horse Sales:
Hope's Auction Mart, High Street,
Wigton.
DECEMBER – 2ND WEEK
**Christmas Fayre Motor Racing
Meeting:**
Rowrah Stadium, Cockermouth.

EGREMONT FAIR
The World Champion Gurning Competition must rate as one of the most bizarre of all annual customs. Contestants, like the winner shown here, compete to create some of the worst pulled faces imaginable. See: OLD CUSTOMS.

WASDALE SHOW
Sheep are synonymous with farming in the hill-lands and mountains throughout Cumberland and the Wasdale Show is an opportunity for farmers to meet and deliberate on the various aspects of their trade. See: SHOWS.

UPPIES AND DOWNIES
Members of the team prepare for the start of the annual football match known affectionately as 'Uppies & Downies', a lively game played on the streets of Workington during Easter. See: OLD CUSTOMS.

ESKDALE VILLAGE FÊTE
The beauty of the Eskdale landscape sets the scene for this local village fête. See: FÊTES.

CUMBRIA
◆ Westmorland ◆

Green leaves were here;
But 'twas the foliage of the rocks—the birch,
The yew, the holly, and the bright green thorn,
With hanging islands of resplendent furze:
And, on a summit, distant a short space,
By any who should look beyond the dell
A single mountain-cottage might be seen.

FROM "IT WAS AN APRIL MORNING"
(EASDALE) BY WILLIAM WORDSWORTH

OLD CUSTOMS

JUNE 29
Warcop Rushbearing Ceremony:
Warcop.
JUNE 29
Brough Rushbearing Ceremony:
Brough.
JULY – SATURDAY NEAREST ST.
ANNE'S DAY
Ambleside Rushbearing Ceremony:
St. Mary's Church, Ambleside.
Rushbearing is a survival of the old
religious custom of strewing the church with
rushes in the days when the floors were of
simple beaten earth. At Ambleside the
rushbearings are carried round the town led
by the town band and at the Market Place
the traditional Rushbearing Hymn is sung.
After the procession and the service in the
church all those who carried bearings are
presented with a piece of gingerbread.
JULY – 1ST SATURDAY
Musgrave Rushbearing Ceremony:
Musgrave, Nr. Brough.
Following the traditional events, tea is
served in the Village Hall and also there are
children's sports.
AUGUST – SATURDAY NEAREST 5TH (ST
OSWALD'S DAY)
Grasmere Rushbearing Ceremony:
St. Oswald's Church, Grasmere.

FESTIVALS

MAY – 3RD WEEK (BIENNIAL)
**Mary Wakefield Westmorland Music
Festival:**
Details: Festival Secretary, 13 Hawsmead
Drive, Kendal.
MAY – 4TH WEEK TO JUNE – 2ND
WEEK
Lake District Festival:
Details: Festival Administration,
'Kirkrigg', Lake Road, Windmere.

JULY — IST WEEK
Appleby-in-Westmorland Charter Festival:
Broad Close Recreation Ground, Public Hall, Appleby.
AUGUST — EARLY
Kendal Jazz Festival
Brewery Arts Centre, Kendal.
AUGUST — 4TH WEEK
Kendal Folk Festival:
Brewery Arts Centre, Kendal.

FAIRS

WHIT SATURDAY; FEBRUARY 22; MARCH 22; APRIL 29; NOVEMBER 8
Kendal Fair:
Kendal.
JUNE — 2ND WEEK
Appleby Horse Fair:
Fair Hill Appleby.
JUNE — 3RD WEEK
Folk & Craft Fair:
Kendal Town Hall, Stricklandgate, Kendal.
JULY — 4TH WEEK
The Cumbria Steam Fair & Gathering:
County Showfield, Appleby Road, Kendal.
JULY OR AUGUST
The Lakeland Antiques Fair:
Belsfield Hotel,
Bowness-on-Windermere.
SEPTEMBER — 4TH WEEK
Brough Hill Gypsy Fair:
Brough.
OCTOBER — 4TH WEEK
Grasmere Antiques Fair:
Grasmere Hall, Grasmere.
NOVEMBER — 4TH WEEK
Craft Fair:
Brewery Arts Centre, Kendal.

FAYRES

JULY — 2ND WEEK
Old Time Market Fayre:
Market Square, Appleby.

FÊTES

Kendal Grammar School Annual Fête
Kendal Grammar School, Burton Road, Kendal.

GALAS

AUGUST — 4TH WEEK
Kendal Gathering Gala:
K.R.U.F.C. Rugby Club Ground, Shap Road, Kendal.

GATHERINGS

JULY — 4TH WEEK
Cumbria Steam Gathering:
County Showfield, Appleby Road, Kendal.
SEPTEMBER — IST & 2ND WEEKS
Kendal Gathering:
Kendal.

AGRICULTURAL, HORTICULTURAL & BREED SHOWS

JUNE — MID
Foxhound, Beagle, & Terrier Show:
Helbeck Road, Brough.
AUGUST — 2ND WEEK
Appleby Agricultural Show:
Barley Field Golf Course, Appleby.
AUGUST — 2ND WEEK
Lonsdale Agricultural Show
Underley Park, Kirkby Lonsdale.
AUGUST — 3RD WEEK
Vale of Rydal Hound Show & Sheepdog Trials:
Rydal Park, Ambleside.
AUGUST — 4TH WEEK
Ambleside Flower, Handicrafts & Produce Show:
St. Anne's Hall, Kirkstone Road, Ambleside.
AUGUST — 4TH WEEK
Dufton Agricultural Show:
Church Field, Dufton Village, Appleby.
AUGUST — 4TH WEEK
Lyth Valley Horse Trials:
Row Farm, Lyth, Nr. Kendal.
AUGUST — 4TH WEEK
Ullswater Sheepdog Trials:
Patterdale, Glenridding.
AUGUST — LATE
Rydal Hound Show (including Sheep Dog Trials):
Rydal Park Ambleside.
AUGUST
Applethwaite Sheepdog Trials:
Windermere.
SEPTEMBER IST WEEK
Appleby & District Gardens, Flower & Vegetable Show.
Public Hall, Market Square, Appleby.
SEPTEMBER — IST WEEK
Lunesdale Foxhounds Show:
Lunesdale, Marthwaite, Nr. Sedbergh.
SEPTEMBER — IST WEEK
Milnthorpe Annual Flower & Vegetable Show:
Secondary School, Haverflats Lane, Milnthorpe.
SEPTEMBER — IST WEEK
Westmorland County Show:
County Showground, Kendal.
SEPTEMBER — 3RD WEEK

Westmorland Horticulatural Society Show:
Market Hall, Market Place, Kendal.

SPORTS

FEBRUARY — IST WEEK
Benson Knott Fell Race:
Kendal Show Ground, Appleby Road, Kendal.
MAY — 4TH WEEK
Appleby Spring Harness Races:
Holme Farm, Holme Street, Appleby.
JUNE — 3RD WEEK
Four 3,000 Peaks Marathon Walk:
Details: R. Union Club, Tithebarn Street, Keswick.
JULY — 3RD WEEK
Primary Schools Athletic Festival:
Longland Boys School Track, Kendal.
JULY — 3RD WEEK
Ullswater Long Distance Swimming Championships:
Lake Ullswater, Glenridding to Pooley Bridge.
JULY — 4TH WEEK
Ambleside Sports Meeting:
Rydal Park, Ambleside.
AUGUST — IST WEEK
The Two-Way Windermere Long Distance Swimming Championships:
Lake Windermere, Waterhead to Lakeside & return.
AUGUST — 2ND WEEK
Levens Sports Gala:
The Pasture, Levens.
AUGUST — 4TH WEEK
Grasmere Sports:
Ambleside.
AUGUST — 4TH WEEK
Brough Harness Racing:
Holm Farm Field, Appleby.
SEPTEMBER — IST WEEK
The Windermere Long Distance Swimming Championships:
Lake Windermere, Lakeside to Waterhead.

Regattas:

JULY — 4TH WEEK
Steam Boat Regatta:
Windermere Steamboat Museum, Rayriggs Road, Windermere.

MISCELLANEOUS

AUGUST — 3RD WEEK
Appleby International Week:
Appleby.
NOVEMBER 5
Great Bonfire & Firework Display:
County Showground, Shap/Appleby Road, Kendal.

◆ *Derbyshire* ◆

BENE·CONSULENDO

Good God! how sweet are all things here!
How beautiful the fields appear!
How cleanly do we feed and lie!
Lord! What good hours do we keep!
*   How quietly we sleep!*
What peace, what unanimity!
How innocent from the lewd fashion
Is all our bus'ness, all our conversation!

FROM "THE RETIREMENT" (DOVEDALE)
BY CHARLES COTTON

——— OLD CUSTOMS ———

FEBRUARY – SHROVE TUESDAY
Shrovetide Football
The Green Man Hotel, Ashbourne.
The teams consist of the 'Up'ards' – those
born north of the Henmore stream – and the
'Down'ards' – those born on the south side.
The game starts at 2.00 p.m. and is akin to
rugby, only with the minimum of rules.
FEBRUARY – SHROVE TUESDAY
Winster Pancake Races:
Winster.
An ancient pancake ceremony dating back
to 1870.
EASTER
Egg Rolling:
Bunkers Hill, Derby.
Traditional Easter custom throughout the
North which symbolises the rolling away of
the rock from Jesus's tomb.
APRIL & OCTOBER
Wirksworth Barmote Court:
Wirksworth.

Barmote Courts are the oldest industrial
courts in England and are held to deal with
matters relating to lead mining and the
ownership of mines.
APRIL & OCTOBER
Eyam Barmote Court:
Eyam.
MAY – 3RD OR 4TH WEEK
Etwall Well Dressing:
Etwall.
As a thanksgiving for the supply of pure
water, panels are erected in this and other
Derbyshire villages around the wells. These
are decorated with leaves, mosses and
flowers pressed into clay to form pictures,
usually on a biblical theme.
MAY – 4TH WEEK
Wirksworth Wells Dressing:
Wirksworth.
MAY 29
Oak Apple, or Garland King Day
Castleton, Nr. Tideswell.
Although this day commemorates the

restoration of King Charles II to the throne
(the symbolism of the tree referring to
Charles's refuge in the oak at Boscobel
following the battle of Worcester), the
ceremony probably has its origins in an
ancient May rite. The present celebrations
featuring a bee-hive posy of wild flowers
carried on horseback includes a procession
headed by a 'King' and 'Lady' followed by
a 'silver band' and a troupe of children who
later dance around the maypole.
JUNE 1
Monyash Well Dressing:
Monyash Village.
JUNE 9–18
Ashford-in-the-Water Well Dressing:
Ashford-in-the-Water.
JUNE 24 (MID SUMMER'S DAY)
Hope Well Dressing:
Hope.
JUNE – 3RD OR 4TH WEEK
Tideswell Wells Dressing & Wakes
Carnival:
Tideswell.
JUNE – 3RD OR 4TH WEEK
Litton Wells Dressing:
Litton.
JUNE – THURSDAY NEAREST 24TH
(MIDSUMMER'S DAY)
Buxton Well Dressing:
Buxton.
JUNE – SATURDAY NEAREST 24TH (ST.
JOHN BAPTIST DAY)
Youlgrave Well Dressing:
Youlgrave.
JUNE – LATE
Breaston Wells Dressing:
Breaston.
JUNE – LATE

Rowsley Wells Dressing:
Rowsley.
JUNE – LATE
Edlaston & Wyaston Wells Dressing:
Edlaston & Wyaston.
JUNE – LATE
Bakewell Royal British Legion Wells Dressing
Bath Gardens, Bath Street, Bakewell.
JULY – 1ST SUNDAY
Alport Castle Woodlands Love Feast:
Ladybower Reservoir, Allport Castle Farm. (Grid Ref: SK 135911)
A religious confirmation ceremony in which the worshippers, following a short service, receive a small piece of cake and a sip of water from the loving cup.
JULY 4 (OLD MID SUMMER'S EVE)
Dore Well Dressing:
Dore
JULY – 3RD OR 4TH WEEKS
Whitwell Wells Dressing:
Whitwell.
JULY – 3RD OR 4TH WEEK
Pilsley Wells Dressing:
Pilsley.
JULY – 3RD OR 4TH WEEK
Stoney Middleton Wells Dressing:
Stoney Middleton.
JULY – 3RD OR 4TH WEEK
Ault Hucknall, Holmewood & Heath Wells Dressing:
Ault Hucknall, Holmewood & Heath.
JULY – 4TH WEEK
Bonsall Wells Dressing:
Bonsall.
JULY – LATE
Clipping the Church Ceremony:
Burbage, Nr. Buxton
An ancient form of ceremony dating back to Roman times whereby the church is 'clipped', – i.e. embraced, – by the parishioners who encircle the building holding hands, as a form of affection.
AUGUST – 1ST OR 2ND WEEK
Bradwell Wells Dressing (& Gala):
Bradwell.

◆

YOULGREAVE WELL DRESSING
The dressing of wells with decorated panels and tableaux is firmly rooted in the traditions of Derbyshire. The Youlgreave Well Dressing shown here is a particularly fine example. See: OLD CUSTOMS.

MATLOCK VENETIAN NIGHTS
A spectacular illuminated event staged on the River Derwent and its banks where it passes through Derwent Gardens at Matlock Bath. Beautifully illuminated craft and tableaux put this on an equal footing with Blackpool's illuminations. See: MISCELLANEOUS.

AUGUST – 2ND OR 3RD WEEK
Barlow Wells Dressing:
Barlow.
AUGUST – LAST SUNDAY
Plague Memorial Service (Plague Sunday):
Eyam.
On 'Wakes' or 'Plague' Sunday a special service is held at Cucklet Dell where the Plague Hymn is sung to commemorate the heroic fight against the plague in the village during the plague years long ago.

FESTIVALS

MARCH
Derby Arts Festival:
Details: Mrs. A. Winkler, Windward, Summer Lane, Wirksworth.
APRIL
Alfreton Competitive Musical Festival:
Details: Mrs. M. Tooze, 128 Nottingham Road, Alfreton.
APRIL – 4TH WEEK OR MAY – 1ST WEEK
Brass Band Festival Weekend:
Pavilion Gardens, St. John's Road, Buxton.
APRIL – 4TH WEEK TO MAY – 1ST WEEK
Derwent Festival:
Matlock.
APRIL/MAY
Buxton & North Derbyshire Musical Festival:
Pavilion Gardens, St. John's Road, Buxton.
Details: Mrs. R. M. Downs, 19 Heath Grove, Buxton, SK17 9HH.
JUNE TO SEPTEMBER
Derbyshire Festival:
Various venues throughout Derbyshire.
Details: Festival Director, Central Buildings, Bank Road, Matlock.
JUNE
Buxton Independent One-Act Drama Festival:
The Playhouse Theatre, Buxton.
Details: Festival Director: Charles R. Clowes, 4 Cavendish Circus, Buxton.
JUNE – 1ST WEEK
Chesterfield Amateur Theatre Federation One-Act Drama Festival:
Civic Theatre, Chesterfield.
Details: Mrs. A. Jones (Secretary). 3 Coppice Court, Hasland, Chesterfield.
JUNE – LATE
Buxton Flower Festival:
St. John's Church, St. John's Road, Buxton.
JUNE – LAST WEEKEND
Festival In The Park:
Glossop.
JULY – 2ND WEEK

Arts & Flowers Festival:
Methodist Church, Old Derby – Nottingham Road, Borrowash.
JULY, TO AUGUST – EARLY
Buxton Shakespeare Festival:
The Opera House, Buxton.
AUGUST – 4TH WEEK
Stainsby Folk Festival:
Stainsby.
Details: Brenda Whitmore, 67 Stetlea Lane, Old Higham.
AUGUST – 4TH WEEK
Festival of Art, Craftwork & Music:
St. Edmund's Parish Church, Castle Street, Castleton.
SEPTEMBER – 1ST WEEK
The Ilam Festival:
Ilam Village, Nr. Ashbourne.
OCTOBER
Derby Cathedral Festival:
Derby Cathedral, Derby.
Details: The Provost, Derby Cathedral, College Place, Derby.

FAIRS

FEBRUARY 10; APRIL 1; MAY 2; OCTOBER 28
Buxton Fair:
Buxton.
LAST SATURDAY IN JANUARY; FEBRUARY; APRIL; MAY; JULY; SEPTEMBER & NOVEMBER
Chesterfield Fair:
Chesterfield.
FRIDAY AFTER JANUARY 6; JANUARY 25; MARCH 25; WHIT FRIDAY
Derby Fair:
Derby.
MARCH
Clay Cross Fair:
Clay Cross.
MAY 6; OCTOBER 2
Glossop Fair:
Glossop.
MAY 8; OCTOBER 24
Matlock Fair:
Matlock.
MAY – 3RD WEEK
Buxton Antiques Fair:
Pavilion Gardens, St. John's Road, Buxton.
MAY – 4TH WEEK
Hayfield Craft Fair:
Parish Church, Hayfield.
JULY
Glossop Summer Event & Fair:
Glossop.
OCTOBER 16 – 18
Ilkeston Fair:
Ilkeston.
OCTOBER – LATE
3-Day Craft Fair:
Pavilion Gardens, St. John's Road,

Buxton.
NOVEMBER
Belper Fair:
Belper.

CARNIVALS

JULY – 2ND WEEK
Ashbourne Carnival:
The Recreation Ground, Cockayne Avenue, Ashbourne.
JULY – 3RD WEEK
Elvaston Summer Carnival:
Elvaston Castle Country Park, Borrowash Road, Elvaston.
AUGUST – 2ND WEEK
Matlock Carnival:
Hall Lees Park, Matlock.

GALAS

JUNE – 3RD WEEK
Bolsover Hospital Committee Gala Week:
Bolsover.
JULY – 1ST OR 2ND WEEK
Hathersage Gala:
Hathersage.
SEPTEMBER – 3RD WEEK
Scouts Steam Gala:
Ladywood Road, Kirk Hallam, Ilkeston.

AGRICULTURAL, HORTICULTURAL & BREED SHOWS

JANUARY – 1ST WEEK
Ashfield Canine Society Open Show:
Alfreton Leisure Centre, Alfreton Park, Alfreton.
JANUARY – 1ST WEEK
Mansfield Canine Society Open Show:
Alfreton Leisure Centre, Alfreton Park, Alfreton.
FEBRUARY – 3RD WEEK
Leicester Gun Dog Show:
Alfreton Leisure Centre, Alfreton Park, Alfreton.
MARCH – 1ST WEEK
Collie Club Show:
Alfreton Leisure Centre, Alfreton Park, Alfreton.
APRIL – 3RD WEEK
Chesterfield Canine Society Open Show:
Alfreton Leisure Centre, Alfreton Park, Alfreton.
MAY – 4TH WEEK
Derbyshire County Show:
Showground, Elvaston Castle Country Park, Nr. Derby.
MAY – 4TH WEEK
Bamford Sheep Dog Trials:
Bamford.

JULY — 2ND WEEK
Whitworth Show:
Whitworth Institute & Park, Darsley
Dale, Nr. Matlock.
JULY — 3RD WEEK
Ashby-de-la-Zouch Agricultural Show:
Calke Parke, Ticknall.
AUGUST — 1ST WEEK
Bakewell Agricultural Show:
Showground, Coombes Road, Bakewell.
AUGUST — 3RD WEEK
Asbourne Shire Horse Society Show:
Osmaston Polo Ground, Osmaston.
SEPTEMBER — 1ST WEEK
Sheep Dog Trials:
Longshaw, Sheffield Road, Grindeford.
SEPTEMBER — 2ND WEEK
Hayfield Sheepdog Trials:
Spray House Farm, Little Hayfield.

———Sports———

APRIL — 3RD WEEK
Easter Bowls Tournament:
Alfreton Leisure Centre, Alfreton Park,
Alfreton.

JUNE — 1ST WEEK
**Derbyshire Association of Tug-Of-War
Clubs North of England Outdoor
Championships:**
Cromford Meadows, Cromford, Nr.
Matlock.
AUGUST — 1ST WEEK
**Uppertown Tug-Of-War Club Outdoor
Open Championships:**
Whitworth Institute Park, Darley Dale,
Nr. Matlock.
AUGUST — 4TH WEEK
Shipley Park Horse Trials:
Shipley Park, The Field, Shipley,
Heanor.

———Miscellaneous———

JANUARY — 1ST WEEK
New Year's Steaming:
Dinting Railway Centre, Dinting Lane.
Glossop.
MAY — 4TH WEEK
Spring Bank Holiday Steamings:
Dinting Railway Centre, Dinting Lane,
Glossop.
MAY
MG Owners Motor Rally:
Elvaston Castle Country Park,

⬠
BAKEWELL GALA DAY
*Many towns and villages stage gala days
during the summer months; public festive
holidays where the local residents can forget
their worries and really enjoy themselves.
The gala at Bakewell is noted for its lively
entertainment. See: GALAS.*

◆

Borrowash Road, Elvaston.
JUNE — 2ND WEEK
Elvaston Castle Mobile Radio Rally:
Elvaston Castle Country Park, Elvaston,
Nr. Derby.
JULY — 2ND WEEK
Elvaston Castle Steam Engine Rally:
Elvaston Castle Country Park, Elvaston,
Nr. Derby.
AUGUST — 1ST WEEK
Cromford Steam Rally:
Cromford Meadows, Cromford.
AUGUST — 4TH WEEK TO OCTOBER —
4TH WEEK
**Matlock Illuminations & Venetian
Nights:**
Matlock Baths, Matlock.
*Details: The Secretary, Matlock Bath
Illuminations, 15 Pinewood Close,
Matlock.*

◆ *Devon* ◆

AUXILIO · DIVINO

Here all the summer could I stay,
For there's Bishop's teign
And King's teign
And Comb at the clear teign head –
Where close by the stream
You may have your dream
All spread upon barley bread.

JOHN KEATS.

──── OLD CUSTOMS ────

JANUARY I
Andrew Dole:
Bideford.
In 1605, John Andrew left a plot of land in his will, the rent from which he instructed was to be distributed for the poor. This is still observed and a loaf of bread and ¹/₂lb of butter is given to all those over the age of sixty.
JANUARY – 1ST SUNDAY AFTER TWELFTH NIGHT
Blessing the Plough Ceremony:
Exeter Cathedral, Exeter.
The beginning of the ploughing season is marked with the blessing of a plough and a service in the cathedral.
FEBRUARY – SHROVE TUESDAY
"Tip-Toeing":
Gittisham.
Children in the village visit every house in the village chanting "Tip tip toe, please for a penny then we will go" and ask for money which they divide between them.
GOOD FRIDAY
Bartholomew Borrington Dole:
Ideford.
A charity which dates back to 1585 when Bartholomew Borrington charged certain lands with an annual levy of £1. The money, in the form of twenty new shillings,

is laid upon his tomb and is then distributed to twenty poor or deserving folk in the parish.
MAY – 1ST SATURDAY
May Day Celebrations:
Town Orchard, Lustleigh.
MAY
May Day Celebrations:
Kingsteignton.
ROGATION SUNDAY – 5TH WEEK AFTER EASTER
Blessing the Fishing Fleet Ceremony:
Brixham.
A waterside service in which the boats, nets and all who sail are blessed.
WHIT MONDAY
Ram Roasting Fair:
Kingsteignton.
The decorated carcase of a ram-lamb is carried in procession through the streets and then roasted on a spit before a huge open fire by the side of Oakford Lawn. The cooked meat is then sliced and distributed to the spectators. The fair is said to commemorate the time when rams were sacrificed to pagan gods.
JULY – 2ND WEDNESDAY
Pretty Maid's Charity:
Holsworthy.
The Reverend Thomas Meyrick's brother Owen authorised in his will at his death in

1841 that £2.50 be paid annually "to the young single woman resident in the parish, being under 30 years of age, and generally esteemed by the young as the most deserving and most handsome, and most noted for her qualities and attendance at church." The charity has been faithfully paid ever since.
JULY – TUESDAY BEFORE THE 3RD WEDNESDAY
Proclamation of Lammas Fair. ("Displaying the Glove")
Exeter.
The ancient Saxon Lammas Fair is still ceremonially observed. A white stuffed glove decorated with ribbons and garlands is carried in procession through the streets and positioned in front of the Guildhall. The proclamation is then read out (by officials in ceremonial robes at various points throughout the city including the Cattle Market and the site of the East Gate) saying "Oyez! Oyez! The Glove is up, the fair has begun, no man shall be arrested until the glove is taken down. God Bless the Queen!"
JULY
Ale Tasting Ceremonies:
Ashburton.
The appointed Portreeve Ale Tasters tour the public houses tasting the ale. Those landlords whose ale is satisfactory receive a sprig of evergreen over his or her door.
JULY
Burrator Reservoir Ceremony:
Plymouth.
A custom which celebrates Sir Francis Drake's creation of the water-supply to

◆

DISPLAYING THE GLOVE
The 'Glove' is carried in procession ready to be positioned outside the Guildhall before the proclamation of the Lammas Fair is given at Exeter. See: OLD CUSTOMS. ⟳

⇧ BARNSTAPLE OLD FAIR (ST GILES FAIR)
*The charm of the pleasure fair can be fully
appreciated at night when illuminated by
myriads of coloured lights. See: OLD
CUSTOMS.*

TAR-BARREL ROLLING
*On November 5th at Ottery-St.-Mary in
South Devon the exciting and dramatic
Tar-barrel Parade takes place. Flaming
barrels are carried and rolled through the
village and a mighty bonfire and Guy
Fawkes ceremonially burned. See: OLD
CUSTOMS.*

*Plymouth which he built following the
defeat of the Armada in 1588. The custom
first began around 1603 and is celebrated by
the Lord Mayor and other officials by
drinking and toasting water of the
corporation reservoir from a silver goblet.*
SEPTEMBER – WEDNESDAY BEFORE
20TH
Barnstaple Old Fair (St. Giles's Fair):
Barnstaple.
*One of the oldest and most elaborate fairs
which lasts for three days and includes a
carnival in the streets of Barnstaple.*
OCTOBER 10
Tavistock Goose Fair ("Goosey Fair"):

Tavistock.
NOVEMBER 5
Turning the Devil's Boulder:
Shebbear.
*A ceremony for keeping at bay evil spirits,
in which a ritual stone is heaved over to the
sound of bellringing and by the light of
torches and lanterns.*
NOVEMBER 5
Tar-Barrel Rolling:
Ottery St. Mary.
*Nine burning barrels are first carried and
then rolled through the streets from different
starting points and the evening ends in the
traditional manner with a huge bonfire and
the burning of Guy Fawkes.*
NOVEMBER – 1ST WEDNESDAY
FOLLOWING 5TH
Hatherleigh Fire Festival:
Hatherleigh.
*The present celebrations, rooted as they are
in Celtic witch-lore and hill-top fires for the
guidance of dead spirits, is now a carnival
with many activities going on all day. The
highlight of the celebrations, however, is the
drawing through the town of a sledge
carrying lighted tar-barrels, accompanied
by the Hatherleigh Jazz Band.*
DECEMBER 31 – NEW YEAR'S EVE
Wassailing Ceremonies:
Various orchards throughout the county.
*Every New Year's Eve the ancient custom
of Wassailing still survives among some
Devonshire farmers who proceed to the
apple orchards and toast the trees with cider
to ensure good crops for the following
season.*

FESTIVALS

MARCH – 2ND – 4TH WEEK
Devon & Exeter Festival:
Barnfield Theatre, Maynard School and
Priory High School, Exeter.
APRIL
**County Music Festival (Devon
Federation of Women's Institutes):**
The Priory School, Exeter.
*Details: Winifred Edge, "Rope's End",
Berryharbour, Nr. Ilfracombe.*
APRIL/MAY
**Torbay & South West of England
Festival:**
Palace Avenue Theatre, Paignton.
*Details: Ms. B. M. Whitby, 2a Heath
Rise, Brixham.*
APRIL/MAY
Sidmouth Arts Festival:
Sidmouth.
MAY – 3RD WEEK
Newton Abbot Festival:
Newton Abbot.
Details: Colehays, Bovey Tracey.
Exmouth Summer Festival:

Exmouth.
Details: Festival Office, 21 Rolls Street, Exmouth.
MAY – 3RD WEEK, TO JUNE – 2ND WEEK
Exeter Festival:
Exeter.
MAY – LATE, TO JUNE – EARLY
Barnstaple Folk Festival:
Barnstaple.
Details: Barbara Verdigi, 2 Gubbs Tenement, Bratton Fleming, Barnstaple.
JUNE – 2ND TO 4TH WEEK
Seaton Festival:
Town Hall, Fore Street, Seaton.
JUNE – 3RD & 4TH WEEKS
Dawlish Arts Festival:
Dawlish.
Details: Festival Secretary, 5 Weech Close, Dawlish.
WHITSUN
Upottery Festival:
Upottery.
Details: J. W. Trobridge, 12 Vapron Road, Plymouth.
JULY – 4TH WEEK
Dartmouth Town Week Festival:
Avenue Gardens, Coronation Park and Guildhall, Dartmouth.
AUGUST – 1ST WEEK
Sidmouth International Folklore Festival:
Sidmouth.
Details: The Festival Director, International Folklore Festival, 10 Richmond Road, Exeter.
AUGUST – 1ST OR 2ND WEEK
Dartmoor Folk Festival:
Wood Country Hotel,
Details: Bob Cann, 4 Hillcrest, South Tawton, Nr. Okehampton.

———————**Fairs**———————

2ND TUESDAY EACH MONTH
Dartmouth Fair:
Dartmouth.
FEBRUARY 14
Bideford Fair:
Bideford.
3RD WEEK IN FEBRUARY; MAY & JULY; 2ND WEEK IN DECEMBER
Exeter Fair:
Exeter.
MAY
Salcombe Regis County Fair:
Salcombe Regis.
MAY
Great Torrington May Fair:
Great Torrington.
JULY – 4TH WEEK
Kingsbridge Fair:
Kingsbridge.
JULY – 4TH WEEK

Chumleigh Old English Fair:
Chumleigh.
AUGUST – 2ND WEEK
Bicton County Fair:
Bicton Arena, Yettington, East Buddleigh.
AUGUST – 4TH WEEK
Marldon Apple Fair:
The Meadow (opposite Church House Inn) Marldon.
1ST SATURDAY AFTER AUGUST 22
Ilfracombe Fair:
Ilfracombe.
4TH MONDAY & TUESDAY IN AUGUST
Torquay Fair:
Torquay.
SEPTEMBER – 2ND WEEK
Widecombe-In-The-Moor Fair:
Widecombe-in-the-Moor.
1ST WEDNESDAY AFTER SEPTEMBER 10
Newton Abbott Fair:
Newton Abbott.
WEDNESDAY, THURSDAY & FRIDAY BEFORE SEPTEMBER 30
Barnstaple Fair:
Barnstaple.
SEPTEMBER
Cheese & Onion Fair:
Newton Abbot.
2ND WEDNESDAY IN OCTOBER & 2ND & 4TH WEDNESDAY IN EACH MONTH
Tavistock Fair:
Tavistock.
OCTOBER
Brendon Pony Fair:
Brendon.

———————**Carnivals**———————

MAY – 4TH WEEK
Ilfracombe Spring Carnival:
Ilfracombe.
MAY
Great Torrington Carnival:
Great Torrington.
JUNE – 3RD WEEK
Babbacombe Carnival Fayre:
Babbacombe Downs, Babbacombe.
JUNE – 4TH WEEK
Torbay Carnival Week:
Torbay.
JULY – 1ST WEEK
Dartmouth Carnival:
Dartmouth.
JULY – 1ST WEEK
Grand Carnival:
Fore Street, Buckfastleigh.
JULY – 1ST & 2ND WEEK
Tavistock Carnival Fortnight:
Tavistock.
JULY – 4TH WEEK
Torbay Fayre & Carnival:
Central Park, Promenade, Paignton.

JULY – 4TH WEEK
Exmouth Carnival:
Sea Front, Esplanade, Exmouth.
AUGUST – 2ND WEEK
Totnes & District Carnival Week:
Totnes.
AUGUST – 3RD WEEK
Dawlish Carnival Week:
The Lawn, Dawlish.
AUGUST – 4TH WEEK
Ilfracombe Carnival procession:
Ilfracombe.
OCTOBER –3RD WEEK
Exeter Carnival procession:
Exeter.
OCTOBER – 3RD WEEK
Okehampton & District Swimming Pool Association Carnival:
Okehampton.

———————**Shows**———————

MAY – 4TH WEEK
West Country Boat Show:
Plymouth Hoe, Plymouth.
JUNE – LAST WEEK, OR JULY – 1ST WEEK
Exeter Air Show:
Exeter Airport, Exeter.

———**Agricultural,**———
———**Horticultural &**———
———**Breed Shows**———

FEBRUARY
Devon Cattle Breeders' Society Spring Show
Exeter.
APRIL – 3RD WEEK
Easter Four-Day Horse Show:
Bicton Arena, Yettington, East Buddleigh.
MAY – 3RD WEEK
The Devon County Show:
Devon County Showground, Whipton, Exeter.
MAY– 3RD WEEK
West of England Championship Horse Show:
Bicton Arena, Yettington, East Buddleigh.
MAY – 4TH WEEK
Spring Bank Holiday Horse Show:
Bicton Arena, Yettington, East Buddleigh.
MAY
Ilfracombe Canine Society Open Dog Show:
Ilfracombe.
JUNE – 2ND WEEK
Exmouth Horse Show:
Bicton Arena, Yettington, East Budleigh.
JUNE – 3RD WEEK

Chudleigh Knighton Rose Show:
Village Hall, Chudleigh Knighton, Nr.
Newton Abbott.
JUNE – 3RD WEEK
June Two-Day Horse Show:
Bicton Arena, Yettington, East
Buddleigh.
JUNE – LAST WEEKEND
Flower Festival:
St. Gregory's Church, Coles Lane,
Kingskerswell, Nr. Newton Abbott.
JULY – 2ND WEEK
Championship Dog Show:
Clennon Valley, Paignton.
JULY – 4TH WEEK
Yealmpton Agricultural Show:
The Showground, Yealmpton, Nr.
Plymouth.
JULY – 4TH WEEK
Totnes & District Agricultural Show:
Berry Pomeroy, Nr. Totnes.
JULY
Tiverton Agricultural Show:
Tiverton.
AUGUST – 1ST WEEK
**Brixham Horticultural Society Summer
Show:**
Scala Hall, New Road, Brixham.
AUGUST – 1ST WEEK
Flower Festival:
Oldway Mansion, Torquay Road,
Paignton.
AUGUST – 2ND WEEK
Summer Flower Show:
Pavilion, Ilfracombe.
AUGUST – 2ND WEEK
Chudleigh Knighton Flower Show:
Village Hall, Chudleigh Knighton, Nr.
Newton Abbott.
AUGUST – 3RD WEEK
**St. Budeaux & District Gardeners'
Association Annual Summer Show:**
St. Budeaux Methodist Church Hall,
Victoria Road, St. Budeaux.
AUGUST – 4TH WEEK
**Marldon Flower and Heavy Horse
Show:**
The Meadow (opposite The Church
House Inn), Marldon, Paignton.
AUGUST
Exeter Flower Show:
Exeter.
AUGUST
Okehampton Agricultural Show:
Okehampton.
AUGUST
Brendon Horse & Agricultural Show:
Brendon.
AUGUST
**Ilfracombe & District Horticultural
Society's Annual Summer Flower
Show.**
Ilfracombe.
AUGUST

Bideford Horse Show:
Bideford.
AUGUST
**Devon Closewool Sheep Breeders'
Society Annual Show & Sale:**
Barnstaple.
SEPTEMBER – 1ST WEEK
**Kingsbridge Agricultural and
Horticultural Show:**
Borough Farm, Nr. Kingsbridge.
SEPTEMBER – 3RD WEEK
Autumn Flower Show:
Pavilion, Ilfracombe.
SEPTEMBER – 4TH WEEK
**South Western Counties
Championship Cat Show:**
Newton Abbott Racecourse,
Kingsteignton, Newton Abbott.
SEPTEMBER
**Widecombe-In-The-Moor Annual
Horse, Pony & Sheep Show:**
Widecombe-in-the-Moor.
NOVEMBER – 2ND WEEK
Autumn Open Flower Show:
Scala Hall, New Road, Brixham.
NOVEMBER
Barnstaple & District Dairy Show:
Barnstaple.

——SPORTS——

JANUARY – 2ND WEEK
Devon Badminton Championships:
Town Hall, Torquay.
JANUARY – 3RD WEEK
**Michael Spiers Invitation Squash
Matches:**
Plymouth.
MARCH – LAST WEEKEND
Torquay Bridge Congress:
Palace Hotel, Babbacombe, Torquay.
MARCH – LAST WEEKEND
East Devon Chess Congress:
Exeter University, Prince of Wales
Road, Exeter.
APRIL – 1ST WEEK
**West of England Women's Squash
Championships:**
Plymouth.
APRIL – 4TH WEEK
Bicton Horse Trials:
Bicton Arena, Yettington, East
Budleigh.
MAY – 4TH WEEK
Lyn & District Traders Trophy Trial:
Holman Park, Lynton.
JUNE – 2ND WEEK
Golf Open Week:
Ilfracombe Golf Club, Ilfracombe.
JUNE – 3RD WEEK
**Lympstone Tug-of-War Club Annual
Tournament:**
Lympstone, Nr. Exmouth.
JUNE – 3RD WEEK

**Teignmouth Open Amateur Bowling
Tournament:**
The Den & Bitton Park Bowling Greens,
Teignmouth.
JUNE – 4TH WEEK
Port of Brixham Trawler Race:
Brixham.
JUNE – 4TH WEEK
**Annual Torbay Gentlemen's Bowls
Tournament:**
Torquay.
JUNE – 4TH WEEK & JULY – 1ST WEEK
**Ilfracombe Open Bowling
Tournament:**
Bowling Green, Highfield Road,
Ilfracombe.
JULY
Plymouth Yachting Week:
Plymouth.
AUGUST – 1ST WEEK
**Woodtown Breakaways Tug-of-War
Club Annual:**
Hockridges Woodtown, Fairy Cross,
Bideford.
AUGUST – 2ND WEEK
**Benson & Hedges International Open
Golf:**
Mellion, Plymouth.
AUGUST – 2ND WEEK
**Fastnet Race and Admirals Cup Yacht
Race:**
Plymouth Sound and Millbay Docks,
Plymouth.
AUGUST – 4TH WEEK
**Cockwood Harbour Revels: Mud and
Water Sports:**
Cockwood Harbour, Nr. Starcross.
AUGUST – 4TH WEEK
Ippleton Tug-of-War Annual Event:
The Playing Field, Ipplepen, Nr.
Newton Abbott.

——MISCELLANEOUS——

JUNE – 2ND WEEK
Hotels Week:
AUGUST – 4TH WEEK
Plymouth Navy Days:
H.M. Naval Base, Plymouth.
AUGUST – 4TH WEEK
Hope Cove Week-end:
Hope Cove, Nr. Kingsbridge.
AUGUST – 4TH WEEK
Old Fashion Day at the Seaside:
Teignmouth.
OCTOBER – 4TH WEEK
Grand Fireworks Display:
Bicton Arena, Yettington, East
Buddleigh.
OCTOBER – LATE
**Goodleigh Annual Conker
Championships:**
The New Inn, Goodleigh, Nr.
Barnstaple.

◆ *Dorset* ◆

WHO'S AFEARD

Here, in the valley, the word seems to be constructed upon a smaller and more delicate scale; the fields are mere paddocks, so reduced that from this height their hedgerows appear a network of dark green threads overspreading the paler green of the grass. The atmosphere beneath is languorous, and is so tinged with azure that what artists call the middle distance partakes also of that hue, while the horizon beyond is of the deepest ultramarine. Arable lands are few and limited; with but slight exceptions the prospect is a broad rich mass of grass and trees, mantling minor hills and dales within the major. Such is the vale of Blackmoor.

FROM "TESS OF THE D'URBERVILLES"
BY THOMAS HARDY.

——— OLD CUSTOMS ———

FEBRUARY – SHROVE TUESDAY
Shrovetide Football:
Corfe Castle.

FEBRUARY – SHROVE TUESDAY
Annual Meeting of the Company of Marblers & Stone-Cutters of the Isle of Purbeck:
Corfe Castle.
Purbeck marble is renowned throughout England and can be found in many great cathedrals and churches. The Marblers formed a guild during the Middle Ages and they have met annually ever since, playing a traditional game of Shrovetide Football as part of the proceedings.

MAY 13 (OLD MAY DAY)
Garland Day:
Abbotsbury.
A custom dating back to 1752 and celebrated with the construction of three garlands which are carried through the village at varying times throughout the day and a collection made for charity.

MAY – ASCENSION DAY (EVERY SEVEN YEARS – NEXT ONE 1981)
The Perambulation of the Bounds:
The Island and Royal Manor of Portland.

JULY – MID
Beating of the Bounds:
Poole Quay & Harbour, Poole.
An ancient ceremony which has developed

in recent years into a fun occasion comprising of various water events involving the Mayor, 'buccaneers' and 'pirates' and many local groups. There is also a Parade and Fayre on the quay and a number of displays throughout the day.

JULY – 3RD SUNDAY
Tolpuddle Martyrs Procession:
Tolpuddle.
Organised by the National Union of Agricultural Workers. Six labourers from the village, who organised themselves into the first Trade Union in 1834, are remembered by a procession through the village.

OCTOBER
Pack Monday Fair:
Sherborne.
The villagers commemorate the completion of Sherborne Abbey in the 14th century with a midnight march through the streets.

NOVEMBER – A FRIDAY
Wareham Court Leet:
Wareham.
The 'Court Leet' was a tribunal set up after the Norman Conquest to exercise the right to regulate civil matters, including the 'view of frankpledge'. Held at the Town Hall, the Wareham Court Leet is attended by the bailiff, steward, officers of the court and members of the jury, and matters concerning grazing rights are normally discussed. During the preceeding week the bailiff is

accompanied by officers of the court and bread-weighers, ale-tasters and chimney sweeps. They visit the pubs and hotels of Wareham in the evenings to check the quality and quantity of the food and drink, and the state of the chimneys.

DECEMBER 25 (CHRISTMAS DAY)
Christmas Pennies Distribution:
Sherborne Castle, Sherborne.
This custom originated back in the eighteenth century and the pennies are still distributed every Christmas morning.

——— FESTIVALS ———

EASTER
Weymouth Easter Hockey Festival:
Redlands Sports Ground, Dorchester Road, Weymouth.

MAY – 3RD WEEK
Wessex Brass Band Festival:
Pavilion Theatre, Weymouth.

JUNE – 3RD & 4TH WEEKS
Dorchester Abbey Festival:
Dorchester.

JUNE – JULY
Shaftesbury Festival:
Enmore Green, Shaftesbury.

JULY – 1ST WEEK
Childrens' Festival:
Various venues, Bournemouth.

JULY – 1ST WEEK
Sherborne Abbey Festival:

Abbey Close, Sherborne.
AUGUST – 2ND WEEK
Sherborne Summer Festival:
Sherborne House, Sherborne.
AUGUST – 3RD WEEK
Wimborne Country Festival:
Town Centre, Wimborne.
AUGUST – 3RD WEEK
Wimborne Festival:
Wimborne.
AUGUST – 4TH WEEK
Church Flower Festival:
St. Mary's Church, 1 Werne Minster,
Blandford.
SEPTEMBER – MID
Wareham Folk Festival:
Details: Alan White, 10 Old Wareham
Road, Parkstone, Poole.
SEPTEMBER – 4TH WEEK
Steam Engine Festival:
Stourpaine Bushes, Blandford.

FAIRS

1ST WEEK IN APRIL; 1ST WEEK IN
OCTOBER
Bridport Fair:
Bridport.
FEBRUARY 14; JULY 6; AUGUST 6;
SEPTEMBER 30; OCTOBER 25
Dorchester Fair:
Dorchester.
MAY 1; NOVEMBER 2
Poole Fair:
Poole.
JUNE – 3RD WEEK
Wessex Antiques Fair:
Corn Exchange, Market Place,
Blandford Forum.
JULY – 3RD WEEK
Lions Club Country Fair:
Sandpit Field, De Moulham Road,
Swanage.
AUGUST – 1ST WEEK
Crafts & Hobbies Fair:
Allendale Community Centre, Hanham
Road, Wimborne.
AUGUST – 3RD WEEK
Langton Matravers Fair:
Langton Matravers, Nr. Swanage.
SEPTEMBER – 3RD WEEK
St. John's Ambulance Autumn Fair:
Allendale Community Centre, Hanham
Road, Wimborne.
NOVEMBER – 4TH WEEK
Wessex Book Fair:

GARLAND DAY
Children who carry the Abbotsbury
Garland through the village stop at the local
pottery to collect a donation for charity. See:
OLD CUSTOMS.

The Church Hall, Digby Road,
Sherborne.

FÊTES

JUNE – LATE
Melbury Abbas & Cann Village Fête:
School Grounds, Melbury Abbas.
JULY – MID
Swanage British Legion Fête:
Sandpit Field, De Moulham Road,
Swanage.

FAYRES

JUNE – 2ND OR 3RD WEEK
Rotaraction Summer Fayre:
Poole.
DECEMBER – 2ND WEEK
Christmas Fayre:
Church House, 22 High Street,
Wimborne Minster.

CARNIVALS

JUNE – 3RD WEEK
Lytchett Matravers Carnival:
Lytchett Matravers, Nr. Poole.
JUNE – 3RD WEEK
Wimborne Carnival:
Various venues, Wimborne.
WHITSUN
Poole Carnival:
Poole.
JULY – 4TH WEEK
Wareham Round Table Carnival:
Recreation Ground, Worgrist Road,
Wareham.
AUGUST – 1ST WEEK
Swanage Carnival:
Swanage.
AUGUST – 1ST & 2ND WEEKS
Lyme Regis Carnival:
Lyme Regis.
AUGUST – 3RD WEEK
Weymouth Carnival:
Esplanade, Weymouth.
AUGUST
Sturminster Newton Carnival & Fair:
Sturminster Newton.
SEPTEMBER – 2ND WEEK
Wimborne Carnival:
Redcotts Recreation Ground, Victoria
Road, Wimborne.
SEPTEMBER
Shaftesbury Carnival:
Shaftesbury.

GALAS

AUGUST – 2ND WEEK
Poole Hospital Gala:
Poole Park, Poole.

AGRICULTURAL, HORTICULTURAL & BREED SHOWS

APRIL – 2ND WEEK
**Dorset County Canine Society Dog
Show:**
Pavilion Ballroom, Weymouth.
AUGUST – 1ST WEEK
Swanage Carnival Novelty Dog Show:
Sandpit Field, De Moulham Road,
Swanage.
AUGUST – 3RD WEEK
Championship Dog Show:
The Showground, Canford Magna,
Wimborne.
AUGUST – 4TH WEEK
Horticultural Society Show:
Allendale Community Centre, Hanham
Road, Wimborne.
AUGUST – 4TH WEEK
Melplash Agricultural Show:
West Bay Road, Bridport.
SEPTEMBER
Dorchester Show:
Dorchester.

SPORTS

JUNE – 1ST WEEK
Weymouth Olympic Week:
Weymouth Beach, The Esplanade,
Weymouth.
JULY – 3RD WEEK
**Two-Ton World Yachting
Championships:**
Poole Bay, Poole.
JULY – 4TH WEEK
**Dorset Tug-Of-War Association
Annual Barbecue:**
Bowleaze Cove, Weymouth.
AUGUST – 1ST WEEK
Poole Borough Bowling Tournament:
Poole Park, Poole.
AUGUST – 1ST WEEK
**British Rail Wareham Tug-Of-War
Club Annual Event:**
Swanage & Wareham R.F.C. Bestwall
Road, Wareham.
AUGUST – 4TH WEEK
Poole Yachting Week:
Poole Harbour, Poole.

Regattas:

JULY
Poole Regatta:
Poole.
JULY – 4TH WEEK
Swanage Regatta:
Swanage Beach, Shore Road, Swanage.
JULY – 4TH WEEK, TO SEPTEMBER –
2ND WEEK

WAREHAM COURT LEET
The customary 'Weighing of the Bread' takes place at the Antelope Hotel as part of Wareham's 'Court Leet'. See: OLD CUSTOMS.

BEATING OF THE BOUNDS
Piracy and all manner of watery pranks make Poole's annual 'Beating of the Bounds' ceremony a real fun event. See: OLD CUSTOMS.

EASTER HOCKEY FESTIVAL
A traditional sporting occasion which is one of the major hockey events in the West Country attracting enthusiasts from many counties over the Easter holiday. See: FESTIVALS.

WEYMOUTH CARNIVAL
One of the unusual events in the town's annual carnival is the barrel rolling race, a fun sport which is definitely not as easy as it looks. See: CARNIVALS.

Lyme Regis Regatta and Lifeboat Week:
Lyme Regis.
AUGUST – 1ST WEEK
Swanage Sailing Regatta:
Swanage Sailing Club, Buck Shore, Swanage Bay, Swanage.
AUGUST
Royal Dorset Yacht Club Regatta:
Weymouth.
SEPTEMBER
Weymouth Regatta:
Weymouth.

MISCELLANEOUS

JULY – 4TH WEEK
Navy Open Days:
Portland.

◆ *Durham* ◆

(INCLUDING SOUTH TYNE & WEAR)

──Old Customs──

FEBRUARY — SHROVE TUESDAY
Shrovetide Football:
Sedgefield.
The game commences at 1 pm when the verger throws a specially made ball into the air. The goals are a pond and a stream 500 yards apart and the game is declared finished when one of the players scores the first goal.
GOOD FRIDAY
Good Friday Parade:
Seaham Harbour, Nr. Sunderland.
On this day it has long been the tradition for children who attend sunday school classes to walk in procession around the town as part of the Easter religious ceremonies.
GOOD FRIDAY
Pram Races:
Sunderland & other Tyneside Towns.
Pram races are a traditional custom in this part of the country with the contestants, usually the men, dressing up in drag for the occasion.
MAY 29 (OAK APPLE DAY)
Tower Top Singing:
Durham Cathedral, Durham.
In honour of the restoration of Charles II anthems are sung from the Cathedral tower.
DECEMBER 26 (BOXING DAY)
Sword Dancers:
Greatham.

──Festivals──

FEBRUARY — MARCH
Middlesborough Competitive Musical Festival:
Middlesborough.
Details: Mrs. F. C. Grunwell, 53 Emerson Avenue, Middlesborough, Teeside.
FEBRUARY — MARCH
Ryton & District Musical Festival:
Ryton.
Details: E. H. Taylor, Dunedin, Beechwood Avenue, Ryton, Tyne & Wear.
MARCH
Darlington Competitive Musical Festival:
Darlington.
Details: Mrs. D. Waterfall, 62 Grange Road, Darlington.
MAY
Consett Muscial Festival:
Consett.
Details: A. Robson, 61 Villa Real Road, Consett.
JUNE — 1ST WEEK
Festival Spectacular:
South Park, Darlington.
JUNE — LATE
Durham Cathedral Festival of Flowers:
Durham Cathedral, Durham.
JULY — 1ST WEEK
American Independence Day Celebration & Festival:

Washington Old Hall, The Avenue, Washington New Town.
JULY — MID
Cleveland Inter-TIE (formerly: Teeside International Eisteddfod)
Details: Secretary, Inter-TIE Headquarters, 27 Baker Street, Middlesborough, Cleveland TS1 2LE.
AUGUST — EARLY
Oriental Music Festival:
Durham.
Details: Festival Secretary, School of Oriental Studies, Elvet Hill, Durham DH1 3TH.
AUGUST — 1ST WEEK
Durham City Folk Fesitval:
Durham.
Details: Ian McCulloch, 8 Cedar Close, Gilesgate Moor, Durham.
AUGUST — 2ND & 3RD WEEKS
Billingham International Folklore Festival:
Billingham.
Details: Philip Conroy, 39 St. Christopher's Road, Sunderland, Tyne & Wear.
AUGUST — 4TH WEEK
Durham Beer Festival:
Dunelm House, New Elvet, Durham City.
OCTOBER
Stanley U.D.C. Choral Festival:

SHROVETIDE FOOTBALL
Shrovetide football still survives in the north as a tradition and the match which occurs in Sedgefield shows no sign of losing its popularity. See: OLD CUSTOMS.

◆

Stanley.
Details: W. Wilson, 13 Lyndhurst Road, Oxhill, Stanley.
OCTOBER – NOVEMBER
Stockton-on-Tees Musical Festival:
Stockton-on-Tees.
Details: A. Palant, 39 Richardson Road, Stockton-on-Tees, Teeside.
OCTOBER – 3RD WEEK, TO NOVEMBER – 2ND WEEK
Durham Music Festival:
Durham.
Details: Festival Secretary, 9 Neville's Cross Villas, Durham DH1 4JR.

FAIRS

1ST MONDAY IN MARCH; EASTER MONDAY; MAY 9; WHIT MONDAY; NOVEMBER 21
Darlington Fair:
Darlington.
LAST FRIDAY IN MARCH; FRIDAY BEFORE MAY 13, SEPTEMBER 15, NOVEMBER 23
Durham Fair:
Durham.
WEDNESDAY BEFORE & AFTER MAY 1 & NOVEMBER 11
South Shields Fair:
South Shields.
2ND WEDNESDAY BEFORE MAY 13 &

NOVEMBER 23
Stockton-On-Tees Fair:
Stockton-on-Tees.
JULY – 1ST WEEK
Medieval Fair:
Market Place, Durham City.

CARNIVALS

JUNE – 4TH WEEK
Whitsuntide Meet Carnival:
Town Centre, Galgate, Barnard Castle.
AUGUST – 4TH WEEK
Durham City Carnival:

Durham City.

GALAS

JULY – 1ST WEEK
Red House Gala Week:
Red House District, Sunderland.
JULY – 3RD WEEK
Durham Miners Gala:
Racecourse & Streets, Durham.

SHOWS

AUGUST – MID
Teeside Air Show:
Teeside Airport, Darlington.

AGRICULTURAL, HORTICULTURAL & BREED SHOWS

AUGUST – 1ST WEEK
Sunderland Flower Show:
Seaburn, Sunderland.
AUGUST – 3RD WEEK
Darlington Agricultural Show:
South Park, Darlington.
SEPTEMBER – 1ST WEEK
Seaham Show (Civic Show):
Seaham Secondary Modern School Playing Fields, New Drive, Seaham.

◆

SUNDAY PARADE
Children from local Sunday Schools, together with the Salvation Army, are seen here attending the 'Procession of Witnesses' during Good Friday in Sunderland. See: OLD CUSTOMS.

Spennymoor.

CHAMPION LEEK SHOW
The growing of leeks enjoys the status of a religion in parts of Derbyshire. Fantastic competition between eminent rival growers and secret cultivation methods guarded by elaborate security measures to prevent sabotage of specimens make for one of our more fascinating local traditions. See: SHOWS.

SEPTEMBER – 2ND WEEK
Darlington Championship Dog Show:
South Park, Darlington.
SEPTEMBER – 2ND WEEK
Bowes Agricultural Show:
Gilmonby, Nr. Bowes.
SEPTEMBER – 3RD WEEK
Eggleston Agricultural Show:
High Shipley Farm, Nr. Eggleston, Barnard Castle.
AUTUMN/WINTER
Leek Growing Shows:
Details: Champion of Champions Leek Club. F. Hall, 7 Massingham Way, School Lorning, South Shields.

SPORTS

MAY – 3RD WEEK
Area 9 Far North Tug-of-War Championships:
Merrington Lane Playing Field, Spennymoor.
JUNE – 2ND WEEK
Milk Race (Cycling):
Barnard Castle.
JUNE – 2ND WEEK

Durham County Schools Athletics Championships:
Gateshead Stadium, Neilson Road, Gateshead.
JULY – 2ND WEEK
Philip Gateshead Games:
Gateshead Stadium, Nielson Road, Gateshead.
AUGUST
Middleton St. George Air Races:
Middleton St. George.
SEPTEMBER – 1ST WEEK
Durham Tug-of-War Championships:
Merrington Lane Playing Field,

MISCELLANEOUS

JUNE – 3RD WEEK
Vintage Car Rally: Beamish Reliability Run:
Beamish Museum, Nr. Stanley, Durham.
AUGUST – 4TH WEEK
Rolls Royce Rally:
The Castle, Durham City.
SEPTEMBER – 1ST WEEK
Beamish Commercial Vehicle Event:
Beamish Museum, Nr. Stanley, Durham.
SEPTEMBER – 2ND WEEK
R. R. E. C. Durham Castle Weekend Rally:
The Castle, Durham City.
SEPTEMBER – 3RD WEEK
Vintage Motorcycle Rally: Beamish Trophy Trial:
Beamish Museum, Nr. Stanley, Durham.
OCTOBER – 2ND WEEK
Houghton Feast:
Rectory Field, Dairy Lane, Houghton-le-Spring.

TEES-SIDE AIR SHOW
Tees-side Airport is the venue for one of the north's most popular air displays. A parachute stunt team is pictured here performing an impressive spectacle of effect and skill. See: MISCELLANEOUS.

◆ Essex ◆

How beautiful this hill of fern swells on!
So beautiful the chapel peeps between
The hornbeams—with its simple bell. Alone
I wander here, hid in a palace green.
Mary is absent—but the forest queen,
Nature, is with me. Morning, noon and gloaming,
I write my poems in these paths unseen;
And when among these brakes and beeches roaming,
I sigh for truth, and home, and love and woman.

   FROM "IN EPPING FOREST" BY JOHN CLARE.

──Old Customs──

WHITSUNTIDE (IRREGULARLY)
The Dunmow Flitch:
Talberds Ley, Great Dunmow
*This is an award of a flitch of bacon to any
couple who can prove that they have not
quarrelled or regretted their marriage for a
year and a day. It goes back at least as far
as the 13th century, and is referred to by
Chaucer, and also in 'Piers Plowman':
"For since the Plague hundreds of couples
have married yet the only fruit they have
brought forth are foul words . . . If they
went to try for the Dunmow Flitch they
wouldn't stand a chance without the Devil's
help". The 'trial' of couples was regarded
much more seriously in the old days and few
awards were made.*
SEPTEMBER – LATE
Blessing of the Fishes Ceremony:
Southend-On-Sea.
*Following the special service there is a
banquet where fish is the main course.*

OCTOBER – LAST FRIDAY
Oyster Festival:
Colchester.
*The mayor and other town dignitaries set off
in a fishing boat to make the first
commemorative oyster dredge of the season.
Later a toast of gin is drunk to the Queen
and gingerbread is served both to officials
and to guests.*

──Festivals──

JANUARY – 3RD WEEK
The Pavilion Festival:
Cliffs Pavilion, Station Road, Westcliff.
MARCH – LATE
**South East Essex Drama Association
Independent Amateur Drama Festival:**
Palace Theatre, London Road,
Westcliff.
*Details: J. White, 292 Church Road,
Benfleet.*
MARCH – APRIL

**Colchester & East Essex Co-Operative
Society Festival of Music, Elocution &
Drama:**
*Details: J. Macey, Member Relations
Dept., P.O. Box 4, Victoria Place, Old
Lane, Colchester.*
EASTER – SUNDAY & MONDAY
Southend Easter Sports Festival:
Southend-on-Sea.
APRIL – 3RD WEEK
**Havering Independent One-Act Drama
Festival:**
Spa Pavilion, Felixtowe.
APRIL – 4TH WEEK
**Southend-on-Sea Spring Flower
Festival:**
Cliff Pavilion, Southend-On-Sea.
APRIL/MAY – BIENNIAL (EVEN YEARS)
Saffron Walden Arts Festival:
Saffron Walden.
APRIL/MAY
Braintree Arts Festival:
*Details: Braintree & District Arts Council,
Braintree College, Church Lane,
Braintree.*
APRIL/MAY
Chelmsford Arts Festival:
*Details: Arundel House, The Street,
Hatfield Peverel, Chelmsford.*
APRIL/MAY
**Redbridge (Wanstead & Woodford)
Musical Festival:**
*Details: Redbridge Festival, Mr. J. L.
Tomlinson, LB of Redbridge (Arts
Council), 22–26 Clements Rd., Ilford.*
MAY – 3RD WEEK
Harlow Museum Festival:
Harlow Museum, Third Avenue,
Harlow.

MAY
Essex Festival:
Details: Students Council, University of Essex, Wivenhoe Park, Colchester.
MAY
National Accordian Organisation of Britain Festival:
Colchester.
MAY
Leigh-On-Sea Musical Festival:
Details: F. Nightingale, 8 Clattefield Gardens, Westcliffe-on-Sea.
JUNE – 4TH WEEK
Barking Children's Festival:
Barking.
Details: Dagenham Women's Action Group, 2 Flamstead Road, Dagenham.
JUNE – LATE, OR JULY – EARLY
Essex Folk Festival:
Details: Rocheway Centre, Rocheway, Rocheford, Nr. Smithend.
AUGUST – 1ST WEEK
Colchester Festival:
Colchester.
AUGUST – 4TH WEEK
Flower Festival:
Parish Church of St. Mary the Virgin, Saffron Walden.
SEPTEMBER – 4TH WEEK
Stanstead Flower Festival:
Stanstead.
SEPTEMBER – 4TH WEEK
Harvest Festival of Flowers:
Halstead Parish Church, Halstead.
OCTOBER
St. Botolph's Music Society Festival:
Details: 14 Roman Road, Colchester.
OCTOBER – TRIENNIAL (NEXT 1982)
Southend Festival of Music & the Arts:
Details: Cliff Pavilion, Station Road, Westcliffe-on-Sea.
NOVEMBER
Southend-on-Sea Musical Festival:
Details: Mrs. S. H. Heppel, 18 Kenilworth Gardens, Westcliffe-on-Sea.
NOVEMBER
Chelmsford Competitive Festival of Music & Drama:
Details: Mrs. B. Carey, 151 Mildmay Road, Chelmsford.

FAIRS

MAY – 1ST WEEK
Holland Fair:
Cliffs Pavilion, Station Road, Westcliffe-on-Sea.
WHITSUN
17th Century Fair:
Basildon.
WHIT TUESDAY; OCTOBER 11; NOVEMBER 13 – 14
Epping Fair:
Epping.

OCTOBER 15
Brentwood Fair:
Brentwood.
OCTOBER 20
Colchester Fair:
Colchester.
MAY 2; NOVEMBER 12
Chelmsford Fair:
Chelmsford.

FÊTES

MAY – 4TH WEEK
Harwich Redoubt Fête:
Harwich Redoubt, Main Road, Harwich.
MAY – 4TH WEEK
Dunmow Round Table Fête:
Dunmow Cricket Club, Dunmow.

CARNIVALS

MAY – 4TH WEEK
Harwich & District Summer Carnival:
Harwich.
JUNE – 2ND OR 3RD WEEK
Carnival Procession:
Rolph School, High Street, Thorp-le-Soken.
JULY – 3RD WEEK
Dagenham Carnival & Town Show:
Central Park, Wood Lane, Dagenham, Essex.
JULY – LATE
Colchester Carnival:
Cavalry Barracks, Castle Park, Colchester.
AUGUST
Southend-on-Sea Carnival:
Southend-on-Sea.

TATTOOS

JULY – LATE, OR AUGUST – EARLY
Colchester Searchlight Tattoo:
Lower Castle Park, Colchester.

AGRICULTURAL, HORTICULTURAL & BREED SHOWS

APRIL
Colchester Rose & Horticultural Society Spring Show:
Colchester.
JUNE – 3RD WEEK
Essex County Show:
The Showground, Great Leighs, Chelmsford.
JUNE – LAST WEEKEND
Colchester Rose Show & Floriade:
Lower Castle Park, Colchester.
JULY – 2ND WEEK
Tendring District Agricultural Show:

Lawford House Park, N. Manningtree.
JULY
Rayleigh Agricultural Show:
Rayleigh.
AUGUST – 4TH WEEK
Harlow Show:
Showground, Harlow.

SPORTS

APRIL – 4TH WEEK
Essex 3 Star Open Table Tennis Championships:
Wanstead Sports Centre, Redbridge Lane West, Wanstead.
MAY – 4TH WEEK
English Open Draughts Championships:
Town Hall, Station Road, Clacton-on-Sea.
JULY – 2ND WEEK
Barking Tug-of-War Club Dagenham Town Show:
Dagenham.
AUGUST – 3RD WEEK
12-Hour National Cycling Championship:
Abess Roding.

Regattas:

MAY
Royal Harwich Regatta:
Harwich.
JUNE
Southend-on-Sea Regatta:
Southend-on-Sea.
AUGUST
Burnham-On-Crouch Regatta:
Burnham-on-Crouch.

MISCELLANEOUS

MAY – 4TH WEEK
Traction Engine & Road Run Rally:
Saling Airfield, Great Saling.
JULY – 4TH WEEK
Valley Vans & Cruisers One-Day Custom Show:
Valentine's Park, Melbourne Road, Ilford.
AUGUST – MID (BEGINS FINAL DAY OF CARNIVAL)
Autumn Illuminations:
The Seafront, Southend-On-Sea.
AUGUST – MID
Children's Fun Week:
Chelmsford & Essex Museum, Moulsham Street, Chelmsford.
AUGUST – 4TH WEEK
Vintage Air Display:
Essex Showground, Great Leighs, Nr. Chelmsford.

Gloucestershire ◆

(INCLUDING AVON)

PRORSUM SEMPER

Beggarley Bisley, Strutting Stroud,
Mincing Hampton and Painswick Proud.

OLD JINGLE.

Old Customs

EASTER WEEK TUESDAY
Distribution of Twopenny Starvers:
St. Michael-on-the-Mount Without,
Bristol, Avon.
Choirboys of the church receive enormous
buns called Twopenny or 'Tuppeny'
Starvers. A custom which dates back to the
days when poor people could only obtain
black bread and on this special day received
white bread instead.
MAY 1 (MAY DAY)
Cheese Rolling:
Randwick.
Three cheeses which have been garlanded
with flowers are ceremonially borne on a
litter to the churchyard and solemnly rolled
three times around the church. The cheeses
are then carried to the village green and cut
into pieces for distribution to the
parishioners.
SPRING BANK HOLIDAY MONDAY
Cheese Rolling:
Coopers Hill, Birdlip.

A custom which originally exercised the
villagers' rights to graze sheep on the hill.
Youths line up at the top of the hill and roll
down the cheese, quickly followed by
themselves and the first competitor to reach
the bottom is declared the winner and
collects all the cheese.
MAY 12
Randwick Wap:
Randwick, Stroud.
MAY 24
Blessing of the Wells:
Bisley, Nr. Stroud.
WHIT SUNDAY
Bread & Cheese Dole:
St. Briavels.
After Evensong in the Parish Church of St.
Mary's, small pieces of bread and cheese are
doled out to the waiting crowd outside by
throwing into the air from large baskets.
The custom was first recorded in 1799. For
the privilege of the dole the parishioners
used to have to pay a penny, which also
secured them the right to cut and take wood

in Hudnalls or the Free Woods.
WHIT SUNDAY
Rushbearing Ceremony:
St. Mary Radcliffe Church, Bristol,
Avon.
During the 15th century a mayor made a
bequest for the church to be strewn with
rushes to help keep the church warm.
Today, the Lord Mayor of Bristol goes into
procession to the Rush Service.
WHITSUN
Scuttlebrooke Wake:
Chipping Camden.
Once known as the Cotswold Games, this
event, which dates back to 1605, is a
collection of various games and trials of
strength, as well as other forms of
entertainment.
AUGUST 10 – 13
Cranham Feast with Deer Roast:
Overton Farm, Cranham.

◆

PAPER BOYS
Gloucestershire abounds in fascinating
customs and the Marshfield 'Paper Boys' is
one of the more curious. The procession of
characters strangely attired in paper clad
costumes is led through the streets by the
town crier. See: OLD CUSTOMS.

⌂
TWOPENNY STARVERS

A custom still observed and much enjoyed by those involved. Huge buns or 'Twopenny Starvers' are distributed to the members of the choir of St. Michael-on-the-Mount-Without Church. See: OLD CUSTOMS.

◆

AUGUST 20
Frampton Deer Roast:
The Greens, Frampton-on-Severn.
AUGUST BANK HOLIDAY
The Water Game:
Burton-On-The-Water.
This relatively recent custom takes place on the day of the local football club fête. A game of football is played in the stream of the River Windrush which runs alongside the village stream. Two teams, five-aside, play under F.A. rules. The game was first played to celebrate the coronation of Edward VII.
SEPTEMBER 14
Avening Feast & Queen Matilda Pageant:
Avening.
A commemoration service for Matilda, wife of William the Conqueror, who consecrated the Church of the Holy Cross, Avening in 1080. The event is known locally as 'Pig-Face Day' and a feast is re-enacted in the village hall after evensong.
SEPTEMBER 19
Painswick Ancient Clypping Ceremony:
Painswick Parish Church, Painswick.
Here, 'clypping' means 'enclosing' and the

ceremony – originally part of an ancient village fair, dating back to 1321 – is made up of children who encircle the church holding hands and who sing the "Clypping Hymn".
SEPTEMBER 30
Opening of the Pie Powder Court:
Stag & Hounds, Old Market Street, Bristol, Avon.
These courts were originally set up at fairs to determine a lawful outcome of disputes between those attending who had fallen out with each other.
OCTOBER
Cirencester Mop Fair:
Cirencester.
(See under Warwickshire for explanation of Mop Fairs).
DECEMBER 26 (BOXING DAY)
Paper Boys:
Marshfield.
A procession around the streets is led by a town crier ringing his bell, as well as a mummers play who's hero is King William, supported by Saucy Jack, Little Man John and Tenpenny Nit.

FESTIVALS

MARCH
Stroud Junior Schools Music Festival:
Stroud.
APRIL – 4TH WEEK
Thornbury Arts Festival:
Thornbury.
Details: Director, Thornbury Arts Festival, 12 Castle Street, Thornbury, Bristol, Avon.

APRIL/JUNE
Oldbury Court Music Festival:
Details: G.H.F. Crabb, 19 Dangerfield Avenue, Bishopsworth, Bristol, Avon.
MAY – 1ST & 2ND WEEKS
Wotton-under-Edge Arts Festival:
Wotton-under-Edge.
MAY – 2ND WEEK
Barnwood Festival of Worship and the Arts:
Gloucester.
Details: Barnwood Festival, 42 Barnwood Avenue, Gloucester.
MAY – 2ND & 3RD WEEKS
Bristol Proms:
Details: Bristol Proms., Colston Hall, Colston Street, Bristol.
MAY
Cheltenham Open Competitive Festival of Speech, Drama and Dancing:
Town Hall, Cheltenham.
Details: K. Dash, Belvedere, Tryers Road, Cheltenham.
MAY
National Accordian Organisation of Great Britain Festival:
Bristol, Avon.
JUNE – 1ST WEEK
Cheltenham Proms:
Cheltenham.
Details: Proms Office, Town Hall, Imperial Square, Cheltenham.
JUNE – 4TH WEEK
Bristol Folk Festival:
Bristol, Avon.
Details: Reg. Mann, Tweenways, Chilcompton, Nr. Bath.
JUNE
Bristol University Summer Music Festival:
Bristol, Avon.
Details: Music Dept., Royal Fort House, University, Bristol.
JUNE
Gloucestershire Music Festival:
Details; Music Advisor, Shire Hall, Gloucester.
JULY – 1ST OR 2ND WEEK
The Cotswold Folk Festival:
Stroud.
Details: Roger Grimes, 66 Granville Street, Gloucester.
JULY – 2ND WEEK
Cheltenham International Festival of Music:
Cheltenham.
Details: Music Festival Organiser, Cheltenham Arts Festivals Ltd., Town Hall, Imperial Square, Cheltenham.
AUGUST – 1ST & 2ND WEEKS
Gloucester Festival:
Gloucester.
Details: Entertainment & Leisure Centre,

CHELTENHAM INTERNATIONAL
FESTIVAL
*The Pitville Pump Room shown here is the
venue where chamber music recitals take
place during the festival. The organisers of
this long established festival always aim to
present first performances of works by
British composers. See: FESTIVALS.*

◆

*Gloucester Leisure Centre, Station Road,
Gloucester.*
AUGUST – EARLY
Tewkesbury – Musica Deo Sacra:
Tewkesbury Abbey, Tewkesbury.
AUGUST – EARLY
Cheltenham Cricket Festival:
College Grounds, Sandford Road,
Cheltenham.
AUGUST – 2ND WEEK
Sherborne Summer Festival:
Sherborne House, Sherborne.
AUGUST – MID
Iron Acton Folk Festival:
*Details: Maureen Marshall, 6 Richmond
Road, Mangotsfield, Bristol, Avon.*
SEPTEMBER
**Cheltenham Festival for Creative
Thinking:**
Cheltenham.
Details: P.O. Box 88, Cheltenham.
OCTOBER – 2ND & 3RD WEEKS
Stroud Arts Festival:
Stroud.
*Details: Director, Stroud Festival Ltd.,
Highmead, Field Road, Stroud.*
OCTOBER – NOVEMBER
Longwell Green Eisteddfod:
Bristol, Avon.

NOVEMBER – 1ST WEEK
Cheltenham Festival of Literature:
Cheltenham.
*Details: Cheltenham Festival of Literature,
Town Hall, Imperial Square, Cheltenham.*
NOVEMBER – 3RD WEEK
Great Western Beer Festival:
Exhibition Centre, Canon's Road,
Bristol, Avon.

FAIRS

1ST THURSDAY & 2ND WEDNESDAY IN
MARCH; 1ST THURSDAY & 2ND
WEDNESDAY IN SEPTEMBER
Bristol Fair:
Bristol, Avon.
1ST & 2ND WEEKS IN OCTOBER
Cheltenham Fair:
Cheltenham.
EASTER MONDAY; MONDAY BEFORE &
AFTER OCTOBER 11; 1ST MONDAY IN
NOVEMBER
Cirencester Fair:
Cirencester.
1ST SATURDAY IN APRIL, JULY &
SEPTEMBER; SEPTEMBER 28; LAST
SATURDAY IN NOVEMBER
Gloucester Fair:
Gloucester.
MAY – 2ND WEEK
Dodington Steam & Vintage Fair:
Dodington House, Park & Carriage
Museum, Chipping Sodbury, Bristol,
Avon.
MAY – 4TH WEEK
Craft Fair:
Sudeley Castle, Winchcombe.
JULY – 3RD & 4TH WEEKS
World Wine Fair:
Exhibition Centre, Bristol, Avon.
AUGUST – 3RD WEEK
Ecology Fair:
Subscription Rooms, Stroud.
AUGUST – 4TH WEEK
Dodington Century Battle and Fair:
Dodington House, Park & Carriage
Museum, Chipping Sodbury, Bristol,
Avon.
AUGUST – LATE
Medieval Fair:
Sudeley Castle, Winchcombe.

FAYRES

JULY – MID
Clifton Village Fayre:
Clifton Downs & the Mall Gardens.

CARNIVALS

JULY – 1ST WEEK
Cirencester Carnival:
Cirencester.

INTERNATIONAL BRICK AND ROLLING
PIN CONTEST
*Of the numerous entertainments which go to
make up Stroud's annual show the
International Brick and Rolling Pin
Contest is perhaps the most unusual. Here a
contestant is being judged for his brick
throwing skills. See: SHOWS.*

◆

JULY – 4TH WEEK
Gloucester Carnival Procession:
Gloucester.
NOVEMBER – 3RD WEEK
Bristol Hospital Carnival Procession:
Anchor Road, Bristol, Avon.

SHOWS

APRIL – 3RD WEEK
Dodington Easter Show:
Dodington House, Park & Carriage
Museum, Chipping Sodbury, Bristol,
Avon.
MAY – EARLY
Bristol Boat Show:
Exhibition Centre, Bristol, Avon.
JULY – 3RD WEEK
**Stroud Show (Including International
Brick and Rolling Pin Throwing
Contest):**
Stratford Park, Stratford Road, Stroud.

AGRICULTURAL, HORTICULTURAL & BREED SHOWS

JANUARY – 1ST WEEK
City of Bristol Canine Society Annual

DODINGTON STEAM AND VINTAGE FAIR
Vintage Rallies are attended by thousands of enthusiasts throughout the country especially when, as is shown here, those majestic masterpieces of engineering the steam traction engines are on display. See: FAIRS.

◆

Dog Show:
Wills Recreation Halls, Bedminster, Bristol, Avon.
APRIL
West of England Flowers, Gardens and Horticultural Show:
Exhibition Centre, Bristol, Avon.
APRIL – 2ND WEEK
Dodington Horse Show:
Dodington House, Park & Carriage Museum, Chipping Sodbury, Bristol, Avon.
JULY
Cheltenham Horse Show:
Cheltenham.
AUGUST – 1ST WEEK
Dodington Heavy Horse Show:
Dodington House, Park & Carriage Museum, Chipping Sodbury, Bristol, Avon.
AUGUST – 4TH WEEK, OR SEPTEMBER – EARLY
Bristol Flower Show:
The Downs, Bristol, Avon.
AUGUST
Painswick Agricultural Show:
Painswick House, Painswick.
SEPTEMBER – 1ST WEEK
Moreton-in-Marsh & District Agricultural and Horse Show:
Moreton-in-Marsh.

JUNE – MID
Bristol Horse Show:
Ashton Court Estate, Bristol.
Details: 10 Longwood House, Failand, Bristol, BS8 3TL.
JULY – 3RD WEEK
Northavon Tug-of-War Club Open Day:
Pucklechurch Recreation Ground, Pucklechurch, Bristol, Avon.
JULY – 4TH WEEK
Western Counties Senior & Junior Water Polo Finals:
Bristol University, Bristol, Avon.
AUGUST – 1ST WEEK
English Girls' Close Amateur Golf Championship:
Cirencester Golf Club, Cirencester.
AUGUST – 1ST WEEK
Yatton R.C.C. Tug-of-War Open Day:
Yatton, R.F.C., Northend, Yatton.
AUGUST – 2ND WEEK
Upton Tug-of-War Open Day:
Village Hall, Upton, St. Leonards.
AUGUST – 4TH WEEK
Polo: Cheltenham Cup:
Cirencester Park, Cirencester.
SEPTEMBER
Pony Club Horse Trials Championships:
Cheltenham.
DECEMBER – 1ST WEEK
Indoor National Tug-of-War Championships:
Sports Centre, Gloucester.

Regattas:

JUNE OR JULY
Bristol Harbour Regatta & Rally of

Boats:
City Docks, Bristol, Avon.

SPORTS

FEBRUARY – 3RD WEEK
Gloucestershire Open Badminton Championships:
Gloucester Leisure Centre, Station Road, Gloucester.
FEBRUARY – 4TH WEEK
Ashton Court Invitation Squash Matches:
Ashton Court Country Club, Bristol, Avon.
APRIL – 3RD WEEK
Badminton Horse Trials:
Badminton.
MAY – 2ND WEEK
South West Area Tug-of-War Championships:
Sports Stadium, Whitchurch, Bristol, Avon.
MAY – 3RD WEEK
Weston Farmers Tug-of-War Club Annual Competition:
Recreation Ground, Redhill, Nr. Bristol, Avon.
JUNE – 1ST WEEK
Royal Oak Tug-of-War Club Portishead Annual Competition:
Flower Show Field, Clevedon Road, Portishead, Bristol, Avon.

MISCELLANEOUS

MARCH – 3RD WEEK
West of England Qualifying Brass Band Championships:
Colston Hall & Victoria Rooms, Bristol, Avon.
APRIL – LATE
Bristol Ideal Home Exhibition:
Bristol Exhibition Complex, Canons Road, Bristol, Avon.
MAY – 2ND WEEK
Commencement of South West Coast Run of the Vintage Motorcycle Club:
Canons Marsh Car Park, Bristol, Avon.
JUNE – 3RD WEEK
National Folk Day Displays:
Broadmead Shopping Precinct, Bristol, Avon.
JULY – 1ST WEEK
Air Day:
Sudeley Castle, Winchcombe.
AUGUST – 1ST & 2ND WEEKS
International Caravan Rally:
Cheltenham.
SEPTEMBER
Bristol International Balloon Fiesta:
Ashton Court Estate, Bristol, Avon.

◆ *Hampshire* ◆

FORDINGBRIDGE RUSTIC SPORTS
A day of fun and frolics is guaranteed to all who attend this popular local shindig. The Barrel Riding event pictured is one of a number of decidedly unusual sports and activities open to the public. See: OLD CUSTOMS

◆

Old Customs

MARCH 25 (LADY DAY)
The Tichborne Dole:
Tichborne.
This curious custom, which began in the 12th century, is a yearly re-enactment of Lady Mabella Tichborne's deathbed wish. It is said her husband promised to give the poor people in the village the yield from as much land as she could crawl around before the flame from a burning faggot which he took from the fire expired. The resulting 23 acres, known as The Crawls, produces about 30 hundredweights of flour each year.
ROGATION SUNDAY
Blessing the Sea Ceremony:
Mudeford.
ROGATION SUNDAY
Blessing of the Waters:
Southampton.
Members of the clergy, civic dignitaries and other officials proceed in procession to the Ocean Dock where a service is held. The blessing itself is performed from a small boat moored inshore, followed by another service on the Town Quay.
MAY 1 (MAY DAY)
Singing on Bargate:
South Lawn, Bargate, Southampton.
The choir of King Edward VI school sing carols to greet the 1st of May.
JULY 28
Fordingbridge Rustic Sports:
Recreation Ground, Ringwood Road, Fordingbridge.
AUGUST 1
Knighthood of the Old Green:
Southampton.
The game of bowls in England has ancient origins and the green at Southampton is reputed to be the oldest in the world. This particular competition was first held in 1776 and the various players go under the title of

'gentlemen commoners' and are supervised by 'knights of the green', dressing for the occasion in top hats and tails.
OCTOBER 7
Bell-Ringers' Feast:
Twyford.
One of the Twyford landowners, William Davis, was narrowly saved from death by the sound of the bells in the parish church while returning home in a fog one night. Therefore in his will dated April 22 1754, he bequeathed the sum of £1 to the parish bell-ringers to be paid on October 7, for ever, providing the bells were rung on the morning and evening of that day. A feast follows the traditional evening ringing which is paid by the ringers and their guests every other year.
OCTOBER 21
Trafalgar Day Ceremonies:
Portsmouth.
A service is conducted on board H.M.S. Victory, and a wreath is laid on the spot that Lord Nelson was alleged to have fallen.
DECEMBER 24 (CHRISTMAS EVE)
Andover Mummers Play:
Andover.
An 800 years old play performed by players dressed in costumes of paper streamers.
DECEMBER 26 (BOXING DAY)
Mummers' Play:
Crookham.
This particular Mumming play has been performed for over a century and is distinguished by the fact that many of the players are dressed in paper strips.

Festivals

FEBRUARY – APRIL
Portsmouth Musical Competition Festival:
Portsmouth.
Details: Mrs. R. Ryan, Eveleigh Road, Farlington.
MARCH – 3RD WEEK
Petersfield Musical Festival:
Petersfield.
Details: Ms. W. K. Purches, Landfall, Tilmore, Petersfield.
MARCH
Winchester & County Music Festival:
Winchester.
MARCH/APRIL
Fareham Musical Festival:
Fareham.
Details: Mrs. D. Kilford, 67 Park Lane, Fareham.
EASTER
Bournemouth Easter Festival:
Bournemouth.
MAY – EARLY OR MID
Winchester Folk Festival:
Details: David Slater, Woodfidley Cottage, New Road, Swanmore.
MAY – 4TH WEEK, TO JUNE – 2ND WEEK
Portsmouth Festival:
Portsmouth.
Details: Portsmouth Festival, Guildhall, Portsmouth.
MAY/JUNE
Aldershot Musical Festival:
Aldershot.
Details: G. Waller, 6 Birchett Road, Aldershot.
MAY/JUNE
Bournemouth Festival of Dance:
Bournemouth.
Dept. of Tourism & Publicity, Westover Road, Bournemouth.

JUNE – 1ST WEEK
Atton Folk Festival:
Atton.

JUNE – 1ST WEEK
Flower Festival:
The Abbey, Farnborough.

JUNE – 2ND WEEK
Children's Festival:
Salisbury.

JUNE – 2ND WEEK
Christchurch Folk Festival:
Christchurch.
*Details: Nikki White, 10 Old Wareham
Road, Parkstone, Poole, Dorset.*

JUNE – 2ND WEEK
Eastleigh Arts Association Festival:
Town Hall, Leigh Road, Eastleigh.

JUNE – MID
Christchurch Folk Festival:
Christchurch.

JUNE – 4TH WEEK
Flower & Music Festival:
The Vicarage, Burley.

JUNE – LAST WEEKEND
Flower Festival:
The Vyne, Sherborne St. John.

JUNE/AUGUST
Fair Oak Theatre Festival:
Fair Oak Theatre, Rogate Village, Nr.
Petersfield.

SUMMER
Winchester Summer Festival:
Winchester.
*Details: 52 Ravensdale Avenue, London,
N12 9HT.*

JULY – 1ST & 2ND WEEKS
Winchester Festival of Music:
Winchester.
*Details: c/o Publicity Secretary, 5 The
Close, Winchester.*

JULY – 3RD WEEK
Buckler's Hard Village Festival:
Buckler's Hard, Beaulieu.

JULY – 4TH WEEK
Portsmouth County Cricket Festival:
United Services Ground, Burnaby Road,
Portsmouth.

JULY
Southern Cathedrals' Festival
Salisbury/Winchester.

AUGUST – 3RD WEEK
The Wine Festival:
The Town Hall, Leigh Road, Eastleigh.

AUGUST – 4TH WEEK
The Wessex Flower Festival:
College of Nautical Studies, Newtown
Road, Warsash.

AUGUST
Edington Music Festival:
Edington Priory Church, Edington.

AUGUST/OCTOBER/NOVEMBER
Basingstoke Music Festival:
Basingstoke.
Details: Ms. J. H. Paterson, Manor

*Farm, Farleigh Wallop, Basingstoke
RG25 2HR.*
Brownsea Open Air Theatre Festival:
Brownsea.
*Details: c/o Publicity Officer, 13 Somerset
Road, Boscombe, Bournemouth.*

SEPTEMBER – 1ST WEEK
Waterlooville Folklore Festival:
Waterlooville.
*Details: P. Chadbund, 82 Sandy Lane,
Fair Oak, Eastleigh.*

SEPTEMBER – 2ND WEEK
Whitchurch Folk Festival:
Whitchurch.
*Details: Rip Rippingdale, 49 Monserat
Road, Popley, Basingstoke.*

SEPTEMBER – 2ND & 3RD WEEKS
Salisbury Festivities:
Salisbury.

SEPTEMBER – 4TH WEEK
**Alton One Day Festival of Dance &
Music:**
Alton.
*Details: Graham Roberts, 30 Abbey Road,
Alton.*

SEPTEMBER – 4TH WEEK
**Southampton Old Time Dance
Festival:**
Guildhall, West Morlands Road,
Southampton.

OCTOBER – 3RD WEEK
**Southampton Ballroom Dance
Festival:**
Guildhall, West Morlands Road,
Southampton.

OCTOBER
Gosport Music Festival:
Gosport.
*Details: Ms. E. M. Wood, 4 Bury
Crescent, Gosport.*

FAIRS

LAST SUNDAY IN FEBRUARY; OCTOBER
– 4TH WEEK
Winchester Fair:
Winchester.

TRINITY MONDAY (8 DAYS AFTER
WHIT SUNDAY)
Southampton Fair:
Southampton.

MAY – 4TH WEEK
Annual Forest Fair:
New Park Showground, Brockenhurst.

JUNE – 2ND WEEK
Medieval Fair:
Lyndhurst First School, Lyndhurst.

JUNE – 2ND WEEK
Portchester Village Fair:
Portchester Castle Recreation Ground,
Fareham.

JUNE – 3RD WEEK
Spice Island "Waterman's Fair":
Bath Square, Portsmouth.

JUNE – 4TH WEEK
Summer Fair:
Warsash Recreation Ground, Fareham.

WHITSUN
Whitsun Fair:
Southampton.

JULY – 1ST WEEK
Freemart Fair:
Governors Green, Old Portsmouth.

JULY – 2ND WEEK
Hampshire County Fair:
Queen Elizabeth Country Park, Gravel
Hill, Horndean, Portsmouth.

JULY – 4TH WEEK
Thorney Hill Country Fair:
Playing Field, Burley Road, Thorney
Hill, Nr. Bransgore.

AUGUST – 3RD WEEK
**Annual Country Sports and Crafts
Fair:**
National Motor Museum, Beaulieu.

AUGUST – LAST WEEKEND
Antiques Fair:
The Guildhall, Portsmouth.

SEPTEMBER – 2ND WEEK
Petersfield Antiques Fair:
Town Hall, Heath Road, Petersfield.

SEPTEMBER – 2ND WEEK
Fondroyant Fair:
On board Frigate 'Fondroyant',
Portsmouth Harbour, Portsmouth.

SEPTEMBER – 4TH WEEK
Antiques & Collectors' Fair:
Town Hall, Leigh Road, Eastleigh.

SEPTEMBER – 4TH WEEK
National Wildlife Fair:
Marwell Zoological Park, Nr.
Winchester.

OCTOBER – 1ST WEEK
Taro Fair
The Heath, Heath Road, Petersfield.

OCTOBER 11
Basingstoke Fair:
Basingstoke.

OCTOBER – 3RD WEEK
Eastleigh United Charities Fair:
Town Hall, Leigh Road, Eastleigh.

NOVEMBER – 1ST WEEK
Craft Fair:
The Guildhall, Portsmouth.

NOVEMBER – 1ST WEEK
Fireworks Fair:
National Motor Museum, Beaulieu.

NOVEMBER – 4TH WEEK
Bournemouth Book Fair:
Linden Hall Hotel, Bournemouth.

NOVEMBER 17
Andover Fair:
Andover.

FAYRES

JUNE – EARLY
Old English Fayre:

RINGWOOD CARNIVAL
The newly crowned Queen of Ringwood sits on her throne surrounded by her attendants which include Pearly Kings and Queens. See: CARNIVALS.

KNIGHTHOOD OF THE OLD GREEN BOWLING MATCH
Believed to be the oldest in the world, the bowling green at Southampton is the setting for the game of bowls' most unusual contest which dates back to 1776. See: OLD CUSTOMS.

Walpole Park, Gosport.

BAZAARS

NOVEMBER
P.D.S.A. Bazaar:
The Guidhall, Portsmouth.

CARNIVALS

MAY – 4TH WEEK
Alton Spring Carnival:
Anstey Park, Anstey Lane, Alton.
WHITSUN

Portchester Carnival:
Portchester.
JUNE – 3RD WEEK
Waterside Carnival (& Fair):
Fawley Parish, Fawley.
JUNE – 3RD WEEK
Hythe Carnival:
Hythe.
JUNE – 3RD WEEK
Sarisbury Annual Carnival:
Sarisbury Green, Fareham.
JUNE – 4TH WEEK
Totton & Eling Carnival
Totton.

JUNE – 4TH WEEK
West End Carnival:
Hatch Grange, Hedge End.

JUNE – 4TH WEEK
Fleet Carnival:
Fleet.

JULY – 1ST WEEK
Hedge End Carnival Week:
Recreation Ground, Hedge End.

JULY – 1ST WEEK
Andover Carnival Procession:
Town Centre, Andover.

JULY – 2ND WEEK
Basingstoke Carnival:
Basingstoke.

JULY – 2ND WEEK
Southampton Carnival:
Southampton.

JULY – 2ND WEEK
Portsmouth Carnival Day:
Portsmouth.

JULY – 2ND WEEK
Winchester Carnival:
Winchester.

JULY – 3RD WEEK
Hamble Carnival:
Mount Pleasant Rectory, Hamble.

JULY – 3RD WEEK
Fair Oak Carnival:
Recreation Ground, Shorts Road, Fair
Oak.

JULY – 4TH WEEK
Romsey Town Carnival Week:
Crosfield Hall, Broadwater Road,
Romsey.

JULY – 4TH WEEK
**Lee-on-the-Solent Carnival (& Solent
Show):**
Recreation Ground, Salisbury Terrace,
Lee-on-the-Solent, Gosport.

AUGUST – 2ND & 3RD WEEKS
Lyndhurst Carnival:
Football Ground, Wellands Round, &
various venues, Lyndhurst.

AUGUST – 3RD WEEK
Eastleigh Carnival:
Town Centre, Eastleigh.

AUGUST – 3RD WEEK
Lymington Carnival:
Woodside Park, Lymington.

SEPTEMBER – 3RD WEEK
Ringwood Carnival:
Carvers Recreation Ground, Ringwood.

GALAS

JUNE – 1ST WEEK
**R.N.L.I./Calshot Activities Centre
Galal Day:**
Calshot Activities Centre, Calshot.

JULY – 2ND WEEK
Lymington Gala Day:
Wellworthy Ampress, Southampton
Road, Lymington.

OCTOBER – 2ND WEEK
Johann Strauss Gala:
The Guildhall, Portsmouth.

PAGEANTS

JULY – 3RD WEEK
Bournemouth Air Pageant:
Hurn Airport, Christchurch.

SHOWS

AUGUST
Water Show:
Wellington Country Park, Riseley.

SEPTEMBER – 3RD WEEK
Southampton International Boat Show:
Mayflower Park, Town Quay,
Southampton.

TATTOOS

JUNE – LAST WEEKEND
S.S.A.F.A. Aldershot Tattoo:
Rushmore Arena, Aldershot.

JULY – 4TH WEEK
**Royal Marine Volunteer Cadets
Tattoo:**
H.M.S. Barracks, Easteny, Southsea.

SEPTEMBER – 3RD WEEK
H.M.S. Vernon Searchlight Tattoo:
H.M.S. Vernon, Portsmouth.

AGRICULTURAL, HORTICULTURAL & BREED SHOWS

JUNE – EARLY
**National Cactus & Succulent Society
Show:**
Holy Spirit Church Hall, Fawcett Road,
Southsea.

JUNE – 1ST WEEK
Country Show:
Wellington Country Park, Riseley.

JUNE – 2ND WEEK
Exemption Dog Show:
Burridge Recreation Ground, Fareham.

JUNE – MID
Fareham Show:
Cams Hall, Portchester Road, Fareham.

JUNE – MID
Bishop Waltham Agricultural Show:
Bishop Waltham.

JUNE
Royal Counties Show:
Kingsclere

JUNE – 4TH WEEK
Harefield Show:
Moorhill School, Minstead Avenue,
Harefield, Southampton.

JUNE – 4TH WEEK
Cacti Show:

Town Hall, Leigh Road, Eastleigh.

JULY – 2ND WEEK
Country Agricultural Show (& Fayre):
Queen Elizabeth Country Park, Gravel
Hill, Horndean, Portsmouth.

JULY – 2ND WEEK
Southampton Show:
The Common, The Avenue,
Southampton.

JULY – 2ND WEEK
Salisbury Hobbies & Leisure Show:
St. Edmund's Art Centre, Salisbury.

JULY – 3RD WEEK
Championship Obedience Dog Show:
Cam Alders Stadium, Fareham.

JULY – 4TH WEEK
New Forest Agricultural Show:
New Park, Brockenhurst.

JULY
Fordingbridge Agricultural Show:
Fordingbridge.

JULY
Southampton Horticultural Show:
Civic Centre, Southampton.

AUGUST – 1ST WEEK
Heckfield Agricultural Show:
Wellington Country Park, Riseley.

AUGUST – 1ST WEEK
Southsea Show:
Southsea Common, Southsea.

AUGUST – EARLY
**The Great Christchurch Show (&
Wine Festival):**
Bernard's Mead, Christchurch.

AUGUST – 2ND WEEK
Ellingham Show:
Somerley Park, Ringwood.

AUGUST – 3RD
Mid Southern Counties Show:
Rushmoor Arena, Aldershot.

AUGUST – 4TH WEEK
Stocklands Show:
Equestrian Centre, Stocklands.

AUGUST – 4TH WEEK
**August Bank Holiday Agricultural
Show:**
Anstey Park, Anstey Lane, Alton.

AUGUST
**New Forest Pony Breeding and Cattle
Society's Summer Show:**
Burley.

SEPTEMBER – 1ST WEEK
Alresford Agricultural Show:
Tichborne Park, Alresford.

SEPTEMBER – 2ND WEEK
Romsey Agricultural & Horse Show:
Broadlands Park, Romsey.

SEPTEMBER – 2ND WEEK
**National Cactus & Succulent Society
Show:**
Holy Trinity Church Hall, West Street,
Fareham.

SEPTEMBER – 4TH WEEK
Basingstoke Show:

The Common, London Road,
Basingstoke.
OCTOBER – 4TH WEEK
**Portsmouth Horticultural Society
Autumn Show:**
The Guildhall, Portsmouth.

SPORTS

MAY
**British Long Bow Society Annual
Meet:**
Winchester.
JUNE – 2ND WEEK
Archery Championships:
Overton Black Arrows Field,
Kingsclere.
JUNE – 3RD WEEK
**Bordon Tug-of-War Open
Competition:**
Mill Chase Recreation Ground, Bordon.
JUNE – 4TH WEEK
Southern Horse Show:
Langford Farm, Woodlands,
Southampton.
JULY – 2ND WEEK
Hampshire & Isle of Wight Games:
Applemore Recreation Centre, Hythe,
Southampton.
JULY – 2ND WEEK
Southsea Lawn Tennis Tournament:
Canoe Lake Grounds, Southsea.
JULY – 4TH WEEK
**Lawn Tennis County Championships
(Prudential County Cup):**
Canoe Lake Grounds, Southsea.
AUGUST – EARLY
Southsea Bowls Tournament:
Castle Green, Southsea.
AUGUST – MID
Southsea Junior Tennis Tournament:
Southsea Castle Hard Courts, Southsea.
SEPTEMBER – 1ST WEEK
Pier to Pier Swimming:
South Parade Pier to Clarence Pier,
Southsea.
OCTOBER – 1ST WEEK
New Forest Horse Trial:
New Park, Brockenhurst.
OCTOBER – 1ST WEEK
**Southern England Open Majorette
Championships:**
Guildhall, West Midlands Road,
Southampton.
OCTOBER – 4TH WEEK
Hampshire Archery Championships:
Kingsclere.

MISCELLANEOUS

JUNE – 2ND WEEK
Andover Steam Rally & Country Show:
Balkesbury Hill, Salisbury Road,
Andover.

JUNE – 2ND WEEK
Southsea Vintage Vehicle Rally:
Southsea Common, Southsea.
JUNE – 3RD WEEK
**Re-Enactment of the Napoleonic
Battles:**
Wellington Country Park, Nr.
Basingstoke.
JUNE – 4TH WEEK
**Southern Counties Youth Band
Championships:**
Barton Peveril College, Cherbourg
Road, Eastleigh.
JUNE – 4TH WEEK
English Civil War Battle:
Breamore House, Breamore.
JUNE – 4TH WEEK
Austin 750 Club Rally:
National Motor Museum Complex,
Beaulieu.
JUNE – ALL MONTH
**Portsmouth Command Field Gun Crew
Displays:**
H.M.S. Excellent, Whale Island,
Portsmouth.
JULY – 1ST WEEK
Austin 750 Club Rally:
National Motor Museum, Beaulieu.
JULY – 1ST WEEK
Summer Market:
Normansland Green, Normansland, Nr.
Salisbury.
JULY – 2ND WEEK
**Military Parade: Royal Green Jackets
Sounding the Retreat:**
Peninsula Barracks, Romsey Road,
Winchester.
JULY – MID

NATIONAL NURDLING
CHAMPIONSHIPS
*It is not surprising to learn that the
comedian Michael Bentine of Goon fame
was the inspiration behind the now annual
Nurdling Championships in which
contestants have to carry a 16-foot pole over
an obstacle course. See:
MISCELLANEOUS.*

◆

National Nurdling Championships:
Hill View Farm, Grateley, Nr. Middle
Wallop.
JULY – 3RD WEEK
**Annual Netley Marsh Steam & Vintage
Rally:**
Meadow Farm, Ringwood Road, Netley
Marsh, Southampton.
JULY – 3RD WEEK
Lee-on-Solent Air Day
H.M.S. Daedalus, Nottingham Place,
Lee-on-Solent.
AUGUST – 4TH WEEK
Navy Days:
H.M. Dockyard, The Hard,
Portsmouth.
SEPTEMBER, TO OCTOBER – EARLY
**Hambledon Vineyard & Wine Press
Open Days:**
Hambledon.
OCTOBER – 1ST & 2ND WEEKS
Ideal Home Exhibition:
Guildhall, Portsmouth.
OCTOBER – 2ND WEEK
Round Up Of Ponies:
New Forest.

HAMPSHIRE
◆ *Isle of Wight* ◆

ALL THIS BEAUTY IS OF GOD

White yacht small as a dot
Just a tissue wing on the sea,
Sailing on a tack past Colwell Head
Past the Needles surreal promontory.

Bramble Chine on the far skyline
No longer a picturesque view,
Yet touches remain of a time gone by
When Bramble's was worth passing through.

FROM 'ISLAND OF DREAMS'
BY BERNARD SCHOFIELD

OLD CUSTOMS

JANUARY — EARLY
Blessing of the Plough:
Parish Church, Newchurch.
MAY — 4TH WEEK
Ventnor Crab Fayre:
Botanic Gardens, Steephill, Ventnor.
As the name implies this Victorian fayre
was once a thriving event for the buying and
selling of crabs and other seafood which
featured strongly as an industry in the area.
Today the fair is a pleasure occasion which
attracts visitors from all over the island and
is organised by the Ventnor Lions charity
group.

FESTIVALS

MARCH
**Isle of Wight Musical Competition
Festival:**
Details: Ms. D. Hodgkins, 2 Cornwall
Street, Ryde.
SEPTEMBER — 2ND WEEK
Isle of Wight Wine & Beer Festival:
Town Hall, Ryde.

FAIRS

JUNE — LATE
Shorewell Midsummer Fair:
Northcourt Manor, Shorwell.

CARNIVALS

JULY — 2ND WEEK
West Cowes Carnival:
Cowes.
JULY — 4TH WEEK
Shanklin Carnival:
Shanklin.
AUGUST — 1ST WEEK
Sandown Carnival:
Sandown.
AUGUST — EARLY
**Freshwater & Totland Carnival
Procession:**
Freshwater & Totland
AUGUST — 2ND WEEK
East Cowes Carnival:
East Cowes.
AUGUST — 2ND & 3RD WEEKS
Yarmouth Carnival Week:
Offshore and Onshore, Yarmouth.
AUGUST — 3RD WEEK
Ventnor Illuminated Carnival:
Ventnor.

AUGUST — 3RD WEEK
East Cowes Illuminated Carnival:
East Cowes.
AUGUST — 4TH WEEK
Sandown Illuminated Carnival:
Sandown.
AUGUST — 4TH WEEK
Newport Illuminated Carnival:
Newport.
AUGUST — 4TH WEEK
St. Helens Carnival & Sports
Main Streets and Village Green, St.
Helens.
SEPTEMBER — 1ST WEEK
Ryde Illuminated Carnival:
Ryde.
SEPTEMBER — 1ST WEEK
Shanklin Illuminated Carnival:
Shanklin.
SEPTEMBER — 1ST WEEK
**Cowes Illuminated Carnival
Procession:**
Main Streets, Cowes.

GALAS

JULY — EARLY
Annual Youth Swimming Gala:
Seaclose, Newport.

NEWPORT CARNIVAL
As with the West Country the Island is
renowned for its carnivals. One of the many
floats from the Newport Carnival procession
is shown here. See: CARNIVALS.

TIN BATH RACE
The perfectly daft Tin Bath Race brings a
touch of lunacy to the otherwise serious and
professional sailing mentality of famous
Cowes. See: SPORTS.

SHOWS

EASTER SUNDAY
Easter Parade:
The Esplanade, Sandown.
JULY – 4TH WEEK
Summer Show:
Recreation Ground, Brighstone.

AGRICULTURAL, HORTICULTURAL & BREED SHOWS

JUNE – LATE
Rose, Carnation & Sweet Pea Show:
Nine Acres School, South View, Newport.
JULY – 3RD WEEK
Royal Isle of Wight Agricultural Show:
County Showground, Northwood.
JULY – 4TH WEEK
Brighstone Horticultural Show:
Brighstone.
AUGUST – 1ST WEEK
Chillerton Horticultural Show:
The School, Chillerton.
AUGUST – 2ND WEEK
Chale Horticultural Show:
Hill Crest Farm, Military Road, Chale.
AUGUST – 2ND WEEK
Niton & Whitwell Summer Horticultural Show:
County Primary School, Niton.
AUGUST – 3RD WEEK
Carisbrooke Cottage Garden Society Show:
Recreation Grounds, Carisbrooke.
AUGUST – 4TH WEEK
Northwood Village Produce Association Show:
W.I. Institute Hall, Northwood.
AUGUST – 4TH WEEK
Ventnor Horticultural Show:
Ventnor Park, Ventnor.
SEPTEMBER – 2ND WEEK
Plessey Garden Club Show:
Plessey's Fields, Three Gates, Nr. Cowes.
SEPTEMBER – 2ND WEEK
Wootton Horticultural Show:
Church Hall, Wootton.
SEPTEMBER – 3RD WEEK
Isle of Wight Chrysanthemum & Dahlia Show:
Village Hall, Godshill.
OCTOBER – 1ST WEEK
Carisbrooke Garden Society Autumn Show:
Village Hall, Carisbrooke.
OCTOBER – 4TH WEEK
Open Dog Show:
Town Hall,

SUMMER STEAM SHOW
Model traction engines, like the one pictured here, are a regular feature of vintage steam shows on the island. See:
MISCELLANEOUS.

◆

SPORTS

JUNE – 3RD WEEK
Round the Island Yacht Race:
Depart from: Cowes.
JUNE – 3RD WEEK
Croquet Tournament:
Play Street Lane, Ryde.
JULY – 4TH WEEK
Ryde Open Annual Tournament:
Ryde.
JULY – 4TH WEEK
Dinghy Week:
Cowes.
AUGUST – 2ND WEEK
Cowes Week (Yacht Racing):
Cowes.
AUGUST – 2ND WEEK
The R.O.R.C. Fastnet Race (Yacht Racing):
Depart from: Cowes.
AUGUST – 2ND WEEK
Tin Bath Race:
Offshire, The Parade, Cowes.
AUGUST – 3RD WEEK
Newtown Randy:
Main Street, Newtown.
AUGUST – 3RD WEEK
Yarmouth Folk Boat Week:
Yarmouth.
AUGUST – 4TH WEEK
Cowes to Torquay Power Boat Race:
Depart from: Cowes.

AUGUST – 4TH WEEK
Round the Island Power Boat Race:
Depart from: Cowes.
SEPTEMBER – 2ND WEEK
South Coast Amateur Rowing Championships:
Shanklin.
SEPTEMBER – 3RD WEEK
Open Croquet Tournament:
Playstreet Lane, Ryde.

Regattas:

JULY – LATE
The Royal Solent Yacht Club Regatta:
The Solent, Yarmouth.
JULY – LATE, OR AUGUST – EARLY
Colwell, Freshwater & Totland Regatta:
Colwell Beach and Colwell Common, Colwell.
JULY – 4TH WEEK
Ryde Regatta:
Ryde.
AUGUST – 2ND WEEK
Sandown Bay Regatta:
Shore and offshore, Esplanade, Sandown.
AUGUST – 3RD WEEK
Shanklin Regatta:
Seafront, Shanklin.
AUGUST – 3RD WEEK
Bembridge Sailing Club Regatta:
Bembridge.
AUGUST – 3RD WEEK
Seaview Regatta:
Seaview.
AUGUST – 4TH WEEK
Bembridge Village Regatta:
Bembridge.
SEPTEMBER – 2ND WEEK
Folly Regatta:
Off the Folly Inn, The River Medina, Whippingham, Nr. East Cowes.

MISCELLANEOUS

AUGUST – 4TH WEEK
Summer Steam Show:
Isle of Wight Steam Railway, Haven Street Station, Nr. Ryde.

HEREFORD & WORCESTER
◆ *Herefordshire* ◆

The ground seemed cut up from the fellowship
Of verdure, field from field, as man from man;
The skies themselves looked low and positive,
As almost you could touch them with a hand,
And dared to do it they were so far off
From God's celestial crystals; all things blurred
And dull and vague. Did Shakespeare and his mates
Absorb the light here? – not a hill or stone
With heart to strike a radiant colour up
Or active outline on the indifferent air.

FROM 'AURORA LEIGH REACHES HEREFORDSHIRE
FROM ITALY' BY ELIZABETH BARRETT BROWNING

OLD CUSTOMS

EASTER – PALM SUNDAY
Pax Cakes Distribution:
Hentland, Sellack & Kings Caple, Nr.
Ross-on-Wye.
A custom which began in the 16th century
when a Lady Scudamore distributed cakes
and ale to the villagers in the belief that
those who shared a common meal on Palm
Sunday would refrain from quarrelling for
the year ahead.
MAY 29
Oak Apple Day Ceremony:
Fownhope.
The local Heart of Oak Friendly Society
commemorate Oak Apple Day by parading
to the church bearing club sticks which have
been specially adorned with wooden oak
apples and flowers.

FESTIVALS

MAY – 4TH WEEK
Hereford Cider Festival:
The Cider Gardens, River Wye,
Hereford.
MAY
Herefordshire Musical Festival:
Shirehall, Hereford.
MAY
Herefordshire Festival:
Details: 25 Castle Street, Hereford, HR1
2NW.
JULY
Madley Festival:
Details: Madley Festival Society, The
Forge, Tyberton, Madley, Hereford, HR2
9PT.
SEPTEMBER – 3RD WEEK
Bromyard Folk Festival:
Bromyard.
Details: Doug Isle, Wayside Cottage, Mile
End Road, Coleford, Gloucester.

FAIRS

WEDNESDAY AFTER FEBRUARY 2; 1ST
WEDNESDAY AFTER MARCH 2; 1ST
WEDNESDAY IN APRIL; 1ST
WEDNESDAY AND THURSDAY AFTER
MAY 2; 1ST WEDNESDAY IN JULY; 3RD
WEDNESDAY IN AUGUST; 3RD
WEDNESDAY IN OCTOBER; 2ND
WEDNESDAY IN DECEMBER
Hereford Fair:
Hereford.
AUGUST – 3RD WEEK
Hereford Annual Antiques Fair:
Green Dragon Hotel, Hereford.

PARADES

MAY
Mayor's Sunday Parade:
Hereford.

AGRICULTURAL, HORTICULTURAL & BREED SHOWS

JULY – 3RD WEEK
City of Herefordshire Show:
Hereford Racecourse, Hereford.
AUGUST – 4TH WEEK
Leominister Show:
Leominister.

SPORTS

Regattas:

JUNE
Hereford City Regatta:
Details: Mark Jabale, Belmont Abbey,
Hereford.
AUGUST
Ross-on-Wye Regatta:
Details: W.J. Watkins, 'Onaway', Kerne
Bridge, Ross-on-Wye.

MADLEY FESTIVAL
The magnificent 13th century Parish Church at Madley lying in beautiful surroundings near the River Wye is the idyllic setting for a music festival, a week-long affair which also features exhibitions of local arts and crafts. See: FESTIVALS.

CYDER FESTIVAL
The Market Fayre pictured here is one of many individual events staged during Hereford's old Cyder Festival which takes place in the Cider Gardens in Hereford City. The ladies who serve their wares dressed in historical costume add an air of authenticity to the occasion. See: FESTIVALS.

HEREFORD & WORCESTER
◆ *Worcestershire* ◆

But on a May morning, on Malvern Hills,
A marvel befel me, sure from Faery it came;
I had wandered me weary, so weary, I rested me
On a broad bank by a merry-sounding burn;
And as I lay and leaned and looked into the waters
I slumbered in a sleeping, it rippled so merrily,
And I dreamed – marvelously.

WILLIAM LANGLAND

Old Customs

JANUARY I (NEW YEAR'S DAY)
Winbury Dole:
Castlemorton.
This particular dole is over four hundred years old and consists of a specially baked cake which is distributed after the morning service.

MAY 29
Oak Apple Day Ceremony:
Guildhall, Worcester.
In commemoration of Charles II triumphant entry into London after the Reformation of 1660, the Guildhall gates are adorned with oak boughs and a commemorative service held.

JUNE 24
Peace & Good Neighbourhood Dinner
Church Street, Kidderminster.
A fifteenth century bequest by an unknown lady stipulated that forty shillings be used annually for the benefit of the inhabitants of Church Street. Dinner is served at St. Mary's Church and Church Warden pipes are also traditionally smoked.

Festivals

MARCH
Worcestershire Orchestral Society Competitive Music Festival:
Details: B.A. Plant, 48 The Drive, Colletts Green, Powick.
APRIL
Worcestershire Federation of Women's Institutes Annual Music Festival:
Details: Ms. J.R. Habgood, Well Cottage, Loggerheads, Mere Green, Nr. Droitwich.
MAY – IST & 2ND WEEKS

Bromsgrove Festival:
Details: Bromsgrove Festival Ltd., 10 Kidderminster Road, Bromsgrove, B61 7JW.
MAY – 3RD & 4TH WEEKS
Dudley Spring Festival
Details: Director of Leisure & Recreation, Dudley Metropolitan Borough, 3 St. James' Road, Dudley, DY1 1HU.
MAY – 3RD WEEK, TO JUNE – IST WEEK
Malvern Festival:
Details: Artistic Director, Malvern Festival, Harold Holt Ltd., 134 Wigmore Street, London, W1.
JUNE/JULY
Pershore Festival:
Details: Ms. R.S.D. Veal, Hill Cottage, Tyddesley Wood, Pershore.
JULY
Catshill Music Festival:
Details: Ms. M. Wheeler, 54 Meadow Road, Catshill, Bromsgrove.
AUGUST – IST WEEK
Malvern Health Festival:
Malvern.
Details: Malvern Hills Health Foundation, 249 Worcester Road, Malvern Link.
OCTOBER – BIENNIAL
Stoke Prior Autumn Arts Festival:
Details: L.G. Harris & Co Ltd., Stoke Prior Brushworks, Bromsgrove, B60 4AE.

OCTOBER – BIENNIAL (NEXT ONE 1983)
Pershore Organ Festival:
Details: 76 Bridge Street, Pershore, WR10 1AX.
NOVEMBER
Worcester College of Education Arts Festival:
Details: Worcester College of Education, Oldbury Road, Worcester.

FAIRS

1ST MONDAY IN MARCH, MAY & OCTOBER; 2ND MONDAY IN AUGUST
Dudley Fair:
Dudley, West Midlands.
FRIDAYS BEFORE AND AFTER OCTOBER 11
Evesham Fair:
Evesham.
2ND TUESDAY EVERY MONTH; MARCH 25; APRIL 18; 3RD THURSDAY IN JULY
Kidderminster Fair:
Kidderminster.
SEPTEMBER 19
Worcester Fair:
Worcester.

CARNIVALS

JULY – 1ST WEEK
Worcester City Carnival:
Pithcroft, Worcester.
JULY – 1ST WEEK
Droitwich Carnival:
Droitwich.

GALAS

JUNE – 4TH WEEK
Droitwich Gala:
Lido Park, Droitwich.

AGRICULTURAL, HORTICULTURAL & BREED SHOWS

JUNE – 2ND WEEK
Three Counties Agricultural Show:
Showyard, Malvern.
JULY – 4TH WEEK
Worcester City Show:
Perdiswell, Worcester.
AUGUST – 4TH WEEK
Evesham Flower Show:
Evesham.
AUGUST – 4TH WEEK
Droitwich Annual Horticultural Show:
Droitwich.
AUGUST
National Pony Society Annual Show:
Malvern.
AUGUST
Madresfield Agricultural Show:
Madresfield, Nr. Malvern.

▷ DROITWICH GALA
Medieval games and other historical re-enactments take place at Droitwich's colourful gala in and around the Lido Park during midsummer. See: GALAS.

WORCESTER CITY CARNIVAL
A magnificent traction engine thunders through the city streets thronged with onlookers during carnival week. See: CARNIVALS.

THREE COUNTIES SHOW
One of the most important events in the farming year takes the form of the Three Counties Show, a major attraction not just to the farming community but to thousands of visitors from all over the West Midlands. See: SHOWS.

◆

Hertfordshire ◆

TRUST AND FEAR NOT

OLD CUSTOMS

DECEMBER 26 (BOXING DAY)
St. Albans Mummers:
St. Albans.
Mumming is an ancient Christmas sport where men and women exchanged clothes and went visiting houses, making merry and partaking of Christmas cheer. From this activity arose mumming plays which still survive here and in other parts of the country.

FESTIVALS

APRIL – 4TH WEEK
Ashwell Music Festival:
Ashwell.
Details: Festival Organiser, The Rectory, Ashwell, Baldock.
MAY
Watford Music Festival:
Watford.
Details: R.F. George, 38 Orchard Drive, Watford, WD1 3DY.
MAY
Disco Festival:
Knebworth House, Knebworth.
JULY – BIENNIAL (NEXT ONE 1983)
St. Albans International Organ Festival:
St. Albans.
Details: Secretary, International Organ Festival Society, P.O. Box 80, St. Albans.
JULY – 1ST WEEK
International Folk Festival:
City Hall, Civic Centre, St. Albans.
JULY – 3RD WEEK
Flower Festival:
Hemel Hempstead.

JULY – 3RD & 4TH WEEK
Barnet Festival:
Barnet.
Details: Pam Edwards, Old Bull Gallery, 68 High Street, Barnet.
SEPTEMBER – 3RD WEEK
Aylett's Dahlia Festival:
Aylett Nurseries, North Orbital Road, Colney, St. Albans.
SEPTEMBER – 4TH WEEK
Festival of Real Bread:
Country College, 11 Harmer Green Lane, Digswell, Welwyn, AL6 0A7.
OCTOBER – 3RD & 4TH WEEK
Hemel Hempstead Arts Trust Festival:
Hemel Hempstead.
Details: Hemel Hempstead Arts Trust, 34 George Street, Hemel Hempstead, HP2 5JH.
OCTOBER
Bishop's Stortford Music Festival:
Bishop's Stortford.
Details: Ms. M. Savage, 7 Havers Lane, Bishop's Stortford.
NOVEMBER
St. Albans & District Music Festival:
St. Albans.
Details: R.G. Woodhouse, 13 Farringford Close, St. Albans.

FAIRS

APRIL 8 & 9; SEPTEMBER 4 – 6;
NOVEMBER 21
Hatfield Fair:
Hatfield.
3RD SATURDAY BEFORE EASTER; MAY 12; JULY 5; NOVEMBER 8
Hertford Fair:
Hertford.

EASTER TUESDAY AND WEDNESDAY;
WHIT TUESDAY AND WEDNESDAY;
OCTOBER 12
Hitchin Fair:
Hitchin.
MAY – 1ST WEEK
Spring Bank Holiday Fair:
Gadebridge Park, Hemel Hempstead.
JUNE – EARLY
Milton keynes Bow Country Fair:
Milton Keynes.
AUGUST – 4TH WEEK
Antiques & Collectors Fair:
Knebworth House, Nr. Stevenage.
SEPTEMBER
Stevenage Fair:
Stevenage.
WEDNESDAY AND THURSDAY AFTER
OCTOBER 11
Royston Fair:
Royston.

CARNIVALS

MAY – WEEK BEFORE BANK HOLIDAY
Rickmansworth Week (Carnival):
Rickmansworth.
MAY – 4TH WEEK
Whitsun Carnival:
Cassiobury Park, Watford.
JUNE – 3RD WEEK
Welwyn Garden City Carnival:
Town Centre, Welwyn Garden City.
JUNE – MID
Leighton-in-Slade Carnival:
Leighton-in-Slade.
JULY – 2ND WEEK
Radlett Carnival:
Harperbury Hospital, Harper Lane, Shenley.

AUGUST – 4TH WEEK
Hemel Hempstead Carnival:
Cadebridge Park, Hemel Hempstead.
SEPTEMBER – 3RD WEEK
Water Carnival:
Stamborough Park, Stanborough Road,
Welwyn Garden City.

GALAS

EASTER – SUNDAY & MONDAY
Easter Gala:
Woodside Arena, Horseshoe Lane,
Garston, Watford.
MAY DAY WEEK
May Day Gala:
Watford Shopping Precinct, High
Street, Watford.

SHOWS

AUGUST – 4TH WEEK
Watford Show Week:
Watford Precinct, Watford.
SEPTEMBER – 4TH WEEK
Hertfordshire Ideal Home Show:
Pavilion, Marlowes, Hemel Hempstead.
OCTOBER – LATE
Welwyn Woodstove Show:
Country College, 11 Harmer Green
Lane, Digswell, Welwyn, AL6 0A7.

AGRICULTURAL, HORTICULTURAL & BREED SHOWS

JANUARY – 4TH WEEK
**East of England Afghan Hound
Championship:**
*Watford Leisure Centre, Horseshoe Lane,
Garston, Watford.*
EASTER WEEKEND
Daffodil Weekend:
Thriplow, Royston.
MAY – 4TH WEEK
Hertfordshire Show:
Friars Wash, A5 Watling Street,
Redbourn.
JUNE & SEPTEMBER
Royal National Rose Society Show:
Chiswell Green Lane, St. Albans.
SEPTEMBER – 3RD WEEK
**St. Albans Horticultural Society
Autumn Flower Show:**
Aylett Nurseries, North Orbital Road,
St. Albans.

SPORTS

JANUARY
**All England Junior Badminton
Championships:**
Watford Leisure Centre, Horseshoe
Lane, Garston, Watford.

JUNE – EARLY
**Metropolitan Police Athletic
Association Annual Open Police Sports
Day:**
Aldenham Road, Bushey.
JUNE – MID
Highland Gathering:
Rothampsted Park, Harpenden.

MISCELLANEOUS

JUNE – MID
Bovingdon Revels:
Bovingdon.
JULY – 2ND WEEK
Punch Bowl Rally:
Redbourne, Nr. St. Albans.
AUGUST OR SEPTEMBER
Croxley Revels:
Croxley.
SEPTEMBER – 2ND WEEK
Dacorum Steam Rally & Fayre:
Six Tunnels Farm, Gaddesden Row,
Hemel Hempstead.

ST. ALBAN'S MUMMERS
*The celebrated mummers of St. Alban's are
seen here performing their traditional
Christmas play as one of the great surviving
traditions of the British Isles. See: OLD
CUSTOMS.*

ROYAL NATIONAL ROSE SHOW
*For rose lovers everywhere the yearly rose
displays on view at the Royal National
Rose Society grounds at St. Alban's are
pure delight. The gardens are brilliant with
an abundance of blooms from July to
September. See: SHOWS.*

COUNTY SHOW
*A prize beast is led around the arena at the
main Hertfordshire County Show held at
Friars Walsh. See: OLD CUSTOMS.*

BOVINGDON REVELS
*'Revels', as festive celebrations with music,
dancing and spontaneous entertainment, are
traditional to this part of the country.
Bovingdon's Revels make for a good day
out for all the family. See:
MISCELLANEOUS.*

◆ Kent ◆

Look to the smiling shores, to the villages set in the woodland,
Orchards and red-roof'd farms, churches and castles and all.
then to the west turn round, and see right on to the landward,
Fold upon fold, the hills rising like waves of the sea:
FROM 'ABOVE THE MEDWAY' BY A.J. MUNTY

Old Customs

JANUARY
Blessings of the Sea:
Margate.
As a celebration of Epiphany, members of the Greek community, including the Greek Orthodox Archbishop of Thyateria and Great Britain, take part in a service in which a crucifix decorated with flowers is thrown into the sea and then retrieved by a bather.

FEBRUARY – SHROVE TUESDAY
Pancake Day Races:
Northfleet.

EASTER MONDAY
Biddenden Dole:
Biddenden.
Said to have originated sometime in the 12th century by two sisters who were Siamese Twins. This charity is also known as the Biddenden Maids Charity. It has become customary over the last 200 years to present all visitors and parishioners who attend the ceremony with a biscuit bearing an impression of the sisters.

APRIL – 4TH WEEK
Blessing of the Waters & Boats:
The Jetty, Nelson Place, Broadstairs.

MAY 1 (MAY DAY)
Tilting the Quintain:
Offham.
This was once a popular medieval game and consists of a post positioned on the village green, on which a bucket of water is fixed for swinging – the Quintain, – by riders on horseback, – the Tilters.

MAY – CHERRY BLOSSOM TIME
Blessing of the Cherry Orchards:
Newington, Nr. Sittingbourne.
This recent custom takes place in an orchard near to the church where the blessing takes place.

JULY – 1ST SATURDAY
The Admiralty Court:
Ceremonial Barge, Rochester Pier, Rochester.
An act of Parliament of 1728 established the Admiralty Court which is concerned with the various matters arising over the administration of the Oyster Fisheries. The Mayor of Rochester proceeds with other dignitaries in procession to a decorated barge where the Court is held.

JULY
Blessing of the Sea:
Folkestone.

AUGUST – MID (BIENNIAL – NEXT ONE 1982)
The Venetian Festival:
Royal Military Canal, Hythe.
This impressive and colourful water pageant is presented by the Hythe Venetian Fête Society and consists of a procession of carnival floats, often depicting local historical events of interest, followed by a display of aquatic fireworks. The event, which began in 1854, commemorates the Napoleonic invasion which never occurred
in 1804–1805.

AUGUST 24
Bun & Biscuit Dole:
St. Bartholomew's Chapel, Sandwich.
Following a service in the chapel, buns and biscuits are distributed to children who have run around the chapel in order to qualify for the dole.

SEPTEMBER
Beating of the Bounds:
River Medway, Rochester.

SEPTEMBER – 1ST SATURDAY
Hop Hoodening:
Kent Hop Fields.
Details of this hop harvest celebration can be obtained from the East Kent Morris Men, 53 Rylands Road, Kennington, Ashford.

DECEMBER 24 (CHRISTMAS EVE)
Hoodening:
Folkestone.
A ceremonial horse figure which has a real horse's skull with working jaws and often a lantern inside is taken around the village from house to house to the accompaniment of carol singing and merriment. This particular Hooden Horse is accompanied by the Leader, the Rider, The Old Woman and various musicians or bellringers.

Festivals

JANUARY
Bexley Festival of Music, Speech and Dancing:
Details: London Borough of Bexley Administrative & Legal Service, Town Hall, Erith, Kent. DA8 1TL.

FEBRUARY – 3RD WEEK
Folkestone Audio Visual Festival:
Leas Cliff Hall, Folkestone.

FEBRUARY – LATE

**Medway Championship Dance
Festival:**
Corn Exchange, Rochester.
FEBRUARY – MARCH
**Tunbridge Wells Festival of Music,
Speech & Drama:**
*Details: V.J. Benning, 13 Hilden Avenue,
Hildenborough, Kent, TN11 9BY.*
MARCH – MID
Gillingham Arts Festival:
Gillingham.
*Details: Chief Amenities Officer,
Gillingham Borough Council, Municipal
Buildings, Gillingham, ME7 5LA.*
MARCH
Bromley Musical Festival:
*Details: Mrs. M.J. Rees, 10 Benenden
Street, Bromley, Kent.*
MARCH
Thanet Music & Drama Festival:
*Details: Ms. M. Raven, Paragon Lodge,
Thanet Close, Crow Hill, Broadstairs,
Kent.*
APRIL – JULY
Broadstairs Festival of Music:
*Details: Broadstairs Music Club, 5
Lanthorne Road, Broadstairs, Kent, CT10
3NH.*
APRIL – 1ST WEEK
William Harvey Festival Celebrations:
The Leas, Folkestone.
APRIL – 4TH WEEK
Thanet International Hockey Festival
Jackey Bakers Ground, Ramsgate.
MAY – 3RD WEEK
Gravesham Glad Day Festival:
Gravesham.
*Details: Education Liason Officer,
Gravesham Education Centre, 6–8
Overcliffe, Gravesend.*
MAY – MID
Caravan Festival:
Brands Hatch, Fawkham, Nr. Dartford
MAY – 4TH WEEK
Choral Festival (Free Church Choir):
Leas Cliff Hall, Folkestone.

◇ VENETIAN FESTIVAL
*A spectacular water festival held on the
Royal Military Canal and presented by the
Hythe Venetian Fête Society, a charity
organisation run by volunteers. Along the
tree-lined canal carnival floats depicting
tableaux of historical, local or humorous
interest, pass in procession which at night
are beautifully illuminated. See: OLD
CUSTOMS.*

FAVERSHAM TORCHLIGHT CARNIVAL
*One of the few torchlight carnivals of Kent
and therefore impressive by virtue of the
uniqueness of the occasion. See:*
◇ *CARNIVALS.*

MAY – 4TH WEEK
Festival of Dedication of the High Altar:
St. Augustine's Abbey, Canterbury.
MAY
Kent Competitive Festival:
Details: Ms. E.V. Anthony, 11 Swalecliffe Road, Tankerton, Whitstable, Kent, CT5 2PR.
MAY – LAST WEEKEND
Dickens Festival:
Various venues throughout the Borough of Medway.
MAY/SEPTEMBER
Canterbury Summer Arts Festival:
Details: Canterbury Arts Council, 1 New Street, Ash, Nr. Canterbury, Kent.
JUNE – 3RD WEEK
Broadstairs Dickens Festival:
Broadstairs.
JUNE – 3RD & 4TH WEEK
Festival of Music in Kent:
Details: Festival Society, Barton Cottage, 22 The Street, Kennington, Ashford, Kent, TN24 9HB.
JUNE – LATE
Stour Music Festival:
Church of All Saints, Boughton Aluph.
Details: Mrs. P. Deller, Barton Cottage, The Street, Ashford, Kent, TN24 9HB.
JUNE – 4TH WEEK (BIENNIAL)
Folkestone International Folklore Festival:
Civic Centre, Folkestone.
JUNE – LATE, TO JULY – EARLY
Bexley Arts Council Festival:
Bexley.
Details: – The Secretary, Bexley Arts Council, Hall Place, Bourne Road, Bexley.
JUNE
Sevenoaks Three Arts Festival:
Ms. J.M. Hargreaves-Browne, Flat 6, 34 High Street, Sevenoaks, Kent, TN13 1JG.
JUNE
Canterbury Cathedral Music Week:
Canterbury Cathedral, Canterbury.
JUNE
Star Festival:
Boughton Aluph.
JULY – 2ND WEEK
Cranbrook Festival:
Cranbrook.
JULY – 3RD WEEK
Tunbridge Wells Shakespeare Festival:
Tunbridge Wells.
JULY – LAST 10 DAYS OF SUMMER TERM
Canterbury Kings Week Festival:
The Kings School, Canterbury.
JULY – SATURDAY FOLLOWING KINGS WEEK FESTIVAL
Friends of the Cathedral One Day

Festival:
Canterbury Cathedral, Canterbury.
JULY – 3RD WEEK
Sevenoaks Summer Festival:
Details: Festival Manager, Sevenoaks School, High Street, Sevenoaks, Kent, TN13 1HU.
JULY – 4TH WEEK
Racing Saloon Car Festival:
Brands Hatch, Fawkham, Nr. Dartford.
AUGUST – 1ST & 2ND WEEKS
Broadstairs Folk Festival:
Details: Linda Wood, 108 Westwood Road, Broadstairs, CT10 2PB.
AUGUST – 2ND WEEK
Festival of Speed:
Brands Hatch, Fawkham, Nr. Dartford.
SEPTEMBER – 2ND WEEK
Flower Festival:
St. Christopher Church, Newington, Ramsgate.
SEPTEMBER – MID
Youth Festival:
Pantiles, Tunbridge Wells.
SEPTEMBER
Great Comp Festival:
Great comp.
Details: R. Cameron, Great Comp, Borough Green, Sevenoaks.
SEPTEMBER
Malling Festival:
Malling.
Details: Festival Chairman, Abingdon, 74 Station Road, Ditton, Nr. Maidstone.
OCTOBER – MID
Tonbridge Festival:
Tonbridge.
Details: Organiser, Lidwells House, Goudhurst, Cranbrook.
OCTOBER – 4TH WEEK
Festival of Remembrance:
Winter Gardens, Margate.
NOVEMBER – EARLY
Tunbridge Wells Independent Amateur Drama Festival:
Details: Entertainments Manager, Town Hall, Tunbridge Wells, Kent.
NOVEMBER
Folkestone Competitive Musical Festival:
Details: J. Whittaker, 4 West Cliff Gardens, Folkestone, Kent, CT20 1SR.
NOVEMBER
Beckenham Festival:
Details: G.B. Withers, 10 Highland Croft, Beckenham, Kent, BR3 1TB.
DECEMBER – 1ST WEEK
Literature Festival:
Gravesham.
Details: Literature Officer, South East Arts, 9–10 Crescent Road, Tunbridge Wells.

FAIRS

MARCH – EARLY
South East England Antiques & Collectors Fair:
Woodville Halls, Gravesham.
APRIL 7; SEPTEMBER 8; OCTOBER 27
Ashford Fair:
Ashford.
APRIL 8; OCTOBER 11
Deal Fair:
Deal.
EASTER THURSDAY
Folkestone Fair:
Folkestone.
MAY 12; JUNE 20; OCTOBER 17
Maidstone Fair:
Maidstone.
MAY
National Motor Caravan Fair:
Brands Hatch, Fawkham, Nr. Dartford.
AUGUST – 1ST WEEK
Phoenix Fair:
Ellington Park, Ramsgate.
AUGUST – 2ND WEEK
Summer Fair:
General Hospital, Margate.
OCTOBER
Hythe Fair:
Hythe.
OCTOBER – LAST FRIDAY
Tonbridge Fair:
Tonbridge.
NOVEMBER 22
Dover Fair:
Dover.

CARNIVALS

JUNE
Margate Carnival Week:
Margate.
JUNE – LATE
Higham Carnival:
Higham.
JULY – 1ST WEEK
Tunbridge Wells Carnival:
Tunbridge Wells.
JULY – 4TH WEEK
Maidstone Carnival (& River Regatta):
Maidstone.
JULY – 4TH WEEK
Birchington Carnival:
Birchington.
JULY – 4TH WEEK
Water Carnival:
Royal Harbour, Ramsgate.
JULY – 4TH week
Carnival Procession:
Ramsgate.
AUGUST – 1ST WEEK
Broadstairs Carnival:
Broadstairs.
AUGUST – 2ND WEEK

Margate Carnival Procession:
Margate.
AUGUST – MID
Folkestone Carnival Week:
Folkestone.
AUGUST
Dover Carnival:
Dover.
AUGUST
Canterbury Carnival Week:
Canterbury.
AUGUST
Herne Bay Carnival Week:
Herne Bay.
OCTOBER
Faversham Carnival and Torchlight Procession:
Faversham.

GALAS

AUGUST – 4TH WEEK
Broadstairs Water Gala:
Broadstairs.

PARADES

DECEMBER – IST WEEK
Christmas Lighting Ceremony & Parade:
Sittingbourne.

AGRICULTURAL, HORTICULTURAL & BREED SHOWS

APRIL – IST WEEK
Spring Horticultural Show:
Willson Hall, Ramsgate.
JULY – 2ND WEEK
Kent County Show:
County Showground, Detling, Maidstone.
JULY – 4TH WEEK
Bexleyheath & District Annual Rose Show:

Dickinson Hall, Graham Road, Bexleyheath.
JULY – 3RD WEEK
Danson Park Show:
Danson Park, Bexleyheath.
JULY – 3RD WEEK
London Borough of Bromley Family Dog Show:
Recreation Ground, Croydon Road, Bromley.
JULY
Folkestone Flower Show:
Folkestone.
JULY
Tunbridge Wells & South Eastern Counties Agricultural Show:
Tunbridge Wells.
AUGUST – 2ND WEEK
Sevenoaks Agricultural Show:
Sevenoaks.
AUGUST – 4TH WEEK
Edenbridge & Oxted Annual Horse & Agricultural Show:
Edenbridge.
SEPTEMBER
Marden Fruit Show:
Jarmons Farm, Collier Street, Marden, Tonbridge.
NOVEMBER – IST WEEK
Autumn Horticultural Show:
Winter Gardens, Margate.

SPORTS

JANUARY – IST WEEK
New Year Motor Cycle Races:
Brands Hatch, Gawkham, Nr. Dartford.
JANUARY – 4TH WEEK
Kent County Senior Table Tennis Championships:
Marine Pavilion, Folkestone.
APRIL – 4TH WEEK
Criterion Cycle Races:
Promenade, Westbrook, Margate.
APRIL – 4TH WEEK
Kent Under 13 Open Badminton Championship:
Stour Centre, Ashfield.
APRIL – 4TH WEEK
County Tennis Championships Senior Challenge:
Tunbridge Wells.
APRIL
European Touring Car Championships:
Brands Hatch, Fawkham, Nr. Dartford.
MAY – 2ND WEEK
S.A.G.A. Bowls Championships:
St. Georges Lawns, Cliftonville.
MAY – 2ND WEEK
Kent Under 16 Junior Open Badminton Championship:
Stour Centre, Ashford.
MAY – MID

Historic Car Races:
Brands Hatch, Fawkham, Nr. Dartford.
MAY – LATE
International Motor Cycle Races:
Brands Hatch, Fawkham, Nr. Dartford.
JUNE – IST WEEK
Fireball Open Sailing Competition:
Minnis Bay, Birchington.
JUNE – 4TH WEEK
Thames Barge Race:
Gravesend to Pinmill, Suffolk.
JULY – IST WEEK
London Power Boat Race – London to Calais:
The Harbour, Ramsgate.

MISCELLANEOUS

JANUARY – 4TH WEEK
Burns Supper:
Birchington Village Centre, Alpha Road, Birchington.
THROUGHOUT THE SPRING AND SUMMER
Tournament of Knights (Combat Re-enactment):
Chilham Castle, Chilham, Nr, Canterbury.
APRIL – LATE
Accordian Championship:
Winter Garden, Margate.
MAY – 3RD WEEK
Biggin Hill Air Show:
Biggin Hill.
MAY – 4TH WEEK
Navy Days:
H.M. Naval Base, Chatham.
JUNE – IST WEEK
World Custard Pie Championship:
Coxheath, Maidstone.
JUNE – 3RD WEEK
National Folk Day:
Broadstairs.
JUNE – 3RD WEEK
Medieaval Market:
Allington Castle, Maidstone.
AUGUST – 3RD WEEK
Brands Hatch Traction Engine and Historic Vehicle Rally:
Brands Hatch, Fawkham, Nr. Dartford.
SEPTEMBER – IST WEEK
Detling Steam and Historic Vehicle Rally:
Detling Showground, Maidstone.
SEPTEMBER – 2ND WEEK
Tunbridge Lions Rally:
Hall Place, Leigh, Nr. Tonbridge.

◆

WORLD CUSTARD PIE CHAMPIONSHIPS
A brilliantly funny and insane slapstick occasion which really speaks for itself and now gaining worldwide recognition. See: MISCELLANEOUS.

◆ Lancashire ◆

(INCLUDING MERSEYSIDE & GREATER MANCHESTER)

OLD CUSTOMS

FEBRUARY – SHROVETIDE
Pancake Day Races:
Liverpool.
MAUNDY THURSDAY
Travice Dole:
Leigh.
A charity derived from the bequest in his will of Henry Travice who died in 1627 in which forty poor people are provided for by a distribution at his tomb of five shillings each.
GOOD FRIDAY
Burning Judas:
Liverpool.
Early morning, the minute it is light, children appear on the streets at the South End of Liverpool carrying a straw-stuffed effigy in old clothes. As the sun rises, the figure is hoisted up a pole while houses are knocked up for pennies. The effigy is later ceremonially burned in the street.
EASTER SUNDAY
Nutters Dance (Brittania Coco-Nut Dancers):
Bacop.
Dressed in black breeches, white barrel skirts, decorated clogs, with their faces blacked, the coconut dancers – the 'coconuts' being wooden discs (the tops of cotton bobbins) tied to their knees – dance through the streets of the town to the accompaniment of the town band. Originally, the dancers were made up of married men who worked at the Royal Britannia Mill in Bacup.
EASTER SUNDAY
Egg Rolling:
Avenham Park, Preston.
Children roll hard-boiled coloured eggs down a slope in Avening Park to

commemorate the stone being rolled away from Christ's tomb at Easter time.
EASTER MONDAY
Riding the Black Lad.:
Ashton-Under-Lyme.
This custom is believed to have had its origins in the Knighthood bestowed on Thomas Ashton by Edward III which proved to be a most unpopular gesture. During the day a figure of a man from an old suit is carried through the town on a horse. The figure is then tied to a post and set on fire.
EASTER
Egg Rolling:
West Derby.
During the last century at Easter it was customary for the men of the village to meet on Sunday wearing patched inside-out clothing. They paid visits to houses to beg for eggs, oatmeal, cakes and money, after which they made their way to the alehouse for celebrations. The custom is still observed.
EASTER
Easter Pace Eggers:
A nine member group from the Bury Folk Club perform an authentic version of the Easter Pace Egg Play – an old mummers play – in local pubs and shopping precincts in the town.
APRIL – EARLY
Furnace Pace Egging Play:
Various venues in South Lakeland.
ALL SOULS DAY
Hunting the Witches:
Pendle Hill.
MAY 1ST (MAY DAY)
Gawthorpe May Day:
Gawthorpe.
A really ancient May Day celebration, the

present one being unchanged for over one hundred years. The centre piece of the procession is a young couple on horseback who are said to represent Snow White and Prince Charming.
MAY
Mayor Making Ceremony:
Clitheroe.
A local pageant where members and officers of the Council walk in procession to the Town Hall while the Town Sergeant, ceremonially robed, visits each school ringing a bell, which signifies a declaration of a holiday for the children.
MAY
Cockle & Mussel Feast:
Clitheroe.
This event has taken place for several centuries and today occurs before the first council meeting where tinned shellfish are served to the councillors.
WHITSUN
Manchester Whit Walks:
Manchester.
Originally these occasions were religious affairs and were very popular during the last century. Nowadays they are mainly festive galas with impressive processions.
JUNE – FRIDAY NEAREST 30TH
Warrington Walking Day:
Warrington.
As many as 50,000 people line the streets to see the walkers in procession. It was begun

---

WARRINGTON WALKING DAY
Originally this annual parade of children was a religious occasion but although Sunday Schools still take part, the walk has now much more of a carnival atmosphere. See: OLD CUSTOMS.

⬑
BRITANNIA COCONUT DANCER
The 'Nutters Dance' of the Britannia Coconut Dancers presents a striking and curious spectacle as the men, dressed in their vivid costumes set against the hard landscape of the town, make their way through the streets. See: OLD CUSTOMS.

━━━━━━━━━◆━━━━━━━━━

in 1832 by the Rev. H. Powys, then Rector of Warrington, who instituted the 'procession of witness' by children to divert the attention of parishioners away from the Latchford and Newton races which were held nearby on the same day.
JULY
Admission of Freemen:
Lancaster.

An oath is sworn by all those officials who serve in obedience to the Crown, the Mayor, and Magistrates.
AUGUST — FROM THE 24TH
Wakes Week:
St. Bartholomew's Church, Westhoughton.
On this, the Feast Day of St. Bartholomew, the occasion is still observed and the locals are still affectionately known as "cow-heads" after the old Feast Day custom of baking a large communal pie in the shape of a cow's head.
SEPTEMBER 29
Urswick Rushbearing:
Urswick, Bardsea.

FESTIVALS

JANUARY
Rochdale Annual Brass Band Festival:
Rochdale.
MARCH — LATE
Leeds College of Music Festival:
Details: Leeds College of Music, Cookridge Street, Leeds, LS2 8BH.
MARCH
Horwich Festival of Music & Verse:
Details: Mrs. F.E. Robinson, 6 Hughes Avenue, Horwich.
MARCH/APRIL
Bromborough Festival of Music, Speech, Dancing & Drama:
Details: A.N. Philips, 14 Princes Boulevard, Wirral, Merseyside, L63 5LP.
MARCH/APRIL
Liverpool Festival of Music, Speech & Drama:
Details: G.R. Roger, The Mansion House, Calderstone Park, Liverpool, L18 3JD.
MARCH/APRIL
Nelson Festival:
Details: Ms. S.M. Sarginson, 44 Park Avenue, Carr Hall, Nelson, BB9 6BU.
MARCH/APRIL
Rochdale Youth Festival of Music & Speech:
Details: C.E. Noble, 19 Manley Road, Rochdale.
MARCH/APRIL
South Cumbria Musical Festival:
Details: Ms. E.C. Croskey, 187 Roose Road, Barrow-in-Furness.
MARCH/APRIL
Wigan & District Competitive Music Festival:
Details: R. St. C. Bassett, Heathfield, Minley Wood Lane, Heskin, Nr. Chorley PR7 5NT.

⬑
EGG ROLLING
An Easter custom still enthusiastically observed by children each year on the grassy slopes of Avenham Park. See: OLD CUSTOMS.

APRIL
Blackpool International Hockey Festival:
Stanley Park, West Park Drive, Blackpool.
APRIL
Crosby Festival of Music & Dancing:
Details: Mrs. A.W.S. Johnson, 2 Glendower Court, 7 Warren Road, Blundellsands, Liverpool L23 6TY.
APRIL
Lytham St. Annes Musical Festival:
Details: W.R. Dutton, 178 Church Road, St. Annes, Lytham St. Annes, FY8 3NJ.
APRIL
Leyland Music Festival:
Details: Jean Moffat, 68 Langdale Road, Leyland, Preston, PR5 2AS.
APRIL/MAY
Morecambe Musical Festival:
Details: N.O. Mayor, 4–6 New Street, Morecambe, LA4 4BW.
APRIL/MAY
Manchester Independent One-Act Drama Festival:
Lesser Free Trade Hall, Manchester.
MAY – IST WEEK
Clitheroe Full Length Drama Festival:
Civic Hall, Clitheroe.
MAY – IST WEEK
Lancaster Festival of Literature:
Dukes Playhouse, Moor Lane, Lancaster.
Details: Festival Director, St. Leonard's House, St. Leonard's Gate, Lancaster.
MAY
Ashton-in-Makerfield Competitive Festival:
Details: Mrs. E. Taylor, 59 Bolton Road, Ashton-in-Makerfield, Wigan, WN4 8AA.
MAY
Blackburn Festival of Ballet, Music &

⬇
HALLE SUMMER PROMS
An exciting musical climax with James Loughran and the Hallé Orchestra in concert at the Free Trade Hall, Manchester. See: FESTIVALS.

Drama:
Details: Ms. M. Wilson, Hollymount, 3 Hollowhead Lane, Wiltshire, Blackburn.
MAY/JUNE
Southport Spring Festival:
Details: Festival Director, The College Library, Mornington Road, Southport, PR9 OTS.
MAY – LATE
Warrington Festival:
Details: Festival Co-ordinator, Festival Centre, 80 Sankey Street, Warrington.
MAY – LATE, OR JUNE EARLY
Blackpool Dance Festival:
Winter Gardens, Church Street, Blackpool.
JUNE – IST & 2ND WEEKS
Trinity Arts Festival:
Southport.
JUNE – 2ND & 3RD WEEKS
(Sheffield) Radio Hallam International Jazz Festival:
Details: Jazz centre Society, c/o North West Arts, 52 King Street, Manchester, M2 4LY.
JUNE – 4TH WEEK
Thornton Festival:
Details: Thornton Festival Committee, c/o Barclays Bank, 391 Thornton Road, Thornton, Bradford.
JUNE – 4TH WEEK, TO JULY – 2ND WEEK
Halle Summer Proms:
Free Trade Hall, Manchester.
JUNE
Manchester Independent Full Length Drama Festival:
Lesser Free Trade Hall, Manchester.
JUNE
Barrowford St. Thomas's Music & Arts Festival:
School House, Church Street, Barrowford, Nelson.
JUNE – QUADRENNIAL (NEXT ONE – 1983)
Saddleworth Festival of the Arts:
Details: c/o Secretary, 33 Clough Lane, Grascroft, Via Oldham, OL4 4EW.
JUNE – ALL MONTH
Hope Street Arts Festival:
Hope Street, Liverpool.
JUNE
Red Rose Festival:
Various towns, North East Lancashire.
JULY – LATE (BIENNIAL – NEXT ONE 1982)
Manchester International Organ Festival:
Details: Artistic Director, Festival Office, Central Library, St. Peter's Square, Manchester, M2 5PP.
JULY
Whitworth Arts Festival:
Details: Council Offices, Whitworth,

Rochdale, OL12 8JJ.
JULY
Blackpool Dairy Festival:
Blackpool.
JULY
Morecambe & Heysham Dairy Festival:
Morecambe.
AUGUST – EARLY
Grange-Over-Sands Music Festival:
Grange-Over-Sands.
AUGUST – 4TH WEEK (BIENNIAL)
Bolton Festival:
Details: Festival Director, c/o Arts Dept., Bolton Metropolitan Borough Council, Le Mans Crescent, Bolton.
SEPTEMBER – 4TH WEEK
Fylde Folk Festival:
Details: Alan Bell, 55 The Strand, Fleetwood.
SEPTEMBER
Fleetwood Music & Arts Festival:
Details: R. Heggie, 22 Custom House Lane, Fleetwood, FY7 6BY.
SEPTEMBER/OCTOBER
Southport Music Festival:
Details: Ms. Knowles, 20a Curzon Road, Southport, PR8 6PL.
OCTOBER – 2ND & 3RD WEEK
Crosby Arts Festival:
Details: Crosby Arts Association, 36 Kings Road, Crosby, Liverpool, L23 7TW.
OCTOBER – LATE
Blackpool Music Festival:
Winter Gardens, Church Street, Blackpool.
Details: Ms. E.M. Riley, 98, Church Street, Blackpool, FY1 1JA.
OCTOBER/NOVEMBER
Fylde Arts Festival:
Details: 55a Cookson Street, Blackpool, FY1 3DA.
OCTOBER/NOVEMBER
Radcliffe Arts Festival:
Details: 119 Mather Road, Bury, Manchester.
NOVEMBER – 3RD & 4TH WEEKS
Fleetwood Independent Full Length Drama Festival:
Marina Hall, Fleetwood.
NOVEMBER/DECEMBER
(Colne) Luther Greenwood Memorial Festival:
Details: V. Birtwistle, 158 Keighley Road, Colne.
DECEMBER
Freckleton Music Festival:
Details: R. Spencer, Brades Farm, Freckleton, Nr. Preston.

FAIRS

EASTER monday; MAY 12; 2ND
MONDAY IN JUNE & OCTOBER
Blackburn Fair:
Blackburn.
2ND MONDAY IN JANUARY; EASTER
MONDAY; LAST WEDNESDAY &
THURSDAY IN JULY; 2ND WEDNESDAY
& THURSDAY IN OCTOBER
Bolton Fair:
Bolton.
MARCH 6; EASTER SATURDAY; 2ND
THURSDAY IN JULY
Burnley Fair:
Burnley.
MARCH 5; MAY 5; SEPTEMBER 13
Bury Fair:
Bury.
MARCH 26 EASTER MONDAY; MAY 5;
AUGUST 20; 1ST WEEK IN SEPTEMBER;
OCTOBER 21
Chorley Fair:
Chorley.
NEW YEAR; 1ST WEDNESDAY IN MAY,
JULY, AUGUST, OCTOBER, DECEMBER;
2ND SATURDAY IN NOVEMBER
Lancaster Fair:
Lancaster.
MONDAY AFTER FEBRUARY 5;
MONDAY AFTER MAY 1; JULY 25; LAST
MONDAY IN AUGUST; MONDAY AFTER
NOVEMBER 20; 2ND MONDAY IN
DECEMBER
Liverpool Fair:
Liverpool.
THURSDAY AFTER FEBRUARY 2; MAY
2; JULY 8; LAST SATURDAY IN
AUGUST; WEDNESDAY AFTER OCTOBER
11
Oldham Fair:
Oldham.
JANUARY 10; FEBRUARY 15 MARCH 15
& 27; APRIL 15; 2ND WEDNESDAY &
THURSDAY IN MAY; AUGUST 26;
OCTOBER 3; NOVEMBER 6
Preston Fair:
Preston.
MAY 14; WHIT TUESDAY; NOVEMBER 7
Rochdale Fair:
Rochdale.
JULY 1, 9 & 17; NOVEMBER 29
Warrington Fair:
Warrington.
HOLY THURSDAY (3 DAYS); JULY 27;
3RD WEDNESDAY IN OCTOBER
Wigan Fair:
Wigan.
FEBRUARY
Orell Fair:
Wigan.
MARCH – 1ST WEEK
National Carpet Fair:
Winter Gardens, Blackpool.

MARCH – 3RD WEEK
International Hair & Beauty Fair:
Winter Gardens, Blackpool.
EASTER – SUNDAY & MONDAY
Hornsey Pottery Fair:
Wyresdale Road, Lancaster.
EASTER SUNDAY
Boggart Hole Clough Pleasure Fair:
Rochdale Road, Blackley, Manchester.
JUNE – 2ND WEEK
Restoration Fair:
Conishead Priory, Priory Road,
Ulveston.
AUGUST
Preston Pot Fair:
Preston.
SEPTEMBER
**Manchester Book, Magazine & Comic
Fair:**
Piccadilly Plaza Exhibition Hall, York
Street, City Centre, Manchester.

CARNIVALS

WHITSUN
Lytham St. Annes Carnival:
Lytham St. Annes.
WHITSUN
Bury Carnival:
Bury.
SUMMER
Hulme Carnival:
Hulme.
*Details: Pierre West, c/o Hulme Library,
Hulme Walk, Hulme, Manchester 15.*
SUMMER
Manchester Alexandra Park Carnival:
Alexandra Park, Manchester.
*Details: Mrs. Guishard, 170 Chepstow
Avenue, Sale, Cheshire.*
SEPTEMBER – 2ND WEEK
Wigan XL Carnival:
Greater Manchester Police, Haigh Hall
Country Park, Wigan.

PARADES

JUNE – 1ST WEEK
Lord Mayor's Parade:
City, Centre, Liverpool.
JUNE – 1ST WEEK
Lord Mayor's Parade:
City Centre, Manchester.
*Details: Publicity Dept., Town Hall,
Manchester.*

PAGEANTS

Blackpool Air Pageant:
Squires Gate Airport, Squires Gate
Lane, Blackpool.

AGRICULTURAL, HORTICULTURAL & BREED SHOWS

JUNE
Blackpool Championship Dog Show:
Blackpool.
JULY – 1ST WEEK
**Dalton & District Horticultural
Society Roses & Sweet Pea Show:**
Wellington Hotel, Market Street,
Dalton-in-Furness.
JULY – MID
**Lakeland Rose Show & Royal National
Rose Society's Northern Show:**
Holker Hall, Grange-over-Sands.
JULY – 4TH WEEK
St. Helens Annual Show:
St. Helens.
JULY
North Lonsdale Agricultural Show:
Ulverston.
JULY
Blackburn Agricultural Show:
Blackburn.
JULY
Liverpool Show:
City of Liverpool, The Mansion House,
Calderstone Park, Liverpool.
JULY
West Lancashire Show:
Blagnegate Playing Fields,
Skelmersdale.
JULY/AUGUST
Royal Lancashire Summer Show:
*Details: Royal Lancashire Agricultural
Society, Ribby Hall, Wrea Green, Preston.*
AUGUST – EARLY
Cartmel Agricultural Show:
Cartmel Park, Cartmel.
AUGUST – LATE
Southport Flower Show:
Victoria Park, Rotten Row, Southport,
Merseyside.
AUGUST – LATE
**Dalton & District Horticultural
Society Annual Show:**
St. Margaret's Church Hall, Ulverston
Road, Dalton.
AUGUST
**Garstang & District Agricultural
Show:**
Garstang.
SEPTEMBER – 1ST WEEK
**Barrow Horticultural Society Annual
Flower Show:**
Civic Hall, Duke Street,
Barrow-in-Furness.
SEPTEMBER – 1ST WEEK
Lowick Agricultural Show:
Lowick Bridge, Nr. Ulverston.
SEPTEMBER – 1ST WEEK
Hawkshead Agricultural Show:
Hawkshead Hall Farm, Hawkshead.

SPORTS

MARCH – 4TH WEEK
Grand National 3 Day Race Meeting:
Aintree Racecourse, Ormskirk Road,
Aintree, Liverpool.

MAY – 1ST WEEK
Lytham Golf Trophy:
Royal Lytham & St Annes Old Golf
Club, Lytham.

MAY – 3RD WEEK
British Orienteering Championships:
Lake District.

MAY – 4TH WEEK
National Swimming Championships:
Derby Bath, Warley Road, Blackpool.

JUNE – 1ST WEEK
**Morecambe Bay Long Distance
Swimming Championships:**
Morecambe Bay.

JUNE – EARLY
**Finish of Round Britain Milk Race
(Cycling):**
Middle Walk, North Promenade,
Blackpool.

JUNE – MID
**Cumbria Amateur Athletic Association
20 Miles Road Race:**
Roose Conservative Club, Roose,
Barrow-in-Furness.

JUNE
National Tug-Of-War Championships:
Stanley Park, West Park Drive,
Blackpool.

JUNE
Sand Yachting Championships:
Lytham St. Annes.

JUNE OR JULY
Lancashire International Horse Show:
Arena North, Charnock Richard, Nr.
Chorley.

JULY – 2ND WEEK
**The Coniston Long Distance
Swimming Championships:**
Coniston Water.

JULY
**Ladies British Open Golf
Championships:**
Southport.

AUGUST – 2ND WEEK
**Veterans Long Distance Swimming
Championships:**
Conisto Water.

AUGUST
Ulverston Annual Sports:
Ulverston.

AUGUST – 4TH WEEK
Cartmel Races:
Cartmel Park, Cartmel, Cumbria.

SEPTEMBER – 3RD WEEK
**Waterloo (Crown Green) Bowling
Handicap Final:**
Waterloo Hotel, Waterloo Road,
Blackpool.

MISCELLANEOUS

MARCH
Oldham Annual Brass Band Contest:
Oldham.

MARCH – EARLY
Blackpool Chess Congress:
Norcalympia, Queens Promenade,
Blackpool.

MAY 4TH WEEK
Hawkshead Folk Day:
The Square, Hawkshead.

JUNE – 2ND WEEK
Highland Gathering:
Stanley Park, West Park Drive,
Blackpool.

AUGUST – MID, TO OCTOBER – MID
Morecambe Illuminations:
Central Promenade, Morecambe.

SEPTEMBER – 2ND WEEK, to OCTOBER
Blackpool Illuminations:
The Seafront, Blackpool.

SEPTEMBER
**Skelmersdale Annual Brass Band
Contest:**
Skelmersdale.

NOVEMBER
Barnsley Annual Brass Band Contest:
Barnsley.

NOVEMBER
Tyldesley Annual Brass Band Contest:
Tyldesley.

◆

PRESTON POT FAIR
*The pots are nowadays more likely to be
cheap tea and dinner services but this
ancient fair is still worth a visit. See:
FAIRS.*

LORD MAYOR'S PARADE
*In Liverpool the annual Parade is a grand
occasion with an impressive procession of
bands, floats and other groups. See:
PARADES.*

SAND YACHT CHAMPIONSHIP
*Sand yachting is a specialist sport which is
gaining in popularity year by year. At
Lytham St. Anne's with its marvellous
beaches the annual championships take
place in a holiday atmosphere. See:
SPORTS.*

BLACKPOOL ILLUMINATIONS
*The illuminations were first introduced as
an additional attraction to the town's music
festivals of 1912 and 1913 and are now one
of the biggest draws in the North. Six miles
of lights throng the promenade which are
ceremonially switched on by a famous
personality each year. See:
MISCELLANEOUS.* ◊

◆ Leicestershire ◆

*Fine sharp but easy hills, which reverently are crowned
With aged antique rocks, to which the goats and sheep
(To him that stands remote) do softly seem to creep.*
FROM "CHARNWOOD FOREST"
BY MICHAEL DRAYTON

Old Customs

EASTER MONDAY
**Bottle Kicking and Hare Pie
Scrambling:**
Hallaton.
*This custom originated in 1771. After the
children's parade to the church during the
morning, a hare pie is blessed during the
service and following lunch the villagers
converge on the church gates where the
rector distributes one half of the pie to be
eaten. The villagers then parade through the
village to the Butter Cross in the market
where red, white and blue ribbons are
attached to small wooden barrels referred to
as 'bottles'. This is followed by a march to
the top of the village where everyone
assembles outside the Fox Inn and,
accompanied by a band, everyone goes back
down the village to Hare Pie Bank where
the remnants of the pie are thrown about or
'scrambled for'. Next there comes the 'bottle
kicking' between players from the two
villages of Medbourne and Hallaton in
which two of the three bottles are filled with
beer and the object of the game being for
Hallaton to try and get the bottle over a
small stream which runs between the bank
and the village.*
EASTER THURSDAY
Spring Setting the Lanes:
Gate Inn, Ratcliffe Culey.
*Grass verges for grazing cattle are sold
annually at the Gate Inn.*
EASTER EVE
Easter Hymn Singing Ceremony:
St. Mary in Arden, Market Harborough.

*When William Hubbard died in 1786 he
left one guinea to the Church Choir with the
provision that the Easter Hymn should be
sung annually over his grave.*
EASTER – FIFTH SUNDAY AFTER
ROGATIONTIDE
Rogationtide Procession & Blessing:
Whetstone.
MAY
Mayor Making Ceremony:
Leicester.
MAY – LATE
Orange Dole:
Sileby Churchyard, Sileby.
*The vicar distributes the fruit on the Sunday
School anniversary beneath an old oak tree
in the churchyard.*
WHIT MONDAY
Selling the Wether:
The Nag's Head Inn, Enderby.
*A fourteenth century custom still observed in
which a piece of land – the Wether – is sold
annually to provide entertainment for a
feast.*
JULY – THURSDAY AFTER 6TH
New Mown Hay Ceremony:
Glenfield Church, Glenfield.
NOVEMBER 5
**Guy Fawkes Celebrations & Fireworks
Display:**
Gt. Central Railway, Rothley Station,
Rothley.

Festivals

EASTER MONDAY
Hallaton Easter Festival:

Hallaton.
APRIL – 3RD WEEK
Charnwood Festival of Dance:
Charnwood Theatre, Loughborough
Town Hall, Market Place,
Loughborough.
APRIL – (BIENNIAL)
**Leicestershire Schools Festival of
Music:**
County School of Music, Longslade
School, Birstall.
JUNE – 1ST WEEK
Leicester Proms:
*Details: Entertainments Manager,
Department of Recreation & Culture, New
Walk Centre, Welford Place, Leicester.*
JUNE
Kite Festival:
Stanford Hall, Lutterworth.
JUNE – 4TH WEEK
East Midlands Wine Festival:
Stapleford Park, Nr, Melton Mowbray.
JUNE
Leicester Festival:
Leicester.
*Details: Leicester City Council, New Walk
Centre, Welford Place, Leicester.*

◆

BOTTLE KICKING & HARE-PIE
*Dozens of enthusiastic players struggle to
kick one of the three beer-filled bottles
during the annual Bottle-kicking custom at
Hallaton. See: OLD CUSTOMS.*

⬦

MARKET BOSWORTH AGRICULTURAL
SHOW
*At one time rodeos could only be enjoyed in
America's wild west but they now seem to be
catching on over here. The picture shows a
dramatic end to one contestant's ambitions to
win a prize. See: SHOWS.*

SEPTEMBER – 3RD WEEK
National Festival of Youth Dance:
Knighton Fields Drama Centre, Herrick
Road, Leicester.
SEPTEMBER
Ashby-de-la-Zouch Festival of Arts:
Ashby-de-la-Zouch.
OCTOBER
**Leicester Competitive Festival of
Music:**
*Details: Ms. J.E. Orringe, 16 Hall Close,
Kibworth.*

FAIRS

2ND FRIDAY IN MARCH; SATURDAY
BETWEEN EASTER SUNDAY AND WEEK;
2ND THURSDAY IN MAY; 2ND FRIDAY
IN MAY, JULY, OCTOBER &
DECEMBER; THURSDAY BEFORE 2ND
FRIDAY IN OCTOBER
Leicester Fair:
Leicester.
2ND THURSDAY IN NOVEMBER
Loughborough Fair:
Loughborough.
APRIL 29; OCTOBER 19
Market Harborough Fair:
Market Harborough.

FAYRES

MAY – 4TH WEEK
Hungarton Church Fayre:
Quenby Hall, Hungarton.

CARNIVALS

JULY – 4TH WEEK
Kegworth Carnival:
Hall Stone Meadows, Mill Lane,
Kegworth.
SEPTEMBER

Loughborough Carnival:
Loughborough.

SHOWS

JUNE – 2ND WEEK
Leicester Lord Mayor's Show:
City Centre, Leicester.

TATTOOS

JUNE – LATE
Military Tattoo:
Sports Centre, Saffron Lane, Leicester.

AGRICULTURAL, HORTICULTURAL & BREED SHOWS

JUNE
**Leicestershire County Agricultural
Show:**
Braunstone Park, Leicester.
*Details: Leicester Agricultural Society
County Show, 219 London Road,
Leicester.*
JULY
**Market Bosworth Agricultural and
Horticultural Society's Annual Show:**
Bosworth Park, Market Bosworth.
AUGUST
Wymeswold Flower Show:
Wymeswold.
AUGUST
Leicester Sheepdog Trials:
Leicester.
SEPTEMBER
**Leicester City Championship Dog
Show:**
Braunstone.

SPORTS

JUNE – 4TH WEEK
**Midland Counties Amateur Athletic
Association Senior Youth Athletic
Championships:**
Leicester Sports Centre, Saffron Lane,
Leicester.
JUNE/SEPTEMBER
International Motorcycle Racing:
Mallory Park, Kirkby Mallory.
JULY – 4TH WEEK, TO AUGUST – 1ST
WEEK
**British Cycling Federation Track
Championships:**
Leicester Sports Centre, Saffron Lane,
Leicester.

MISCELLANEOUS

APRIL – LATE
National Brass Band Championships:
De Montfort Hall, Leicester.

APRIL
**International Food, Wine & Kitchen
Exhibition:**
Granby Halls, Leicester.
MAY – 1ST WEEK
**Annual Art Exhibition of the Oadby
Society of Artists:**
The Church of Christ, Rosemead Drive,
Oadby.
MAY – 2ND WEEK
Volkswagon Owners Rally:
Stanford Hall, Lutterworth,
MAY – 3RD WEEK
Rudge Owners' Motorcycle Club Rally:
Stanford Hall, Lutterworth.
MAY – 4TH WEEK
**Vintage Motorcycle Club Founder's
Day Rally:**
Stanford Hall, Lutterworth.
JUNE – 1ST WEEK
**Leicester Rod and Custom Club
Annual Rod Run:**
Barrow, Nr. Loughborough.
JUNE – 2ND WEEK
Roundhead & Cavalier Mock Battles:
Stanford Hall, Lutterworth.
JUNE – 2ND WEEK
**Spartan Car Owners' Club Rally &
Concours d'Elegance:**
Stanford Hall, Lutterworth.
JUNE – 2ND WEEK
Lea Francis Owners' Club Rally:
Stanford Hall, Lutterworth.
JUNE – 3RD WEEK
Riley Owners' Club National Rally:
Stanford Hall, Lutterworth.
JUNE – 4TH WEEK
British Two-stroke Club Rally:
Stanford Hall, Lutterworth.
JULY – 3RD WEEK
Rempstone Traction Engine Rally:
Rempstone, Nr. Loughborough.
JULY – 4TH WEEK
Velocette Owners Club Rally:
Stanford Hall, Lutterworth.
AUGUST – 3RD WEEK
**Morris Register and Wolseley Register
Rally & Concours d'Elegance:**
Stanford Hall, Lutterworth.
AUGUST – 4TH WEEK
Brough Superior Club Rally:
Stanford Hall, Lutterworth.
SEPTEMBER – 1ST WEEK
**Midlands Austin 7 Club Rally &
Concours d'Elegance:**
Stanford Hall, Lutterworth.
SEPTEMBER – 1ST WEEK
Scotts Owners' Club Rally:
Stanford Hall, Lutterworth.
SEPTEMBER – 2ND WEEK
Le Velo Club Rally:
Stanford Hall, Lutterworth.

LEICESTERSHIRE
◆ *Rutland* ◆

Multum·in·Parvo

OLD CUSTOMS

JUNE 29
Rush Strewing Ceremony:
The Church, Barrowden.
Rushes from nearby fields are used for this ceremony in keeping with a provision once made to ensure the tenant of the fields – the Church – keeps up the rush strewing custom each year.
JUNE – SUNDAY FOLLOWING 29TH
Hay Strewing Ceremony:
The Church Langham.
JUNE – SUNDAY NEAREST JUNE 29TH
Hay Strewing Ceremony (Hay Sunday):
The Church, Braunstone.
The Lord of the Manor originally made a hay legacy to the parish clerk as a thankyou for finding his daughter. Today the East Midlands Gas Board provide a payment in lieu of hay as the original meadow now lies under the gas works.
AUGUST
Mayor Making Ceremony:
Oakham.

MAYOR MAKING
The old Mayor greets the new Mayor during Oakham's Mayor Making Ceremony. See: OLD CUSTOMS.

FAIRS

MAY
Oakham Fair:
Oakham.

AGRICULTURAL, HORTICULTURAL & BREED SHOWS

AUGUST – 1ST WEEK
Rutland Agricultural Show:
The Showground, Barleythorpe Road, Oakham.
AUGUST – BANK HOLIDAY
Oakham Horticultural Show:
Oakham.

SPORTS

MAY – 4TH WEEK
Burley-on-the-Hill Jumping Show:
Burley-on-the-Hill, Burley Village, Oakham.

87

◆ Lincolnshire ◆

CIVITAS : LINCOLNIA

How often when a child I lay reclined:
I took delight in this fair land and free:
Here stood the infant lion of the mind,
And here the Grecian ships all seemed to be.
And here again I come, and only find
The drain-cut level of the marshy lea
Grey sandbanks, and pale sunsets, dreary wind,
Dim shores, dense rains, and heavy-clouded sea.

A. TENNYSON

OLD CUSTOMS

JANUARY 6 (TWELFTH DAY &
TWELFTH DAY EVE)
Haxey Hood Game:
Haxey.
*This boisterous version of rugby football is
thought to have its origins in a sacrificial
Celtic game but was conceived in its present
form after an incident involving the first
Lady de Mowbray of the late 13th century.
It is said that while out riding her hood was
blown off and thirteen farm workers gave
chase to retrieve it. Lady de Mowbray was
suitably impressed by such a show of
gallantry and in her will she left a piece of
land called the 'Hoodlands' to the village
providing the villagers re-enacted the event
every year. The ritual hood-throwing game
comprising of the Fool and twelve Boggans
(i.e. thirteen farmers) has been held ever
since.*
EASTER MONDAY
Egg Rolling:
Barton-upon-Humber.
EASTER
Running Auction:
Bourne.
First instigated in 1770 by Richard Clay,

*this curious custom came into being through
the legacy of a piece of land called White
Bread Meadow which he left for annual
letting, the rent from which was to be used
for providing bread for the needy in the
Eastgate Ward. Each Easter the land is let
by auction and the bidding only remains
valid while two boys are running up and
down a prescribed length of road.*
MAY – LATE, OR JUNE – EARLY
Mayor's Sunday:
Boston.
*The day's proceedings begin with a civic
service in St. Botolph's church attended by
the Mayor who has walked in procession
accompanied by three Halberdiers and three
mace bearers. This is followed by a
reception and the traditional toast to the
Mayor and Mayoress given by the local
M.P.*
MAY
Sermon Against Drunkenness:
Grantham.
*On the eve of Mayor's Sunday a curious
sermon is preached in Grantham as a
request made be the landlord of the local inn
in years gone by. He left the sum of forty
shillings per annum to provide the sermon*

*which "the subject shall be chiefly against
drunkenness."*
DECEMBER – 2ND WEEK
Boston Beast Mart:
Boston.
*Under a charter granted in 1573 by
Elizabeth I a proclamation opening the
Beast Mart is read at noon by the Town
Clerk. Though nowadays the Mart is
largely a pleasure fair, sheep are still sold
each year.*
DECEMBER 21
Candle Auction:
Old Bolingbroke.
*This custom goes back to a church charity
whereby a particular piece of land called
'Poor Folks Close' is let every five years by
candle auction. Here the Chairman of the
Parish Council or the Vicar sticks a pin in a
tallow candle about an inch from the top
and when the flame burns down sufficiently
for the pin to drop out, this signals the end of
the bidding, where upon the last bidder
becomes the new tenant.*

FESTIVALS

JANUARY – 1ST WEEK
Humberside Stage Dance Festival:
Town Hall, South Street, Hessle, South
Humberside.
FEBRUARY/MARCH
Lincoln Music Festival:
*Details: R.H. Ponting, 7 Westwood Close,
Swanpool, Lincoln, LN6 0HG.*
MARCH
**North Lincolnshire Music and Drama
Festival:**
*Details: S.G. Jarvis, 59 Rigby High
Road, Brigg, South Humberside, DN20
9HB.*
APRIL – 1ST & 2ND WEEKS
Cleethorpes Dance Festival:

Pier Promenade, Cleethorpes, South Humberside.

APRIL

Grimsby & District Guild of Music & Drama Festival:
Details: Ms. F.I. Young, 9 St. Thomas Close, Humberston, Grimsby, South Humberside, DN36 4HS.

MAY – 4TH WEEK

Cleethorpes Festival:
Details: 7 Bestall Road, Grimsby, South Humberside.

MAY – 4TH WEEK

Cleethorpes Folk Festival:
Details: 6 Walker Avenue, Grimsby, South Humberside.

MAY – 4TH WEEK

Junior Stage Dance Festival:
Festival Pavilion, Tower Esplanade, Skegness.

MAY – BIENNIAL (NEXT ONE 1983)

Sleaford Arts Festival:
Carre's Grammar School, Sleaford.

MAY

Grantham Music Festival:
Details: R.A. Jeffrys, 43 Manthorpe Road, Grantham, NG31 8PA.

JUNE – 2ND WEEK

Lincoln Water Festival:
Brayford Pool & High Street, Lincoln.

JUNE – EARLY/MID

Boston Festival:
Details: Festival Director, Sam Newson Music Centre, South Street, Boston, PE21 6HT.

◆————————

BEAST MART
The Proclamation opening the Mart is read out at noon by the town clerk at Barter Grammar School and followed by the customary 'Three Cheers' by the pupils on hearing they have the half day off. See: OLD CUSTOMS.

SPALDING FLOWER PARADE
Spalding is the centre of a vast bulb growing area – 'Little Holland' – and the Easter Flower Parade is closely linked to the industry. A mile-long procession of dazzling floral floats are created from thousands of spring blooms to create one of the most delightful of English events. See: PARADES.

BELTON ANNUAL SHOWS
Throughout the spring and summer Belton House, set in 600 acres of beautiful parkland, is the scene for a number of fascinating entertainments. Pictures show the Re-enactment of the Battle of Gettysburg from the American Civil War. See: MISCELLANEOUS. ⇗

JUNE – 4TH WEEK
Walesby Festival:
All Saints Church, Walesby.
JUNE/JULY
Stamford Arts Festival:
Details: 17 Rutland Terrace, Stamford,
PE9 2QD.
JULY – 2ND WEEK
Diocesan Royal School of Church
Music Festival:
Lincoln Cathedral, Lincoln.
JULY – 2ND WEEK
Flower Festival:
St. James Church and Rectory, Wetgate,
Louth.
JULY
Cleethorpes Festival of Music and
Words:
Details: Ms. K.J. Cox, 183 Clee Road,
Cleethorpes.
AUGUST – 3RD WEEK
Belton Hot-Air Balloon Festival:
Belton Park, Belton, Grantham.
AUGUST – 4TH WEEK
Flower Festival:
St. Wilfrid's Church, Alford.
AUGUST – 4TH WEEK
Festival of Youth:
Belton Park, Belton, Grantham.
AUGUST – 4TH WEEK
Flower Festival:
St. Matthew's Church, Lumley Avenue,
Skegness.
SEPTEMBER – 4TH WEEK
Inter-Town Sports Festival:
Various venues in Lincolnshire.
AUGUST – 4TH WEEK
Alford Festival:
Details:
P.O. Box 1, Alford, LN13 9DJ.
OCTOBER
Market Rasen Music Festival:
Details: Ms. M.J. Schupham, 32
Willingham Road, Market Rasen, LN8
3DX.
OCTOBER
Grantham October Festival:
Grantham.
Details: R. Bailey, 2 Station Cottages,
Honington, Grantham.
AUTUMN
Bourne Festival:
Bourne.
Details: G. Harmston, 40 Coggles
Causeway, Bourne.

FAIRS

MAY 5; 1ST WEDNESDAY IN AUGUST;
SEPTEMBER 15; NOVEMBER 18
Boston Fair:
Boston.
5TH MONDAY IN LENT; EASTER EVE;
OCTOBER 26; DECEMBER 17

Grantham Fair:
Grantham.
1ST MONDAY IN APRIL; 1ST MONDAY
IN OCTOBER
Grimsby Fair:
Grimsby.
2ND MONDAY IN AUGUST & THE
FOLLOWING THURSDAY
Horncastle Fair:
Horncastle.
LAST WHOLE WEEK IN APRIL; 1ST
FRIDAY IN JULY; FRIDAY FOLLOWING
SEPTEMBER 12; 3RD FRIDAY IN
OCTOBER, NOVEMBER
Lincoln Fair:
Lincoln.
MONDAY & TUESDAY BEFORE
FEBRUARY 13; MONDAY BEFORE
MID-LENT; MONDAY OF MID-LENT;
MONDAY BEFORE MAY 12; 2ND
MONDAY IN NOVEMBER
Mid-Lent Pleasure Fair:
Stamford.
APRIL – 4TH WEEK
April Pleasure Fair:
South Common, Lincoln.
EASTER SUNDAY
Easter Fair and Spectacular:
Belton Park, Belton, Grantham.

CARNIVALS

JUNE – 1ST & 2ND WEEKS
Mayor's Carnival:
High Street, Lincoln.
JULY – 3RD WEEK
Skegness Carnival Week:
Skegness.
JULY – 3RD WEEK
Barton-on-Humber Carnival:
Baysgarth Park, Brigg Road,
Barton-on-Humber.

GALAS

JULY – 2ND WEEK
Lincoln Lions Gala:
North Kesteven Sports Centre, Newark
Road, Lincoln.
Horbling Misfits Annual Gala:
Details: P. Sentance, 83 Kingscliffe Road,
Grantham.

PARADES

MAY – 2ND WEEK
Spalding Flower Parade:
Spalding.

SHOWS

JULY – MID
Air Show:
R.A.F. Coningsby, Coningsby.

AGRICULTURAL, HORTICULTURAL & BREED SHOWS

MARCH – LATE
East Midlands Orchid Society Annual
Show:
Belton House, Belton, Grantham.
MARCH – 1ST WEEK
Springfields Horticultural Show:
Spalding Bulb & Produce Auction Halls,
Winfrey Avenue, Spalding.
MAY – 4TH WEEK
Woodhall Spa Agricultural Show &
Gymkhana:
Jubilee Park, Stixwould Road, Woodhall
Spa.
JUNE – 1ST WEEK
Messingham Horse & Foal Show:
The Showground, Northfield Road,
Messingham, Nr. Scunthorpe, South
Humberside.
JUNE – 3RD WEEK
Lincolnshire Show:
Lincolnshire Showground, 3½ miles
North of Lincoln on A15 Lincoln to
Brigg road.
JUNE/JULY
Winterton Show:
Showground, Park Street, Winterton,
Humberside.
JULY – 1ST WEEK
German Shepherd Dog British
Championships:
Belton Park, Belton, Grantham.
AUGUST – EARLY
Midland Shetland Pony Show:
Belton House, Belton, Grantham.
AUGUST – 1ST WEEK
Cleethorpes Show:
Leisure Park, North Sea Lane,
Cleethorpes, South Humberside.
AUGUST
Annual Competitive Cactus &
Succulent Show:
Bailgate Methodist, Church Hall,
Bailgate, Lincoln.

MISCELLANEOUS

EASTER
Hunt the Outlaws (The Robin Hood
Society):
Belvoir Castle, Grantham.
MAY – 4TH WEEK
The Siege of Belton – Historic
Re-enactment:
Belton Park, Belton, Grantham.
NOVEMBER – 1ST WEEK
Caravan Club of Great Britain Bonfire
Rally:
Jubilee Park, Stixwould Road, Woodhall
Spa.

London ◆

(INNER BOROUGHS)

What's not destroyed by Time's devouring hand?
Where's Troy, and where's the Maypole in the Strand?
Peases, cabbages and turnips grew, where
Now stands New Bond Street and a newer square,
Such piles of buildings now rise up and down,
London itself seems growing out of town.

JAMES BRAMSTON.

——Old Customs——

JANUARY 6 (TWELFTH DAY, &
TWELFTH DAY EVE)
Cutting The Baddeley Cake:
Theatre Royal, Drury Lane.
This Twelfth Night celebration
commemorates the pastry cook Robert
Baddeley who managed to secure a part in
a Drury Lane production through the offices
of Samuel Foote, who very much
appreciated his cooking. Baddeley
forthwith left £100 in his will for a cake to
be baked and eaten every Twelfth Night by
the cast for the evening performance.

JANUARY 6
Royal Epiphany Gifts:
St. James' Palace.
A medieval ceremony in origin which
commemorates the bringing of gifts to the
Infant Jesus by the Three Kings. The
ceremony takes place in the Chapel Royal
where Gentleman Ushers offer gold,
frankincense and myrrh in silk purses on
behalf of the Queen.

JANUARY 30
King Charles I Ceremony:
A parade proceeds down Whitehall from
Trafalgar Square and gathers beneath
Hubert Le Suer's statue of King Charles I.
Wreaths are laid and a ceremony follows in
Banqueting House, only one hundred yards

from the statue, the spot where King
Charles was executed in 1649.

FEBRUARY 3
Blessing of the Throats:
St. Ethelreda's Church, Ely Place,
Holborn WC1.
On this, the Feast Day of St. Blaise,
pilgrims who suffer from disease or
imperfections of the throat are welcomed in
the ancient crypt of St. Ethelreda's Roman
Catholic Church where the priest
administers a blessing.

FEBRUARY – 1ST WEEK
Clowns' Service:
Holy Trinity Church, Dalston,
Hackney.
A colourful event in which clowns who
belong to the Clowns Club of Great Britain
have their own special service. A tribute is
paid to Grimaldi and there follows after the
service a show for the children in which all
the clowns perform.

FEBRUARY – SHROVE TUESDAY
Pancake Greaze:
Westminster School.
Said to have first started before the 18th
century though the first written record was
by Jeremy Bentham during his time as
scholar in the late 1750's. Basically the idea
is for the pancake to be tossed by the cook
over the bar to a line of boys who then

commence on a greaze; the boy with the
most cake being declared the winner and his
prize being a golden guinea. The occasion is
also commemorated by a half-holiday by all
the school.

FEBRUARY – SHROVE TUESDAY
JIF National Pancake Race:
Lincolns Inn Fields.
This famous pancake race is sponsored by
Jif Ltd in which Jif lemon packs are given
out free to spectators.

FEBRUARY (ASH WEDNESDAY)
Cakes and Ales Ceremony:
St. Paul's Cathedral.
When Norton died in 1612 he left a bequest
in his will that members of the Stationers'
Company should hear a special sermon in
St. Faith's Chapel in the crypt of St.
Paul's Cathedral and later partake of cakes
and ale at Stationers' Hall.

FEBRUARY 20
Sir John Cass Memorial Service:
St. Botolph's Church, Aldgate.
Pupils from Sir John Cass College attend
this memorial service which pays tribute to
Sir John Cass who died while making out
his will. All those who attend wear red
quills.

FEBRUARY OR MARCH
The Trial of the Pyx:
Goldsmith's Hall, Foster Lane, EC2.
This ceremony originates from the ancient
custom of coin testing at the Mint where the
accuracy, composition and weight of the
coins of the Realm were put to an annual
scrutiny by a chosen jury of distinguished
business men, as decreed by King Henry III
in 1248.

MARCH
Mothering Sunday:
Chapel Royal, Tower of London.
A custom which began in Tudor times.
Young people who attend the service receive
Simnel cakes and flowers to mark the

occasion.

MARCH 21

Spring Equinox Ceremony:

Tower Hill Terrace.

The beginning of Spring is celebrated by Druids.

MARCH 31

Oranges and Lemons Ceremony:

St. Clement Danes, The Strand.

Children from the nearby primary school attend a short service of hymns and prayers. Once over, the melody of the nursery rhyme "Oranges and Lemons" is played on handbells by members of the London County Association of Change Ringers. Each child is given an orange and a lemon as they leave. The custom dates back to 1920 and is symbolic of the fact that when oranges and lemons first arrived in England, they arrived at the Pool of London, near to the site of the Church.

GOOD FRIDAY

Butterworth (Poor Widows) Charity:

St. Bartholomew the Great, Smithfield.

During the morning, twenty-one sixpences are ceremonially placed upon a flat stone in the churchyard for the benefit of poor widows. Each lady kneels in turn to pick up a coin and then steps across the stone where she receives an extra 25p and a hot cross bun. The dole derives from a bequest dating back to 1686 left by Joshua Butterworth.

EASTER – 2ND WEDNESDAY FOLLOWING

Annual Spital Sermon:

St. Lawrence Jewry Church, Spitalfield.

The sermon is attended by the Mayor and his Aldermen and dates back to the time of the Great Fire of London.

SPRING

Swearing on the Horns:

The Wrestlers Inn, Highgate.

"It's a custom at Highgate that all who go through must be sworn on the horns, sir, and so sir, must you".

In the days of stage coach travel it was the custom for certain London bound travellers to be 'sworn' at the various coaching Inns. One evening in spring, this is still observed at the Wrestlers Inn where 'The Judge' in wig and black gown and accompanied by "The Clerk" carrying horns administers the oaths.

APRIL 5

John Stow Memorial Service:

St. Andrew Undershaft Church.

The Mayor and his Aldermen attend and a

◆

SPRING EQUINOX CEREMONY

At the Equinox of Spring London's Tower Hill is witness to the gathering of latter-day Druids who welcome the season with a special rite. See: OLD CUSTOMS.

new quill is placed in the hand of the statue of John Stow following the service.

APRIL – LAST SUNDAY

Martyrs Pilgrimage:

Old Bailey to Marble Arch.

In memory of the religious persecution of martyrs during the 16th and 17th centuries, pilgrims walk in procession from the site of the Tyburn Gallows at Marble Arch.

APRIL – MAUNDY THURSDAY

Royal Maundy:

Westminster Abbey.

The distribution of Royal Maundy by the reigning monarch is still given to as many people as there are years in the Queen's age. They receive specially minted silver pieces.

MAY 21

Oak Apple Day (Founders Day):

Royal Hospital, Chelsea.

This Restoration Festival which commemorates the day Charles II made his escape in the Boscobel Oak is marked by a march and inspection parade of Chelsea Pensioners followed by a feast of plum pudding and beer. King Charles II statue is also decorated with sprigs of oak.

MAY 24 (ASCENSION DAY)

Beating the Bounds:

Temple Steps, St. Clement Danes, and around the Tower of London.

The ceremony of Beating the Bounds is a survival from way back in the Middle Ages when town and parish officials were charged with the duty of surveying the boundaries once a year in the form of beating certain landmarks with long canes. In London, choirboys perform the ceremony.

JUNE 24 (MID-SUMMERS DAY)

Election of Sheriffs:

Great Hall, Guildhall.

JUNE 24

The Knollys Red Rose:

Mansion House, City of London.

Back in the 14th century Sir Robert Knollys was ordered by the City Corporation to pay an annual rent of one red rose on Mid-Summer's Day to the Lord Mayor of London for permission to construct a gallery between his two houses. Today, the Rose Payment is carried on a velvet cushion by the Churchwardens of All-Hallows-by-the-Tower and is presented to the Lord Mayor at the Mansion House.

JUNE 26

Beating the Bounds:

Greenwich, Woolwich, Blackheath & Deptford.

JUNE – THURSDAY FOLLOWING TRINITY SUNDAY

Skinners' Company Procession:

Dowgate Hill, EC4.

Members proceed from Skinners' Hall to the Church of St. Mary Aldermanbury, all of

whom carry posies of flowers.

JULY – THURSDAY FOLLOWING 4TH

Vintners' Company Procession:

Upper Thames Street, EC4.

From their Hall members proceed to the Church of St. James, Garlickhythe, for a special service. For the occasion, two wine porters dressed in smocks and top hats lead the procession and ceremonially sweep the path with birch brooms.

AUGUST 1

Doggett's Coat and Badge Race:

This is the oldest surviving sailing race in the world. Entrants race from London Bridge to Chelsea and the occasion itself commemorates the acession to the throne of George I. The race first was instigated in 1715 by Thomas Doggett and the prize then, as now, is an orange coat and silver badge.

Details: The Clerk, The Fishmonger's Company, Fishmonger's Hall, London, EC4.

SEPTEMBER 21

St. Matthew's Day March:

Christ's Hospital School.

Three hundred Bluecoat boys from Horsham School and twenty-five girls from Hertford School congregate at Sepulchre's Church in Newgate and march to Mansion House. There they receive a coin from the Mayor.

SEPTEMBER 23

Autumn Equinox Ceremony:

Primrose Hill, Regents Park.

SEPTEMBER 28

Election of Sheriffs:

Guildhall.

A procession from Mansion House to Guildhall is attended by the Mayor and his Aldermen where the election takes place.

OCTOBER – 1ST SUNDAY

Harvest of the Sea Ceremony:

Church of St. Mary-at-Hill, Lovat Lane, EC3.

OCTOBER – 1ST SUNDAY

St. Martin-in-the-Fields

Costermongers' Harvest Festival:

An annual service held at St. Martin-in-the-Fields is attended by the Pearly Kings and Queens of London dressed in their traditional attire of suits sown with hundreds of pearl buttons.

OCTOBER 16

Lion Sermon:

St. Katherine Cree, Leadenhall Street, EC3.

In accordance with the bequest in the will of Sir John Gayer who died in 1649, a sermon which commemorates his miraculous escape from death from a lion while abroad is preached in the Church.

OCTOBER 18 (ST. LUKE'S DAY)

Charlton Horn Fair:

93

Charlton House, Charlton.
An ancient fair which dates back to the days when animal horns were ritually displayed; an association with St. Luke who was often represented with a cow or an ox by his side.

OCTOBER – BETWEEN THE MORROW OF ST. MICHAEL AND THE MORROW OF ST. MARTIN

Horseshoe and Faggot Cutting Quit Rents Ceremony:
Royal Courts of Justice.
There are two services which deal with the confirmation of tenancy of two pieces of land, – the Moors at Eardington, Shropshire, and The Forge at St. Clement Danes. For the first, the City Solicitor pays the Queen's Rembrancer a hatcher, bill hook, and two faggots, and for the second, six horseshoes and sixty-one nails.

OCTOBER – NEAREST SUNDAY TO 21ST

Trafalgar Day Celebrations:
Trafalgar Square.
This occasion marks the great Trafalgar Battle of Lord Nelson. A procession from Horse Guard's Parade proceeds to Nelson's Column for a ceremony which includes a fanfare and the singing of the Lord Nelson Hymn.

OCTOBER – LAST WEDNESDAY

Basketmakers Service:
Church of St. Margaret Patterns, Eastcheap, EC3.
The service occurs at noon and is attended by officials of the Worshipful Company of Basketmakers.

NOVEMBER – 2ND SATURDAY

Election of Lord Mayor:
The Guildhall.
London's biggest and most spectacular custom, with its great procession from Guildhall to Temple Bar (headed by the Lord Mayor's horse-drawn coach), and back to Mansion House.

NOVEMBER – 1ST WEEK

State Opening of Parliament:
Houses of Parliament, Westminster.

AUTUMN

Procession of Judges:
Westminster Abbey.
Every year in the Autumn at the opening of the Michaelmas Term of Law Sittings in London, the judges, wearing their official robes of office of the King's Bench and Court of Common Pleas, proceed in company to attend service at Westminster Abbey. This is followed by luncheon at the House of Lords with the Lord Chancellor.

DECEMBER – WEDNESDAY BEFORE CHRISTMAS

Boar's Head Feast:
Warwick Lane.
A similar event to the feast held in Oxford in which members of the Worshipful Company of Cutlers attend.

DECEMBER 26 (BOXING DAY)

The Opening of the Pantomime Season:
This day marks the official opening of the pantomime season.

DECEMBER 31 (NEW YEAR'S EVE)

New Year's Eve Celebrations:
Trafalgar Square.
This particular New Year's Eve celebration which could mark the beginning of the silly season is now well known because of the revelry which occurs, including the obligatory midnight bathing in the fountains.

ALTERNATE SATURDAYS

Farthing Bundles:
Fern Street Settlement, Bow.
This particular settlement was founded on behalf of the Devon's Junior School in 1907. The school's Headmistress, Miss Clara Grant, had begun an imaginative scheme known as 'farthing bundles' in 1900 whereby any child who owned a farthing and could pass under a wooden arch forty-eight inches in height without bending received a 'bundle' – i.e. toys, pencils, paper, etc. Nowadays the farthing has been replaced by a half-penny.

DAILY

Kings Keys:
Tower of London.
This ceremony takes place every night at the Tower when the wardens lock the gates. An escort carrying the keys is challenged with the question "Whose Keys?" to which the answer given is "Queen Elizabeth's Keys".

FESTIVALS

JANUARY

Park Lane Group Festival Week of Young Artists and Twentieth Century Music:
Details: Secretary, Park Lane Group Ltd., 1 Montague Street, London, WC1B 5BP.

FEBRUARY – 1ST & 2ND WEEKS

London Mime Festival:
Cockpit Theatre and various other venues in London.

FEBRUARY – MID

Folk Festival:
Royal Albert Hall, Kensington.
Details: English Folk, Dance, & Song Society, Cecil Sharpe House, 2 Regents Park Road, London, NW1 7AY.

FEBRUARY/MARCH

Wimbledon Music Festival:
Details: Ms. E. Cameron, 43 Tybenham Road, London, SW19.

FEBRUARY/MARCH

Camden Music Festival:
Details: Libraries & Arts Dept., St. Pancras Library, 100 Euston Road, London, NW1 2AJ.

MARCH/APRIL

Young Writers' Festival:
Royal Court Theatre, Sloane Square, London, SW1.

MAY

Covent Garden Proms:
Royal Opera House, Covent Garden, London, WC2.

APRIL – 4TH WEEK

St. George's Folk Festival:
Cecil Sharpe House, 2 Regents Park Road, London, NW1 7AY.

APRIL/MAY

English Bach Festival:
Details: 15 South Eaton Place, London, SW1.

APRIL/SEPTEMBER

Bear Gardens Bankside Festival:
Bear Gardens Museum & Arts Centre, 1 Bear Gardens, Bankside, London, SE1.

MAY–JULY

National Festival of Music for Youth:
Details: L. Westland, 23A Kings Road, London, SW3 4RP.

JUNE – 2ND & 3RD WEEKS

Hackney Festival:
Details: Cultural Activities Organiser, London Borough of Hackney, Central Library, Mare Street, London, E8 1HG.

JUNE – 2ND & 3RD WEEKS

London Handel Festival:
Details: Festival Secretary, St. George's, Hanover Square, London, W1.

JUNE – 3RD & 4TH WEEKS

Greenwich Festival:
Details: Greenwich Entertainments Service, 25 Woolwich New Road, London,

JUNE

Westminster Hospital Summer Arts Festival:
Details: The Festival Director, Westminster Hospital Medical School, Horseferry Road, London, SW1.

JUNE

Sanskritik Festival of Arts of India:
Details: 17 Holdenhurst Avenue, London, N12 0JA.

JUNE/JULY

BBC International Festival of Light Music:
Royal Festival Hall, South Bank.

JUNE/AUGUST

Bankside Summer Festival:
World Centre for Shakespeare Studies, 40 Bankside, The Liberty-of-the-Clink, Southwark.

JULY – 1ST, 2ND & 3RD WEEKS

Young Vic Summer Festival:
The Young Vic, 66 The Cut, Waterloo, London, SE1 8LP.

JULY – 2ND WEEK

Tower Hamlets Island Festival:
Millwall Park, Isle of Dogs.

JULY – 2ND WEEK

National Festival of Music for Youth:
Fairfield Halls, Croydon.
Details: National Festival of Music for Youth, 23a Kings Road, London, SW3 4RP.
JULY – EARLY
St. George's Festival:
St. George's Church, Westcombe Park.
JULY – EARLY
Newington Green Festival:
Details: Maryville Community Centre, Woodville Road, N16.
JULY – EARLY
Jester Festival:
West Hampstead Community Association, 60/62 Mill Lane, London, NW6.
JULY – MID
Whittington Park Community Festival:
Details: Whittington Park Community Centre, Yerbury Road, N19.
JULY – MID
Hackney Marsh Fun Festival:
Details: Alan Rossiter, Chats Palace, 42 Brooksby's Walk, E9.
JULY
Capitol Radio London Jazz Festival:
Clapham Common, SW4.
JULY
Southwark Youth Festival:
The Young Vic, The Cut, Waterloo, London, SE1 8LP.
JULY/AUGUST
Hackney Young People's Festival:
Hackney, E.8.
JULY/SEPTEMBER
Henry Wood Promenade Concerts:
Royal Albert Hall, Kensington.
AUGUST – 4TH WEEK
European Festival of Model Railways:
Central Hall, Westminster.
AUGUST
International Festival for Youth Brass & Symphonic Bands:
Organisers: 24 Cadogan Square, London, SW1X 0JP.
AUGUST
International Festival of Youth Orchestras:
Details: 24 Cadogan Square, London, SW1X 0JP.
AUGUST
South Bank Summer Music Festival:
Royal Festival Hall, South Bank.
SEPTEMBER – EARLY
Covent Garden Neighbourhood Festival:
Details: C G Festival Committee, Tish Francis, 45 Short Gardens, London WC2.
OCTOBER – 1ST WEEK
National Brass Band Festival:
National Brass Band Championships, 11 Bath Road, Heathrow, Middlesex, TW6 2AA.

NOVEMBER
English Folk Dance & Song Society Folk Festival:
Cecil Sharpe House, 2 Regents Park Road, London, NW1 7AY.
NOVEMBER
London Folk Music Festival:
Mike Barraclough, 99 Nelson Road, London, N8.
DECEMBER – MID
Lambeth Walk Xmas Festival:
Details: Ms Deborah Sharp, c/o Lady Margaret Hall Settlement, 131 Kennington Road, London SE11.

FAIRS

FEBRUARY – EARLY
London Catering Fair:
New Horticultural Halls, Westminster.
FEBRUARY – EARLY
International Knitwear Fair:
Royal Horticultural Halls, Westminster.
FEBRUARY – 3RD WEEK
St. James' Spring Antiques Fair:
Piccadilly Hotel.
FEBRUARY – 4TH WEEK
Silhouette Fairs' Annual Fair:
Horticultural Halls, Vincent Square, SW1.
MARCH – 1ST, 2ND & 3RD WEEKS
Chelsea Spring Antiques Fair:
Old Town Hall, Chelsea.
MARCH – 4TH WEEK
Camden Antiques Fair:
Camden Arts Centre, Arkwright Road.
EASTER – SUNDAY AND MONDAY
Blackheath Fair:
Blackheath.
EASTER – SUNDAY AND MONDAY
Wormwood Scrubbs Fair:
Wormwood Scrubbs.
EASTER – SUNDAY AND MONDAY
Hampstead Heath Fair:
Hampstead Heath.
EASTER WEEKEND
Decorative Arts Fair:
Camden Arts Centre, Arkwright Road, NW3.
MAY – EARLY
May Book Fair:
Details: Ms, Nikki Marriott, The Book Place, 13 Peckham High Street, London SE15.
JUNE – 2ND WEEK
Fine Arts & Antiques Fair:
Olympia.
JUNE – 3RD WEEK
Southwark Summer Fair:
Bel Air Mansion, Gallery Road, Dulwich, London, SE1.
JUNE – 3RD WEEK
Antiquarian Book Fair:
Europa Hotel, Grosvenor Square.

JULY – 1ST WEEK
Puck Fair:
Gt. Russell Square, London, WC1.
JULY – 2ND WEEK
Chelsea Village Fair:
Burton Court, St. Leonards Terrace, London, SW3.
SEPTEMBER – 3RD WEEK
Chelsea Autumn Antiques Fair:
Chelsea Old Town Hall, Chelsea.
SEPTEMBER – 4TH WEEK
Leicester Square Book Fair:
Notre Dame Hall, Leicester Square, London, W1.
OCTOBER – 1ST & 2ND WEEKS
Burlington International Fine Art Fair:
Royal Academy of Arts, Piccadilly.
OCTOBER – 3RD & 4TH WEEKS
Motor Fair:
Earls Court.
OCTOBER
London Book Fair:
Grosvenor House, Park Lane.

FAYRES

MAY – EARLY
Covent Garden May Fayre:
Details: Maggie Pinhorn and Rosalind Dodd, 1 Shelton Street, London WC2.
SEPTEMBER – LATE
Psychics and Mystics Fayre and UFO Show:
Alexandra Palace.
JUNE – LATE
Ferrier Fayre:
Details: Mrs. S.R. Vint, Secretary, Ferrier Fayre Committee, 28 Ebdon Way, Ferrier Estate, Kidbrooke, SE3.

BAZAARS

DECEMBER – EARLY
Animal Welfare Annual Bazaar:
Chelsea Town Hall, Kings Road, Chelsea.

CARNIVALS

JULY – 2ND WEEK
Cranford Carnival:
Cranford.
JULY – 2ND WEEK
Finchley Carnival:
Victoria Park, Ballards Lane, Finchley, N3.
JULY – 2ND WEEK
Tooting Bec Carnival:
Tooting Bec.
JULY – LATE
Belvedere Carnival:
Belvedere.
JULY
Chelsea Carnival:

SHOWS

JANUARY – 1ST AND 2ND WEEKS
London International Boat Show:
Earls Court, SW5.
FEBRUARY – MID
Racing and Sporting Motorcycle Show:
Royal Horticultural Society Halls,
Vincent Square, SW1.
AUGUST – BANK HOLIDAY
Thamesmead Show:
Thamesmead.
AUGUST – BANK HOLIDAY
Erith Show:
Erith.
AUGUST – 4TH WEEK
International Motor Cycle Show:
Earls Court, SW5.
OCTOBER
Caravan Camping Holiday Show:
Earls Court, SW5.
OCTOBER
National Honey Show:
Caxton Hall, SW1.
NOVEMBER – 2ND WEEK
Woodworker Show:
Royal Horticultural Halls, Westminster.

TOURNAMENTS

JULY
Royal Tournament:
Earls Court.

AGRICULTURAL, HORTICULTURAL & BREED SHOWS

FEBRUARY – 2ND WEEK
Crufts Dog Show:
Earls Court, SW5.
MARCH – 2ND WEEK
Early Spring Show:
Royal Horticultural Society Halls,
Westminster.
MAY – 4TH WEEK
Chelsea Flower Show:
Royal Hospital Grounds, Chelsea.
JULY – 4TH WEEK
Lambeth Country Show:
Details: Lambeth Amenity Services, 14
Knights Hill, SE27.
AUGUST – 3RD WEEK
Friern Barnet Summer Show:
Friary Park, Friern Barnet Lane,
London, N12.
AUGUST
Greater London Horse Show:
Clapham Common, London, SW11.
DECEMBER – 1ST WEEK
Royal Smithfield Show & Agricultural
Machinery Exhibition:
Earls Court.

SPORTS

MARCH – 3RD WEEK
Oxford v Cambridge University Boat
Race:
Putney Bridge to Mortlake, River
Thames.
MARCH – LATE, OR APRIL – EARLY
Gillette London Marathon
JUNE – 2ND WEEK
Stella Artois Grass Championships
(Tennis):
Queens Club, W14.
JUNE – 4TH WEEK, TO JULY – 1ST
WEEK
Lawn Tennis Championships:
Wimbledon.
JULY – 2ND WEEK
Amateur Athletic Association National
Championships:
National Sports Centre, Crystal Palace.
JULY – MID
Benson & Hedges Cricket Cup Final:
Lord's Cricket Ground.
JULY – 4TH WEEK
Southwark Festival of Sport:
Southwark Park, Southwark, London,
SE16.
JULY – 4TH WEEK
Women's Amateur Athletic
Association National Championships:
National Sports Centre, Crystal Palace.

MISCELLANEOUS

JUNE – 1ST & 2ND WEEKS
Beating Retreat:
JUNE/AUGUST
Annual Summer Exhibition:
Royal Academy of Arts, Piccadilly.
DECEMBER – 1ST WEEK
London to Brighton Veteran Car Run:
Hyde Park to Brighton, East Sussex.
CHRISTMAS
Annual Xmas Dinner:
St. Peter's Community Centre,
Woolwich, SE18.

CLOWNS' REMEMBRANCE SERVICE
To witness a congregation full of clowns is a
rare treat for children and adults alike
though, in effect, the occasion is a serious
one. The show presented by the clowns for
children after the service is pure delight.
See: OLD CUSTOMS.

ST. GEORGE'S FESTIVAL OF DRAGONS
St. George's Church in Westcombe Park is
the inspiration behind the Festival of
Dragons which celebrates St. George's fight
with the Dragon. One of the colourful
dragons is shown here as it winds its way
around the grounds of Kidbrooke House.
See: FESTIVALS.

GREENWICH FESTIVAL
The Greenwich Festival is one of the biggest
and most comprehensive of its kind in the
country with literally dozens and dozens of
various events which cater for everyone.
See: FESTIVALS.

PEARLY QUEEN'S CHRISTMAS DINNER
The Pearly Queen of Woolwich sits down to
a slap-up Christmas dinner with local
pensioners at the St. Peter's Community
Centre. See: MISCELLANEOUS.
▽

◆ *Middlesex* ◆

▽
WHEELBARROW RACE
The annual wheelbarrow race down Pinner High Street is an interesting variation on the traditional charity pram races much loved in the North of England. See: MISCELLANEOUS.

◆

*Out into the outskirt's edges
Where a few surviving hedges
Keep alive our lost Elysium
Rural Middlesex again.*
SIR JOHN BETJEMAN.

OLD CUSTOMS

WHIT WEDNESDAY
Pinner Fair:
Pinner.
In 1336 Pinner was granted by Edward III two fairs every year – one on the vigil day and morrow of the Nativity of St. John and the other on the day and morrow of the beheading of St. John the Baptist. From these ancient fairs has developed the now renowned Pinner Pleasure Fair.

FESTIVALS

FEBRUARY – 1ST WEEK
Winter Brass Band Festival:
Wembley Conference Centre, Wembley.
JANUARY/FEBRUARY
Brent Festival:
Details: Arts & Entertainments Dept., London Borough of Brent, Town Hall, Forty Lane, Wembley, Middlesex, HA9 9HT.
FEBRUARY/MARCH
Enfield Highway Co-Operative Festival of Music & Verse Speaking:
Details: I.J. Evans, 446 Hertford Road, Enfield.

MARCH
Enfield Musical Festival:
Details: Ms. E. Frost, 13 Conical Corner, Chase Green, Enfield, EN2 6SL.
MARCH/APRIL
Southall Festival of Music, Speech and Dancing:
Details: S. Watson, 23 Bradenham Road, Hayes.
APRIL – 1ST WEEK
Festival of Country and Western Music:
Wembley Arena, Wembley.
APRIL – MAY
Ruislip and Northwood Festival of Music, Speech, Drama & Dancing:
Details: Mrs. R.H. Maple, 107 Cardinal Road, Eastcote, Ruislip.
MAY – 1ST WEEK
Enfield Folk Festival:
Details: Cyril Jones, 3 Uplands Way, Grange Park, London N21.
OCTOBER/NOVEMBER
Hounslow Music & Drama Festival:
Details: Ms. A. Yorke, 5 Orchard Court, Thornbury Avenue, Isleworth.

FAIRS

MAY 17; SEPTEMBER 12
Brentford Fair:
Brentford.
MAY 11; SEPTEMBER 19
Staines Fair:
Staines.
JUNE
Stanwell Donkey Derby Fair:
Stanwell.
AUGUST – 3RD & 4TH WEEKS
International Craft & Hobby Fair:
Wembley Conference Centre, Wembley.

PAGEANTS

JUNE – 4TH WEEK
Wembley Military Pageant:
Wembley.
EASTER SUNDAY
Easter Sunday Carnival Queen Parade and Show:
Alfred Beck centre, Grange Road, Hayes.

SHOWS

MAY – 3RD WEEK
Fleet Motor Show:
Wembley Conference Centre, Wembley.

AGRICULTURAL HORTICULTURAL & BREED SHOWS

AUGUST – 4TH WEEK
Southall Park Show:

97

⬅ PINNER FAIR
This ancient fair which dates back as far as 1336 has developed over the years into a major pleasure fair, filling the High Street every year with thousands of people. See: FAIRS.

◆

Southall Park, Uxbridge Road, Southall.
JUNE – 4TH WEEK
Hillingdon Show:
Hillingdon.
AUGUST – BANK HOLIDAY
Harrow Show:
Headstone Recreation Ground, Harrow.
SEPTEMBER
Borough of Enfield Horticultural Show:
Enfield.
SEPTEMBER
Brent Town Horticultural Show:
Brent.

——————SPORTS——————

FEBRUARY – 1ST WEEK
Benson and Hedges Snooker
Tournament:
Wembley Conference Centre, Wembley.
MARCH – 3RD WEEK
Miss Ballroom Dancing:
Wembley Arena, Wembley.
MARCH – 3RD & 4TH WEEKS
All England Badminton Championships:
Wembley Arena, Wembley.
MARCH – 4TH WEEK
John Player All England Badminton Championships:
Wembley Arena, Wembley.
MARCH – LATE
Football League Cup Final:
Wembley Stadium, Wembley.
MAY – 1ST WEEK
Rugby League Cup Final:
Wembley Stadium, Wembley.
MAY – MID
St. Claret's Open Tug-of-War Competition:
Hayes Stadium, Judge Heath Lane, Hayes.
MAY
Football Association Cup Final:
Wembley Stadium, Wembley.
JUNE
News of the World Darts Championship:
Wembley Arena, Wembley.
JULY – 1ST WEEK
Old Spice Water Skiing International:
Ruislip Water Skiing Club, Ruislip.
JULY – MID
Royal International Horse Show:
Wembley Arena, Wembley.
OCTOBER – 1ST WEEK
Horse of the Year Show:
Wembley Arena, Wembley.
OCTOBER – 3RD WEEK
International Police Tatoo:
Wembley Arena, Wembley.

——————MISCELLANEOUS——————

JANUARY – EARLY
Model Engineer Exhibition:
Wembley Conference Centre, Wembley
JUNE OR JULY
Annual Wheelbarrow Race:
Pinner High Street, Pinner.

Norfolk

ICH DIEN

When the sea comes in at Horsey Gap
Without any previous warning,
A swan shall build its rushy nest
On the roof of the Swan at Horning.
FROM 'HORSEY GAP',
TRADITIONAL VERSE

Old Customs

JANUARY – LATE
Blessing of the Plough (Plough Sunday):
Cawston.
FEBRUARY – SHROVE TUESDAY
Pancake Races:
Thorpe Abbots.
AUGUST – 1ST SUNDAY
Blessing the Broads:
The ruins of St. Benet's Abbey, Horning, River Bure.
Service conducted by the Bishop of Norwich.
EVERY SATURDAY AFTERNOON
Greneway Dole:
Church of St. Mary, Wireton Green.
When Ralph Greneway died in 1558 he left a bequest for old age pensioners. Several still receive the sum of five shillings after a short service held in the church.

Festivals

JANUARY – 2ND WEEK
Mini Dance Festival:
Tiffany's, Marine Parade, Great Yarmouth.
MARCH – 3RD WEEK
Great Yarmouth & Gorleston Dance Festival:
Caister Holiday Centre, Caister-on-Sea.
MAY – 2ND WEEK (BIENNIAL)
Fakenham Festival of Music & the Arts:
Details: Festival Secretary, 32 Sandy Lane, Fakenham, NR21 9EZ.
MAY – 3RD WEEK
Hunstanton Festival of Arts:
Details: Ms. M. Sexton, 17 Victoria Avenue, Hunstanton, PE36 6BY.
MAY – 3RD WEEK
Cley Little Festival of Poetry:
Details: Mrs. Elsa Martin, Golden Goose Cottage, Chapel Lane, Wiveton, Holt.
MAY
Great Yarmouth Festival of Music and Art:
Details: 5 Seafield Close, Great Yarmouth.
MAY
Cromer & North Norfolk Festival of Music & Drama:
Details: Ms. J. Gilbert, Scotch Cottage, Hanworth.
MAY – 1ST ,WEEK TO JUNE – 1ST WEEK
Downham Market Festival Week:
Downham Market.
JUNE – LATE
Norwich Folk Festival:
University Village, Norwich.
Details: Douglas Gowans, 128 Portland Street, Norwich MR2 3LR.

JULY – 4TH WEEK, OR AUGUST – 1ST WEEK
Kings Lynn Festival:
Festival Administrator, Fermoy Centre, King Street, Kings Lynn, PE30 1HA.
OCTOBER – 3RD WEEK
Norfolk & Norwich Triennial Festival of Music and the Arts:
Norwich Cathedral & St. Andrews Hall, Norwich.
NOVEMBER – 1ST & 2ND WEEKS
St. Andrew's Festival of Music and the Arts:
Gorleston.

Fairs

WHIT MONDAY
Cromer Fair:
Cromer.
FEBRUARY 14 – 19; 2ND TUESDAY IN APRIL; OCTOBER 17; 2ND TUESDAY IN NOVEMBER
Kings Lynn Mart:
Tuesday Market, Kings Lynn.
MAUNDY THURSDAY; EASTER SATURDAY, MONDAY & TUESDAY; DECEMBER 24, 27 & 28
Norwich Fair:
Norwich.
EASTER FRIDAY & SATURDAY
Great Yarmouth Fair:
Great Yarmouth.
JANUARY – 4TH WEEK, TO FEBRUARY – 1ST WEEK
Norfolk Trade Fair:
Caister Holiday Centre, Caister-on-Sea.
THROUGHOUT THE YEAR
Antique & Collectors' Fair:
Carnegie Room, Guildhall, Thetford.
JANUARY – 2ND WEEK
Norwich Annual Antiques Fair:

PANCAKE RACES
One of the few pancake races in costume is held at Thorpe Abbotts. See: OLD CUSTOMS.

◆

St. Andrews and Blackfriars Halls, Norwich.
JUNE
Aldborough Pleasure Fair:
Aldborough.
AUGUST – 4TH WEEK
Holkham Country Fair:
Holkham Park, Wells-Next-The-Sea.

FÊTES

MAY – LATE
Earlham Free Fête:
Earlham Park, Earlham Road, Norwich.
AUGUST – LATE
Earlham Mammoth Fête:
Earlham Park, Earlham Road, Norwich.
WHIT MONDAY
Bank Holiday Fête (& Regatta):
Nicholas Everitt Park, Oulton Broad.
AUGUST
Oulton Broad Fête (& Regatta):
Oulton Broad.

CARNIVALS

MAY – 4TH WEEK
Lord Mayor's Procession & Carnival:
City Centre, Norwich.
JULY
Cromer Carnival:
Cromer.

JULY
Diss Carnival:
Diss.
JULY
Wymondham Carnival:
Wymondham.

AGRICULTURAL, HORTICULTURAL & BREED SHOWS

EASTER
Daffodil Day:
Langley Park, Nr. Loddon.
APRIL – 1ST WEEK
District Kennel Society Dog Show:
Corn Exchange, Tuesday Market, Kings Lynn.
JUNE – 3RD WEEK
Flower Festival:
St. Nicholas Church, Dersingham, Kings Lynn.
JUNE – 4TH WEEK
Royal Norfolk Show:
Showground, Dereham Road, New Costessey, Norwich.
JUNE
Norfolk & Norwich Horticultural Society Rose Show:
Norwich.
JULY – 4TH WEEK
Kings Lynn Horticultural Society Show:
Corn Exchange, Tuesday Market, Kings Lynn.
JULY – 4TH WEEK
Sandringham Estate Cottage Horticultural Society Flower Show:
Sandringham Estate, Nr. Kings Lynn.

AUGUST
Cromer & District Horticultural Society Flower Show:
Cromer.
SEPTEMBER
Watton Agricultural Show:
Watton.
SEPTEMBER
Norfolk & Norwich Horticultural Society Early Autumn Flower Show:
OCTOBER – 4TH WEEK
Kings Lynn & District Horticultural Society Show:
Corn Exchange, Tuesday Market, Kings Lynn.
NOVEMBER – 3RD WEEK
Gorleston Flower Show:
Alderman Leach School, Gorleston, Great Yarmouth.

SPORTS

JANUARY – 3RD WEEK
Norfolk County Badminton Matches:
Breckland Sports Centre, Croxton Road, Thetford.
JANUARY – 4TH WEEK
Bury & District Badminton League Tournament:
Breckland Sports Centre, Croxton Road, Thetford.
FEBRUARY – 2ND & 3RD WEEKS
Norfolk County Hockey Association Matches:
Breckland Sports Centre, Croxton Road, Thetford.
MARCH – 1ST WEEK
East of England Squash Championships:
Hunter Squash Club, Edward Street, Norwich.
MAY – 3RD WEEK
Reedham Vikings Tug-of-War Club Annual Gala:
Reedham.
MAY – 4TH WEEK
Hempnall Lions Tug-of-War Club Open Competition:
School Field, Hempnall.
JULY – 3RD WEEK
International "Race of Aces" (Motorcycling):
Snetterton Circuit, Norwich.
AUGUST – LATE
Hunstanton Open Lawn Tennis Tournament:
Recreation Ground, Hunstanton.
SEPTEMBER – 1ST WEEK
English Bowling Association Men's Open Bowls Tournament:
Great Yarmouth Borough Council,

Bowling Greens, Great Yarmouth.
CHRISTMAS DAY
Christmas Day Sponsored Swim:
The Sea, Hunstanton.

Regattas:

AUGUST
Oulton Broad Regatta Week:
Oulton Broad.
AUGUST
Beccles Town Regatta:
Beccles.

───MISCELLANEOUS───

AUGUST
The Lavender Harvest:
Caley Mill, Heacham.

DISS CARNIVAL
*The country town of Diss presents an
annual carnival of colour and pageant. See:
CARNIVALS.*

LAVENDER HARVEST   ▷
*Lavender has been grown in England since
the Romans introduced it almost 2,000
years ago. Today, the acknowledged centre
of the English Lavender industry is Norfolk
Lavender Ltd., at Caley Mill, Heacham,
in North West Norfolk, a particularly
suitable area; the well-drained sandy soil
and low rainfall are the conditions most
favouring this aromatic and beautiful
shrub. See: MISCELLANEOUS.*

◆ Northamptonshire ◆

CASTELLO · FORTIOR · CONCORDIA

The lake that held a mirror to the sun
Now curves with wrinkles in the stillest place.
The autumn wind sounds hollow as a gun,
And water stands in every swampy place.
Yet in these fens peace, harmony, and grace,
The attributes of nature, are allied.
The barge with naked mast, in sheltered place
Beside the brig, close to the bank is tied,
While small waves plash by its bulky side.
FROM 'NORTHAMPTONSHIRE FENS' BY
JOHN CLARE

──── OLD CUSTOMS ────

MAY 1
May Day Celebrations:
Flore, Nr. Weedon.
*Children from the school lead the
celebrations in which a floral crown which
they have made is carried round the village
on two long poles. Afterwards there is the
crowning of the May Queen.*
MAY – LAST THURSDAY
Wicken Love Feast:
Wicken.
*The parishioners attend a short service at the
parish church and are then led by the vicar
to the 'gospel Elm' next to the Old Rectory
where they share in a feast of cake and ale.
This is in remembrance of the day that the
Rectories of Wickamon and Wickdive were
united into one parish.*
MAY 29
Oak Apple Day Celebrations:

*The Mayor and members of the Corporation
carry bunches of oak apples and gilded
leaves in procession from the Town Hall to
All Saints Church where a service is held.
Inside the Church itself a statue of Charles
II is decorated with oak boughs by the
choiresters.*
WHIT MONDAY – EVERY 20 YEARS
(NEXT ONE 1982)
Corby Pole Fair:
Corby.
*An ancient Charter Fair which
commemorates the charter granted by
Elizabeth I in 1585 in which exemptions
from certain toll-payments and various jury
and military services were conferred on the
people. The name itself comes from the
custom of carting off those who refused to
pay the toll leading to the town. The men
were straddled aside a pole and the women*

on a chair.
DECEMBER – 3RD SUNDAY
Tin Can Band:
Broughton.
*Since the days long ago when a gypsy
woman gave birth to an illegitimate child on
one of the camp sites near the village, it has
been the custom for a crowd of youths and
men to gather outside Broughton village
church and, when midnight strikes, to
parade around the village banging kettles,
tin cans, plates, etc. This was once thought
a good way to frighten off gypsies who were
feared as weavers of spells.*
DECEMBER 26 (BOXING DAY)
Mummers Play & Morris Dancing:
Stocks Hill, Church Street, Moulton.

──── FESTIVALS ────

FEBRUARY/APRIL
Kettering & District Eisteddfod:
*Details: Ms. M.L. Wall, 123 Reservoir
Road, Kettering.*
MARCH/APRIL
Oundle Music Festival:
*Details: Ms. D. Bates, Conegar Halt, 32
Church Lane, Cranford St. John,
Kettering.*
MAY – 3RD WEEK
Moulton Village Festival:
Moulton.

◆

WICKEN LOVE FEAST
*Villagers partake in cakes and ale (wine) at
the annual remembrance service held
beneath the Gospel Elm at Wicken. See:
OLD CUSTOMS.*

TIN CAN BAND
A thoroughly noisy and boisterous occasion is guaranteed at Broughton's midnight Tin Can Band ceremony. See: OLD CUSTOMS.

JULY — 3RD WEEK
Corby Festival:
Details: Entertainments Manager, Festival Office, Civic Centre, George Street, Corby, NN17 1QB.

FAIRS

THURSDAY BEFORE EASTER; FRIDAY BEFORE WHITSUN SATURDAY; FRIDAY BEFORE OCTOBER 11; THURSDAY BEFORE DECEMBER 21
Kettering Fair:
Kettering.
3RD FRIDAY IN FEBRUARY AND NOVEMBER; NEAREST SATURDAY TO JUNE 24; SEPTEMBER 19; 1ST THURSDAY IN NOVEMBER
Northampton Fair:
Northampton.
DECEMBER
Northampton Christmas and New Year Fair:
Northampton.

CARNIVALS

MAY — 3RD WEEK
Moulton Village Carnival:
Moulton.
AUGUST — 3RD WEEK
Kettering Carnival:
Town Centre, Kettering.

AGRICULTURAL, HORTICULTURAL & BREED SHOWS

MAY — 3RD WEEK
Exemption Dog Show:

Long Buckby.
JULY — 4TH WEEK
Northampton Show:
Abingdon Park, Park Avenue North, Northampton.
AUGUST — 4TH WEEK
British Timken Show:
Showground, Duston, Nr. Northampton.
SEPTEMBER
Northamptonshire County Agricultural Show:
Northampton.

SPORTS

JULY — 2ND WEEK
British Grand Prix Motor Racing Finals:
Silverstone Circuit, Nr. Towcester.
JULY — 2ND WEEK

Corby Highland Gathering:
Recreation Club, Corby.

MISCELLANEOUS

JULY
Corby Military Tattoo:
Recreation Club ground, Corby.
OCTOBER — 2ND WEEK
World Conker Championships:
The Chequered Skipper, Ashton, Nr. Oundle.

WORLD CONKER CHAMPIONSHIPS
The noble art of conkers is elevated to an art form inside the Chequered Skipper Inn at Ashton as champion players compete for the honoured cup. See: MISCELLANEOUS.

Northumberland ◆

(INCLUDING NORTH TYNE & WEAR)

O *ye Northumbrian shades! which overlook*
The rocky pavement and the mossy falls
Of solitary Wensbeck's limpid stream,
How gladly I recall your well-known seats,
Beloved of old; and that delightful time,
When all alone, for many a summer's day,
I wander'd through your calm recesses, led
In silence, by some powerful hand unseen.
WILLIAM BASSE.

─── Old Customs ───

JANUARY I
Morris Dancing:
The Ship, Front Street, Monkseaton.
JANUARY I
Wheelbarrow Race:
Ponteland.
FEBRUARY – SHROVE TUESDAY
Ringing of the Pancake Bell:
Berwick-On-Tweed.
The bell is ritually rung at 8.00 p.m.
FEBRUARY – SHROVE TUESDAY
Shrovetide Football:
Alnwick.
The teams, representing the local parishes, receive a new football for the event from the lodge of Alnwick Castle, seat of the Duke of Northumberland. Following a mad scramble the ball is kicked into the river and the first player to reach it is allowed to keep it as a prize.
FEBRUARY 14
Blessing the Salmon-Net Fisheries:
Pedwell Beach, Norham-On-Tweed.
The various fisheries on the River Tweed are blessed during a short open air service held just before midnight. The service is timed to allow the first boat of the season to leave for the fishing grounds immediately after midnight.
MAY I (MAY DAY)
Perambulation of the Bounds:
Guildhall, Marygate,
Berwick-on-Tweed:
The occasion is attended by the Mayor and other officials who beat the Bounds on horseback.
MAY I – AT DAWN
Welcoming The May:
Town Moor, Newcastle.
Morris Dancing.
MAY – ROGATION SUNDAY
Blessing the Sea Ceremony:
Cullercoats.
JUNE – 4TH WEEK
Alnwick Fair:
Market Square, Alnwick.
This fair is a re-enactment of the ancient 18th century Spring Hiring Fair.
MAY – WEDNESDAY NEAREST 18TH
Dunting the Freeholder:
Newbiggin-by-the-Sea.
A freeholding ceremony pertaining to the rights of those in the village whose assets include 'stints' (i.e. plots of land) on Newbiggin Moor. Any new freeholder is initiated at the 'dunting stone' (once an original Druid stone but since replace by a concrete pillar) on the moor.
JULY 4 (OLD MID-SUMMER'S EVE)
Whalton Bale:
Whalton.
Also known as Baal Fire and is simply a Mid-Summer Solstice bonfire on the village green.
DECEMBER 31 (NEW YEAR'S EVE)
Tar-Barrel Parade:
Allendale.
This New Year's Eve celebration was first recorded in 1884, though it probably dates back earlier. Accompanied by the Allendale band, the 'guisers' (those men privileged to carry the barrels) in fancy dress, parade from the church to the market place where the barrels are lit, ending with the traditional 'Auld Lang Syne' singing and 'first-footing' (i.e. visiting houses to receive refreshments and good wishes for the coming year).

─── Festivals ───

MARCH
Tynedale Musical Festival:
Details: C. Smith, 9 Carham Close, Carbridge, NE45 5NA.
MARCH
Wansbeck Music Festival:
Details: Ms. M. Dunn, 140 Middlesgate, Loansdean, Morpeth, NE61 2DD.
MAY – MID OR LATE
Ashington Festival:
Details: Festival Director, Mid-Northumberland Arts Group, Wansbeck Square, Ashington, NE63 9RG.
JUNE – 3RD WEEK
English Folk Dance & Song Society

Festival:
Wallington Hall, Cambo, Morpeth.
JUNE – 3RD WEEK
Newcastle Festival:
*Details: The Director, Newcastle Festival,
7 Saville Place, Newcastle-upon-Tyne,
NE1 8DQ.*
JUNE – 4TH WEEK
Annual Flower Festival:
Oxford Street Methodist Church,
Whitley Bay.
JULY – 3RD WEEK
**Northumberland Traditional Music
Ceremony:**
Rothbury.
JULY – 3RD WEEK
**Whitley Bay Two-Day Festival
Spectacular:**
Churchill Playing Fields, Marine
Avenue, Whitley Bay.
OCTOBER – 2ND WEEK
Hexham Abbey Festival:
*Details: Festival Director, "The Whiggs",
Great Whittington, Newcastle-upon-Tyne,
NE19 2HD.*
OCTOBER – 4TH WEEK
Newcastle Jazz Festival:
Newcastle-upon-Tyne.

FAIRS

LAST FRIDAY AND SATURDAY IN MAY
Berwick Fair:
Berwick-upon-Tweed.
1ST WEDNESDAY IN MARCH, MAY &
NOVEMBER
Morpeth Fair:
Morpeth.
LAST WEDNESDAY IN MARCH; 2ND
WEDNESDAY IN AUGUST; LAST
WEDNESDAY IN OCTOBER; LAST
WEDNESDAY IN NOVEMBER
Newcastle-Upon-Tyne Fair:
Newcastle-upon-Tyne.
MAY – 3RD WEEK
Tyneside Country Fair:
North of England Equestrian Centre,
Stannington, Morpeth.
JUNE – 4TH WEEK
Town Moor Fair:
Town Moor, Newcastle-upon-Tyne.
JUNE – 4TH WEEK
**Northumbrian Wildlife Trust Summer
Fair:**
Etal Manor, Etal.
JUNE – LATE
Alnwick Fair:
Market Square, Alnwick.
JULY – 4TH WEEK
Summer Fair:
Beaconfield, Grand Parade, Tynemouth.

FÊTES

JULY
Delavel Annual Garden Fête:
Delavel Hall, Seaton Delavel.

CARNIVALS

MAY – 3RD WEEK
Seahouses May Carnival Week:
Seahouses.
JULY – MID
Mediaeval Carnival:
Whitley Bay.
JULY – 4TH WEEK
Carnival Parade:
The Links, Whitley Bay.
JULY – 4TH WEEK, TO AUGUST – 1ST
WEEK
Carnival Fortnight:
North Shields.
AUGUST – 4TH WEEK, TO AUGUST –
1ST WEEK
Carnival Fortnight:
North Shields.

SHOWS

JULY – 3RD WEEK
North of England Motor Show:
The Links, Whitley Bay.
AUGUST – 4TH WEEK
Stocksfield Village Show:
Stocksfield.

AGRICULTURAL, HORTICULTURAL & BREED SHOWS

MAY – 4TH WEEK
Allendale Sheepdog Trials:
The Hope Farm, Allendale.
JUNE – 2ND WEEK
Roman Wall Agricultural Show:
Twice Brewed Military Road,
Northumberland.
AUGUST – 2ND WEEK
**Great Northumberland Agricultural
Show:**
North of England Equestrian Centre,
Stannington, Morpeth.
AUGUST – 2ND & 3RD WEEKS
Allendale Agricultural Show:
Showfield, Allendale.
AUGUST – 4TH WEEK
Bellingham Agricultural Show:
Bellingham.
AUGUST – 4TH WEEK
**Whitley Bay Summer Horticultural
Show:**
The Links, Whitley Bay.
AUGUST – 4TH WEEK
Glandale Agricultural Society Show:
Wooler.

SPORTS

JUNE – 2ND WEEK
Annual Pram Race:
Front Street, Tynemouth.
JULY – 4TH WEEK
Temple Thornton Highland Games:
Meldon Park, Morpeth.
AUGUST – 4TH WEEK
**National 12 Class Sailing
Championships:**
Tynemouth.

Regattas:

JULY – 2ND WEEK
Morpeth Regatta & Safety Day:
Town Hall, Carlisle Park, Morpeth.
JULY – 4TH WEEK
**Radio Controlled Model Powerboat
Regatta:**
Tynemouth Park, Promenade,
Tynemouth.

◆

SHROVETIDE FOOTBALL
*Players and spectators proceed in procession
past Alnwick Castle to the pastures where
the game is played. If the ball is kicked into
the river – as it often is – the players dive in
to retrieve it. See: OLD CUSTOMS.*

DELAVEL GARDEN FÊTE
*The Fête Queen is crowned by the Mayor of
Blyth Valley after the opening of the parish
of Delavel annual garden fête at Delavel
Hall. See: FÊTES.*

ASHINGTON FESTIVAL
*Children's entertainer Phil Spellacy paints
willing faces during the 'Captain Rainbow
Fun Show', part of the Ashington Festival.
See: FESTIVALS.*

ALNWICK FAIR
*A ducking takes place at Alnwick's
re-enactment of the 18th century Spring
Hiring Fair. See: FAIRS.*

MODEL POWER BOAT REGATTA
*Winning craft on display at Tynemouth's
famous model regatta. See: SPORTS.*

PRAM RACE
*Pram races are particularly popular in this
part of the country. The race at Tynemouth
is organised by the local Round Table
organisation to raise funds for charity. See:
SPORTS.*

◆ Nottinghamshire ◆

SAPIENTER PROFICIENS

OLD CUSTOMS

FEBRUARY – SUNDAY NEAREST 2ND
Cradle Rocking Ceremony:
Church of St. Mary, Blidworth.
On this, the day of the Feast of the Purification of the Blessed Virgin Mary, the presentation of the young Christ at the Temple is symbolised. A cradle which has been adorned with flowers is placed by the altar and the most recently baptised boy is placed within and rocked during the dedication for several minutes.
SPRING BANK HOLIDAY
Maypole Dancing:
Wellow.
A huge sixty-five foot Maypole on top of which sits a golden vane and weathercock is the scene of this traditional celebration which dates back to the beginning of the nineteenth century.
JULY – SUNDAY NEAREST 8TH
Armada Sermon:
St. Peter's Church, Nottingham.
OCTOBER – 1ST WEEK
Nottingham Goose Fair:
Goose Fair Site, Recreation Ground, Gregory Boulevard.
The first Goose Fairs appeared in 1542 and were held at the time of year when geese were in their prime for eating, in readiness for the Michaelmas feasts where roast goose was the traditional dish.
NOVEMBER – SUNDAY NEAREST 5TH
Gunpowder Plot Sermon:
St. Peter's Church, Nottingham.
CHRISTMAS – 5 SUNDAYS PREVIOUS
Gopher Ringing:
Newark.
In commemoration of the Flemish merchant who was guided out of the marshes by the sound of the Newark Bells, the annual ringing occurs on each of the five Sundays

before Christmas.
DECEMBER
Laxton Jury Day & Court Leet:
Laxton.
The last place in England still practising the old feudal system of farming. The administration of the fields is handled by a 'field jury' responsible to the Court Leet, which sits in judgement on farm business carried out in the manor – now owned by the Ministry of Agriculture.

FESTIVALS

FEBRUARY – MARCH
Nottingham University Cripps Hall Arts Festival:
Cripps Hall, University, Nottingham.
MARCH
Worksop Music & Drama Festival:
Details: J.S Warden, 47 Arundel Drive, Carlton-in-Lindrick, Worksop.
APRIL
Long Eaton Festival of Music & the Arts:
Details: 32 Charnwood Avenue, Long Eaton, NH10 3HB.
MAY – 1ST WEEK
Nottingham at Home to Holland Festival:
Various venues throughout, Nottinghamshire.
MAY – 3RD WEEK
CAMRA Beer Festival:
Victoria Leisure Centre, Gedling Street, Nottingham.
MAY
Beeston Musical Festival:
Details: H.P. Allton, 59 Sidney Road, Beeston, NG9 1AN.
MAY
Mansfield Music & Drama Festival:

Details: A. Steele, 14 Clipstone Avenue, Mansfield, NG18 2AR.
JUNE
Nottingham Festival:
Details: Joe Nuttridge, Nottingham City Council, 51 Castlegate, Nottingham.
JUNE
Nottinghamshire Miners' Welfare Music Festival:
Details: J.A. Wilkinson, 21 Warren Road. Kirkby-in-Ashfield, NG17 9AX.
JUNE
Nottingham Festival Fringe:
Details: Simon Shepherd, English Department, Nottingham University, Nottingham.
JUNE
Pinxton Music Festival:
Details: Mrs. S. Martin, 16 Town Street, Pinxton, Nottingham.
JULY – 1ST WEEK
Flower Festival:
All Saints Church, Main Street, Thrumpton.
JULY
Nottingham Playhouse Art Festival:
Nottingham.
OCTOBER – 2ND, 3RD & 4TH WEEKS
Mansfield Festival:
Details: Amenities Organiser, Mansfield District Council, Civic Theatre, Leeming Street, Mansfield.
OCTOBER
Selston Musical Festival:
Details: Mrs. E.O. Haddon, Fan Fields, Pye Hill, Jacksdale.
NOVEMBER
Nottingham Music & Drama Festival:
Details: W. Barlow, 8 Storey Gelding, Nottingham, NG4 46NT.

GOOSEY FAIR
The Nottingham Goose Fair is steeped in tradition and folk-lore. Nowadays only a pleasure fair remains of this ancient event. See: OLD CUSTOMS.

LAXTON JURY DAY & COURT LEET
Laxton is the only village in England which still practises the feudal system of farming. The Court Leet, which deals with matters relating to farming, is pictured here in session. See: OLD CUSTOMS.

FAIRS

FRIDAY OF MID-LENT; MAY 14; WHIT
TUESDAY; AUGUST 2; WEDNESDAY
BEFORE OCTOBER 2; NOVEMBER 1;
MONDAY BEFORE DECEMBER 11
Newark Fair:
Newark.
EASTER MONDAY & TUESDAY; WHIT
MONDAY & TUESDAY; 1ST THURSDAY
IN OCTOBER FOR 3 DAYS
Nottingham Fair:
Nottingham.
NOVEMBER – 5TH WEEK
Kirton Bonfire Fair:
Kirton.

AGRICULTURAL, HORTICULTURAL & BREED SHOWS

MAY – 1ST WEEK
**Newark & Nottinghamshire
Agricultural Show:**
The Showground, Winthorpe, Newark.
JULY – 3RD WEEK
**The Nottingham (St Ann's) Rose
Show:**
The Rose Gardens (C.W. Gregory & Son
Ltd.) Toton Lane, Stapleford,
Nottingham.
AUGUST – 2ND WEEK
Southwell Show:
Norwood Park, Southwell.
AUGUST
Kingston-On-Soar Agricultural Show:
Kingston-on-Soar.
SEPTEMBER – 4TH WEEK
Collingham Show:
Newark & Notts. Showground,
Winthorpe, Newark.

SPORTS

JUNE – 4TH WEEK
**Rotary Club of Warsop Open
Tug-of-War Competition:**
Warsop.
JUNE
Around the Houses Cycle Race:
Nottingham.
JULY – 4TH WEEK
National Rowing Championships:
National Water Centre, Holme
Pierrepont, Nottingham.
AUGUST – 4TH WEEK
Power Boat Championships:
National Water Sports Centre, Adbolton
Lane, Holme Pierrepont, Nottingham.
OCTOBER – 1ST WEEK
Osberton Horse Trials:
Osberton.

Regattas:

APRIL – 4TH WEEK & MAY – 4TH
WEEK
**British Canoe Union Committee Sprint
Canoe Regatta:**
National Water Sports Centre, Adbolton
Lane, Holme Pierrepont, Nottingham.
MAY – 1ST WEEK
Dutch Week Regatta:
Trent Bridge, Victoria Embankment,
Nottingham.
MAY – 2ND WEEK
Royal Air Force Rowing Regatta:
National Water Sports Centre, Adbolton
Lane, Holme Pierrepont, Nottingham.
MAY – 2ND WEEK
Inter-Services Regatta:
National Water Sports Centre, Adbolton
Lane, Holme Pierrepont, Nottingham.
MAY – 3RD WEEK
Nottingham City Regatta:
National Water Sports Centre, Adbolton
Lane, Holme Pierrepont, Nottingham.
MAY – 3RD WEEK
Regional Freesailing Regatta:
Colwick Park, off Mile End Row,
Nottingham.
JUNE – 2ND WEEK
Loughborough Regatta:
National Water Sports Centre, Adbolton
Lane, Holme Pierrepont, Nottingham.
JUNE – 2ND WEEK
National Schools Regatta:
National Water Sports Centre, Adbolton
Lane, Holme Pierrepont, Nottingham.
JUNE – 4TH WEEK
International Canoe Regatta:
National Water Sports Centre, Adbolton
Lane, Holme Pierrepont, Nottingham.
JUNE – LAST WEEKEND
Nottinghamshire International

◆

'AROUND THE HOUSES' CYCLE RACE
*This popular cycling contest is one of the
many individual events which go to make
up the Nottingham Festival. See:
SPORTS.*
▽

Regatta:
National Water Sports Centre, Adbolton
Lane, Holme Pierrepont, Nottingham.
JULY – 2ND WEEK
National Scout Regatta:
National Water Sports Centre, Adbolton
Lane, Holme Pierrepont, Nottingham.
JULY – MID
**British Canoe Union National Canoe
Regatta:**
National Water Sports Centre, Adbolton
Lane, Holme Pierrepont, Nottingham.
JULY – 4TH WEEK
National Rowing Regatta:
National Water Sports Centre, Adbolton
Lane, Holme Pierrepont, Nottingham.
SEPTEMBER – 1ST WEEK
National Sailboarding Regatta:
National Water Sports Centre, Adbolton
Lane, Holme Pierrepont, Nottingham.

MISCELLANEOUS

FEBRUARY – 2ND WEEK
CISWO Open Brass Band Contest:
West Nottinghamshire College of
Further Education, Mansfield.
APRIL
**Annual Open Brass Band
Championship:**
Nottingham.
SPRING BANK HOLIDAY
Spring Bank Holiday Steaming:
Papplewick Pumping Station, off
Langdale Lane, Ravenshead.
JUNE – 2ND WEEK
Hunt the Outlaw:
Sherwood Forest, Edwinstowe,
Mansfield.
*Details: Mrs. Chamberlain, 37 Moorsholm
Drive, Wollaton.*
JUNE – 3RD WEEK
**Nottingham Festival Water
Spectacular:**
Trent Bridge, Victoria Embankment,
Nottingham.

OXON
Oxfordshire ◆

SAPERE · AUDE

A *land of waters green and clear*
Of willows and of poplars tall,
And in the Spring-time of the year,
The white may breaking over all
And pleasure quick to come at call;
And Summer rides by marsh and wold,
And Autumn with her crimson pall
About the towers of Magdalen roll'd:
And memories of the friends of old,
And strong tradition binding fast
The flying terms with bands of gold –
All these hath Oxford . . .

ANDREW LANG.

Old Customs

JANUARY I
Needle and Thread Ceremony:
The Queen's College, Oxford.
Begun in 1341 in honour of Christ and the Apostles, the ceremony is enacted by a Provost and twelve Fellows.
JANUARY 14; ONCE A CENTURY (NEXT ONE 2000)
Hunting the Mallard:
All Saints College, Oxford.
A ceremonial search for the tutelary bird of All Souls, a mystical creature who, according to legend, was discovered in a drain beneath the college.
APRIL 23
Shakespeare Memorial Ceremony:
Cornmarket, Oxford.
Accompanied by civic officials, the Mayor leads a procession to the Painted Room in the Cornmarket where they drink to the poet's health in sack and malmsey.

MAY I (MAY DAY) AND SEPTEMBER 19TH (VILLAGE FEAST DAY)
Garland Dressing:
Charlton-on-Otmoor.
Inside the church of Charlton-on-Otmoor there is a large wooden cross, permanently adorned with clipped box and yew, known as "The Garland". Twice a year it is taken down and freshly dressed with greenery and flowers.
MAY I (MAY DAY)
May Morning Celebrations:
Magdalen Tower, Magdalen College, Oxford.
In 1491, following his death, Lord Berkeley bequeathed the advowson of Slymbridge parish church to Magdalen College in order that Scholars and Fellows might pray for his soul. Ever since then the choristers of Magdalen greet the sunrise at the top of the tower with a Latin hymn.
MAY

Beating the Parish Boundaries:
Oxford.
WHITSUNTIDE
Morris Dancing:
Bampton.
The ancient West Oxfordshire village of Bampton is the home of the famous Bampton Morris Dancers and on this day they dance amid flowers and garlands from morning to evening in the square, streets and gardens.
WHIT SUNDAY – AND THE SUNDAY AFTER
Grass Strewing Ceremony:
Holy Trinity Church, Sherington.
Banbury grass is strewn in the church and renewed a week later.
WHIT MONDAY
The Great Shirt Race:
Bampton.
An occasion dating back to 784 which celebrates the day when Ethelred the Shirtless pursued the town Burghers through the street in order to acquire a shirt for his back.
JUNE 19 (OR THE SATURDAY NEAREST THIS DATE)
Election of the Mayor of Ock Street:
Abingdon.
Candidates for the post are normally Morris dancers who live on the street. Morris dancing is performed in his honour and the new Mayor is chaired down the street and back.
JUNE – SUNDAY FOLLOWING 24TH
Wall Pulpit Sermon:
Oxford.
A sermon is delivered from the pulpit which is set in the wall of the first quadrangle of Magdalen College and is said to commemorate a Hospital on the site. The

111

◁ **MAYOR OF OCK STREET**
During the Mayor Making ceremony the new Mayor is carried through the streets by the renowned Bampton Morris Men. See: OLD CUSTOMS.

ST. GILES FAIR
This is one of England's oldest and most famous fairs which is a major attraction in Oxford during the autumn. See: OLD CUSTOMS.

THE GREAT SHIRT RACE
At Bampton the villagers stage their annual street race in which entrants in fancy dress ride a motley array of improvised vehicles. See: OLD CUSTOMS.

◆

ceremony dates back about 500 years.
ST PETER'S DAY — 1ST MONDAY FOLLOWING
Yarnton Meadow Mowing Rights:
Yarnton.
Here the rights of tenancy of the meadow are auctioned each year.
AUGUST 27
Ancient Donkey Derby & Fete:
Old School Field, Church View, Bampton.
SEPTEMBER — 1ST MONDAY & TUESDAY FOLLOWING 1ST SUNDAY AFTER 1ST (ST GILES DAY)
St. Giles Fair:
St. Giles, Oxford.
The fifth largest fair in England and, established in the 11th century, one of the oldest. As with other fairs of mediaeval origin St. Giles has ceased to be a trading fair but is still held on the original site in Magdalen Street and St. Giles, Oxford.
DECEMBER 24 (CHRISTMAS EVE)
Bampton Mummers:
Bampton-in-the-Bush.
DECEMBER 26 (BOXING DAY)
Headington Mummers:
Headington Quarry.
DECEMBER
Boars Head Ceremony:
Queen's College, Oxford.
A boars head is carried ceremonially through the college as part of the Christmas feast and an ancient hunting horn is sounded to summon the Provost, Fellows and Dons.

FESTIVALS

MARCH
Chipping Norton Musical Festival:
Details: Ms. M. Lee, Sarsbank, Old London Road, Chipping Norton.
MAY — 1ST WEEK
May Festival:
Towersey.

MAY — JUNE
English Bach Festival:
Oxford.
JUNE — 3RD WEEK
Dorchester-on-Thames Festival:
Dorchester-on-Thames.
JULY — 1ST WEEK
Thames Festival & Carnival:
Various venues: Thames.
JULY — 2ND WEEK
St. Denys Festival:
Stanford-in-the-Vale, Nr. Wantage.
JULY/AUGUST
Oxford Festival:
Details: Festival Director, Festival Office, Oxford Playhouse, Beaumont Street, Oxford, OX1 2LW.
AUGUST — 4TH WEEK
Towersey Village Festival:
Towersey.
AUGUST — 4TH WEEK
Salford Village Festival:
Salford.
AUGUST
International Music Festival of Oxford:
University Church of St. Mary the Virgin, Oxford.
Details: Kato Evans, Studio, 63 Victoria Road, Oxford, OX2 7Q9.
OCTOBER
Dorchester Abbey Festival:
Dorchester Abbey, Dorchester-on-Thames.
Details: Anne Born, 14 Hawkswell Gardens, Oxford.
(BIENNIAL)
Oxford Festival of English Song:
Details: Box 4, Tavistock House, 12 James Street, Laondon, WC2.

FAIRS

1ST THURSDAY AFTER JANUARY 13; OCTOBER 13
Banbury Fair:
Banbury.
MARCH 7; HOLY THURSDAY; THURSDAY AFTER TRINITY SUNDAY; SEPTEMBER 21
Henley Fair:
Henley-on-Thames.
MAY 3; 2ND WEDNESDAY IN AUGUST; MONDAY & TUESDAY AFTER SEPTEMBER 1; THURSDAY BEFORE SEPTEMBER 29

◆

TOWERSEY VILLAGE FESTIVAL
Primarily a folk-orientated occasion, the celebrations at Towersey embrace both carnival and festival including many side shows and events such as the modern version of the ducking stool shown here. See: FESTIVALS.

Oxford Fair:
Oxford.
MARCH
Gypsy Horse Fair:
Stow-in-the-Wold.
MAY
St. Mark's Fair:
Abingdon.
MAY – 2ND WEEK
Henley-on-Thames Antique Fair:
Town Hall, Henley-on-Thames.
MAY – 2ND WEEK
Oxford Polytechnic Book Fair:
Headington, Oxford.
JUNE
St. Edmund's Fair:
Abingdon.
JUNE – MID
Burford Street Fair:
Burford.
JULY
Cropredy Country Fair:
Banbury.
JULY – 4TH WEEK
Free Steam Fair:
Henley-on-Thames.
SEPTEMBER
Chipping Norton Mop Fair:
Chipping Norton.
SEPTEMBER
Wallingford Michaelmas Fair:
Wallingford.
SEPTEMBER
Woodstock Street Fair:
Woodstock.
OCTOBER
Abingdon Michaelmas Fair:
Abingdon.
OCTOBER
Banbury Michaelmas Fair:
Banbury.

FAYRES

JUNE – 4TH WEEK
Banbury Steam Society Fayre and Rally:
Wroxton, Banbury.

FÊTES

SPRING
Spring Fête:
Old School Field, Church View,
Bampton.
JUNE – EARLY
Broughton Castle Fête:
Broughton Castle, Nr. Banbury.
JUNE – LATE
Shotleswell Village Fête:
Shotleswell.
JULY – EARLY
Friends of Abingdon Annual Fête:
Abbey Buildings, Thames Street,

Abingdon.

CARNIVALS

JUNE – 4TH WEEK
Banbury Carnival:
Banbury.
JUNE – 4TH WEEK
Fitzharry's School Carnival:
Northcourt Road, Abingdon.

SHOWS

NOVEMBER
Banbury Motor Show:
Spiceball Park Sports Centre, Banbury.

AGRICULTURAL, HORTICULTURAL & BREED SHOWS

MAY – 4TH WEEK
Oxfordshire Federation of Young Farmers Clubs County Show:
Oxfordshire Showground, Junction of
A34 and A4095.
JUNE – 2ND WEEK
Cotswold Harness Horse & Pony Show:
Cotswold Wild Life Park, Nr. Burford.
AUGUST – 4TH WEEK
White Horse Show:
Cravenfield, Uffington, Nr. Faringdon.
SEPTEMBER – 1ST WEEK
Wootton-by-Woodstock Flower Show:
Wootton Place,
Wootton-by-Woodstock.
SEPTEMBER – 2ND WEEK
Henley Show:
Lower Bolney Farm,
Henley-on-Thames.
SEPTEMBER – 3RD WEEK
Chipping Norton Flower Show:
Chipping Norton.
SEPTEMBER – MID
Thame Agricultural Show:
Showground, Risborough Road, Thame.

SPORTS

MAY – 3RD WEEK
May Eights Week: The University Rowing Races:
The Isis, River Thames, Oxford.
JUNE – 2ND WEEK
Teacle Miners Tug-of-War Club Event:
Faringdon.
JULY
National Archery Championships:
Oxford.
OCTOBER
Banbury Fun Run:

Town Centre, Banbury.
*Details: Countrywide Communications
Ltd, 23 West Bar, Banbury.*
SEPTEMBER – 1ST WEEK
Witney Tug-of-War Club Annual Open:
West Witney Sports Ground, Witney.

Regattas:

JULY – EARLY
Henley Royal Regatta:
*Details: R.S. Goddard, Regatta
Headquarters, Henley-on-Thames.*

MISCELLANEOUS

JUNE – EARLY
Holton Working Steam Rally:
Windmill Field, Waterperry Road,
Holton.
SEPTEMBER – EARLY
Transport Trust Rally:
Blenheim Palace, Woodstock.

HOLTON WORKING STEAM RALLY
*A great day for steam enthusiasts where
traction engines from far and wide converge
on Windmill Field, Holton, for the annual
rally. See: MISCELLANEOUS.*

◆ *Shropshire* ◆

FLOREAT · SALOPIA

Cathercot upon the hill
Wildely down in the dale
Churton for pretty girls
And Pulverbatch for good ale.
TRADITIONAL RHYME

OLD CUSTOMS

MAY 29
Arbor Tree Day:
Aston-on-Clun.
A black poplar tree is dressed with flags, a ceremony which was first celebrated at the wedding of Mary Charter and John Marston in Aston-on-Clun in 1786, though the custom is said to survive from an ancient era in the worship of St. Bridget, a goddess whose shrine was a tree.
NOVEMBER (ALL SOULS DAY)
Souling:
Parts of Shropshire.
DECEMBER 26TH (BOXING DAY)
Mock Battles:
Bridgenorth.
An old custom is still observed in which youths perform mock battles with singlesticks and collect money from passers by.

FESTIVALS

MARCH – 1ST WEEK
Shropshire Drama Festival:
Music Hall, Shrewsbury.
MARCH – 3RD WEEK
British International Song Festival:
Music Hall, Shrewsbury.
MARCH

Minsterley & District Eisteddfod:
Details: H.W. Bishton, 35 Snailbeach, Shrewsbury, SY5 0NS.
APRIL – 2ND WEEK
Wrekin & Telford Festival:
Details: Festival Secretary, Telford Development Corporation, Malinslee House, Telford.
MAY/JUNE
Newport Music Festival:
Details: E.J. Carter, 6 Westfield Terrace. Newport, TF10 7EL.
JUNE – MID
All Folk Round the Wrekin:
Madeley Court Centre, Madeley, Telford.
Details: 17 Wesley Crescent, Shifnal.
JUNE – 4TH WEEK, TO JULY – 1ST WEEK
Ludlow Summer Festival:
Details: Secretary, Ludlow Summer Festival, Castle Square, Ludlow, SY8 1AX.
JULY – 3RD WEEK
International Festival of Youth Orchestras:
Shrewsbury.
JULY – 4TH WEEK, TO AUGUST
Church Stretton & South Shropshire Arts Festival:
Details: General Secretary, Church

Stretton & South Shropshire Arts Festival, 1 Alison Drive, Church Stretton, SY6 7AU.
(BIENNIAL)
Oswestry & District Festival:
Details: Festival Secretary, 'Townscliffe', Croeswylan Crescent, Oswestry.

FAIRS

FEBRUARY – MID
Shropshire Antiques Fair:
Lion Hotel, Shrewsbury.
MARCH
Oswestry Pleasure Fair:
Oswestry.
2ND MONDAY IN JANUARY, MARCH, JUNE & OCTOBER; MAY 1
Ludlow Fair:
Ludlow.
SEPTEMBER
Church Stretton Sheep Fair:
Church Stretton.
OCTOBER
Market Drayton Pleasure Fair:
Market Drayton.

CARNIVALS

MAY – 4TH WEEK
Shrewsbury Carnival:
Shrewsbury.
AUGUST
Oswestry Carnival:
Oswestry.

AGRICULTURAL, HORTICULTURAL & BREED SHOWS

MAY – 3RD WEEK
Mid West Show:

115

⌂
ARBOR DAY
This celebrated tree is still occasionally
dressed with flags and bunting on Arbor
Day at Aston-on-Clun. See: OLD
CUSTOMS.

SHREWSBURY CARNIVAL
Shrewsbury's carnival is a memorable
occasion during the year with many
residents entering into the day's
entertainment in fancy dress. See:
CARNIVALS.

◆

Showground, Berwick Road,
Shrewsbury.
JUNE
National Hunter Show:
Shrewsbury.
JULY
Oswestry & District Agricultural
Show:
Oswestry.
AUGUST
Church Stretton Flower Show:
Church Stretton.
AUGUST – 2ND WEEK
Shrewsbury Flower Show:
Shrewsbury.

⌂
SHREWSBURY HORTICULTURAL SHOW
Prize exhibits beautifully displayed await
the judges' decision at Shrewsbury's annual
show. See: SHOWS.

SPORTS

FEBRUARY – 3RD WEEK
Women's Lacrosse Territorial
Championship:
Moreton Hall, Oswestry.

◆
MID-WEST SHOW
Shropshire is very much an agricultural
county and this can be fully appreciated at
the prestigious Mid West Show, the premier
agricultural event of the year. See:
SHOWS.

116

Somerset

(INCLUDING AVON)

SUMORSÆTE · EALLE

Here the winds rule with uncontested right,
The wanton Gods at pleasure take their flight;
No sheltering hedge, no tree, or spreading bough
Obstruct their course, but unconfined they blow;
With dewey wings they sweep the wat'ry meads
And proudly trample o'er the bending reeds.

FROM 'BRENT' (SEDGEMOOR)
BY WILLIAM DIAPER

OLD CUSTOMS

JANUARY 17 (OLD TWELFTH NIGHT)
Wassailing the Apple Trees:
Carhampton.
The largest apple tree in the cider orchards is toasted by the villagers and cider is thrown over its trunk.

FEBRUARY – SHROVE TUESDAY
Egg Shackling:
Shepton Beachamp and Stoke St. Gregory.
This Easter custom is principally a northern sport in which hard-boiled eggs, firmly gripped in the right hand, are used as weapons to strike eggs of opposing players. Nowadays children take eggs to school, all of which are individually marked, and during a procedure where the eggs are gently sieved in a tray, the child owning the remaining unbroken egg wins a prize.

APRIL – TUESDAY FOLLOWING
SUNDAY AFTER 6TH
Candle Auction:
Tatworth.
A piece of land known locally as Spowell Meadow is let by auction in which a candle is lit, the last bid before it expires being the successful one.

MAY I (MAY DAY)
Hobby Horse Festival:
Minehead.
A canvas horse decked out with ribbons is accompanied through the streets by musicians and dancers.

OCTOBER – LAST THURSDAY
Punky Night
Hinton St. George.
A custom whose origins have to do with the return of the dead on All Hallows' Eve but particularly to some time in the Middle Ages when the men of Hinton St. George visited a fair at Chiselborough, and after failing to return by nightfall, the women went out with punkies in search of them. A 'punkie' is a hollowed out mangel-wurzel with a burning candle inside (It is customary for the children to go begging for candles and is considered bad luck to refuse them). Nowadays, after the procession around the boundaries of the village, a competition is held to judge the punky with the best design.

OCTOBER – LAST THURSDAY
Sandglass Auction:
Guildhall, Chard.

A FEW DAYS BEFORE CHRISTMAS
Cutting the Glastonbury Thorn:
Glastonbury.
The tree or 'Holy Thorn' at Glastonbury, perhaps the most famous tree in Christendom, relating as it does to many legends and events in Christian history, is cut by the vicar of the church of St. John the Baptist and sprays are sent to the Queen for the royal table on Christmas Day. The tree flowers on Old Christmas Day – January 6.

DECEMBER 24 (CHRISTMAS EVE)
Burning the Ashen Faggot:
Luttrell Arms Hotel, Dunster.
A bunch of ash twigs bound together with green ash bands is ceremonially burned on Christmas Eve; a round of cider being served each time a band burns through and bursts. The custom is a throwback to the days when superstition had it that ash wood was a protection against evil witches.

FESTIVALS

MARCH
Mid-Somerset Competitive Festival:
Pump Room, Guildhall, Bath, Avon.

APRIL
Weston-Super-Mare Junior Arts, Music & Dancing Festival:
Details: Director of Leisure Services, Woodspring District Council, Winter Gardens, Weston-Super-Mare, BS23 1AQ.

HOBBY HORSE FESTIVAL
Minehead's famous hobby horse winds its way through the streets on May Day. See: OLD CUSTOMS.

MIRACLES OF GLASTONBURY
Miracles at Glastonbury perform each year in the ruins of Glastonbury abbey and have been doing so for the past eleven years. See: FESTIVALS.

◆

WELLS ILLUMINATED CARNIVAL
The illuminated carnival reigns supreme in the West Country and the Wells annual celebration is noted for the ingenuity and beauty of the floats which make up the carnival procession. See: CARNIVALS.

APRIL – 3RD WEEK
St. George Day Festival & Parade:
Watchet.
MAY
Highbridge Festival of the Arts:
Details: Mrs. S. Dunbavan, 6 Donstan Road, Highbridge.
MAY – 1ST WEEK
Dunster Festival:
Dunster, Nr. Minehead.
MAY – 4TH WEEK, TO JUNE – 1ST WEEK
Bath Festival:
Details: Bath Festival Society, Linley House, 1 Pierrepoint Place, Bath, BA

1JY, Avon.
JUNE – 3RD OR 4TH WEEK
South Petherton Festival:
Details: Graham White, 23 Summerlands Park Avenue, Ilminster.
JUNE – MID
South Petherton Folk & Craft Festival:
Blake Hall, The Square, South Petherton.
JUNE
Montacute Falconry & Jousting Festival:
Montacute House.
JUNE
Taunton Folk Festival:
Taunton.
Details: Paul Mills, 4c Fons George Road, Taunton, TA1 3JU.
JULY – 2ND WEEK
Floral Festival:
Bath, Avon.
JULY – 2ND WEEK
Village Pump Festival:
Trowbridge.
Details: Judy King, 85 The Butts, Frome.
JULY – 3RD & 4TH WEEKS
Minehead & Exmoor Festival:
Minehead & surrounding area.
JULY – 4TH WEEK
Bath Folk & Dance Festival:
Bath, Avon.
JULY – 2ND WEEK, TO AUGUST – 2ND WEEK
Miracles at Glastonbury:
Details: c/o Secretary, 2 Wirral Close, Glastonbury.
AUGUST – 2ND WEEK
Yeovil Festival of Transport:
Barwick Park, Dorchester Road, Yeovil.
AUGUST – 4TH WEEK
Dulverton Festival:
Dulverton.
AUGUST – 4TH WEEK
The Walcot Beans (Bath Festival):
Details: 14b Walcot Street, Bath, Avon.
OCTOBER
Bath Bach Festival:
Details: c/o Organising Secretary, 120 Midford Road, Coombe Down, Bath, Avon.
NOVEMBER
Taunton & Somerset Music & Drama Festival:
Details: L. Rogers, 183 Cheddon Road, Taunton.
NOVEMBER
Worthing Music Festival:
Details: James Croom, Town Hall, Worthing.

FAIRS

FEBRUARY 14; JULY 10; DECEMBER 11
Bath Fair:

Bath, Avon.
LAST WEDNESDAY IN FEBRUARY &
SEPTEMBER
Frome Fair:
Frome.
JUNE 17; JULY 7
Taunton Fair:
Taunton.
MARCH — 4TH WEEK
Bath Spring Antiques Fair:
The Octagon, Milsom Street, Bath,
Avon.
MAY
Midsomer Norton Fair:
Midsomer Norton.
JUNE — 3RD WEEK
Antique & Collectors' Fair:
Assembly Rooms, Bath, Avon.
JUNE — 4TH WEEK
Flowerdown Fair:
R.A.F. Locking, Weston-Super-Mare.
JULY — 4TH WEEK
County Fair:
Dunster Lawns, Dunster.
AUGUST — 2ND WEEK
Glastonbury Tor Fair:
Fairfield, Street Road, Glastonbury.
AUGUST — MID
Annual Priddy Agricultural Fair:
Priddy Green, Priddy, Nr. Wells.
AUGUST — 4TH WEEK
St. Matthew's Fair:
St. Matthew's Field, Bridgewater.
OCTOBER — 3RD WEEK
Bath Autumn Antiques Fair:
The Assembly Rooms, Bennett Street,
Bath, Avon.

FAYRES

JUNE — 2ND WEEK
Draycott Strawberry Fayre:
Recreation Ground, Wells Road,
Draycott, Nr. Cheddar.

CARNIVALS

JUNE — 4TH WEEK
Porlock Carnival:
Porlock.
JULY — 3RD WEEK
Summer Carnival Procession:
Weston-Super-Mare.
AUGUST — 3RD WEEK
Frome Carnival Week:
Frome.
AUGUST — 4TH WEEK
Wellington Carnival:
Wellington.
AUGUST
Portishead Summer Carnival:
Portishead.
OCTOBER — 2ND WEEK
Chard Carnival Week:

High Street, Chard.
OCTOBER — 3RD WEEK
**Taunton's Annual Illuminated Carnival
Procession and Cider Barrel Rolling
Race:**
Taunton.
OCTOBER — 3RD WEEK
Wincanton Carnival:
Wincanton.
OCTOBER/NOVEMBER
Wells Illuminated Carnival:
Wells.
NOVEMBER — 1ST WEEK
**Bridgewater Illuminated Guy Fawkes
Carnival Procession:**

⇧
RIVER TONE STRUGGLE
*Beginning at Tonedale on the River Tone,
the contestants work downstream towards
Taunton hauling a vehicle over several
weirs and waterfalls en route. See:
MISCELLANEOUS.*

◆

SNUFF CONTESTS
*Snuff enthusiasts gather each year at the
Sports Centre, Wellington, for the contests.
See: MISCELLANEOUS.*
⇧

Bridgewater.
NOVEMBER – 1ST WEEK
**North Petherton Illuminated Carnival
Procession:**
North Petherton, Nr. Bridgewater.
NOVEMBER – 1ST WEEK
**Burnham-on-Sea Illuminated Carnival
Procession:**
Burnham-on-Sea.
NOVEMBER – 2ND WEEK
Glastonbury Guy Fawkes Carnival:
Glastonbury.
NOVEMBER – 3RD WEEK
**Weston-Super-Mare November
Carnival:**
Weston-Super-Mare.

GALAS

MAY – 4TH WEEK
R.C. Church Spring Gala:
Manor Gardens, Burnham-On-Sea.
AUGUST – 2ND WEEK
Minehead Gala Week:
Minehead.

AGRICULTURAL, HORTICULTURAL & BREED SHOWS

MARCH – 4TH WEEK
**Taunton & District Gardeners'
Association Flower Show:**
Indoor Cricket School, St. James,
Taunton.
APRIL – 3RD WEEK
Spring Heifer Show:
Shepton Mallet.
APRIL
Bath Championship Dog Show:
Bath, Avon.
MAY – 4TH WEEK
North Somerset Agricultural Show:
Ashton Court Estate, Bristol, Avon.
MAY – LAST WEEK
Royal Bath & West Show:
Bath, Avon.
JULY – 4TH WEEK
Porlock Horse Show & Gymkhana:
West Luccombe, Nr. Minehead.
JULY
Clevedon Horse Show:
Clevedon.
AUGUST – 1ST WEEK
Taunton Flower Show:
Vivary Park, Taunton.
AUGUST – 3RD WEEK
The Dunster Show:
Dunster Castle Lawns, Dunster.
AUGUST – 3RD WEEK
Wiveliscombe Horticultural Show:
Kingsmead Comprehensive School,
Wiveliscombe.

AUGUST
Mid-Somerset Show:
Shepton Mallet.
NOVEMBER – 1ST WEEK
Annual Chrysanthemum Show:
Winter Gardens, Beach Road,
Weston-Super-Mare.
NOVEMBER – 4TH WEEK
**Vale of Avalon National Cage Bird
Show:**
Glastonbury.
AUGUST – LAST WEEKEND
Pilton Show:
Summer's End, Pilton, Shepton Mallet.
AUGUST – LATE
Annual Cheese Show:
The Showground, Rodden Road,
Frome.
DECEMBER – 2ND WEEK
**North Somerset Labour Party's Flower
Show:**
*Details: A. Everard, Dymboro Villa,
Providence Place, Midsomer Norton,
Bath, Avon.*

SPORTS

FEBRUARY
**Avon & Somerset Badminton
Championships:**
Bath Sports & Leisure Centre, Bath.
APRIL – 3RD WEEK
International Easter Hockey Event:
Clarence Park, Beach Lawns, Drove
Road, Weston-Super-Mare.
MAY – 3RD WEEK
Battle of the Barle Boat Race:
Landacre Bridge to Tarr Steps.
MAY – 4TH WEEK
Milk Race:
Beach Lawns, Weston-Super-Mare.
JUNE – 3RD WEEK
National Volleyball Cup Finals:
Bath Sports Centre, North Parade, Bath.
JUNE
**British Long Bow Society Annual
Event:**
Dunster Castle, Dunster.
JUNE – 3RD WEEK
Dunster Archery Week:
Dunster Lawns, Dunster.
JUNE – 4TH WEEK
**Weston-Super-Mare Open Bowling
Tournament for Men:**
Clarence Park, Weston-Super-Mare.

AUGUST – 1ST WEEK
**Royal Bath & West Summer Jumping
Show:**
Shepton Mallet.
AUGUST – 1ST & 2ND WEEKS
Porlock Rodeo:
Porlock.
AUGUST – 1ST WEEK
**West of England Open Golf
Championships:**
Burnham & Barrow Golf Club,
Burnham-On-Sea.
AUGUST – 3RD WEEK
**Burnham-On-Sea Senior Tennis
Tournament:**
Avenue Lawn Tennis Club, The Grove,
Burnham-On-Sea.
AUGUST
**Weston-Super-mare Open Bowling
Tournament for Ladies:**
Clarence Park, Weston-Super-Mare.
AUGUST – 4TH WEEK
Wiveliscombe Gymkhana:
Greenway, Wiveliscombe.
AUGUST – 3RD WEEK
River Tone Struggle:
On River Tone, Wellington to Taunton.
AUGUST – 4TH WEEK
Daily Mail Amateur Golf Foursomes:
Burnham & Berrow Golf Club,
Burnham-On-Sea.
SEPTEMBER – 4TH week
**Cobdens Tug-of-War Club Annual
Competition:**
Martlock.

MISCELLANEOUS

JANUARY
Snuff Taking Championships:
Sports Centre, Corams Lane,
Wellington.
EASTER MONDAY
Outdoor Easter Entertainment:
Palace Fields, Nr. Bishop's Palace,
Wells.
EASTER
British Snuff Taking Championships:
Cleve Hotel, Mantle Street, Wellington.
JUNE – 2ND WEEK
**Annual Clifton Diocesan Pilgrimage to
Glastonbury:**
Glastonbury Tor & Convent Field,
Glastonbury.
JUNE – 3RD WEEK
Annual Crafts Exhibition:
Sampford Brett, Nr. Williton.
AUGUST – 4TH WEEK
Annual Stamp Exhibition:
Methodist Church Hall, Minehead.
NOVEMBER 5
Bonfire Night:
Bridgewater.

Staffordshire

THE · KNOT · UNITES

O *have you you seen, on Cannock Chase,*
The Birches, queens of Silver Grace,
When Autumn's magic Hand hath set
On each a golden coronet?

CECIL JAMES TILDESLEY

Old Customs

FEBRUARY 27
Lichfield Oldfair: Pancake Race:
Guildhall & Market Square, Bore Street,
Market Square, Lichfield.
APRIL – EARLY
Egg Rolling and Pace Egg Play:
Draycott-in-the-Clay.
APRIL 23 (ST GEORGE'S DAY)
St George's Day Court:
Guildhall, Bore Street, Lichfield.
The court dates back to the 16th century
when King Edward VI transferred the
Bishop's manorial rights to the Mayor,
Sheriff & Aldermen. Today the court hears
complaints and appoints two High
Constables, a Bailiff and various other
officers.
MAY I
Newborough Well Dresing:
Newborough, Nr. Burton-on-Trent.
MAY 28
Court of Arraye & Bower Procession:
Lichfield.
The court dates back to the time when the
city was obliged to provide armour for the
Crown. Over the years the event became
linked with the Bower, a medieval pleasure
fair, and today it takes the form of a grand
procession, with youths dressed in ancient
coats of mail parading for inspection by
town officials.
MAY – ASCENSION DAY
Beating of Ecclesiastical Bounds:
Lichfield.
Cathedral officials, including the choir,
visit the boundaries of the cathedral

carrying elm boughs and sing psalms
whenever they stop.
JUNE 24
Burton Barrel Race:
High Street, Burton-on-Trent.
SPRING BANK HOLIDAY WEEKEND
Endon Well-Dressing:
Endon.
A well-dressing Queen is crowned at this
particular ceremony which dates back to
1845.
SPRING BANK HOLIDAY MONDAY
The Greenhill Bower:
Lichfield.
Once a pagan flower celebration but now a
fair and a floral procession.
ALL SOULS DAY
Souling:
Staffordshire Border.
A custom which is still practised by children
in some parts, in which Soul Cakes (or
'Dole Bread') are begged for from door to
door. The cakes were originally collected on
All Saints Day for the souls of the dead.
SEPTEMBER 4
The Sheriff's Ride:
Lichfield.
A throng of riders acompany the sheriff and
encircle the ancient boundaries of Lichfield,
as instructed by an act decreed by Mary
Tudor in 1553. There then follows a formal
parade through the streets to the Guildhall.
SEPTEMBER – MONDAY FOLLOWING
SAMUEL JOHNSON BIRTHDAY
CELEBRATION
Dr Johnson Birthday Ceremony:
Uttoxeter.

A wreath is placed on a plaque fixed to the
wall of an ancient stone kiosk in the Market
Place in commemoration of an event long
ago when the child Johnson stood on the
spot as a penance for disobedience.
SEPTEMBER – MONDAY FOLLOWING
1ST SUNDAY AFTER 4TH
Abbots Bromley Horn Dance:
Abbots Bromley, Nr. Rugeley.
One of England's oldest and most
traditional dances, dating back to
pre-Christian times and said to be rooted in
hunting or fertility rites. The dancers carry
reindeer horns and are accompanied by a
Fool, Hobby Horse, Male-Female, Robin
Hood and his Merry Men, and various
musicians. The procession winds its way
through the parish visiting cottages and
farm-houses and, significantly, Blithfield
Hall.
SEPTEMBER – SATURDAY NEAREST
18TH
Samuel Johnson Birthday Celebration:
Market Square, Lichfield.
A wreath is laid on Dr. Johnson's statue by
the Mayor & Sheriff during a procession
through the streets. In the evening local
dignitaries are served with Dr. Johnson's
favourite meal of steak and kidney pudding,
and apple tart with cream, ale and hot
punch at a commemoration supper.
NOVEMBER 23
St. Clements Day Ceremony:
Enville.
A procession of children from the local
school proceeds to Enville Hall where the
Clemery-song of the district is sung. They
are given an apple apiece and then scramble
for hot pennies.

Festivals

MARCH
Newcastle-Under-Lyme Musical
Festival:
Details: C. Clowes, 10 Como Place,

123

Newcastle-under-Lyme, ST5 2QN.
MARCH/APRIL
Stone & District Music Festival:
*Details: Mrs. G. Priddey, 12 The
Redlands, Stone, ST15 8PX.*
APRIL
**Burton-on-Trent Competitive Music
Festival:**
*Details: G. Handley, 1a Rosliston Road,
Stapenhill, Burton-on-Trent.*
MAY
Tamworth & District Music Festival:
*Details: Ms. M. Barrs, Stanley Place,
Thomas Street, Tamworth, B77 3PS.*
MAY
Rolleston Festival:
*Details: Rolleston Music Circle, 31
Burnside , Rolleston-on-Dove.*
MAY
Stoke-on-Trent Festival:
University of Keele, Newcastle.
JUNE – 2ND WEEK
Corning U.K. Stone Festival:
Westbridge Park, Stone.
JUNE – LATE
Big Band Festival:
Tutbury Castle Grounds, Tutbury.
JUNE – LATE
**Lichfield Festival of Traditional Song
& Dance:**
Arts Centre, Bird Street, Lichfield.
JUNE – LATE
**Wolverhampton Annual Music
Festival:**
*Details: R. Parsons, Civic Hall, North
Street, Wolverhampton.*
JULY – LATE
Shakespeare Festival:
Blithfield Hall, Nr. Abbots Bromley.
SEPTEMBER
Biddulph & District Music Festival:
*Details: E.A. Bracegirdle, 52 Mowlop
Road, Mow Cop, Stoke-on-Trent, ST7
4NA.*
OCTOBER
**Brownhills Competitive Festival of
Music and Verse Speaking:**
*Details: J. Pearce, 30 Chester Road,
Brownhills, WS8 6DX.*
NOVEMBER
**Stafford & District Council of
Churches Music Festival:**
*Details: J.H. Duncan, 102 Porlock
Avenue, Weeping Cross, Stafford.*
NOVEMBER
**Stoke-on-Trent Music and Drama
Festival:**

◆

ABBOTS BROMLEY HORN DANCE
*The Horn Dance is one of England's oldest
and most fascinating customs and is centred
around the historic residence of Blithfield
Hall. See: OLD CUSTOMS.*

*Details: Ms. M.M. Howle, "Westwood",
32 Palmers Green, Hartshill,*

FAIRS

1ST MONDAY IN OCTOBER; OCTOBER
28
Burton-on-Trent Fair:
Burton-on-Trent.
MARCH 4; APRIL 22; JUNE 10;
AUGUST 3
Hanley Fair:
Hanley.
MAY 14; DECEMBER 4 & 27
Stafford Fair:
Stafford.
WHIT TUESDAY; TUESDAY AFTER
AUGUST BANK HOLIDAY; TUESDAY
BEFORE SEPTEMBER 29
Walsall Fair:
Walsall.
WHIT MONDAY; JULY 10
Wolverhampton Fair:
Wolverhampton.
JANUARY – 2ND WEEK
Antique Fair:
Town Hall, Burton-on-Trent.
FEBRUARY – SHROVETIDE
Langton Shrovetide Fair:
Langton.
FEBRUARY – SHROVETIDE
Lichfield Shrovetide Fair:
Lichfield.
MARCH – 4TH WEEK
Stafford Antiques Fair:
Bingley Hall, County Showground,
Junction 14 and M6.
EASTER – SUNDAY AND WEEK
FOLLOWING
Drayton Manor Park Fair:
Drayton Manor Park, Nr. Tamworth.
JUNE
Rugeley Pleasure Fair:
Rugeley.
SEPTEMBER
Burton-on-Trent Pleasure Fair:
Burton-on-Trent.
OCTOBER – 1ST WEEK
Statutes Fair:
Market Place, Burton-on-Trent.

FAYRES

JUNE – 2ND WEEK
**Antique Fayre & St. Michael's
Medieval Market:**
St. Michael on Greenhill, Church Yard,
Lichfield.

CARNIVALS

JUNE – 4TH WEEK
Tamworth Carnival:
Tamworth.

JUNE
Stafford Carnival & Pageant:
Stafford.
JUNE
Tutbury Carnival:
Tutbury, Nr. Burton-on-Trent.
JULY – 1ST WEEK
Uttoxeter Carnival:
Uttoxeter.

AGRICULTURAL, HORTICULTURAL & BREED SHOWS

MAY
Staffordshire County Show:
Stafford.
JULY – 4TH WEEK
**Kings Bromley & District
Horticultural Show:**
Kings Bromley.
AUGUST – 1ST WEEK
Mid Shires Horse Show:
Wolverhampton, West Midlands.
SEPTEMBER – 1ST WEEK
**South Stapenhill Allotment & Cottage
Garden Association Show:**
Town Hall, Burton-on-Trent.
NOVEMBER – 2ND WEEK
**Burton Chrysanthemum Society
Annual Show:**
Town Hall, Burton-on-Trent.

SPORTS

MARCH – 1ST WEEK
**Women's Midlands Schools' Lacrosse
Tournament:**
Abbots Bromley.
MAY – 3RD WEEK
Brabazon Golf Tournament:
Little Aston.
JUNE – 2ND WEEK
**Pirelli Tug-of-War Club Annual Pirelli
Sports & Social:**
Derby Road, Stretton, Burton-on-Trent.
SEPTEMBER
Uttoxeter Cross Country Race:
Uttoxeter.

Regattas:

JULY – 2ND WEEK
Burton Regatta & Riverside Show:
Branston Road, Burton-on-Trent.

MISCELLANEOUS

JUNE/JULY
Mediaeval Market:
Lichfield.
SEPTEMBER – 4TH WEEK
Fole Steam & Presentation Rally:
Fole, Nr. Uttoxeter.

◆ *Suffolk* ◆

OPUS · NOSTRUM · DIRIGE

OLD CUSTOMS

JANUARY – THURSDAY AFTER PLOUGH
MONDAY FOLLOWING 6TH
Cakes and Ale Ceremony:
St. Mary's Church and The Guildhall,
Bury St. Edmunds.
*A commemoration service for Jankyn
Smyth, the town's benefactor who died in
1480. Today the ale has been replaced by
sherry, and cakes are now also served.*
FEBRUARY 2
Carlow's Charity (or Bread Dole):
Woodbridge.
*George Carlow was a member of a religious
sect called 'Separate Congregation'. When
he died in 1738 he instructed in his will that
the rent from his premises should go towards
the maintenance of his tomb and that the
churchwardens from the church of St.
Mary's should purchase twenty shillings
worth of loaves from the town's two poorest
bakers for distribution to the needy. The
charity has continued and the bread is today
distributed by the rector, the verger and two
churchwardens.*
JUNE – 2ND WEEK (TRINITY MONDAY)
Merry-Go-Round Mayor:
South Green, Southwold.
*The ancient Charter Fair at Southwold is
curiously opened by the Mayor, and then
members of his Corporation, by riding on
the roundabout. The Mayor then gives
school children 3p each to spend at the fair.*
SATURDAYS
John Sayer Charity:
Woodbridge.
*Similar to Carlow's Charity, except this
was John Sayer, who, at his death in 1638,
instructed in his will that the rent from his
15 acres of arable land should go towards
providing bread for the poor of Woodbridge
every Sunday, for ever. The day for
distribution has since been changed to
Saturday to ensure the loaves reach the
recipients in a fresh condition.*

FESTIVALS

MARCH/APRIL
Clare Music Festival:
*Details: B. Rose, 10 Chestnut Close, Great
Waldringfield, Sudbury.*
EASTER – SUNDAY AND MONDAY
Lowestoft Easter Hockey Festival:
Lowestoft.
MAY – 3RD WEEK
**Felixtowe Folk Festival (Folk
Weekend):**
Pier Pavilion and Spa Pavilion, The
Esplanade, Felixtowe.
MAY – 4TH WEEK
Felixtowe Drama Festival:
Spa Pavilion, Undercliff Road West,
Felixtowe.
MAY
**Beales Non-Competitive Music
Festival:**
*Details: Ms. V.C. Walker, 26 Beverley
Close, Oulton Broad, Lowestoft.*
JUNE – 2ND, 3RD & 4TH WEEKS
**Aldeburgh Festival of Music and the
Arts:**
Details: Festival Office, High Street,

Aldeburgh, IP15 5AX.
JUNE
Lavenham Church Flower Festival:
Lavenham.
JULY – 2ND WEEK
Wangford Festival:
*Details: c/o Festival Secretary, Festival
Office, Wangford, Beccles.*
JULY
Hintlesham Summer Festivals:
*Details: Honourable Organiser,
Hintlesham Hall, Hintlesham.*
AUGUST – 1ST WEEK
Festival of Wild Flowers and Music:
Long Melford.
*Details: Long Melford Festival Office,
Aldeburgh.*
OCTOBER – 1ST WEEK
**Benson & Hedges Festival of Chamber
Music:**
*Details: Festival Office, High Street,
Aldeburgh, IP15 5AX.*
OCTOBER
Felixtowe Autumn Festival of the Arts:
*Details: 91 Undercliffe Road West,
Felixtowe, IP11 8AE.*
OCTOBER
Suffolk Music Festival:
*Details: Ms. A. Livett, 35 Ipswich Road,
Stowmarket.*

◆

ALDEBURGH FESTIVAL
*Richter plays the Britten Piano Concerto at
the Snape Maltings, the handsome building
used for performances of what are
esssentially English works of music for the
renowned Aldeburgh Festival. See:
FESTIVALS.*

FAIRS

1ST TUESDAY IN SEPTEMBER &
DECEMBER; OCTOBER 2
Bury St. Edmunds Fair:
Bury St. Edmunds.
1ST & 3RD TUESDAY IN MAY;
AUGUST 22
Ipswich Fair:
Ipswich.
MAY 12; OCTOBER 10
Lowestoft Fair:
Lowestoft.
WHIT TUESDAY; NOVEMBER 8
Newmarket Fair:
Newmarket.
VARIOUS MONTHS IN THE YEAR
Antique & Collectors' Fair:
Corn Exchange, Bury St. Edmunds.
MAY — 4TH WEEK
Annual Snape Antiques Fair:
The Maltings, Snape.
JUNE — 2ND WEEK
**Southwold Trinty Fair (Ancient
Charter Fair):**
South Green, Southwold.
JULY — LATE
Stour Valley Moon Fair:
East Bergholt.
SUMMER
Stradbroke Street Fair:
Stradbroke.
SEPTEMBER — 1ST WEEK
East Anglia Antiques Fair:
Athenaeum, Bury St. Edmunds.

FAYRES

MAY — 4TH WEEK
Needham Market Spring Fayre:
Needham Market.

STRADBROKE PRAM RACE
*Pram races are a regular ingredient in
Stradbroke's annual street fair. See:
MISCELLANEOUS.*

128

CARNIVALS

MAY — 4TH WEEK
Round Table Carnival:
South Green, Southwold.
JUNE
Lakenham Carnival (and Fair):
Lakenham.
JUNE
Bury St. Edmunds Carnival:
Bury St. Edmunds.
AUGUST — 2ND WEEK
**Lowestoft Carnival (Fête &
Procession):**
Recreation Ground, Walmer Road,
Lowestoft.
AUGUST — 2ND WEEK
Ipswich Carnival:
Ipswich.
AUGUST — 3RD WEEK
Aldeburgh Carnival:
Moot Green, Aldeburgh.

GALAS

MAY — 4TH WEEK
Framlingham Gala:
Castle Framlingham.

SHOWS

Needham Market Easter Art Show:
Middle School, Needham.
JUNE — 2ND WEEK
East Coast Boat Show:
Bourne Park and Fox Marina, Ipswich.
JUNE — 2ND WEEK, TO SEPTEMBER —
1ST WEEK
Felixtowe Summer Show:
Spa Pavilion, Felixtowe.

AGRICULTURAL, HORTICULTURAL & BREED SHOWS

MARCH
Woodbridge Horse Show:
Woodbridge.
MAY — 4TH WEEK
Suffolk Show:
The Showground, Bucklesham Road,
Ipswich.
JUNE — 2ND WEEK
East Anglian Native Pony Show:
Millfields Riding Establishment,
Stretchworth, Nr. Newmarket.
AUGUST — 3RD WEEK
Lowestoft Annual Horticultural Show:
Royal Green, The Esplanade, Lowestoft.
AUGUST — 4TH WEEK
Eye Agricultural Show:
Dragon Hill, Eye.
AUGUST — 4TH WEEK
Martlesham Horse Show:

Suffolk Showground, Bucklesham Road,
Ipswich.

SPORTS

JANUARY — 3RD WEEK
Suffolk Open Badminton Tournament:
Haverhill Sports Centre, Haverhill.
MAY — 2ND WEEK
Felixtowe Autotests:
Sea Front, Felixtowe.
JULY — 2ND WEEK
Canoe Polo Tournament:
Suffolk Canoe Club, Lonely Farm
Pleasure Park, Saxmundham.
JULY — 4TH WEEK
Prudential Tennis County Cup:
Felixtowe Lawn Tennis Club, Bath
Road, Felixtowe.
AUGUST — 4TH WEEK
**Felixtowe Junior Lawn Tennis
Tournament:**
Felixtowe Lawn Tennis Club, Bath
Road, Felixtowe.
AUGUST — 4TH WEEK
**Lowestoft & East Suffolk Junior Open
Tennis Tournament:**
Normanston Park, Normanston Drive,
Lowestoft.
OCTOBER — 4TH WEEK
Autumn Tug-of-War:
Denes Suffolk Holiday Village,
Lowestoft.

MISCELLANEOUS

MAY — 1ST WEEK
May Day Street Sale:
The Street, East Bergholt.
MAY — 2ND WEEK
Historical Vehicle Road Run:
Ipswich to Felixtowe.
MAY — 4TH WEEK
**R.A.F. Mildenhall Open Day & Air
Show:**
R.A.F. Mildenhall.
JUNE — 2ND WEEK
**Debenham Veteran & Vintage Fire
Engine & Vehicle Rally:**
Community Centre, Gracechurch Street,
Debenham.
JULY — 3RD WEEK
Weeting Steam Engine Rally:
Fengate Farm, Weeting, Brandon.
JULY — 4TH WEEK
International BMW Motorcycle Rally:
Lonely Farm Leisure Park,
Saxmundham.
AUGUST — 1ST WEEK
**Rally of the Federation of Sidecar
Clubs:**
Lonely Farm Leisure Park,
Saxmundham.

✦ *Surrey* ✦

*The breezy Downs and a spirited horse
And the honeyed breath of the golden gorse,
And the twinkling bells of the bleating ewes
And a bright panorama of changing views
And all that is peaceful and cheerful besides.*
MARTIN TUPPER.

OLD CUSTOMS

JANUARY 31
Dicing for Old Maid's Money:
Guildford.
John How directed in his will of January 29 1674 that two poor serving maids should be chosen by the Mayor or magistrate of Guildford and that they both should throw dice. The maid with the highest score was then paid one year's clear profit of the four hundred pounds he invested in South Sea Annuities, an amount known as Maid's Money. Later, in 1702, a John Parson created Apprentices' Money which was to have been paid annually to a young poor apprentice. As no apprentice came forward the money was, and still is, paid to the loser of the Maid's Money dice throwing charity.
FEBRUARY 2 (CANDELMAS DAY)
Forty Shilling Day:
Wotton.
A bequest in the will of William Glanville who died in 1717 provided that a payment of forty shillings be given to each of five boys in need, the condition being that each must lay their hands on his tomb and recite from memory the Lord's Prayer, The Apostles Creed, and the Ten Commandments. They must also read out aloud the 15th Chapter of the first Epistle of St. Paul to the Corinthians and write two verses of the tract in decent handwriting.

MARCH 22
Founders Day Ceremony:
The Parish, Croydon.
The Service commemorates the founder of the old Almshouses in Croydon, Archbishop Whitgift, and is attended by boys and teachers from Whitgift School, together with members of the Fishmongers' Company and occupants of the Almshouses.
SEPTEMBER
Apron & Clog Race:
Royal Botanical Gardens, Kew.
60 years ago this now established custom began as a fun event for the many students who work inside the Royal Botanical Gardens at Kew. The race is along a prescribed length of garden and competitors wear the regulation issue aprons and clogs. The winner receives a bottle of wine and has his or her name officially recorded for posterity.
HARVEST TIME
Blessing the Crops:
Farnham.

FESTIVALS

FEBRUARY/APRIL
Richmond-Upon-Thames Music Festival:
Details: Ms. D. Nettleton, 24 The Avenue, Twickenham, TW1 1RY.

MARCH
Coulsdon & Purley Festival:
Details: Ms. S. Cameron Kirk, 117 Foxley Lane, Purley.
APRIL – 3RD WEEK
Leith Hill Musical Festival:
Dorking Hills, Dorking.
APRIL – MID
St. Peter's Festival:
Details: Rev. Donald Reeves, St. Peter's Vicarage, Bishopsford Road, St. Helier, Mordon, Surrey.
APRIL – LATE
Sutton Arts Councils' Spring Festival:
Details: Mrs. E. Noble, Secretary – Arts Council of the LB of Sutton, 8 Woodcote Green, Wallington, Surrey.
APRIL – LATE, TO MAY – MID
Tadworth and District Arts Festival:
Tadworth.
Details: Chairman, Tadworth and District Arts Festival, 1 Cross Road, Tadworth, KT20 5SP.
EASTER – SUNDAY AND MONDAY
Easter Flower Festival:
St. Nicholas Church, Charlwood.
MAY – 3RD WEEK
Tilford Bach Festival:
All Saints Church, Tilford.
Details: Hon. Secretary, Ling Lea, Frenshaw, Farnham.
MAY – 3RD WEEK
Charlwood Festival:
Charlwood.
MAY
Farnham Festival of Youth & Music:
Details: 22 Blomfield Street, London, EC2M 7AP.
MAY
Reigate & Redhill Music Festival:
Details: Ms. C. Pearch, 8 Fenton Road, Redhill.
MAY/JUNE

Kingston-Upon-Thames Festival:
Details: 2 Downs Road, Epsom.
JUNE – 1ST OR 2ND WEEK
Boxhill Music Festival:
Cleveland Lodge, Boxhill.
Details: Concert Secretary, Cleveland Lodge, Westhumble, Dorking, RH5 6BT.
JUNE
Richmond Arts Festival:

Details: 19 Paradise Road, Richmond, TW9 1SA.
JUNE – LATE, OR JULY – EARLY
Polesden Lacey Open Air Theatre Festival:
Great Bookham, Leatherhead.
Details: General Manager, 48 The Park, Great Bookham, Leatherhead.
JULY – 2ND WEEK

HISTORICAL PAGEANT
The Pageant of Guildford is part of the town's annual festival and depicts an historical re-enactment associated with the town's history. See: FESTIVALS.

DICING FOR OLD MAID'S MONEY
An applicant in this curious charity throws dice in the presence of the Mayor of Guildford in order to qualify for the dole. See: OLD CUSTOMS.

CLOG & APRON RACE
Students of horticulture dressed in their regulation issue clogs and aprons prepare to race inside the Royal Botanical Gardens at Kew. See: OLD CUSTOMS

TILFORD BACH FESTIVAL
Stephen Ddogson conducts at rehearsal work commissioned from him for a recent festival. The festival began in 1953 as a small village affair in All Saints Church and has subsequently expanded into one of England's most highly regarded serious musical functions which presents the music of Bach and his contemporaries in a style consistent with the composer's lifetime. See: FESTIVALS.

◆━━━━━━━━━━━

Merton Kite Festival:
Mitcham Common, Mitcham.
JULY – 4TH WEEK
Haslemere Festival of Early Music:
Haslemere Hall, Haslemere.
Details: Festival Secretary, Jesses, Grayswood Road, Haslemere.
JULY
Molesey Festival of the Arts:
Details: 61 School Road, East Molesey, KT8 9BL.
SEPTEMBER – 2ND WEEK
Dorking Folk Festival:
Dorking.
Details: D, Lawlor, 49 Agraria Road, Guildford.
OCTOBER/NOVEMBER
Croydon Music Festival:
Details: Ms. M. Wey, Flat 2, 30 Normanton Road, South Croydon, CR2 7AR.
OCTOBER/DECEMBER
Kingston-Upon-Thames Music Festival:
Details: Ms. J.R. Bower, 68 Villiers Avenue, Surbiton, KT5 8BH.
NOVEMBER – 3RD WEEK
Croydon Independent Full Length Drama Festival:
Ashcroft Theatre, Croydon.
NOVEMBER
Sutton Musical Festival:
Details: 9 Great Tattenhams, Epsom Downs, KT18 5RF.
NOVEMBER
Woking Music Festival:
Details: P. Readings, Kilrush, Philpot Lane, Chobham, Woking.

FAIRS

OCTOBER – 1ST WEEK
Croydon Fair:
Croydon.
JULY – 4TH WEEK
Epsom Fair:
Epsom.
MAY – 1ST WEEK & NOVEMBER – 4TH WEEK
Guildford Fair:
Guildford.
AUGUST – 3RD WEEK
Mitcham Fair:
Mitcham.

FAYRES

JULY – 1ST WEEK
Redhill & Reigate Olde English Fayre:
Priory Ground, Reigate.

CARNIVALS

MAY – 4TH WEEK
Croydon Carnival:
Ashburton Park, Lower Addiscombe Road, Croydon.

SHOWS

SEPTEMBER – 1ST WEEK
Farnborough Air Show:
Farnborough.

AGRICULTURAL, HORTICULTURAL & BREED SHOWS

FEBRUARY – 4TH WEEK
'Herald of Spring' Horticultural Show:
Bourne Hall, Ewell.
MAY – 4TH WEEK
Surrey County Show:
Stoke Park, Guildford.
JULY – 3RD WEEK
Epsom Mayday Flower Club Anniversary Show:
Bourne Hall, Ewall.
JULY – 4TH WEEK
Metropolitan Police Horse Show:
Metopolitan Police, Imber Court Sports Centre, Thames Ditton.
AUGUST – 1ST WEEK
Metropolitan Police Dog Championships:
Metropolitan Police, Imber Court Sports Centre, Thames Ditton.
AUGUST – 4TH WEEK
Egham Royal Show:
Runnymeade.
AUGUST/SEPTEMBER
Guildford Town Agricultural Show:
Guildford.

SPORTS

MAY – 4TH WEEK
Festival of Tug-of-War:
St. Thomas the Apostle School, Eastworth Road, Chertsey.
MAY – 4TH WEEK
Crondall Youth Open Tug-of-War Competition:
Hook Meadow Recreation Ground, Crondall, Nr. Farnham.
JUNE – 1ST WEEK
The Derby (Oaks Stakes):
Epsom Racecourse, Epsom.
JUNE – MID
Richmond Royal Horse Show:
Old Deer Park, Richmond.
AUGUST – 2ND, 3RD & 4TH WEEKS
National Rife Association Meeting:
Bisley Camp, Nr. Working.
AUGUST
British Long Bow Society Meet:
"Stoke d'Abernon Clout Shoot":
Stoke d'Abernon.

⬒ SURREY COUNTY SHOW
One of the prize beasts at the agricultural show is proudly exhibited by the owner. See: SHOWS.

◆━━━━━━━━━━━

◆ *Sussex* ◆
(EAST & WEST)

Some folks as come to Sussex,
They reckon as they know –
A darn sight better what to do
Than simple folks like me and you,
Could possibly suppose.
But them as comes to Sussex
They mustn't push and shove,
For Sussex will be Sussex,
And Sussex won't be druv!

VICTOR COOK

——OLD CUSTOMS——

JANUARY I
Morris Dancing & Mummers Play:
Black Lion, Patcham, Brighton.
JANUARY 4
Apple Howling:
Furners Farm, Furners Lane, Henfield.
A curious custom of long standing where-by a troop of boys encircle trees in the orchards and chant doggerel lines, such as:
"Stand fast root, bear well top,
Pray God send us a good howling crop;
Every twig, apples big;
Every bough, apples enough;
Hats full, caps full,
Full quarter sacks full."
JANUARY – SUNDAY AFTER TWELFTH NIGHT
Blessing the Plough:
Chichester Cathedral, Chichester.
FEBRUARY – SHROVE TUESDAY
Pancake Race:
Bodium.
GOOD FRIDAY
Marble Day:
Tinsley Green, Nr. Crawley.
A marbles championship has been played here for 300 years, a traditional springtime game associated with Good Friday.
GOOD FRIDAY
Marbles Match:
Battle.

Teams from Battle and nearby Netherfield enjoy a long established game of marbles, followed by a feast of hot cross buns.
GOOD FRIDAY
Skipping Ceremony:
Rose Cottage Inn, Alciston, South Heighton.
Locals skip on Good Friday morning with a rope provided by the landlord.
MAY – IST SATURDAY
Maypole Dancing:
The Square, St. Mary's Church, Shoreham.
MAY – SUNDAY NEAREST IST
Crowning of the May Queen:
Chichester.
MAY – WEDNESDAY BEFORE ASCENSION DAY
Blessing of the Sea:
Churches of All Saints and St. Clements, Hastings.
A procession leaves the church at 7.00 p.m. and proceeds to the seashore for the blessing.
MAY – 3RD WEEK
Mayoring Day:
Rye.
A custom which commemorates the days when Rye minted its own coinage. At noon the new Mayor of the town and other officials throw hot pennies down onto the street from the Town Hall windows for the

children gathered below.
SPRING BANK HOLIDAY MORNING
Folk Dancing:
Bishop's Palace Gardens, Chichester.
JULY 19
Little Edith's Treat:
Piddinghoe.
In commemoration of the death of Edith Croft who died in 1868 at the age of three months her grandmother made an endowment of £100 to be spent every anniversary of the baby's birthday. Following the church service there are races and tea is served.
JULY 25 (ST JAMES' FEAST DAY)
Horn Fair:
Ebernhoe.
This ancient Saints' Feast Day Fair features the roasting of a horned sheep and a cricket match in which the head and horns are awarded to the winning team.
AUGUST – IST SATURDAY
National Town Criers Championships:
Warrior Square Gardens, St. Leonards-on-Sea.
This popular event usually takes place during the afternoon. There is a parade, a band, and the crier competitions being the main attraction.
NOVEMBER 5
Lewes Bonfire Night Celebrations:
Lewes.
Seven local bonfire societies march in torchlit processions, in fancy dress, ending with the burning of their chosen effigies. A highly colourful occasion made more interesting by virtue of its historic association with the Gunpowder Plot of 1605.
DECEMBER 25 (CHRISTMAS DAY MORNING)
Morn's Dancing:
Chichester.

FESTIVALS

FEBRUARY
Eastbourne Music & Arts Festival:
Details: Spencer W. Freeman, 70 Kings Avenue, Eastbourne.
MARCH
Brighton Competitive Musical Festival:
Details: Festival Office, 90 Montpelier Road, Brighton, BN1 3BE.
MARCH
Competitive Musical Festival:
White Rock Pavilion, White Rock, Hastings.
MARCH
Hastings Musical Festival:
Details: D. Morton, 20 Old Roar Road, St. Leonards-on-Sea.
APRIL
Lewes Music Festival:
Details: 25 North Way, Lewes.
MAY – 1ST WEEK
Rye Spring Music Festival:
Details: Artistic Director: 50 Church Square, Rye.
MAY – 3RD & 4TH WEEKS
Eastbourne Festival of Music & the Arts:
Details: Director of Entertainments & Publicity, Eastbourne Corporation, The Congress Theatre. Eastbourne.
MAY/JUNE
Bexhill-on-Sea Festival of Music:
Details: Festival Director, Rother District Council, De La Warr Pavilion, Marina, Bexhill-on-Sea, TN40 1DP.
MAY – 4TH WEEK, TO AUGUST – 1ST WEEK
Glyndebourne Festival Opera Season:
Details: Information Office, Glyndebourne Festival Opera, Glyndebourne, Ringmer, Lewes, BN8 5UU.
MAY
Eastbourne International Folk Festival:
Details: P.J. Mayes, 8 The Sanctuary, Eastbourne, BN20 8TA.
MAY
East Grinstead Music & Arts Festival:
Details: Mrs. C. Tinworth, 125 Halsford Park Road, East Grinstead.
MAY (BIENNIAL) – NEXT ONE 1982
Mayfield Festival of Music & The Arts:
Details: R.G. Money, 'Conifers', Roselands Avenue, Mayfield.
MAY
Free Church Choir Union Competitions:
Details: John C. Morgan, 25 Oak Hall Park, Burgess Hill.
MAY
Brighton Festival:

BLESSING OF THE SEA
Beneath the Hastings Lifeboat an annual service is conducted by the Bishop of the Diocese, an ancient custom which is said to date back to the Middle Ages. See: OLD CUSTOMS.

MARBLES CHAMPIONSHIP
What may be thought of as a simple children's game is regarded seriously by the contestants who take part in the annual championships outside the greyhound Hotel at Tinsley Green. See: OLD CUSTOMS.

APPLE HOWLING
One of the more curious of customs of the country takes place at Furner's Farm. Trees growing in the orchard are encouraged by 'howling' to produce a bountiful crop. See: OLD CUSTOMS.

◆

Royal Pavilion Estate, Brighton.
Details: Local Administrator, Brighton Festival Society Ltd., Marlborough House, 54 Old Steine, Brighton, BN1 1EO.
MAY – SEPTEMBER
Chichester Festival:
Chichester.

Details: Festival Office, Canon Gate House, South Street, Chichester.
JUNE – 4TH WEEK, TO JULY – 2ND WEEK
Seaford – Charleston Manor Festival:
Festival Organiser, Charleston Manor, West Dean, Seaford, BN25 4AJ.
JUNE/JULY
Charleston Manor Festival:
Charleston Manor, West Dean, Seaford.
JUNE/JULY
East Grinstead Ballet Festival:
Adeline Genee Theatre, Lingfield Road, East Grinstead.
JULY – 3RD & 4TH WEEKS
Chichester Festivities:
Details: Festival Director: Canon Gate House, South Street, Chichester.
JULY – 3RD & 4TH WEEKS
Battle Festival:
Langton House, Battle.
Details: Festival Secretary, Claverham Community College, North Trade Road, Battle.
JULY
Southern Cathedrals Festival:
Rotates between Salisbury, Chichester and Winchester.
Details: 10 the Close, Winchester, SO23 9LS.
AUGUST – 4TH WEEK
Arundel Festival:
Details: Festival Administrator, Lyminster House, Lyminster, Littlehampton.
AUGUST
Alfriston Festival:
Details: 10 Smugglers Close, Alfriston, Polegate, BN26 5TG.
AUGUST
Anglo Festival of Music:
Details: V.G. Slater, 22 Potters Croft, Horsham, RH13 5LR.
SEPTEMBER – 1ST WEEK
Rye Festival of Music and Drama:
Rye.
Details: The Chairperson, The Old Brewery, Wishward, Rye.
SEPTEMBER – 1ST WEEK
Brighton, Hove & District Homes and Pleasure Festival:
No. 1 Western Lawns, The Kingsway, Hove.
SEPTEMBER – 1ST WEEK
Festival of English Grape Wine and Vineyards:
Charlston Manor, Nr. Seaford.
SEPTEMBER – 1ST WEEK
Chichester Festival Theatre Season:
Festival Theatre, Oaklands Park, Chichester.
SEPTEMBER – 3RD WEEK
Petworth Festival:
Details: Festival Secretary, Glebe Cottage, Bartons Lane, Petworth.

SEPTEMBER – 4TH WEEK
Bexhill-on-Sea Light Music Festival:
Bexhill-on-Sea.
SEPTEMBER – 4TH WEEK
Fair Organ Festival:
Tinker Park, Hadlow Down, Uckfield.
OCTOBER – EARLY
Festival for Real Ale:
Druscillas, Alfriston.
OCTOBER/NOVEMBER
Chichester Music Festival:
Mrs. P. Pointing, 19 Grosvenor Road,
Chichester.

FAIRS

MARCH – 3RD WEEK
Brighton Toy Fair:
Brighton Centre, Brighton.
APRIL 5; JULY 18; NOVEMBER 17 & 27
Horsham Fair:
Horsham.
APRIL – 3RD OR 4TH WEEK
Antiques & Collectors Fair:
Winter Gardens, Eastbourne.
MAY 6; SEPTEMBER 21 & 28
Lewes Fair:
Lewes.
JUNE – 1ST WEEK
Antiques Fair:
Town Hall, Hove.
JUNE – 4TH WEEK
Folk & Craft Fair:
Michelham Priory.
*Organiser: Peter Mayes, 8 The Sanctuary,
Eastbourne, BN20 8TA.*
JUNE – 4TH WEEK
Parham Fair:
Parham House, Storrington.
JULY – 4TH WEEK
Brighton Antiques Fair:
Corn Exchange, Brighton.
AUGUST – 2ND WEEK
Town & Country Fair:
Alexandra Park, St. Helen's Road,
Hastings.
AUGUST – 3RD WEEK
Lewes Country Crafts Fair:
Southover Grange, Keere Street, Lewes.
AUGUST – 4TH WEEK
Rottingdean Lions Fair:
The Green, Rottingdean.
AUGUST
Haywards Heath Fair:
Haywards Heath.
SEPTEMBER – 1ST WEEK
Brighton Furniture Fair:
Brighton Centre, Brighton.
SEPTEMBER
Findon Great Sheep Fair:
Old Fair Ground, Findon.
OCTOBER 11
Eastbourne Fair:
Eastbourne.

OCTOBER 20
Chichester Fair:
Chichester.
OCTOBER – 3RD WEEK
Annual Sloe Fair:
Northgate Car Park, Chichester.
NOVEMBER – EARLY
Brighton Toy and Doll Fair:
Metropole Hotel, Brighton.

FAYRES

AUGUST – 2ND WEEK
Grand Summer Fayre:
Community Centre, Saltdean.

CARNIVALS

EASTER MONDAY
Hove Easter Carnival:
Sussex County Cricket Ground, Eaton
Road, Hove.
JUNE
Bexhill Carnival:
Bexhill.
JUNE
Hastings Carnival:
Hastings.
JULY
Eastbourne Carnival:
Eastbourne.
AUGUST – 4TH WEEK
Brighton Lions Carnival:
Brighton.

GALAS

JULY – 1ST WEEK
Chichester Gala:
Priory Park, Priory Road, Chichester.

SHOWS

MAY – 3RD WEEK
Spring Boat Show:
Brighton Marina, Brighton.
JUNE – 1ST WEEK
Lindfield Village Day:
Lindfield.

AGRICULTURAL, HORTICULTURAL & BREED SHOWS

APRIL – 1ST WEEK
Spring Flower Show:
Winter Garden, Eastbourne.
APRIL – 2ND WEEK
**Brighton Flower & Horticultural
Show:**
Brighton Centre, Brighton.
MAY – 3RD WEEK
Sheepdog Trials:
Standean Farm, Patcham.

JUNE – 2ND WEEK
South of England Show:
The Showground, Ardingly, Haywards
Heath.
AUGUST – 2ND WEEK
Rodwell & District Summer Show:
Rodwell.
AUGUST – 2ND WEEK
Pycombe Horse Day:
Pycombe.
AUGUST – 3RD WEEK
Eastbourne Show:
Gildredge Park, Eastbourne.
AUGUST – 4TH WEEK
Icklesham Flower Festival:
Icklesham, Nr. Rye.

SPORTS

JANUARY – 1ST & 2ND WEEKS
Annual Chess Congress:
Falaise Hall & White Rock Pavilion,
Hastings.
FEBRUARY – 2ND WEEK
Colston Chichester Squash Festival:
Chichester Lawn Tennis Club,
Chichester.
FEBRUARY – 4TH WEEK
East Sussex Squash Championships:
Bexhill Squash Raquets Club,
Bexhill-on-Sea.
MARCH – 2ND WEEK
Littlehampton Open Championship:
Littlehampton.
MARCH – EARLY
Indoor Bowls Championships:
Indoor Bowls Centre, Hastings.
APRIL – 2ND WEEK
Show Jumping: Easter International:
All England Jumping Course,
Hickstead.
APRIL – 4TH WEEK
**British Senior Freestyle Wrestling
Championships:**
Crawley Sports Centre, Crawley.
APRIL – SEPTEMBER
Polo Meetings:
Cowdray Park, Midhurst.
MAY – 1ST WEEK
**Women's Professional Golf
Tournament Season:**
Willingdon Golf Club, Eastbourne.
MAY – 2ND WEEK
**Table Tennis: English Junior
International Championships:**
Worthing.
MAY – 4TH WEEK
**Show Jumping: Spring Bank Holiday
International:**
All England Jumping Course,
Hickstead.
MAY
**Nutley Tug-of-War Club Annual
Competition:**

Fords Green, Nutley.
MAY
Dressage Championships:
Goodwood Estate, Nr. Chichester.
MAY
Old Ship Hotel Annual 'Royal Escape' Yacht Race:
Seafront, Brighton.
JULY 1ST, 2ND & 3RD WEEKS
Polo: Cowdray Park Gold Cup:
Cowdray Park Polo Grounds, Midhurst.
JUNE – 3RD WEEK
The Colgate International Women's Tennis Tournament:
Devonshire Park, Eastbourne.
JUNE – LAST WEEKEND
Horse Show: International Dressage:
Goodwood Estate, Goodwood, Nr.
Chichester.
JUNE
Redifon (Crawley) Tug-of-War Club Annual Competition:
Redifon Sports & Social Club, Tinsley Lane, Crawley.
JULY – 3RD WEEK
Arun Bath Tub Race:
River Arun, Arundel.
JULY – AUGUST
Glorious Goodwood:
Goodwood Estate, Nr. Chichester.
JULY
Show Jumping: Lambert & Butler International:
All England Jumping Course,
Hickstead.
JULY
Berwick Tug-of-War Club Berwick Day:
Church Farm, Berwick.
JULY
Turners Hill Lion Tug-of-War Annual Competition:
Turners Hill Recreation Ground,
Crawley.
AUGUST – 3RD & 4TH WEEKS
E.B.A. National Bowls Championships and Middleton Cup Final:
Beach House Park, Worthing.
AUGUST
Seaford Annual Open Games Tournament:
Seaford.
SEPTEMBER – 1ST WEEK
Bowling: National Junior Singles Championships:
Eastbourne.
SEPTEMBER – 1ST WEEK
Midland Bank Horse Trials:
Goodwood Estate, Goodwood, Nr.
Chichester.

——MISCELLANEOUS——

JUNE – 4TH WEEK
Folk Nights at Michelham Priory:
Peter Mayes, The Sanctuary,
Eastbourne, BN20 8TA.
JULY – 4TH WEEK
Lewes Folk Day:
Details: Vic & Christine Smith, 26 Ferrers Road, Lewes, BN7 1PZ.
JULY
Annual Pilgrimage to the Chapel of Our Lady:
Hastings.
AUGUST – 1ST WEEK
Sussex Crafts & Small Industries Exhibition:
Michelham Priory, Hailsham.
AUGUST – 3RD WEEK
Sussex Kite Day:
Telscombe.
AUGUST – 3RD WEEK
Steam Rally & Country Fayre:
Petchworth Park.

AUGUST – 4TH WEEK
World Science Fiction Convention:
Brighton.
AUGUST – 4TH WEEK
Horsham Lions Vintage Transport Rally:
Horsham Park, Horsham.
NOVEMBER – 1ST WEEK
Veteran Car Run: London to Brighton Commemoration Run:
Hyde Park, London to Madeira Drive,
Brighton.
DECEMBER 26 (BOXING DAY)
Boxing Day "Steam-Up"
Bluebell Railway, Sheffield Park.

⇦ MAY DAY CELEBRATIONS
Dozens of improvised rafts take to the water at Shoreham-by-Sea as part of the spring celebrations. See: OLD CUSTOMS.

Warwickshire
(INCLUDING WEST MIDLANDS)

NON · SANZ · DROICT

Sutton for Mutton,
Tamworth for Beef,
Walsall for bandy legs,
And Brum for a thief,
Barton-under-Needwood,
Dunstall in the Dale,
Tattenhill for a pretty girl,
And Barton for good ale,
Walsall town for bandy legs,
Bilston town for bulls,
Hampton town for fancy girls,
And Sedgeley town for trulls!
TRADITIONAL RHYME

——Old Customs——

FEBRUARY – SHROVE TUESDAY
Shrove Tuesday Football:
Atherstone.
This game is said to have originated during the reign of King John when men of Leicestershire and Warwickshire competed for the prize of a bag of gold. Today the teams use a water-filled football decorated with the colours of the local team.
APRIL 23
Shakespeare Birthday Celebrations:
Bridge Street, Stratford-on-Avon.
A procession carrying poles bearing flags of many nations makes its way to the Bard's grave where wreaths are laid.
MAY 1 (MAY DAY)
Maypole Dancing:
Welford-on-Avon.
An ancient striped maypole permanently sited on the village green is one of a long line of poles going back some 200 years.
MAY 21
Cyclists Memorial Service:
Meriden.
A remembrance service commemorating cyclists who died in the war is held beneath the Cyclists' War Memorial and attracts cyclists from all over the country.

JUNE
Coventry Great Fair:
Coventry.
JULY
Grand Wardmote:
Meriden.
Archers belonging to the Woodmen of Arden hold an archery meeting dressed in white breeches, buff waistcoats and green hats. The meeting takes place on the spot that Robin Hood is said to have competed.
OCTOBER 12
Stratford-Upon-Avon Mop Fair:
Stratford-upon-Avon.
Mop fairs were traditionally occasions when agricultural and domestic labour were hired for the coming year. A whole ox is roasted at the Stratford-upon-Avon Mop Fair.
OCTOBER 26
Stratford-Upon-Avon Runaway Mop Fair:
Stratford-upon-Avon.
Anyone who was dissatisfied with their employer when hired at the Mop Fair earlier in October was given the chance of alternative employment at the Runaway Mop Fair held ten days later.

WELFORD-ON-AVON MAY DAY
Traditional dancing around the Maypole by local children is the central theme to this long established May Day celebration. See:
OLD CUSTOMS.

OCTOBER
Warwick Mop Fair & Runaway Mop Fair:
Warwick.

OCTOBER
Warwick Court Leet:
Four chamberlains are appointed to govern matters related to the land; Ale Tasters, Fish and Flesh Tasters, Bread Weighers and Overseers of Pavements.

NOVEMBER 11 (ST MARTIN'S DAY)
Wroth Silver Plaid:
Knightlow Cross, Knightlow Hill.
At dawn on St. Martin's Day representatives of the parishes that make up the Hundred meet the Duke of Buccleuch's agent and, after hearing the charter read out, pay sums of money (the Wroth Silver) onto a stone called Knightlow Cross. Whoever fails to pay this (an amount of about 10p) is fined a pound for each penny not paid, or must present a white bull with a red nose and red ears to the Duke.

FESTIVALS

MARCH
Lanchester Arts Festival:
Lanchester Polytechnic, Coventry.

APRIL – 2ND, 3RD & 4TH WEEKS
Nuneaton Festival of Arts:
Nuneaton.

APRIL
Birmingham Competitive Festival:
Birmingham, West Midlands.

APRIL/JANUARY
Stratford-upon-Avon Royal Shakespeare Theatre Season:
Stratford-upon-Avon.

EASTER MONDAY
West Indian Gospel Festival:
Canon Hill Park, Birmingham.

MAY – 4TH WEEK
Spring Festival:
Cannon Hill Park, Birmingham, West Midlands.

MAY
National Accordian Organisation of Great Britain Festival:
Birmingham, West Midlands.
Details: Ms. E. Beecham, 136 St. Andrews Avenue, Colchester, Essex, CO4 3AQ.

MAY
Northfield Music & Spoken Word Festival:
Details: Ms. F. Workman, 3 Cedar Close, Bournville, Birmingham, B30 1UU, West Midlands.

JUNE – 4TH WEEK
Leamington Folk Festival:
Leamington Spa.

Details: E.F.D.S.S., 75 Green Lane, Kettering, Northants.

JULY – 2ND, 3RD & 4TH WEEKS
Stratford-upon-Avon Poetry Festival:
Details: Director, Shakespeare Birthplace Trust, Shakespeare Centre, Henley Street, Stratford-upon-Avon, CV37 6QW.

JUNE – 4TH WEEK, TO JULY – 2ND WEEK
City of Birmingham Symphony Orchestra Proms:

JUNE
Birmingham Dairy Festival:
Birmingham, West Midlands.

JUNE
Leamington Spa Competitive Music Festival:
Leamington Spa.

JUNE
Bournville Musical Festival:
Details: R.H. Richards, Council Office, Cadbury Schweppes Ltd. Bournville, Birmingham, B30 2LU, West Midlands.

JULY
Solihull Festival:
Civic Hall, Solihull.

AUGUST – 2ND WEEK
Staffordshire and Castle Folk Festival:
Warwick.
Details: Jim Brannigan, 69 Dunster Place, Coventry, CV6 4JD.

AUGUST – 4TH WEEK
Town & Country Festival:
National Agricultural Centre, Stoneleigh, Kenilworth.

SEPTEMBER – TRIENNIAL (NEXT ONE 1983)
Birmingham Triennial Musical Festival:
Details: City of Birmingham Amenities & Recreation Dept., Auchinleck House, Five Ways, Birmingham, B15 1DS, West Midlands.

SEPTEMBER – 4TH WEEK
Brass Band Festival:
Spa Centre, Leamington Spa.

OCTOBER 27 – NOVEMBER 5
Bonfire Festivals:
Birmingham, West Midlands.

OCTOBER – (BIENNIAL)
Birmingham Arts Festival:
St Philip & St. James Youth Centre, Hodge Hill Common, Birmingham, West Midlands.

OCTOBER
Coventry Festival of Music:
Coventry.

OCTOBER
Midland Co-Operative Junior Choral Festival:
Details: Ms. E. Alldrick, 261 Boldmere Road, Sutton Coldfield.

OCTOBER
Rugby Festival of Dance & Drama:

Details: Ms. S.M. Lorden, 173 Clifton Road, Rugby, CV21 3QN.

NOVEMBER
Solihull Society of Arts Competitive Music Festival:
Details: Ms. P.M. Pope, 11 Greyfort Crescent, Solihull, B92 8DN.

FAIRS

WHIT THURSDAY; LAST THURSDAY IN SEPTEMBER FOR 3 DAYS
Birmingham Fair:
Birmingham, West Midlands.

MAY 2; WHIT MONDAY WEEK; NOVEMBER 4
Coventry Fair:
Coventry.

OCTOBER 12
Stratford-upon-Avon Fair:
Stratford-upon-Avon.

2ND MONDAY IN JANUARY, FEBRUARY, MARCH, APRIL, JUNE, JULY, AUGUST, SEPTEMBER, NOVEMBER; MAY 12; OCTOBER 12; DECEMBER 17
Warwick Fair:
Warwick.

FEBRUARY – 1ST WEEK
International Spring Fair:
National Exhibition Centre, Birmingham, West Midlands.

FEBRUARY – EARLY
Film Collectors Fair:
Central Hall, Corporation Street, Birmingham City Centre, West Midlands.

MARCH – 3RD WEEK
British Intenational Footwear Fair:
National Exhibition Centre, Birmingham, West Midlands.

AUGUST – 4TH WEEK
Country Sports Fair:
National Agricultural Centre, Stoneleigh, Kenilworth.

CARNIVALS

WHITSUN
Nuneaton Carnival:
Nuneaton.

JULY – 1ST WEEK
Kenilworth Carnival:
Kenilworth.

JULY – 2ND WEEK
Leamington Carnival:
Leamington Spa.

NOVEMBER – 1ST WEEK
Bonfire & Fireworks Carnival:
Handsworth Park, Birmingham, West Midlands.

PAGEANTS

NOVEMBER – 4TH WEEK
Aston Candlelit Pageant:
Aston Hall, Birmingham, West
Midlands.

SHOWS

FEBRUARY
Boat & Leisure Show:
National Exhibition Centre,
Birmingham, West Midlands.
FEBRUARY
The Energy Show:
National Exhibition Centre,
Birmingham, West Midlands.
APRIL – 2ND & 3RD WEEKS
Birmingham Motor Show:
Bingley Hall, Birmingham, West
Midlands.
AUGUST
Coventry Air Show:
Coventry Airport, Baginton, Coventry.
NOVEMBER
International Furniture Show:
National Exhibition Centre,
Birmingham, West Midlands.

TATTOOS

SEPTEMBER
Military Tattoo:
Houndsworth Park, Birmingham, West
Midlands.

AGRICULTURAL, HORTICULTURAL & BREED SHOWS

JULY – 1ST WEEK
Royal Agricultural Show:
National Agricultural Centre,
Stoneleigh, Kenilworth.
AUGUST
Brewood Agricultural Show:
Brewood.
AUGUST
Bilston Flower Show:
Bilston.
AUGUST – LATE
**Kenilworth & District Agricultural
Show (Town & Country Festival):**
Kenilworth.
AUGUST – LATE, TO SEPTEMBER –
EARLY
City of Birmingham Show:
Perry Park, Birmingham, West
Midlands.
*Details: The Manager, City of
Birmingham Parks Dept., Baskerville
House, Civic Centre, Birmingham, West
Midlands.*
SEPTEMBER

Dairy Farming Show:
National Agricultural Centre,
Stoneleigh, Kenilworth.

SPORTS

FEBRUARY – EARLY
**Midland Open Junior Ten Pin Bowling
Championship:**
Starlanes Bowling Ltd., Westley Road,
Acocks Green, Birmingham, West
Midlands.
FEBRUARY – MID
**Prodorite Invitation Squash
Tournament:**
Edgbaston Priory Club, Edgbaston,
Birmingham, West Midlands.
FEBRUARY – 3RD & 4TH WEEKS
**West Warwickshire Squash Club
Event:**
West Warwickshire Club.
MARCH – EARLY
**Birmingham International Show
Jumping Championships:**
National Exhibition Centre,
Birmingham, West Midlands.
MARCH – LATE
**All England National Schools
Women's Lacrosse Tournament:**
Bournville, Birmingham, West
Midlands.
MARCH – LATE
**Women's World Open Squash
Tournament:**
Edgbaston Priory, Edgbaston,
Birmingham, West Midlands.
JUNE – MID
**Stratford Racecourse Summer
Spectacular:**
Stratford.
JUNE – MID
Ford Sports Tug-of-War :
Ford Sports Ground, Myton Road,
Leamington Spa.
JUNE – MID
**Amateur Weight Lifters British Senior
Power Championship:**
Digbeth Institute, Birmingham, West
Midlands.
JUNE – MID
Ice Skating: Link Trophy:
Silver Blades Ice Rink, Pershore Street,
Birmingham, West Midlands.
JUNE – LATE
**Midland District Amateur Swimming
Association Long Course
Championship:**
Coventry.
JUNE
**British Long Bow Society Annual
Meet: "Meriden Clout Shoot":**
Meriden.

JUNE
**Midland District Amateur Swimming
Association Long Course
Championships:**
Coventry.
JULY – EARLY
National Tug-of-War Championships:
Cannon Hill Park, Birmingham, West
Midlands.
JULY – EARLY
Highland Gathering:
Cannon Hill Park, Birmingham, West
Midlands.
JULY – MID
**The Birmingham Arms Tug-of-War
Club Annual Competitions:**
Summerfield Park, Dudley Road,
Birmingham, West Midlands.
JULY – LATE
**Leamington Spa Men's Open Bowls
Tournament:**
Victoria Park, Leamington Spa.
AUGUST – EARLY
Amateur Swimming Championship:
Coventry.
AUGUST – MID
**Women's National Bowls
Championships:**
Victoria Park, Leamington Spa.
AUGUST – MID
Girls' Golf Internationals:
Edgbaston Golf Club, Edgbaston,
Birmingham, West Midlands.
AUGUST – MID
**Girls' British Open Amateur
Championships:**
Edgbaston Golf Club, Birmingham,
West Midlands.
AUGUST
King's Cup Air Race:
Baginton, Coventry.
SEPTEMBER – EARLY
**Amateur Athletic Association
Championships:**
Spennymoor.
SEPTEMBER – EARLY
**Leamington Spa Ladies' Open Bowls
Tournament:**
Victoria Park, Leamington Spa.

MISCELLANEOUS

OCTOBER – MID
Mid-Warwickshire Caravan Rally:
Newbold Comyn, Leamington Spa.
OCTOBER
**Leamington Spa Annual Brass Band
Contest:**
Leamington Spa.
NOVEMBER – MID
**Midlands Model Engineering and
Hobbies Exhibition:**
Bingley Hall, Birmingham, West
Midlands.

◆ *Wiltshire* ◆

Near Wilton sweet huge heaps of stone are found,
But so confused that neither any eye
Can count them just, nor reason try,
What force brought them to so unlikely ground.
FROM 'STONEHENGE' BY SIR PHILIP SYDNEY

──── OLD CUSTOMS ────

MAY 29
Oak Apple Day:
Wishford.
Oak Apple Day or Royal Oak Day commemorates the escape in 1651 of Charles II after the Battle of Worcester. This celebration now ties in with the Grovely Forest Rights custom (see below).
MAY 29
Grovely Forest Rights Procession:
Wishford Magna.
The villagers celebrate their right to gather from the forest "all kinde of deade snapping woode Boughes and Sticks" for firewood. Following the forest gathering there is a procession to the Cathedral altar at Salisbury where the villagers make their claim in the traditional form by crying "Grovely, Grovely, and all Grovely".

JUNE 22 (MID-SUMMER'S EVE) TO
JUNE 23 (MID-SUMMER'S DAY)
Summer Solstice Ceremony:
Stonehenge, Avebury.
This revival of an ancient Druid ceremony takes place at midnight where members of the Most Ancient Order of Druids witness the rising of the sun over the Heelstone. Sun-worshipping ceremonies such as this are believed to have been held at Stonehenge as many as 4,000 years ago.
SEPTEMBER — MID
Marlborough Mop Fairs:
Marlborough High Street, Marlborough.

──── FESTIVALS ────

MARCH/APRIL
Swindon Festival:
Details: Arts & Recreation Director, Civic Offices, Swindon.
APRIL — 3RD WEEK
Folk Under Aries Folk Festival:
St. Edmunds Arts Centre, Salisbury.
Details: Gary Nunn, St. Edmunds Art Centre, Salisbury.
MAY — LATE
Kite Festival:
Longleat House, Warminster.
MAY — LATE
Lacock and Chippenham Folk Festival:
Town Centres, Lacock and Chippenham.
Details: Dick Stanger, 7 Carnarvon Close, Chippenham.
MAY
Trowbridge & West Wiltshire Music Festival:
Details: F. Lavery, 42 Wingfield Road, Trowbridge.
MAY
Wiltshire Music Festival:
Details: J.R. Denny, High Walls, West Winterslow, Salisbury.
JUNE — LATE, OR JULY — EARLY
Potterne Folk Festival:
Details: M. Hiscock, 34 West View Crescent, Hillworth, Devizes.

JULY – 4TH WEEK
(Salisbury) Southern Cathedrals Festival:
Details: The Festival Office, The Close, Salisbury.
JULY
Salisbury Festival of the Arts:
Details: 7–11 Brown Street, Salisbury.
AUGUST – 4TH WEEK
Edington Priory Festival of Church Music:
Details: The Director, Edington Priory Festival of Church Music, Lower Wormhill, Eaton Bishop, Near Hereford.
SEPTEMBER – 2ND & 3RD WEEKS
Salisbury Festivities:
Details: Festival Director, Castle Mews, 29a Castle Street, Salisbury.

FAIRS

FEBRUARY 14; APRIL 20; OCTOBER 20
Devizes Fair:
Devizes.
WHIT MONDAY; 1ST FRIDAY AFTER JULY 15; TUESDAY AFTER OCTOBER 17
Salisbury Fair:
Salisbury.
2ND AND LAST MONDAY IN EVERY MONTH
Swindon Fair:
Swindon.
EASTER SATURDAY
Easter Folk Fair and Celidh:
Corn Exchange, Market Place, Devizes.
MAY – LATE
Teddy Bear & Honey Fair:

Devizes Carnival Week:
Market Place, Devizes.
SEPTEMBER – 1ST WEEK
Aldbourne Carnival:
Aldbourne, Nr. Marlborough.
SEPTEMBER – 4TH WEEK
Pewsey Carnival & Torchlight Procession:
Pewsey.

SPORTS

APRIL – MID
Slazenger South West Counties Junior Badminton Tournament:
Swindon.
APRIL – LATE
Friends Provident English National

⇧
GROVELY FOREST RIGHTS PROCESSION
The Grovely Procession makes its way to Salisbury Cathedral altar on Oak Apple Day. See: OLD CUSTOMS.

◆

⇧
DEVIZES JUNIOR EISTEDDFOD
Recorder recitals feature strongly in this delightful eisteddfod which is devoted to the talents of children. See: FESTIVALS.

◆

⇧
TEDDY BEAR & HONEY FAIR
Teddy bear fanatics can indulge in their childhood fantasies at this unusual gathering staged at Longleat House. See: FAIRS.

◆

SEPTEMBER – LATE
Swindon Floral Festival:
Swindon.
SEPTEMBER – LATE
Flower Festival:
Thamesdown, Swindon.
NOVEMBER
Devises Junior Eisteddfod:
Details: Ms. M.E. Henley, 33 West View Crescent, Devizes.

Longleat House, Warminster.
OCTOBER
Salisbury Pleasure Fair:
Salisbury.

CARNIVALS

MAY – 4TH WEEK
Marlborough Carnival:
Marlborough.
JUNE – 4TH WEEK
Bromham Carnival:
Bromham, Nr. Chippenham.
AUGUST – 4TH WEEK

Under 21 Badminton Tournament:
Swindon.
MAY – MID
Wiltshire Tug-of-War Association County Championships:
Marlborough.
JUNE – EARLY
Avon Anchors Tug-of-War Club Annual Event:
Recreation Ground, Ashley Road, Salisbury.
JUNE – MID
National Parachuting Championships:

Army Parachute Association Centre, Netheravon.
AUGUST – LATE
North Wiltshire Tug-of-War Club Annual Competition:
Christian Malford Recreation Ground, Nr. Chippenham.
SEPTEMBER – MID
British Junior Power (Weight Lifting) Championships:
Salisbury.

MISCELLANEOUS

JUNE
Radio Society of Great Britain Rally:
Longleat House, Warminster.
JULY – EARLY
American Independence Day Celebrations:
Longleat House, Warminster.
JULY
Beat the Retreat:
Longleat House, Warminster.
SEPTEMBER – 2ND WEEK
B.M.W. Car Rally:
Longleat Grounds, Warminster.

⬆
LACOCK & CHIPPENHAM FOLK FESTIVAL
This premier festival of folk dancing and singing is one of the biggest folk events of the year. Concerts, ceilidhs, dance displays and song sessions take place in the streets and in some of the local pubs. The event also attracts performers from abroad. See: FESTIVALS.

COUNTY TUG-OF-WAR CHAMPIONSHIPS
A moment of great effort and concentration during one of the contests at the county championships held at Marlborough. See: SPORTS.

◆ *Yorkshire* ◆
(INCLUDING NORTH HUMBERSIDE & CLEVELAND)

Sleep, O cluster of friends,
Sleep!—or only when May,
Brought by the west-wind, returns
Back to your native heaths,
And the plover is heard on the moors,
Yearly awake to behold
The opening summer, the sky,
The shining moorland—to hear
The drowsy bee, as of old,
Hum o'er the thyme, the grouse
Call from the heather in bloom!
Sleep, or only for this
Break your united repose!

FROM 'HAWORTH CHURCHYARD'
BY MATHEW ARNOLD

——— Old Customs ———

JANUARY – FIRST SATURDAY AFTER
PLOUGH MONDAY
Goathland Plough Stots:
Goathland.
A revival of an ancient Plough Monday Procession in which a 'lord' and 'lady' lead a group of men in disguise known as 'toms', a group of musicians and sword-dancers, and the 'plough stots' (i.e. youths leading around a bullock) through the village, stopping at various places to collect money.

FEBRUARY – SHROVE TUESDAY
Shrovetide Skipping:
Foreshore, Scarborough.
At one time Shrove Tuesday in Scarborough was known as 'Ball Day' and balls were tossed and kicked around on Southsands. This has now been largely replaced by skipping and hundreds of people of all ages gather on the Southsands Promenade after midday to skip with huge ropes until nightfall.

FEBRUARY – SHROVE TUESDAY
Ringing the Pancake Bell:
Scarborough.
A large bell known as the curfew bell which hung in the entrance to St. Thomas the Martre Hospital used to be rung at 12 noon on Shrove Tuesday as a signal to begin the frying of pancakes. Since the hospital was demolished in 1861 the bell has been housed in the town museum but is still rung at midday by the museum staff.

MARCH – 3RD THURSDAY
Kiplingcotes Derby:
Between South Dalton and Kiplingcotes Farm, Nr. Market Weighton.
Said to be the oldest flat race in Britain, dating back to 1519, and run over a 4 mile course.

GOOD FRIDAY
Pace Egg Play:
Midgley; Mythomroyd; Hebden Bridge; Heptonstall; Luddenden; Todmorden.
This is an Easter Version of the traditional

Mumming Play symbolizing the struggle between good and evil. The Mummers parade through the villages begging eggs and other treats.

EASTER EVE
Pace Egg Play:
Brighouse.

EASTER SUNDAY
Horn Day:
Ripon.
The city houses three ancient horns, the oldest of which, dated AD886, is brought out on the five 'Horn Days' during the year.

EASTER MONDAY
Egg Rolling:
Scarborough & Pocklington.

EASTER MONDAY & WHIT TUESDAY
Barwick-in-Elmet Maypole Raising:
Barwick-in-Elmet.
Every three years, Britain's tallest maypole at Barwick-in-Elmet is taken down, repainted and then raised again (with four new garlands) on Whit Tuesday. Following the raising of the maypole there is a May procession which tours the village, ending up at Hall Tower Field for the traditional maypole dancing and the crowning of the May Queen.

MAY 1
Gawthorpe May Day:
Gawthorpe.
A really ancient May Day celebration, the present one being unchanged for over one hundred years. The centre piece of the procession is a young couple on horseback who are said to represent Snow White and Prince Charming.

MAY 23 (EVE OF ASCENSION)
Planting the Penny Hedge or Horngarth:
Boyes Staithe, Harbourside, Church Street, Whitby.
A penance custom which began in 1159 when three noblemen who had been found

guilty of fighting and manslaughter in church, and hunting without permission, were ordered to plant a hedge of stakes at the brim of the water at Whitby Harbour, strong enough to withstand three tides.

MAY 26
Boars Head Morris Dancing:
The Pierce Hall, Town Centre, Halifax.
SPRING BANK HOLIDAY MONDAY
Bellerby Feast:
Bellerby.
Whitsuntide was, up until the beginning of the 20th century, traditionally celebrated with sports and fetes. At Bellerby, villagers dressed in clowns' uniform make a collection at houses which is used for a children's outing and Christmas party.
JULY
Haworth Rush Bearing Service:
Haworth.
AUGUST 7
Littlebeck Garden Fete & Rose Queen Ceremony:
Old Mill, Littlebeck, Nr. Whitby.
AUGUST — 1ST TUESDAY
Whitby Ancient Gooseberry Contest:
Egton Bridge, Nr. Whitby.
Gooseberries, often the size of hen's eggs and weighing 2 oz. or more, can be seen at this show.
AUGUST 9
Feast of St. Wilfred & Procession:
Ripon.
A custom which commemorates the return of St. Wildred from exile in Rome during the 7th century. A man dressed as the saint rides a white horse through the city accompanied by a band of musicians.
AUGUST — SATURDAY FOLLOWING 24TH
Burning the Bartle:
West Witton.
A large straw effigy called the 'Bartle' is carried in procession down the main street and, stopping outside various houses, the villagers sing a traditional rhyme:
'At Pen Hill crags he tore his rags
At Hunter's Thorn he blew his horn
At Capplebank Stee he brak his knee
At Grassgill Beck he brak his neck
At Waddam's End he couldn't fend
At Grassgill End he made his end'
At the end of the procession a knife is plunged into the effigy and it set on fire. The custom is thought to have originated when a thief was caught long ago in the village.

THE PENNY HEDGE
A 'hedge' of stakes is still constructed every year at the water's edge at Whitby Harbour. See: OLD CUSTOMS.

AUGUST
Blessing of the Fishing Fleet:
Whitby.
SEPTEMBER
Harvest of the Sea Service:
Flamborough.
NOVEMBER 1 (OR FOLLOWING MONDAY)
Caking Night:
Dungworth.
'Caking' means the collection of money, a custom still surviving in the town of Dungworth. This is always preceded by a mask and fancy dress competition held in the local pub with prizes given to the best three contestants.
NOVEMBER 5TH
Mischief Night:
York.
A particularly interesting November 5th celebration seeing how Guy Fawkes was born in a house in York which is now the Youngs Hotel.
DECEMBER 24 (CHRISTMAS EVE)
Tolling the Devil's Knell:
Dewsbury.
A custom said to have been instituted by Sir Thomas de Soothill to atone for a murder he committed. The tenor bell known as Black Tom of Soothill, is rung once for every year passed since the death of Christ, and this before midnight exactly. It is rung in the parish church and is said to proclaim Satan's defeat when Christ was born.
DECEMBER 25 (CHRISTMAS DAY)
Horn Day:
Ripon.
DECEMBER 26 (BOXING DAY)
Sword-Dance:
Handsworth.
A traditional sword-dance said to be part of the death and resurrection celebrations held during mid-winter throughout the country.
DECEMBER 26
Sword-Dance Play:
Ripon.
EVERY NIGHT
Horn Blowing Ceremony:
Ripon.
Every night at 9.00 p.m. the Mayor's official Hornblower blows the city's horn, once outside the Mayor's house and four times in the market place. The custom originated in Saxon times when the 'Wakeman', who was in charge of good order in the town, sounded the horn at the beginning of the night's curfew.

FESTIVALS

JANUARY OR FEBRUARY
CAMRA Beer Festival:
De Grey Rooms, St. Leonards Place, York.

RING THE PANCAKE BELL
The 'Curfew Bell' which hangs in the town museum is rung at mid-day by museum staff and watched appreciatively by a young audience. See: OLD CUSTOMS.

FEBRUARY TO JUNE
Kingston-Upon-Hull Musical Festival:
Details: Ms. M. Ellis, 15 Westwood Road, Beverley HU17 8EN.
FEBRUARY/MARCH

WHITBY ANCIENT GOOSEBERRY CONTEST
Gooseberries of astonishing size compete in one of the oldest horticultural events of the country. See: OLD CUSTOMS.

145

Harrogate Competitive Musical Festival:
Royal Baths Assembly Rooms, Royd
MARCH – LATE, OR APRIL – EARLY

City of Leeds College Music Festival:
Details: City of Leeds College of Music, Leeds Institute Buildings, Cookridge Street, Leeds LS2 8BH.
MARCH

Mexborough & District Musical Competition Festival:
Details: Ms. M. Booker, 17 St. George's Avenue, Swinton.
MARCH

Bradford Festival:
Details: 52 Goodwin Street, Bradford BD1 2SD.
APRIL – EARLY

Whitby Folk Festival:
Spa Theatre & Pavilion, North Promenade, Whitby.
EASTER

Easter Folk Festival:
Civic Hall, Eldon Street, Barnsley.
APRIL – MID

Harrogate International Youth Music Festival:
Harrogate.
APRIL – LATE

West Yorkshire One-Act Drama Festival:
Venn Street Arts Centre, Huddersfield.
APRIL – LATE

Bradford Independent Drama Festival:
Bradford Playhouse, Chapel Street, Leeds Road, Bradford.
APRIL

Horsforth Competitive Festival of Music, Drama and Dance.
Details: D. Halliday, 1 Grange Drive, Hall Lane, Horsforth, Leeds.
APRIL

Robertshaw Music Festival:
Details: Ms. M. Cartwright, 99A Oak Lane, Marringham, Bradford.
APRIL

Elsecar & Hoyland Musical Festival:
Details: Ms. B.E. Clayton, 42 Lansdowne Crescent, Darton, Barnsley.
APRIL

Harrogate International Youth Music Festival:
Royal Baths, Harrogate, and district.
EASTER

Easter Hockey Festival:
Scarborough.
APRIL – LATE, TO MAY – EARLY

Yorkshire Dance Festival:
Details: Yorkshire Arts Association, Glyde House, Glydegate, Bradford.
MAY – 1ST SUNDAY

St. John of Beverley One Day Music Festival:
Beverley.

Details: Information Officer, St. John of Beverley Church, Beverley.
MAY – 2ND WEEK

Holmfirth Folk Festival:
Holmfirth.
Details: David Keys, Rockhouse, Chapelgate, Scholes, Holmfirth, HD7 1SX.
MAY – EARLY

Eskdale Festival of Song, Speech & Drama:
Spa Theatre & Pavilion, North Promenade, Whitby.
MAY – EARLY

Great Pennine Festival:
Holmfirth.
MAY – 4TH WEEK

York Early Music Festival:
York – Various Venues.
MAY – (BIENNIAL)

Leeds Musical Festival:
Details: Leeds Musical Festival Ltd., 40 Park Lane, Leeds LS1 1LN.
MAY

Scarborough Dutch Festival:
Scarborough.
MAY/JUNE

Richmondshire Festival:
Details: Swale House, Frenchgate, Richmond DL10 7JE.
MAY/JUNE

Askrigg Festival:
Details: Jean Thomas, Askrigg, Leyburn.
SPRING BANK HOLIDAY WEEK – (BIENNIAL)

Ilkley Literature Festival:
Details: Festival Office, Ilkley Literature Festival, Ilkley LS29 9JB.
SPRING BANK HOLIDAY

Hebden Bridge New Arts Festival:
Details: New Arts Association, Birchcliffe Centre, Hebden Bridge.
JUNE – EVERY 4 YEARS (NEXT ONE 1984)

York Festival of Mystery Plays:
Museum Gardens, Museum Street, York.
Details: 1 Museum Street, York.
JUNE – MID

International Youth Folklore Festival:
York.
JUNE – MID

National Festival of Youth Theatres Summer School:
Details: Advisory Division, Dudley House, Albion Street, Leeds LS2 8PT.
JUNE – MID

Dutch Festivals:
Whitby and Filey.
JUNE – MID

Halle Festival of Music:
Royal Hall, Ripon Road, Harrogate.
Details: Harrogate District Council, Council Offices, Harrogate, HG1 2SG.

JULY – LATE, TO AUGUST – EARLY

The Harrogate International Festival of Music and Arts:
Harrogate and Ripon – various venues.
JULY – LATE, TO AUGUST – EARLY

Wakefield Music Festival:
Details: Walker House, 22 Bond Street, Wakefield.
AUGUST – MID

Billingham Intenational Folklore Festival:
Details: Festival Office, Municipal Buildings, Town Centre, Billingham, Cleveland TS23 2LW.
AUGUST – MID

International Festival of Sound:
Exhibition Centre, Harrogate.
AUGUST – LATE

Askrigg Church Flower Festival:
The Parish Church, Askrigg.
AUGUST – LATE

Yorkshire Koi Festival:
Harewood House, Harewood, Leeds.
AUGUST

Festival of the Arts in Flowers:
Sledmere House, Sledmere, Driffield, North Humberside.
AUGUST

Whitby Folk Festival:
Details: 5 Norfolk Mount, Chapel Allerton, Leeds LS7 4PU.
AUGUST – SEPTEMBER

Annual Cricket Festival:
Cricket Ground, North Marine Road, Scarborough.
SEPTEMBER – EARLY

Fulneck Festival:
The Fulneck Moravian Settlement, Pudsey.
SEPTEMBER – MID

Guiseborough Weekend Festival:
King George Playing Field, Guiseborough, Cleveland.
SEPTEMBER – LATE (TRIENNIAL)

Leeds International Pianoforte Festival Competition:
Details: The Festival Director, L.I.P.F.C., University of Leeds, Leeds LS2 9JT.
SEPTEMBER

Scarborough Cricket Festival:
Scarborough.
OCTOBER – EARLY

West Riding Cathedrals Festival:
Bradford, Sheffield & Wakefield.
OCTOBER

Sheffield Festival:
Details: Education Buildings, Leopold Street, Sheffield.
OCTOBER

Dearne & District Competitive Musical Festival:
Details: Ms. E. Fitt, 15 Common Road, Thurnscoe, Rotherham S63 OSX.

FAIRS

WEDNESDAY BEFORE FEBRUARY 28,
MAY 13; OCTOBER 11
Barnsley Fair:
MARCH 3, JULY 17, DECEMBER 9
Bradford Fair:
1ST THURSDAY IN FEBRUARY, APRIL,
AUGUST & NOVEMBER
Doncaster Fair:
JULY 24; 1ST SATURDAY IN
NOVEMBER
Halifax Fair:
MARCH 31; MAY 14; OCTOBER 4
Huddersfield Fair:
2ND TUESDAY IN APRIL; EACH
TUESDAY IN JULY; OCTOBER 11
Hull Fair:
3RD WEDNESDAY IN JANUARY, APRIL,
JULY & OCTOBER; 1ST WEDNESDAY IN
MARCH, JULY, SEPTEMBER &
DECEMBER; NOVEMBER 8
Leeds Fair:
MAY 13; 1ST THURSDAY & FRIDAY IN
JULY & NOVEMBER; NOVEMBER 23
Ripon Fair:
HOLY THURSDAY; NOVEMBER 22
Scarborough Fair:
EASTER TUESDAY; LAST MONDAY IN
JULY; 1ST MONDAY IN OCTOBER
Selby Fair:
WHIT TUESDAY; LAST TUESDAY IN
NOVEMBER
Sheffield Fair:
JULY 4 – 6; NOVEMBER 11 – 14
Wakefield Fair:
THURSDAY BEFORE FEBRUARY 14;
WHIT MONDAY FOR 4 DAYS; JULY 10;
AUGUST 12; NOVEMBER 14, 23; WEEK
BEFORE XMAS
York Fair:

FAYRES

APRIL – EARLY
Spring Fayre:
Town Hall, High Street, Skipton.
JUNE – 1ST WEEK
Scarborough Fayre:
Scarborough – various venues

CARNIVALS

MAY
Holmfirth Carnival:
Holmfirth.
MAY – MID
Todmorden Carnival:
Centre Vale Park, Todmorden.
MAY – MID
Aire Faire & Carnival:
Myrtle Park, Bingley.
MAY – LATE
Richmond Meet: Carnival & Fair:

Various venues in Richmond.
JUNE – LATE
Honley Carnival:
Honley, Nr. Huddersfield.
JUNE – LATE
Tadcaster Carnival:
Toulson Polo Ground, Tadcaster.
JULY – MID
**Saltburn, Marse & New Marske
Carnival:**
Civic Hall and other venues, Skelton,
Cleveland.
JULY – MID
Hornsea Carnival:
Hornsea, Humberside.
AUGUST – LATE
Eston Play Week and Carnival:
Eston Recreation Ground (and other
venues), Trunk Road, Eston, Cleveland.
AUGUST
Denby Dale Carnival:
Denby.

GALAS

MAY 1
May Day Gala:
Pierce Hall, Halifax.
MAY – 1ST WEEK AND SEPTEMBER –
1ST WEEK
Railway Gala:
North York Moors Railway,
Pickering/Grasmont.
JUNE – MID
Garforth & District Lions Club Gala:
Glebelands, Garforth.
JUNE – MID
Halifax Charity Gala:
Manor Heath, Skircoat Green, Halifax.
JUNE – MID
Lord Mayor's Parade & Gala:
City Centre & Lister Park, Bradford.
JUNE – MID
Keighley Gala:
Victoria Park, Hardings Road,
Keighley.
JUNE – LATE
Horsforth Gala:
Horsforth Hall Park, Hall Lane,
Horsforth.
JULY – EARLY
St. Austins Annual Gala:
Ings Road Centre, Sports Field, St.
Austins.
JULY – LATE
Drighlington Gala:
Adwalton Common, Drighlington.
AUGUST – MID
Mission to Seamen's Gala:
North Promenade, Whitby.
SUMMER
Arskey Gala:
Arskey.

SHOWS

JANUARY 2ND WEEK
Doncaster Motor Show:
Exhibition Centre, Leger Way,
Doncaster.
EASTER
Easter Model Railway Show:
Assembly Rooms, Blake Street, and De
Grey Rooms, St. Leonard's Place, York.

AGRICULTURAL, HORTICULTURAL & BREED SHOWS

FEBRUARY – MID
Craven Canine Association Show:
Town Hall, High Street, Skipton.
APRIL – EARLY
Northern Siamese Cat Show:
Royal Baths Assembly Rooms,
Harrogate.
APRIL – LATE
Harrogate Spring Flower Show:
Valley Gardens, Harrogate.
MAY – 3RD WEEK
The Great Doncaster Show:
Exhibition Centre, Leger Way,
Doncaster.
MAY – MID
Humberside County Show:
Racecourse, Westwood, Beverley,
Humberside.
MAY – LATE
Rothwell Show:
Springhead Park, Park Lane, Rothwell.
MAY – LATE
Leeds Championship Dog Show:
Temple Newsham Estate, Leeds.
MAY – LATE
Wickersley Agricultural Show:
Springvale Farm, Moorhen Lane,
Wickersley.
MAY – LATE
Wensleydale Horse Show:
Wensley Park, Nr. Leyburn.
MAY – 4TH WEEK
Swaledale Sheep Show:
Tan Hill Inn, Swaledale, Nr. Keld.
MAY
Otley Agricultural Show:
Otley.
MAY
Wetherby Agricultural Show:
Wetherby.
JUNE – MID
Todmorden Agricultural Show:
Centre Vale Park, Todmorden.
JUNE – MID
Northern Horse Show:
Wetherby Grange Park, Wetherby.
JUNE – 4TH WEEK
Harden Moss Sheepdog Trials:
Harden Moss, Greenfield Road,

Holmfirth, Nr. Huddersfield.
JUNE
Batley & District Agricultural Show:
Batley.
JULY – EARLY
Great Yorkshire Agricultural Show:
Great Yorkshire Showground,
Hookstone Oval, Harrogate.
JULY – MID
Husthwaite Agricultural Show:
Acaster Hill, Husthwaite, Nr.
Easingwold.
JULY – LATE
Bishop Wilton Agricultural Show:
Bishop Wilton, Nr. Wilton.
JULY
Malton Agricultural Show:
Malton.
JULY
Driffield Agricultural Show:
The Showground, Driffield, North
Humberside.
AUGUST – EARLY
**Sneaton & Hawkser Agricultural
Show:**
Russell Hall Farm, Stainacrem Whitby.
AUGUST – EARLY
Hull Agricultural Show:
East Park, Holderness Road, Hull,
Humberside.
AUGUST – MID
Leeds Flower Show:
Roundhay Park, Leeds.
AUGUST – MID
Whitby & District Flower Show:
Whitby School, Prospect Hill, Whitby.
AUGUST – LATE
Egton Horse & Agricultural Show:
Egton, Nr. Whitby.
AUGUST – LATE
Wensleydale Agricultural Show:
Myers Farm, Wensley, Nr. Leyburn.
AUGUST – LATE
Burniston Agricultural Show:
Showground, Scalby Road, Burniston,
Nr. Scarborough.
SEPTEMBER – EARLY
Rotherham Horticultural Show:
Clifton Park, Clifton Lane, Rotherham.
SEPTEMBER – EARLY
**Lealholm Farm Produce and
Horticultural Show:**
Lealholm, Nr. Whitby.
SEPTEMBER – EARLY
Reeth Agricultural Show:
Reeth, Nr. Richmond.
SEPTEMBER – EARLY
**Harrogate Great Autumn Flower
Show:**
Valley Gardens, Harrogate.
SEPTEMBER – EARLY
**Castleton & Danby Horticultural
Show:**
Castleton, Nr. Whitby.

⇧
KNARESBOROUGH BED RACE
*Come rain, wind or shine the annual Bed
Race takes place in Knaresborough's
Conynham Hall Grounds and attracts a
large crowd of spectators. See: SPORTS.*

WORLD COAL CARRYING
CHAMPIONSHIP
*This interesting fun event is not for the
faint-hearted as anyone who has picked up
a sack of coal will testify. Entrants race
down a prescribed length of road carrying
the obligatory sacks of coal. See:
SPORTS.*

◆

──────SPORTS──────

JANUARY – LATE
**Yorkshire Amateur Swimming
Association Championships:**
Halifax Pool, Huddersfield Road,
Halifax.
FEBRUARY – LATE
Mintex International Motor Rally:
Bramham Park, Wetherby.
EASTER
Easter Chess Tournament:
Royal Baths Assembly Rooms,
Harrogate.
EASTER MONDAY
World Coal-Carrying Championship:
Dewsbury.
APRIL – 3RD WEEK
**Harewood Spring National
Speedclimb:**
Harewood Avenue, Harewood.
APRIL – LATE
Yorkshire Ladies Golf Championship:
Ganton Golf Club, Ganton, Nr.
Scarborough.
MAY – MID

Wensleydale Horse Trials:
On the banks of the River Ure,
Thornton Steward, Ripon.
MAY – LATE, TO SEPTEMBER – MID
**Gambart Baines Challenge Cup Bowls
Tournament (Crown Greens):**
Alexandra Gardens, Scarborough.
JUNE – EARLY
Bramham Horse Trials:
Bramham Park, Wetherby.
JUNE – EARLY
**Scottish & Northern Osprey Sailing
Championship:**
Filey.
JUNE – EARLY
Harness Racing: Dent Sports:
Jackie Holme Pasture, Dent.
JUNE – EARLY
**International Roller Hockey
Tournament:**
Albert Park Rink, Park Vale Road,
Middlesborough, Cleveland.
JUNE – EARLY
Cycle Milk Race:

──────MISCELLANEOUS──────

JUNE – EARLY
Vintage and Veteran East Coast Run:
Hull to Bridlington.
MAY – LATE
**The Caravan Club East Yorkshire
Rally:**
Carlton Towers, Carlton, Nr. Goole,
Humberside.
SPRING BANK HOLIDAY
**Harrogate Spring Bank Holiday Arts
and Crafts Market:**
Royal Baths Assembly Rooms,
Harrogate.
JUNE – EARLY
S.S.A.F.A. Air Display:
R.A.F. Station, Church Fenton,
Tadcaster.
JUNE – 4TH WEEK
Mock American Civil War Battle:
Oakes Park, Norton, Sheffield.
JUNE – 4TH WEEK
**Rotherham Motoring Weekend (and
Tattoo):**
Herringthorpe Playing Fields, Middle
Lane, Rotherham.

· PART TWO ·
SCOTLAND

BORDERS

◆ *Berwickshire* ◆

OLD CUSTOMS

AUGUST — EARLY
Lauder Common Riding:
Lauder.
Common Ridings are colourful ceremonies traditional to the towns of the Southern Uplands which commemorate important events in local history concerning the warfare between England and Scotland in the late Middle Ages.

FESTIVALS

MAY — 4TH WEEK
Dryborough Border Shore Festival:
Eyemouth.
JULY — 1ST WEEK
Duns Summer Festival:
Duns.

FAIRS

MAY — 4TH WEEK
Borders Country Fair:
The Hirsel, Coldstream.
AUGUST
North Berwick Pipe Band Tartan Fair:
Lodge Grounds, North Berwick.

AGRICULTURAL, HORTICULTURAL, & BREED SHOWS

AUGUST — 1ST WEEK
Berwickshire Agricultural Show:
Duns.

SPORTS

MAY — LATE
Borders Fair Horse Show & Gymkhana:
Cumledge Mill, Preston, Nr. Duns.
MAY — LATE
Horse Show:
Cumledge, Nr. Duns.
JUNE — MID
Hay Golf Trophy:
Duns Golf Club, Duns.
JULY — EARLY
International Horse Driving Trials:
Mellerstain, Nr. Gordon.
SEPTEMBER
Open Mixed Golf Foursomes:
North Berwick Golf Club, Beach Road, North Berwick.
NOVEMBER — EARLY
Scottish Open Surfing Championships:
Pease Bay, Cockburnspath.

Highland Games:

JUNE
Oxton Professional Games:
Justice Hall, Haugh, Oxton.

Regattas:

Berwick-Upon-Tweed Regatta:
Details: J. Cromarty, 21 High Cliffe, Berwick-Upon-Tweed.
Berwick Arc Regatta:
Details: D. Ringland, 11 Bridge Street, Berwick-Upon Tweed.

MISCELLANEOUS

JULY — EARLY
Eyemouth Herring Queen Week:
Gunsgreen Area, Eyemouth.
JULY — EARLY
Duns Reivers Week:
Duns.
JUNE — EARLY
Historic Vehicles Rally and Concours de'Elegance:
Mellerstain, Nr. Gordon.
JULY — MID
Earlston Civic Week:
Earlston.
AUGUST — 2ND WEEK
Coldstream Civic Week:
Coldstream.

HERRING QUEEN WEEK
The Queen and her attendants arrive in Eyemarsh Harbour on local fishing boats for the official crowning ceremony. See: MISCELLANEOUS.

LAUDER COMMON RIDING
Dignitaries from the council, and other official bodies, walk in procession through the town during this important traditional event. See: OLD CUSTOMS.

BORDERS
◆ *Peebles-shire* ◆

ONWARD·TWEEDDALE

**Peebles-shire Agricultural Society
Agricultural Show:**
Hay Lodge Park, Peebles.

OLD CUSTOMS

JUNE 23
Beltane Festival:
Peebles.
*The Beltane Queen is crowned on the steps
of the old Parish Church and this revival of
an ancient fire-lighting ceremony also
includes the Riding of the Marches.*

FESTIVALS

MAY
Border Music Festival:
*Details: Mrs. B. Fialane, Schoolhouse,
Traquair, Innerleithen, EH44 6PL.*

FAIRS

JUNE – 2ND WEEK
Borders Fair:
Hay Lodge Park, Peebles.

AGRICULTURAL, HORTICULTURAL, & BREED SHOWS

JUNE – MID
McEwans Lager Sheepdog Trials:
Hay Lodge Park, Peebles.
AUGUST – 3RD WEEK

◆

PEEBLES HIGHLAND GAMES
*An impressive spectacle of pipers entertain
the spectators at the annual games. See:
SPORTS.*
▽

SPORTS

SEPTEMBER – EARLY
Peebles Highland Games:
Whitestone Park, Peebles.

MISCELLANEOUS

SEPTEMBER – 2ND WEEK
Peebles & District Club Border Run:
Borders.

◆

BELTANE FESTIVAL
*The Beltane Queen is crowned on the steps
of the parish church, Peebles, and following
the ceremony there is a procession with local
bands through the streets. See: OLD
CUSTOMS.*

PEEBLES AGRICULTURAL SHOW
*The Parade of Beasts proceeds around the
arena in Hay Lodge Park during the county's
main agricultural event of the year. See:
SHOWS.*

BORDERS
◆ Roxburghshire ◆

NE·CEDE· ·ITO
MALIS·SED·CONTRA·AUDENTIOR

When distant Tweed is heard to rave,
And the owlet to hoot o'er the dead man's grave,
Then go—but go alone the while—
Then view St. David's ruin'd pile;
And, home returning, soothly swear,
Was never scene so sad and fair!
FROM 'MELROSE ABBEY' BY SIR WALTER SCOTT

OLD CUSTOMS

FEBRUARY 2 (CANDLEMAS DAY)
Jethart Ba':
Jedburgh.
A traditional handball game which is also
played on 'Fastern's E'en (Eve of Lenten
Fast).
JUNE
Common Riding:
Hawick Moor, Hawick.
DECEMBER 27TH (ST. JOHN'S DAY)
Freemasons Walk:
Melrose.
This Saint's Feast Day celebration which
dates back to 1707 takes the form of a
torchlight parade in which members of the
Lodge of Melrose St. John take part.

FESTIVALS

JUNE – 3RD WEEK
Melrose Summer Festival:
Melrose.
JUNE
Newcastleton Traditional Music
Festival:
Newcastleton.
JULY – 1ST & 2ND WEEKS
Jethart Callants Festival:
Jedburgh.

AGRICULTURAL, HORTICULTURAL & BREED SHOWS

MAY – 3RD WEEK
Newtown St. Boswells Vintage
Agricultural Show:
Newtown St. Boswells.
JUNE – 4TH WEEK
Kelso Dog Show:
Springwood Park, Kelso.
JULY – 4TH WEEK
Ponies of Britain Scottish Show:
Springwood Park, Kelso.
JULY – 4TH WEEK
Border Union Show:
Springwood Park, Kelso.
AUGUST – 4TH WEEK
Holm Agricultural Show:
Newcastleton.
AUGUST – 4TH WEEK
Liddesdale Agricultural Show:
Newcastleton.

SPORTS

MAY OR JUNE
Raft Races:
River Tweed, Kelso – Carnham.
JULY & AUGUST
Scottish Horse Show:
Springwood Park, Kelso.
SEPTEMBER – EARLY
Open Amateur Sponsored Golf
Competition:
Hawick Golf Club, Hawick.

Highland Games:

JULY – MID
Jedburgh Border Games:
Riverside Park, Jedburgh.

MISCELLANEOUS

JULY – 1ST WEEK
Border Car Run:

Hawick & Border Car Club.
SEPTEMBER — 2ND WEEK
Kelso Ram Sales:
Kelso.

JETHART BA'
*These games are, by tradition, played
between teams known as the 'Uppies' and
'Doonies' using small leather balls and with
the goals determined arbitrarily as points on
the outskirts of town. See: OLD
CUSTOMS.*

FREEMASON'S WALK
*Members of the Lodge of Melrose St. John
in ceremonial robes in procession to Melrose
Abbey. See: OLD CUSTOMS*

KELSO RAFT RACES
*One of the many improvised rafts built
specially for the occasion makes its way
along the River Tweed during the Kelso to
Carnham raft races. See: SPORTS.*

BORDERS

◆ *Selkirkshire* ◆

LEAL·TO·THE·BORDER

────OLD CUSTOMS────

JUNE – 2ND OR 3RD WEEK
Common Riding:
Selkirk.
JULY
Braw Lads Gathering:
Galashiels.
*This two-day festival known as the 'Braw'
or 'Brave Lads Gathering' commemorates
the history of the town and recalls events in
a pageant on horseback and an enactment of
the routing of a company of marauding
Englishmen by townsmen in 1337.*

────AGRICULTURAL,────
──HORTICULTURAL &──
────BREED SHOWS────

JULY – MID
Flower Show:
St. Cuthbert's Church Hall, Galashiels.
SEPTEMBER – EARLY
**Effrick and Yarrow Pastoral Society
Annual Show:**
Effrick.
NOVEMBER – EARLY
**The Border Canary Association
"Premier All-Border Show":**
Volunteer Hall, Galashiels.

────SPORTS────

MAY – LATE
**Border Amateur Athletic
Championships:**
Galashiels Academy, Galashiels.

Regattas:

MAY – LATE
Borders Fair Sailing Regatta:
St. Mary's Loch, Selkirk.

◊ SELKIRK COMMON RIDING
*The Standard Bearer leads the riders
around the boundaries of the town during
this auspicious ancient ceremony. See:
OLD CUSTOMS.*

CENTRAL
◆ *Clackmannanshire* ◆

LOOK·ABOOT·YE

FESTIVALS

MAY – EARLY
Alloa & District Festival:
Alloa.

GALAS

SUMMER
Menstrie Summer Gala:
Menstrie.

SPORTING EVENTS

JULY – MID
Alva Gymnastic Games:
Johnstone Park, Alva.

MISCELLANEOUS

JUNE – MID
National Pony Society Scottish Show:
West End Park, Alloa.

◁ ALLOA GAMES
Caber tossing is unmistakably a Scottish sport and is one of the many traditional events featured at Alloa's annual Games. See: SPORT.

MENSTRIE SUMMER GALA
Gala Days are held in many villages throughout the county. The picture shows the children's Wheelbarrow Race during the Summer Fayre event of the gala. See: GALAS.

157

CENTRAL
◆ *Stirlingshire* ◆

What would the world be, once bereft
Of wet and of wildness? Let them be left,
O let them be left, wildness and wet;
Long live the weeds and the wilderness yet.
FROM 'INVERSNAID' BY
GERARD MANLEY HOPKINS

FESTIVALS

JANUARY – 4TH WEEK
Full Length Drama Finals Festival:
MacRobert Centre, Stirling.
FEBRUARY
Falkirk One-Act Drama Festival:
Falkirk Town Hall, or MacRobert
Centre, Falkirk.
MAY – 4TH WEEK TO JUNE – 2ND
WEEK
Stirling District Festival:
Stirling.
AUGUST – 2ND WEEK
Falkirk Festival:
Falkirk.
NOVEMBER – 3RD WEEK
Festival of New Drama:
Falkirk.

AGRICULTURAL,
HORTICULTURAL &
BREED SHOWS

MAY – LATE
Drymen Agricultural Show:
Drymen Show Field, Drymen.
MAY

Stirling Agricultural Show:
Stirling.
JUNE – MID
National Pony Society Scottish Show:
Kildean Market, Stirling.
SEPTEMBER
Drymen Sheepdog Trials:
Drymen.

SPORTS

MAY – IST WEEK
The Tryst Golf Trophy:
Tryst Golf Club, Larbert, Nr. Falkirk.
MAY – MID
Men's Festival Golf Trophy:
Stirling Golf Course, Queen's Road,
Stirling.
MAY – MID
Hornall Golf Trophy:
Stirling Golf Course, Queen's Road,
Stirling.
MAY – LATE
Ladies' Festival Golf Trophy:
Stirling Golf Course, Queen's Road,
Stirling.
MAY – LATE

Grangemouth Open Golf Tournament:
Grangemouth Golf Course, Polmonthill,
Grangemouth.
JUNE – EARLY
Hayston Bell Golf Handicap:
Kirkintilloch.
JUNE – EARLY
Open Mixed Golf Foursomes:
Stirling Golf Course, Queen's Road,
Stirling.
AUGUST – EARLY
Wood Golf Trophy:
Falkirk Golf Club, Falkirk.
AUGUST – EARLY
**Champion of Scotland Equestrian
Show:**
Drymen Showground, Drymen.
SEPTEMBER – EARLY
**Watson-Cameron Rosebowl Golf
Handicap:**
Stirling Golf Course, Queen's Road,
Stirling.
OCTOBER – MID
**Commonwealth Spoons Play Off
(Golf):**
Stirling.

Regattas:

JUNE – 4TH WEEK
Stirling Regatta:
Riverside, Stirling.

STIRLING AGRICULTURAL SHOW
Champion sheep are proudly displayed during the annual Stirling Show. See: SHOWS.

RAFT RACE
The raft race is one of the events featured in the annual regatta held on the River Forth. See: SPORTS

DUMFRIES & GALLOWAY
Dumfries-shire ◆

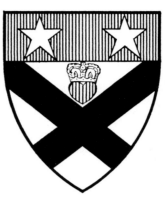

OLD CUSTOMS

JUNE
Riding the Marches:
Annan.
This surviving custom of checking local boundaries was first introduced into Scotland during the Middle Ages.
JUNE 24 TO 30 (MID-SUMMERS DAY AND WEEK)
Guid Nychburris:
Dumfries.
Known locally as the week of "Good Neighbourliness", this festival includes the riding of the marches (see above), trumpet fanfares, the crowning of the Queen of the South, historical Pageants and other events.
JULY
Riding the Marches:
Lockerbie Common, Lockerbie.
JULY
Langholm Common Riding:
High Street & Castleholm, Langholm.
Based on some event in local history. A Cornet or Standard Bearer accompanied by a cavalcade of riders travels over a traditional route.
AUGUST – MID
Riding the Marches:
Sanquhar.

FESTIVALS

MARCH
Dumfries & District Competitive Festival:
Dumfries.
Details: C. Fox, 30 Edinburgh Road, Dumfries.
MAY
Dumfries & Galloway Regional Council of Competitive Music Festival:
Details: Adviser in Music, 10 Market Place, Stranraer.
JUNE – 3RD & 4TH WEEKS
Robert Burns Festival:
Dumfries.

FAIRS

MARCH
Dumfries March Fair:
Dumfries.

CARNIVALS

MAY – 4TH WEEK & JUNE – 1ST WEEK
Lockerbie Carnival Fortnight:
Lockerbie.

GALAS

JUNE – 3RD WEEK
Kirconnel & Kelloholm Gala Week:
Kirconnel.
JULY – 2ND WEEK
Moffat & District Gala Celebrations:
Moffat.

AGRICULTURAL, HORTICULTURAL & BREED SHOWS

JULY
Thornill Agricultural Show:
Thornhill.
JULY – LATE, OR AUGUST – EARLY
Dumfries and Lockerbie Agricultural Show:
The Showfield, Park Farm, Dumfries.
AUGUST – 3RD WEEK
Dumfries & Lockerbie Sheepdog Trials:
Thornhill.
AUGUST – 3RD WEEK
Gretna Annual Open Flower Show:
Gretna.
AUGUST – 4TH WEEK
Langholm Horticultural Society Show:
Buccleuch Hall, Langholm.
AUGUST – 4TH WEEK
Dumfries Flower Show:
Loreburn Hall, Newall Terrace, Dumfries.
AUGUST – LATE

Moffat Society Open Show:
Hope Johnstone Park, Moffat.
SEPTEMBER – 4TH WEEK
Castleholm Agricultural Show:
Langholm.
SEPTEMBER
Beattock Sheepdog Trials:
Beattock.
OCTOBER
Moniave Sheepdog Trials:
Moniave.
OCTOBER – 3RD WEEKS
Dumfries & Galloway Vintage Agricultural Machinery Club Ploughing Match:
Dumfries.

SPORTS

APRIL OR MAY
Moffat Golf Week:
Moffat Golf Course, Coateshill.
MAY – LATE
Mackenzie Grieve & Elliot Golf Cups:
Moffat Golf Course, Moffat.
JUNE – MID
Oswald Cup Open Golf Tournament:
Southerness Golf Club, Dumfries.
JULY – EARLY
Morton Craigielands & Johnston Golf Cups. Reiner Mixed Golf Foursomes:
Moffat Golf Course, Moffat.
JULY – MID
Mundle & Stevenson Golf Cups: Men's Singles:
Lockerbie Golf Course, Lockerbie.
AUGUST – LATE
Thornbank Golf Trophy: Mixed Foursomes:
Lockerbie Golf Course, Lockerbie.
SEPTEMBER – MID
Burnet Golf Cup:
Powfoot Golf Course, Annan, Dumfries.
SEPTEMBER – MID
Smith & Wilson Golf Cup:
Lockerbie Golf Course, Lockerbie.
SEPTEMBER – LATE
Paul Jones Mixed Foursomes Golf Cup:
Southerness Golf Club, Dumfries.

DUMFRIES & GALLOWAY

◆ *Kirkcudbrightshire* ◆

. . . at the top of every rise, as you look across the masses of foliage embowering the river in the depths of the glen, you see the cottages and gardens of Dalry climbing skywards about a mile away. If it is late on a summer evening, you will note also how the little white walls retain the light of the evening day while all surrounding details are sunk in shade.

Even when one is on top of the Kells range, seven or eight miles away, a small splash of white of the east side of the valley enables one to say, "There is Dalry".

ANON

SPORTS

JUNE – LATE
Bainloch Golf Cup (Charity Mixed Foursomes):
Colvend Golf Club, Dalbeattie.
SEPTEMBER – LATE
Drystane Dyking Competition:
Gatehouse of Fleet.

MISCELLANEOUS

AUGUST – LATE
World Flounder Tramping Championship:
Palnackie, Solway Firth.

◆

WORLD FLOUNDER TRAMPING CHAMPIONSHIP
This bizarre charity event began only five years ago on the Urr estuary of the Solway with the object being to tramp through the shallows when the tide is out searching for flounders. On feeling a flounder wriggle underfoot a participant attempts to spear the fish with an improvised trident, usually constructed from a fork lashed to a bamboo cane. See MISCELLANEOUS.
▽

FESTIVALS

FEBRUARY – 4TH WEEK
Stewartry One-Act Drama Festival:
Town Hall, Castle Douglas.

FAIRS

SEPTEMBER (SUMMER FESTIVITIES)
Kirkcudbright Fair:
Kirkcudbright.

GALAS

JULY – LATE, OR AUGUST – EARLY
Dalbeattie Gala Week:
Dalbeattie.

AGRICULTURAL, HORTICULTURAL & BREED SHOWS

JUNE – 1ST WEEK
Carsphairn Pastoral and Horticultural Show:
Carsphairn.
AUGUST – 1ST WEEK
Stewartry Agricultural Society Annual Show:
Ernespie Road, Castle Douglas.
AUGUST – 3RD WEEK
Glenkens Agricultural Society Annual Show:
Mains of Kenmure, Glenkens.

DUMFRIES & GALLOWAY
◆ *Wigtownshire* ◆

Portnessock is a bonnie place,
It lies beside the sea,
If 'twas na for the paikie-dogs,
Portnessock folk wud dee.

OLD LOCAL VERSE

FESTIVALS

FEBRUARY – 3RD WEEK
Wigtownshire West One-Act Drama Festival:
Stranraer Academy Hall, Stranraer.

GALAS

MAY – 1ST WEEK
Golf Gala Day:
Wigtownshire County Golf Club,
Glenluce.

HIGHLAND GATHERINGS

MAY – LATE
Clan Hannay Gathering:
Sorbie Tower, Sorbie.

PAGEANTS

AUGUST – LATE
Galloway Pageant Day:
Newton Stewart.

AGRICULTURAL, HORTICULTURAL & BREED SHOWS

JULY
Stranraer & Rhinns of Galloway Agricultural Show:
Stranraer.
AUGUST – EARLY
Wigtown Agricultural Show:
Southfield Park, Wigtown.
SEPTEMBER – MID
International Sheepdog Trials:
Stranraer.

SPORTS

MAY – MID
Reid & Adams Ford Golf Competition:
Stranraer.
JULY – EARLY
Galloway Gazetter Mixed Golf Foursomes:
Wigtown.
JULY – EARLY
Murdoch Ladies Golf Trophy:

Wigtownshire Golf Club, Glenluce.
JULY – MID
George Porter Golf Trophy:
Stranraer Golf Club, Stranraer.
JULY – MID
Cancer Research Portpatrick Dunskey Golf Club Tournament:
Portpatrick.
AUGUST – EARLY
R.N.L.I. Golf Tournament:
Dunskey Golf Club, Portpatrick.
AUGUST – EARLY
Tenant Caledonian 4-Ball Golf Tournament:
Bladnoch Golf Course, Wigtown.
SEPTEMBER – EARLY
McRobert Silver Salver Men's Golf Tournament:
Stranraer Golf Club, Stranraer.
SEPTEMBER – MID
Luce Bay Rosebowl Golf Tournament:
Wigtownshire County Golf Club,
Glenluce.
SEPTEMBER – LATE
Nan Young ladies' Golf Cup:
Stranraer Golf Club, Stranraer.

MISCELLANEOUS

JUNE – EARLY
Pipe Band Contests:
Stranraer.

◆ *Fife* ◆

VIRTUTE · ET · OPERA

Reikie, farewel – I Ne'er cou'd part
Wi thee but wi a dowy heart;
Aft frae the Fifan coast I've seen
The tow'ring on thy summit green;
So glowr the saints when first is given
A fav'rite keek o' glore and heaven;
On Earth nae mair they bend their ein,
But quick assume angelic mein;
So I on Fife wad glowr no more,
But gallop'd to Edina's shore.

FROM "AULD REIKIE" (1773)
BY ROBERT FERGUSSEN.

Old Customs

APRIL
Kate Kennedy Celebrations (& Historical Pageant)
St. Andrews University, St. Andrews.

Festivals

FEBRUARY – 3RD WEEK (BIENNIAL)
St. Andrews Festival:
St. Andrews.
FEBRUARY – 3RD WEEK
Fife One-Act Drama Festival:
Y.W.C.A. Centre, Kirkcaldy.
FEBRUARY
Fife Co-Operative Edication and Arts Council Musical Festival:
Details: Mrs. J. Balmey, 12 Gordon Street, Lochgelly.

JUNE – LATE
Dunfermline Abbey Festival:
Dunfermline Abbey, Dunfermline.
OCTOBER – 3RD WEEK
St. Andrews Folk Festival:
Town Hall, St. Andrews.
Details: John Milne, 4 Sloan Street, St. Andrews.

Fairs

APRIL
Kirkcaldy Links Fair:
Kirkcaldy.
JULY
Burntisland Fair Week:
Burntisland.
AUGUST – 2ND WEEK
St. Andrews Lammas Fair:
St. Andrews.

Celebrations

NOVEMBER
St. Andrew's Day Celebrations:
St. Andrews.

Agricultural, Horticultural & Breed Shows

MAY – MID
Fife Annual Agricultural Show:
Balcormo Mains, By Levens.
JULY – 3RD WEEK
St. Andrews Rose Society Show:
Town Hall, St. Andrews.

Sports

MAY – MID
British Legion Silver Poppy Golf Competition:
St. Andrews.
MAY – MID
Colgate PGA Golf Championships:
St. Andrews.
MAY – LATE
St. Andrews Boys Golf Championship:
St. Andrews.
JUNE – EARLY
Smith & Braid Memorial Golf Trophies:
Elie.
JUNE – EARLY

Scotscraig Open Amateur Golf Tournament:
Scotscraig Golf Course, Golf Road, Tayport.
JUNE – EARLY
International Golf Tournament:
St. Andrews.
JUNE – MID
Scottish Open Parachute Championships:
Glenrothes Airfield, Glenrothes.
JUNE – MID
Silverlink Open Golf Tournament:
Dunnikier Park Golf Course, Kirkcaldy.
JUNE – LATE
Canmore Open Amateur Golf Tournament:
Canmore Golf Club, Canmore.
JUNE – LATE
East of Scotland Amateur Golf Tournament:
Lundin Links Golf Club, Lundin Links.
JUNE – LATE
Scottish Small Bore Rifle Championships:
St. Andrews.
JUNE – LATE
Thornton Cup Open Golf Tournament:
Thornton Golf Club, Thornton.
JULY – EARLY
Ladies Cup Golf Competition:
Elie.
JULY – MID
Boyd Quaich Golf Tournament:
St. Andrews.
JULY – LATE
Doctor's Trophy Golf Competition:
Elie.

---◆---

LAMMAS FAIR
This ancient fair of St. Andrews is largely a pleasure fair these days. 'Lammas' is a derivation of 'loaf-mass', the ancient festival or feast of August 1st. See: FAIRS.

THORNTON HIGHLAND GAMES
Children compete individually during this contest of traditional dancing at the Games. See: SPORTS

KATE KENNEDY CELEBRATIONS
Kate Kennedy, a noted beauty in her day, was the niece of the founder of St. Andrews University. Her uncle was a builder whose only surviving work is The Church of St. Salvator, the University Chapel. Every year a first year student at the University plays the part of Kate in celebrations commemorating her name. See: OLD CUSTOMS.

JULY – LATE
Baird Coronation Golf Cup:
Elie.
JULY – LATE
Canmore Mixed Golf Foursomes:
Dunfermline.
JULY – LATE
Mixed Open Golf Tournament:
Aberdour Golf Course, Aberdour.
AUGUST – EARLY
Leven Merchants Golf Trophy:
Leven Scoonie Golf Course, Leven.
AUGUST – MID
Boys Open Golf Tournament:
St. Andrews.
AUGUST – MID
Scottish Hard Court Tennis Championships:
Kilburn Park, St. Andrews.
AUGUST – MID
Doctor's Trophy Golf Competition:
Elie.
AUGUST – MID
Pitreavie Open Golf Cup:
Pitreavie Golf Club, Queensferry Road, Dunfermline.
AUGUST – MID
Eden Golf Tournament:
St. Andrews.
AUGUST – MID
Men's Open Amateur Golf Competition:
Crail.
AUGUST – MID
Elie Links Open Golf Championship:
Elie.
AUGUST – MID
Canmore Ladies Open Golf Tournament:
Dunfermline.
SEPTEMBER – EARLY
Open Scratch Tournament:
Thornton Golf Club, Thornton.
SEPTEMBER – EARLY
Scottish Single-Handed Sailing Championships:
St. Andrews.
SEPTEMBER – EARLY
Kinghorn Open Golf Tournament:
Kinghorn.
SEPTEMBER – MID
Bing Crosby Golf Trophy:
St. Andrews.

Highland Games:

MAY – LATE
Pitlessie Highland Games:
Pitlessie.
JUNE – EARLY
Strathmiglo Highland Games:
Stratmiglo.
JUNE – EARLY
Markinch Highland Games:

DUNFERMLINE ABBEY FESTIVAL
In the 910 years since its foundation, Dunfermline Abbey has weathered the storms of time remarkably well and has witnessed the passage of many Kings and Queens including Robert the Bruce who is buried here. Today, its dominant buttressed presence creates a unique historical backdrop against which to set the Dunfermline Abbey Festival. See: FESTIVALS.

FIFE AGRICULTURAL SHOW
Black-faced sheep are judged at Fife's annual show. See: SHOWS.

---◆---

Markinch.
JUNE – LATE
Ceres Highland Games:
Ceres.
JULY – EARLY
Thornton Highland Games:
Thornton.
JULY – LATE
Cupar Highland Games:
Cupar.

GRAMPIAN

Aberdeenshire

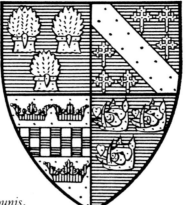

Blyth Aberdeane, thow beriall of all tounis,
   The lamp of bewtie, bountie, and blythnes;
Unto the heaven [ascendit] thy renoun is
   Off vertew, wisdome, and of worthines.
FROM 'TO ABERDIN' BY WILLIAM DUNBAR

FESTIVALS

MARCH – 3RD WEEK
Drama Festival For the Deaf:
Aberdeen Arts Centre, King Street,
Aberdeen.
MAY/JUNE
**Aberdeen and North East of Scotland
Music Festival:**
*Details: Miss L.M. Fraser, 6 Girdlestone
Place, Torry, Aberdeen AB1 3LB.*
JUNE – 2ND WEEK
Kildrummy Castle Festival:
Kildrummy Castle Gardens,
Kildrummy.
JUNE – 3RD WEEK
Castle Fraser Festival:
Castle Fraser, Kemnay.
*Details: The Co-Ordinator, Grampian
Festival Society, Dept. of Leisure &
Tourism, Woodhill House, Ashgrove Road
West, Aberdeen.*
JUNE
Aberdeen Festival:
St. Nicholas House, Broad Street,
Aberdeen AB9 1XJ.
AUGUST – 2ND & 3RD WEEKS
**Aberdeen – International Festival of
Youth Orchestras and the Performing
Arts:**
*Details: Secretary General, International
Festival of Youth Orchestras and the
Performing Arts, 24 Cadogan Square,*
London SW1X 0JP.
AUGUST/SEPTEMBER
Braemar Scottish Festival:
The Invercauld Galleries, Braemar.
*Details: Invercauld Festival Theatre,
Braemar, Deeside.*

FAIRS

JUNE – 3RD WEEK
Aberdeen Annual Antiques Fair:
Tree Tops Hotel, Aberdeen.
JUNE – 3RD WEEK
"Aikey Fair":
Aikey Brae, Old Deer.

GALAS

JUNE – 2ND WEEK
Turriff Gala:
The Haughs, Turriff.
JUNE – 4TH WEEK
Rothienorman Gala Week:
Rothienorman.
JULY – 2ND WEEK
Aboyne Gala:
Aboyne.

HIGHLAND GATHERINGS

AUGUST – LATE
Lonach Highland Gathering:
Bellaby Park, Strathdon.
SEPTEMBER – EARLY
Braemar Highland Gathering:
Princess Royal and Duke of Fife
Memorial, Braemar.

PAGEANTS

AUGUST – LATE
Echt Vintage Vehicle Motor Pageant:
Echt.

AGRICULTURAL, HORTICULTURAL & BREED SHOWS

FEBRUARY
**Aberdeen-Angus Cattle Society Show
& Sale:**
Aberdeen.
FEBRUARY
**Beef Shorthorn Cattle Society Pedigree
Show & Sale:**
Aberdeen.
MARCH – 3RD WEEK
Agricultural Field Day:
Adamston, Huntley.
JUNE – 2ND WEEK
Goat Show:
Turriff Market, Turriff.
JUNE – 2ND WEEK
Monymush Sheepdog Trials:
The Holm Farm, Monymusk.
JULY
Royal Northern Agricultural Show:

Aberdeen.
JULY — 2ND WEEK
Echt Agricultural Show:
Pleasure Park, Echt.
AUGUST — IST WEEK
Turriff Agricultural Show:
The Haughs, Turriff.
JULY/AUGUST
New Deer Agricultural Show:
New Deer.
AUGUST — 2ND WEEK
Tarland Agricultural Show:
Tarland Showyard, Tarland.
AUGUST — 3RD WEEK
Ballater Horticultural Show:
Victorial Hall, Ballater.
SEPTEMBER — 1ST WEEK
Aberdeen Flower Show:
Duthie Park, Aberdeen.

SPORTS

APRIL — MID
Spring Golf Tournament:
Links Golf Course, Aberdeen.
MAY — MID
Royal Deeside Golf Week:
Royal Deeside.
MAY — LATE
Open Mixed Fours Golf Competition:
Tarland.
JUNE — EARLY
Ladies Open Golf Tournament:
Turriff Golf Club, Turriff.
JUNE — EARLY
Rosslyn Open Golf Tournament:
Huntley Golf Course, Cooper Park,
Huntley.
JUNE — MID
Oldmeldrum Sports:
Pleasure Park, Oldmeldrum.
JUNE — LATE
**Scottish Fireball Yachting
Championships:**
Aberdeen & Stone Yachting Club,
Aberdeen.
JULY — EARLY
**Huntly Sponsored Open Golf
Tournament:**
Huntly Golf Club, Huntly.
JULY — EARLY
Mens Open Golf Tournament:
Braemar Golf Course, Braemar.
JULY — MID
Tormintoul Highland Games:
Tormintoul, Nr. Braemar.
JULY — MID
**Gents 18-Hole Open Golf
Tournament:**
Turriff Golf Club, Turriff.
JULY — MID
Aboyne Open Golf Tournament:
Aboyne.
JULY — MID

Mixed Open Golf Tournament:
Huntly Golf Course, Cooper Park,
Huntly.
JULY — LATE
Summer Golf Tournament:
Balnagask Course, Aberdeen.
JULY
Ladies Open Golf Tournament:
Huntly Golf Course, Cooper Park,
Huntly.
AUGUST — MID
Open 18-Hole Mixed Golf Foursomes:
Turriff Golf Club, Turriff.
AUGUST — MID
**Gents 36-Hole Open Golf
Tournament:**
Turriff Golf Club, Turriff.
AUGUST — LATE
Ladies Open Golf Tournament:
Huntly Golf Course, Cooper Park,
Huntly.
OCTOBER — MID
**Senior/Junior 18-Hole Open Golf
Tournament:**
Turriff Golf Club, Turriff.

Highland Games:

JUNE — MID
**World Caber-Tossing Championship
and Aberdeen Highland Games:**
Hazlehead Park, Aberdeen.
AUGUST — LATE
Aboyne Highland Games:
Aboyne.

MISCELLANEOUS

JUNE — 2ND WEEK
Kildrummy Castle Rally:
Kildrummy.
JUNE — 4TH WEEK
New Blyth Steam and Vintage Rally:
Aberdeen.
JULY — 4TH WEEK
Peterhead Scottish Week:
Peterhead.
JULY — 4TH WEEK
**Aberdeen Canine Training Society
Championship:**
Hazlehead, Aberdeen.
AUGUST — IST WEEK
August Finray Hill Climb:
Aberdeen & District Motor Club,
Fintray.

PETERHEAD SCOTTISH WEEK
*The newly crowned Peterhead Queen sits
outside the Council Offices at the beginning
of Scottish Week. The various events
include a Pageant in the streets in which
many interested local groups participate.
See: MISCELLANEOUS*

GRAMPIAN
Banffshire ◆

FESTIVALS

JUNE – MID
Festival of Ceilidhs (Traditional Music and Song Association of Scotland):
Keith.

GALAS

JUNE – MID
Forsyce Annual Gala:
By Portsoy, Forsyce.
JULY – MID
Keith Gala Week:
Keith.
JULY – 4TH WEEK
Dufftown Gala Week:
Dufftown.

AGRICULTURAL, HORTICULTURAL, & BREED SHOWS

JULY – 4TH WEEK
Keith Sheepdog Trials:
Keith.
AUGUST – 2ND WEEK
Banff Flower Show:
Banff.
AUGUST – 2ND WEEK
Keith Agricultural Show:
Seafield Park, Keith.
AUGUST – 3RD WEEK
Aberchirder Flower School:
McRobert Park, Aberchirder.

SPORTS

MAY
Gents Open Golf Tournaments:
Buckpool Golf Club. Barhill Road,
Buckie.
MAY – LATE

Brangan Cup Golf Trophy:
Duff House, Royal Castle, Banff.
JUNE – LATE
Mixed Foursomes Golf Tournament:
Buckpool Gold Club, Barhill Road,
Buckie.
JUNE – LATE
Spencer Merchiston Cup Golf Trophy:
Duff House, Royal Castle, Banff.
JULY – MID
Tankard Golf Trophy:
Duff House, Royal Castle, Banff.
JULY – MID
Dufftown Golf Championships:
Dufftown.
JULY – LATE
Ladies Open Golf Tournament:
Duff House, Royal Castle, Banff.
JULY – LATE
Four Days Open Golf Tournament:
Duff House, Royal Castle, Banff.
AUGUST – LATE
Men's Open Golf Tournament:
Duff House, Royal Castle, Banff.

◆

KEITH GALA
The Gala at Keith, the biggest in this eastern Scottish county, is an occasion in which the Gala Queen is an essential part of the festivities. Here the Queen is shown being crowned on her ceremonial throne. See: GALAS.

FESTIVAL OF CEILIDHS
Ceilidhs are traditional events where musicians, and others involved in Scottish culture gather together to perform. The festival at Keith is a unique occasion in which to enjoy the fine local music. See:
◁ *FESTIVALS*

GRAMPIAN
◆ Kincardineshire ◆

OLD CUSTOMS

DECEMBER 31ST (NEW YEAR'S EVE)
Swinging the Fireballs:
Stonehaven.
The men who take part in this well known New Year fire revel march in procession through the streets swinging balls of fire made from wire netting filled with oil soaked rags.

FESTIVALS

FEBRUARY – 4TH WEEK
Kincardine & North Angus One-Act Drama Festival:
Town Hall, Stonehaven.

AGRICULTURAL, HORTICULTURAL & BREED SHOWS

JUNE – 4TH WEEK
Deeside Agricultural Show:
King George V Park, Banchory.
SEPTEMBER
Inverbie Horticultural Show:
Inverbie.

◆

STONEHAVEN HIGHLAND GAMES
The Young Bells Tug-of-War team from Strichen give a mighty heave during the tug-of-war competition at the Games.
See: SPORTS
▷

SPORTS

MAY
Open Mixed Golf Foursomes and Junior Open Golf Tournament:
Banchory Golf Course, Kinneskie, Banchory.
JUNE – EARLY
Mixed Golf Foursomes:
Stonehaven.
JULY – MID
Mens Open Amateur Golf Tournament:
Stonehaven Golf Course, Cowie, Stonehaven.
AUGUST – MID
Men's Golf Tournament:
Banchory Golf Course, Kinneskie, Banchory.

HIGHLAND GAMES:

JULY – MID
Highland Games:
Mineralwell Park, Stonehaven.

MISCELLANEOUS

JUNE – 1ST WEEK
Annual Feeling Market:
Market Square, Stonehaven.
JULY – 3RD WEEK
R.W. Thomson Vintage Vehicle Tour

of the Town:
Cowie Park, Stonehaven.
JULY – 3RD WEEK (AFTER RALLY, AS ABOVE)
Thomson Rally Ceilidh:
Royal Hotel, Stonehaven.

◆

SWINGING THE FIREBALLS
An evening of excitement takes place at Stonehaven where the fire-swingers take to the High Street. Flaming caskets are swung to and fro in the ritual of the Fireball Parade which is said to recall the superstitions of the early Middle Ages when the town's ancestors tried to charm the sun from the heavens during the cold winter months. See: OLD CUSTOMS.
▷

GRAMPIAN
◆ *Morayshire* ◆

SUB · SPE

OLD CUSTOMS

JANUARY 11
Burning the Clavie:
Burghead.
This is believed to have originated from a custom practised by the Druids. The 'Clavie King' sets alight a tar-filled barrel and this is carried in procession through the town.

FESTIVALS

JUNE — 3RD WEEK
Elgin Fiddle Festival:
Town Hall, Elgin.
JUNE — 3RD WEEK
Archiestown Festival:
Archiestown.
Moray Music Festival:
Details: G.R. Wiseman, Adviser in Music, Div. Education Office, Academy Street, Elgin, IV30 1LL.

GALAS

JULY — 4TH WEEK
Fochabers Gala Week:
Fochabers.

AGRICULTURAL, HORTICULTURAL & BREED SHOWS

AUGUST — 2ND WEEK
Strathspey Farmers Club Agricultural Show:
Grantown-on-Spey.
AUGUST — 4TH WEEK
Elgin Horticultural Society Flower Show:
Elgin.
AUGUST — 4TH WEEK
Strathspey Horticultural Flower Show:
Grantown-on-Spey.

SPORTS

MAY — MID
"Open" Hopeman Foursomes Golf Handicap Cup:
Hopeman.
MAY — MID
Northern Counties Ladies' Golf Association Tournament:
Forres Golf Club, Forres.
JUNE — MID
Ladies' Open Golf Tournament:
Garmouth & Kingston Golf Club, Garmouth & Kingston.
JUNE — MID
Open Macarthur Men's Golf Trophy:
Hopeman Golf Course, Hopeman.
JUNE — LATE
"Jubilee Tray" Open Amateur Golf Tournament:
Forres Golf Club, Forres.
JUNE — LATE
Boyd Anderson 36 Hole Golf Trophy:
Moray Golf Course, Stotfield Road, Lossiemouth.
JULY — EARLY
Open Bowls Competition:
Grant Park Bowling Club.
JULY — MID
Open Ladies' Dee Mohr Golf Trophy:
Hopeman Golf Course, Hopeman.
JULY — MID
Boys' Open Golf Tournament:
Forres Golf Club, Forres.
JULY — LATE
Findhorn Week (Sailing):
Royal Findhorn Yachting Club, Findhorn.
JULY — LATE
Open Amateur Golf Tournament:
Moray Golf Club, Lossiemouth.

HIGHLAND GAMES

JULY — 2ND WEEK
Forres Highland Games:
Forres.

MISCELLANEOUS

AUGUST — 2ND WEEK
Historic Wheel Club Rally:
Elgin.
SEPTEMBER — 1ST WEEK
Fiddlers Rally:
Town Hall, Elgin.

FORRES HIGHLAND GAMES
No Highland Games would be complete without the Throwing the Hammer contest and here a contestant puts everything into his throw during the Forres Games. See: SPORTS.

BURNING THE CLAVIE
This ancient Druid custom takes place in Burghead early in the year. The 'Clavie' is carried through the town and positioned on the top of Loorie Hill. See: OLD CUSTOMS.

HIGHLAND
◆ *Caithness* ◆

FESTIVALS

MARCH OR JUNE
Caithness Music Festival:
Wick.
JULY — 2ND WEEK
Thurso Folk Festival:
Details: Ian Livingstone, 5 Naver Road,
Thurso.
AUGUST — 2ND WEEK
Wick Festival of Poetry, Jazz & Folk:
Details: 3 Moray Street, Wick.

GALAS

JULY — MID
Thurso Gala Week:
Thurso.
JULY — LATE
Wick Gala Week:
Wick.

HIGHLAND
GATHERINGS

JULY — 1ST WEEK
Caithness Highland Gathering &
Games:
Millbank Playing Fields, Thurso.

AGRICULTURAL,
HORTICULTURAL, &
BREED SHOWS

JULY — LATE
Caithness County Agricultural Show:
Wick or Thurso.
AUGUST
Wick Sheepdog Trials:
Wick.

SPORTS

MAY — LATE
Ladies Open Golf Tournament:
Thurso Golf Course, Newlands of Guise,
Thurso.
JULY — EARLY
Caithness Open Golf Tournament:
Wick Golf Course, Wick.
JULY — MID

Gala Week Open Golf Tournament:
Thurso Golf Course, Newlands of Guise,
Thurso.
AUGUST — MID
Thurso Open Golf Tournament:
Thurso Golf Course, Newlands of Guise,
Thurso.

Highland Games:

JULY — MID
Dunbeath Highland Games:
Playing Fields, Dunbeath.
JULY — LATE
Halkirk Games:
Halkirk.

◆

CAITHNESS SHOW
Princess Anne presents a winning cup
and inspects the beasts at a recent Caithness
Agricultural Show. See: SHOWS.

HIGHLAND
◆ *Inverness-shire* ◆

"Why called the White Loch, I do not know, except, as Sir William Maxwell informs me, it be so called because the water (as he saith his property), that it will wash linen as well without soap as many others will do it; and therefore in my opinions it is an excellent place for whitening or bleaching linen, Holland, and muzlin webs".

SYMSON – ON THE WHITE LOCH,
TWO MILES FROM FORT WILLIAM.

FESTIVALS

FEBRUARY – 3RD WEEK
Inverness One-Act Drama Festival:
Eden Court Theatre, Inverness.
MARCH – 1ST WEEK
Badenoch One-Act Drama Festival:
Kingussie High School, Kingussie.
MARCH
Inverness Music Festival:
Inverness.
Details: Divisional Education Office, 1–3 Church Street, Inverness IV1 1LB.
MARCH
Badenoch & Strathspey Music Festival:
Details: Divisional Education Office, 1–3 Church Street, Inverness IV1 1LB.
MARCH
Lochaber Music Festival:
Details: Divisional Education Office, 1–3 Church Street, Inverness IV1 1LB.
APRIL – EARLY
Inverness Folk Festival:
Details: Walter Allan, 62 Academy Street, Inverness.
APRIL – 4TH WEEK

Scottish One-Act Drama Finals Festival:
Eden Court Theatre, Inverness.
MAY
Northern Counties Musical Festival:
Inverness.
AUGUST – 2ND WEEK
International Amateur Open Free Skating Festival:
Aviemore.
SEPTEMBER – 3RD WEEK
Carrbridge Festival of Ceilidhs:
Carrbridge.

FAIRS

JUNE – 4TH WEEK
Antiques Court Theatre, Inverness.
AUGUST – 1ST WEEK
Highland Field Sports Fair:
May Estate, Nr. Inverness.
AUGUST – 1ST WEEK
Annual Antiques Fair:
Caledonian Hotel, Inverness.

GALAS

JUNE – 1ST WEEK
Gala Day:
Police Headquarters, Perth Road, Inverness.
JULY – 4TH WEEK, OR AUGUST – 1ST WEEK
Fort William Gala Week:
Fort William.
AUGUST – 1ST WEEK
Beauly Gala Week:
Beauly.

HIGHLAND GATHERINGS

AUGUST – 3RD WEEK
Glenfinnan Highland Gathering:
Glenfinnan.

TATTOOS

JULY – 4TH WEEK
Inverness Military Tattoo:
Inverness.

AGRICULTURAL, HORTICULTURAL & BREED SHOWS

FEBRUARY
Beef Shorthorn Cattle Society Pedigree Show:
Inverness.
AUGUST – 2ND WEEK
Kingussie Sheepdog Trials:
Kingussie.
AUGUST – 3RD WEEK
Nethybridge Sheepdog Trials:

Nethybridge.
AUGUST — 4TH WEEK
Fort William Agricultural Show:
Fort William.
AUGUST
Inverness Sheepdog Trials:
Inverness.

SPORTS

JULY — MID
Open Golf Championships:
Newtonmore Golf Course, Newtonmore.
JULY — MID
Glen Nevis River Races:
Fort William.
AUGUST — MID
Amateur Open Golf Tournament:
Boat of Garten Golf Course, Boat of
Garten.
AUGUST — MID
Kingussie Open Golf Tournament:
Kingussie Golf Course, Gynark Road,
Kingussie.
SEPTEMBER — EARLY
Ben Nevis Hill Race:
Fort William.

Highland Games:

JULY — MID
Inverness Highland Games:
Inverness.
JULY — LATE
**Fort William (Lochaber) Highland
Games:**

---◆---

BEN NEVIS HILL RACE
*Contestants set off at the beginning of the
strenuous Ben Nevis Hill Race at Fort
William. See: SPORTS.*
▽

Fort William.
JULY — LATE
Arisaig Highland Games:
Arisaig.
AUGUST — EARLY
Caol Highland Games:
Caol.
AUGUST — EARLY
Mallaig Highland Games:
Mallaig.
AUGUST — EARLY
**Newtonmore Highland Games and
Clan MacPherson Rally:**
Newtonmore.
AUGUST — MID
Skye Highland Games:
The Meall, Portree, Isle of Skye.
AUGUST — MID
Glenfinnan Highland Games:
Glenfinnan.
AUGUST — LATE
Glenurquhart Highland Games:
Drumnadrochit.

MISCELLANEOUS

AUGUST
Clan MacPherson Rally:
Kingussie & Newtonmore.
AUGUST OR SEPTEMBER
Silver Charter Piping Competitions:
Dunvegan Castle, Dunvegan, Isle of
Skye.
SEPTEMBER
Northern Piping Competition:
Inverness.

▽

CARRBRIDGE FESTIVAL OF CEILIDHS
*Carrbridge, a small Highland village in the
Spey Valley, gives a warm welcome to
visitors: the Ceilidh Week has ceilidhs,
concerts, crafts, and competitions in piping,
dancing, singing and fiddle-playing. See:
FESTIVALS.*

---◆---

HIGHLAND
Nairnshire

UNITE · AND · BE · MINDFUL

AGRICULTURAL, HORTICULTURAL & BREED SHOWS

AUGUST – EARLY
Nairnshire Farmers' Society Show:
The Showfield, Nairn.

SPORTS

MAY – MID
Nairn Golf Week:
Nairn Golf Club, Nairn.
JUNE – EARLY
British Ladies' Open Amateur Golf Championship:
Nairn Golf Club, Nairn.
JUNE/JULY
Ladies British Open Amateur Golf Championships:
Nairn Golf Club, Nairn.
JULY – MID
King Golf Trophy:
Nairn Golf Club, Nairn.
AUGUST – EARLY
Open Amateur Golf Tournament:
Nairn Golf Club, Nairn.
AUGUST
Nairn Gold Tournament:
Nairn.
SEPTEMBER – LATE
Open Amateur Mixed Foursomes Golf Tournament:
Nairn Golf Club, Nairn.

Highland Games:

AUGUST – MID
Nairn Highland Games:
The Links, Nairn.

NAIRNSHIRE FARMERS' SOCIETY SHOW
Nairn's County Show has been in existence for two hundred years. Here the Supreme Champion strikes a majestic pose with her calf. See: SHOWS.

HIGHLAND
Ross & Cromarty

FESTIVALS

MAY – 3RD WEEK
Wester Ross Mod:
Gairloch.

GALAS

AUGUST
Seabord Gala:
Balintore Harbour, Seabord.

HIGHLAND GATHERINGS

JULY – 2ND WEEK
Dingwall Games and Highland Gathering:
Jubilee Park, Dingwall.
AUGUST – 4TH WEEK
Invergordon Highland Gathering:
Castle Grounds, Invergordon.

AGRICULTURAL, HORTICULTURAL & BREED SHOWS

JULY – 3RD WEEK
Gairloch & District Sheepdog Trials:
Achtercairn, Gairloch.
AUGUST – 1ST WEEK
Black Isle Agricultural Show:
Mansfield, Muir of Ord.
AUGUST – 3RD & 4TH WEEKS
Lairg Crofters' Show:
Lairg.
SEPTEMBER – 2ND WEEK
Gairloch & District Horticultural Show:
Gairloch.

SPORTS

JUNE – MID
36 Hole Open Golf Tournament:
Strathpeffer Golf Course, Strathpeffer.
JUNE – LATE
One Day Open Golf Tournament:
Invergordon Golf Club, Invergordon.

Highland Games:

JULY – MID
Dingwall Games:
Jubilee Park, Dingwall.
AUGUST – MID
Strathpeffer Highland Games:
Castle Leod, Strathpeffer.

Regattas:

JULY – 4TH WEEK, TO AUGUST – 1ST WEEK
Plockton Annual Regatta:
Loch Carron, Plockton.
AUGUST – EARLY
Ullapool Regatta:
Ullapool.

MISCELLANEOUS

AUGUST – 2ND WEEK
Muir of Ord Vintage Rally:
Muir of Ord.

STRATHPEFFER HIGHLAND GAMES
Together with the caber, hammer and other traditional sports, putting the shot is an essential ingredient to many Highland Games. The contestant here, from Muir of Ord, gets set to throw his shot putt. See: SPORTS.

HIGHLAND
◆ *Sutherland* ◆

My heart's in the Highlands, my heart is not here;
My heart's in the Highlands a chasing the deer;
Chasing the wild deer, and following the roe;
My heart's in the Highlands wherever I go.—
FROM 'MY HEART'S IN THE HIGHLANDS'
BY ROBERT BURNS.

FESTIVALS

FEBRUARY – 4TH WEEK
Sutherland One-Act Drama Festival:
Dornoch Academy Hall, Dornoch.
JULY – EARLY
Dornoch Festival Week:
Dornoch.

GALAS

JULY – 2ND WEEK
Helmsdale Gala Week:
Helmsdale.
JULY – 4TH WEEK
Brora Gala Week:
Brora.
AUGUST – 1ST WEEK
Golspie Gala Week:
Golspie.
AUGUST – 3RD WEEK
Lairg Gala Week:
Lairg.

HIGHLAND GATHERINGS

AUGUST – 2ND WEEK
Dornoch Highland Gathering:
Dornoch.

AGRICULTURAL, HORTICULTURAL & BREED SHOWS

JULY – LATE
Sutherland Agricultural Show:
The Links, Dornoch.
AUGUST – 3RD WEEK
Sutherland Sheepdog Trials:
Golspie.
AUGUST – 4TH WEEK
Rogart Sheepdog Trials:
Rogart.
AUGUST – 4TH WEEK
Loch & Helmsdale Flower Show:
Helmsdale.
AUGUST
Lairg Sheep Show:
Lairg.
AUGUST
Golspie Sheepdog Trials:
Golspie.

SPORTS

MAY – EARLY
Dornoch Open Golf Competition:
Dornoch.
JUNE – EARLY

Bank of Scotland Junior Open Golf Championships:
Golspie.
JUNE – MID
Ross-Sutherland Open Golf Competition:
Golspie.
JULY – EARLY
Tri-Am Team Golf Tournament:
Golspie.
JULY – MID
Millicent Bowl Golf Tournament:
Golspie Golf Club, Golspie.
JULY – MID
Sinclair Cup Open Golf Competition:
Dornoch.
AUGUST – EARLY **Golspie Golf (Gala Week):**
AUGUST – EARLY
G.K. Mackay Open Golf Foursomes:
Dornoch.
AUGUST – EARLY
Annual 36 Hole Golf Open:
Golspie.
AUGUST – EARLY
Macleod Golf Trophy:
Dornoch.
AUGUST – MID
Ladies' Annual Open Golf Tournament:
Dornoch.
AUGUST – MID
Captain's Mixed Golf Foursomes:
Dornoch.
AUGUST – MID
Open Ladies' Golf Foursomes:
Golspie.
AUGUST – EARLY
Annual 36 Hole Golf Open

Tournament:
Golspie Golf Club, Ferry Road, Golspie.
AUGUST – MID
**Carnegie Shield Annual Open Golf
Competition:**
SEPTEMBER – EARLY
**Duchess of Sutherland Rosebowl
Ladies' Golf Tournament:**
Golspie.
SEPTEMBER – LATE
Dornoch Golf Week:
Dornoch.

Highland Games:

JULY – LATE
Durness Highland Games:
Shore Park, Durness.
AUGUST – MID
Assynt Highland Games:
Lochinver.

——Miscellaneous——

AUGUST – EARLY
Salmon Queen Week:
Bonar Bridge.

SALMON QUEEN WEEK
*Beneath the bridge at Bonar the newly
elected Salmon Queen is ceremonially
crowned in the presence of local dignitaries.*
See: MISCELLANEOUS.

ISLANDS

◆ Orkney & Shetland ◆

Scant are the few green acres that I till
But arched above them spreads the
boundless sky,
Ripening their crops; and round them lie
Long miles of Moorland hill.

Beyond the cliff-top glimmers in the sun
The far horizon's bright infinity;
And I can gaze across the sea
When my day's work is done

The solitudes of land and sea assuage
My quenchless thirst for freedom unconfirmed;
With independent heart and mind
Hold I my heritage.
       'ON ORKNEY', BY ROBERT RENDALL

Old Customs

JANUARY 1ST (NEW YEAR'S DAY)
Street Football (Kirkwall Ba'Games):
Kirkwall, Orkney.
JANUARY – LAST TUESDAY
Uphalic Day:
Lerwick, Shetland.
*These are celebrations which mark the close
of the Yule festivities. Several hundred men
dressed as Vikings assemble at the Market
Cross at 9.00 p.m. and accompany a 30 ft.
model of a Viking Galley in torchlight
procession through the streets. Later the
Galley is set alight and revelry of various
kinds follow. The celebrations are said to
represent a Viking fire festival called
Up-Helly-Aa.*

Festivals

JUNE – 4TH WEEK
St. Magnus Festival:
Orkney.
Details: Festival Secretary, Lindisfarne,

⇧

ORKNEY COUNTY SHOW
*Orkney's major agricultural event takes
place in the spacious Bignold Park and
offers a good day out for the Islanders. See:
SHOWS.*

◆

Annfield Crescent, Kirkwall, Orkney.
Orkney County Music Festival:
*Details: Festival Director, Education
Office, Kirkwall, Orkney.*

Carnivals

JULY
Lerwick Summer Carnival:
Lerwick.

Agricultural, Horticultural & Breed Shows

Orkney County Show:
Bignold Park, Kirkwell.

◆

KIRKWALL BA' GAMES
*A boisterous New Year's sport similar to
other free-for-all ball games in England
takes place in the town and is immensely
popular to contestants of all ages. See:
OLD CUSTOMS.*

UP-HELLY-A
*This world-famous event is one of the most
dramatic and exciting of all Britain's
customs. Set against the bleak Nordic
background of the Shetland landscape, the
festival is the Islanders' way of
commemorating the way of life of their
hardy ancestors, the Vikings. See: OLD
CUSTOMS.*

LOTHIAN
◆ *East Lothian* ◆

Old Customs

JULY
Riding the Marches:
Musselburgh.

Festivals

MAY – 4TH week
Haddington Festival Week:
Haddington.
AUGUST
**International Festival of Dancing &
The Arts:**
Brunton Hall, Musselburgh.

Fairs

AUGUST – 1ST WEEK
North Berwick Pipe Band Tartan Fair:
North Berwick.

Agricultural, Horticultural & Breed Shows

JULY – 1ST WEEK
**United East Lothian Agricultural
Society Show:**
Aldershot Park, By-pass Road,
Haddington.
AUGUST – LATE
Musselburgh Annual Flower Show:
Brunton Hall, Musselburgh.

Sports

MAY – LATE
Scottish Ladies Golf Championships:
Gullane.
MAY – LATE
The Walker Golf Cup:
Muirfield, Gullane.
JULY – MID
Scottish Girls Golf Championships:
Dunbar.
JULY – MID
Mackie Golf Cup:
Gullane.
JULY – LATE
Merchants Golf Cup:
Dunber Golf Course, East Links,
Dunbar.

Miscellaneous

AUGUST – 4TH WEEK
Dunbar Rally:
Dunbar.

◆

UNITED EAST LOTHIAN
AGRICULTURAL SHOW
*A fine, healthy sheep is displayed by its
owner during the annual County Show at
Alderston Park. See: SHOWS.*
▽

LOTHIAN
◆ *Midlothian* ◆

*S*uch dusky grandeur cloth'd the height,
Where the huge Castle holds its state,
And all the steep slope down,
Whose ridgy back heaves to the sky,
Pil'd deep and massy, close and high,
   Mine own romantic town!
FROM 'EDINBURGH FROM THE
            PENTLAND HILLS
      BY SIR WALTER SCOTT

——Old Customs——

MAY 1
May Day Celebrations:
Arthur's Seat, Edinburgh.

——Festivals——

FEBRUARY – 2ND WEEK
Edinburgh One-Act Drama Festival:
Edinburgh.
MARCH – 4TH WEEK
Edinburgh Folk Festival:
*Details: Promotions Officer, Scottish
Tourist Board, 23 Ravieston Terrace,
Edinburgh, EH4 3EV.*
MAY – 4TH WEEK
**Penicuik & District Flower Club
Festival:**
Penicuik House, Penicuik.

MAY
Edinburgh Musical Festival:
*Details: D.A. Lamb, 49 Queen Street,
Edinburgh.*
MAY/JUNE
Edinburgh Bach Festival:
St. Celia's Hall, Niddry Street, Cowgate,
Edinburgh.
*Details: Department of Music, Edinburgh
University, Alison House, 12 Nicholson
Square, Edinburgh, EH8 9DF.*
JUNE – 1ST WEEK
S.N.O. Proms:
Usher Hall, Edinburgh.
JUNE – 2ND WEEK
Carlton Mini Festival:
Swing Park, Montgomery Street,
Edinburgh.
JUNE – 3RD WEEK
Charlotte Square Festival:

Charlotte Square, Edinburgh.
JUNE – 3RD & 4TH WEEKS
Craigmillar Festival:
Craigmillar Castle, Hunter's Hall Park,
Edinburgh.
JULY – 3RD WEEK
Beer Drinking Festival:
Princess Street, Gardens, Edinburgh.
JULY – 4TH WEEK
International Folk Dance Festival:
Edinburgh and other venues throughout
Scotland.
AUGUST – LATE, OR SEPTEMBER –
EARLY
Edinburgh Fringe Festival:
Various venues, Edinburgh.
*Details: Edinburgh Festival Fringe Society
Ltd., 170 High Street, Edinburgh.*
AUGUST
Ingliston Rock Festival:
Ingliston, Edinburgh.
AUGUST – 3RD & 4TH WEEKS
Edinburgh International Film Festival:
*Details: Edinburgh International Film
Festival, The Film House, 88 Lothian
Road, Edinburgh, EH3 9BZ.*
AUGUST – LATE, TO SEPTEMBER –
EARLY
Jazz Festival:
Various venues, Edinburgh.
AUGUST/SEPTEMBER
Edinburgh International Festival:

Details: Edinburgh Festival Society, 21 Market Street, Edinburgh, EH1 1BW.
SEPTEMBER – 4TH WEEK
Women's & Girls Judo Championships:
Meadowbank Sports Centre, Edinburgh.

―――――**FAIRS**―――――

APRIL
Bo'ness Spring Fair:
Bo'ness.
AUGUST – 2ND WEEK
Edinburgh Annual Antiques Fair:
Roxburghe Hotel, Edinburgh.
DECEMBER – 1ST WEEK
Winter Antiques Fair:
Roxburghe Hotel, Edinburgh.

―――――**GALAS**―――――

JANUARY – 1ST WEEK
New Year Athletics Gala:
Meadowbanks Sports Centre, London Road, Edinburgh.

―――――**HIGHLAND**―――――
―――――**GATHERINGS**―――――

AUGUST – 4TH WEEK
Highland Gathering:
Ross Open Air Theatre, West Princess Street Gardens, Edinburgh.

――**AGRICULTURAL,**――
――**HORTICULTURAL &**――
――**BREED SHOWS**――

MARCH – EARLY
Royal Caledonian Horticultural Flower Show:
Meadowbanks Sports Centre, London Road, Edinburgh.
EASTER SATURDAY
Edinburgh Dog Show:
Thomas Morton Hall, Ferry Road, Edinburgh.
MAY – 3RD WEEK
Scottish Kennel Club Championship:
Edinburgh.
JUNE – 3RD WEEK
Royal Highland Agricultural Show:
Ingliston, Edinburgh.
AUGUST – 4TH WEEK
Scottish Kennal Club Dog Show:
Royal Highland Showground, Ingliston, Edinburgh.

―――――**SPORTS**―――――

JANUARY – LATE
Scottish Open Badminton Championships:
Meadowbanks Sports Centre, London Road, Edinburgh.
FEBRUARY – MID
Scottish Indoor Hockey Championships:
Meadowbanks Sports Centre, London Road, Edinburgh.
APRIL – EARLY
Scottish Schools Fencing Championships:
Meadowbanks Sports Centre, London Road, Edinburgh.
APRIL – EARLY
Scottish Junior Gymnastics Championships:
Meadowbanks Sports Centre, London Road, Edinburgh.
MAY – EARLY
British Age-Group Trampoline Championships:
Meadowbank Sports Centre, London Road, Edinburgh.
JUNE – EARLY
Whiteburgh Cup Open Golf Tournament:
Newbattle Golf Course, Abbey Road, Dalkeith.
JUNE – MID/LATE
Open Milk Championships:
Royal Commonwealth Pool, Edinburgh.
JUNE – LATE
Open Mixed Golf Foursomes:
Murrayfield Golf Course, Edinburgh.
JULY – EARLY
Boys Open Golf Tournament:
Harburn Golf Club, West Calder.
JULY – MID
Boys Open Golf Tournament:
Newbattle Golf Course, Abbey Road, Dalkeith.
JULY – MID
British Junior Skiing Championships:
Hillend Ski Slopes, Edinburgh.
JULY – MID/LATE
Dragon Gold Cup (Sailing):
Royal Forth Yachting Club, Edinburgh.
JULY – MID
Open Handicap Golf Tournament:
Harburn Golf Club, West Calder.
AUGUST – EARLY
Open Scratch Golf Tournament:
Harburn Golf Club, West Calder.
AUGUST – LATE
Skiing Festival Slalom:
Hillend Ski Centre, Edinburgh.
AUGUST – LATE
Edinburgh Croquet Club Annual Tournament:
Dunfermline College, Cramond, Edinburgh.
SEPTEMBER – LATE
Meadowbank Open Table Tennis Championships:
Meadowbank Sports Centre, London Road, Edinburgh.

NOVEMBER – EARLY
European Junior Judo Championships:
Meadowbank Sports Centre, London Road, Edinburgh.
NOVEMBER – LATE
British Artificial Ski Slopes Championships:
Hillend Ski Slopes, Biggar Road, Edinburgh.
DECEMBER – MID
British Schools Ski Championships:
Hillend Ski Centre, Edinburgh.

Highland Games:

AUGUST – MID
Edinburgh Highland Games:
Meadowbank Stadium, Edinburgh.

―――――**MISCELLANEOUS**―――――

MARCH – (BEGINS)
Royal Scottish Academy Annual Exhibition:
Edinburgh.
MAY – 1ST WEEK
National Solo Piping Competition:
Royal Arch Chambers, Edinburgh.
MAY – 3RD WEEK
National Beating Retreat:
Castle Esplanade, Edinburgh.
AUGUST – MID, TO SEPTEMBER – EARLY
Edinburgh Military Tatoo:
The Castle Esplanade, Royal Mile, Edinburgh.
SEPTEMBER – 2ND WEEK
Historical Re-Enactment: Sealed Knot Society:
Edinburgh.
NOVEMBER – 1ST WEEK
Firework Displays:
Meadowbank Sports Centre; Saughton Park Enclosure; City Park, Edinburgh.

―――――――◆―――――――

SCOTTISH NATIONAL ORCHESTRA PROMS
Sir Alex Gibson conducting the last night at the Proms inside the Usher Hall, Edinburgh. See: FESTIVALS.

EDINBURGH MILITARY TATTOO
An impressive and spectacular floodlit occasion at the Castle Esplanade. The Tattoo is one of the most famous of its kind in Britain. See: MISCELLANEOUS

LOTHIAN
◆ *West Lothian* ◆

OLD CUSTOMS

JUNE – 1ST SATURDAY
John Newland's Day:
Bathgate.
John Newland went overseas and made his fortune. When he returned to Bathgate he generously provided the town with money to build schools, a library and other public services. The town remembers his generosity with celebrations every year.
JUNE – TUESDAY AFTER 2ND THURSDAY
Riding of the Marches:
Linithgow Common, Linithgow.
AUGUST – EARLY
Burry Man's Day:
South Queensferry.
A most curious custom whereby a native man of Queensferry is literally covered from head to foot with the burrs of the burdock plant, (this is said to have originated with a man long ago who was shipwrecked and, having no clothes, dressed himself in burrs) and then parades through the streets.

FESTIVALS

JUNE – MID
Livingston Festival & Carnival:
Livingston.

PAGEANTS

JUNE
Bathgate Academy Procession & Pageant:
Bathgate.

SPORTS

AUGUST – LATE
Cummings Golf Trophy:
Greenburgh Golf Course, Bridge Street, Fauldhouse.

Highland Games:

MAY – LATE
Bathgate Highland Games:
Glasgow Road, Bathgate.

◆

THE BURRY MAN
This is, perhaps, the most curious of all Scotland's surviving ancient customs. The Burry Man, covered from head to foot in burrs from the Burdock plant and supported by staves decorated with garlands of flowers, makes his way through the streets of Queensferry. See: OLD CUSTOMS.

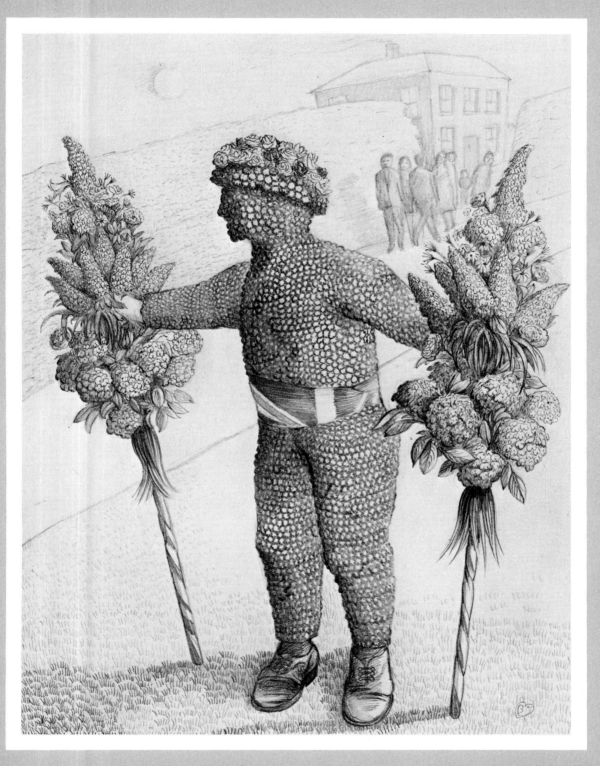

STRATHCLYDE
◆ *Argyllshire* ◆

SEAS · AR · COIR

Here the crow starves, here the patient stag
Breeds for the rifle. Between the soft moor
And the soft sky, scarcely room
To leap or soar.
FROM 'RANNOCH, BY GLEN COE' BY T.S.
ELLIOT.

FESTIVALS

APRIL – 4TH WEEK
Mull Music Society Festival:
Details: The Committee, The Mull Music Festival, Aros Hall, Tobermory, Isle of Mull.
JUNE – LATE, TO JULY – EARLY
Tarbert Loch Fyne Seafood Festival:
Quayside, Tarbert.

FAIRS

JULY – LAST SATURDAY
Tarbert Pleasure Fair:
Tarbert.

HIGHLAND GATHERINGS

AUGUST – 4TH WEEK
The Argyllshire Highland Gathering:
Oban.

AUGUST
Cowal Highland Gathering:
Dunoon.

AGRICULTURAL, HORTICULTURAL & BREED SHOWS

FEBRUARY/MARCH
Highland Cattle Society Spring Show & Sale:
Oban.
AUGUST
Appin Agricultural Show:
Appin.
OCTOBER
Highland Cattle Society Autumn Show and Sale:
Oban.
AUGUST – 1ST WEEK
Scottish National Sheepdog Trials:
Kilmartin.

AUGUST – 2ND WEEK
Strontian Agricultural Show:
Strontian.
AUGUST – LATE
Salen Agricultural Show:
Glenaros, Isle of Mull.
AUGUST
Appin Sheepdog Trials:
Appin.
SEPTEMBER – 1ST WEEK
Dalmally Agricultural Show:
Mart Park, Dalmally.

SPORTS

FEBRUARY
Scottish Kandahar Ski-ing Trophy:
Glencoe.
FEBRUARY
East of Scotland Ski-ing Championships:
Glencoe.
APRIL
Pitman Quaich Ski-ing Cup:
Glencoe.
JUNE – MID
McGilchrist Cup Golf Trophy:
Ardeer Golf Club, Greenhead.
AUGUST – EARLY
West Coast Yachting Week:
Oban, Crinan, and Tobermory Area, Isle of Mull.

Highland Games:

JULY – MID
Mull Highland Games:
Tobermory, Isle of Mull.
JULY – LATE
Inveraray Highland Games:
Inveraray.
JULY
Lochaline Highland Games:
Lochaline.
JULY
Taynuilt Highland Games:
AUGUST – LATE
Dunoon and Cowal Highland Games:
Dunoon.
SEPTEMBER – MID
Oban Highland Games:
Oban.

Regattas:

AUGUST
Tarbert Yacht Regatta:
Tarbert.

OBAN GAMES
Stewards, including the Duke of Argyll, march from Oban railway station to the Games field at the start of the annual Games. See: SPORTS.

TARBERT 'LOCH FYNE' SEAFOOD FESTIVAL
Various entertainments such as the Raft Race pictured here go to make up the week's celebrations and include tug-of-war, concerts, the crowning of the Sea Food Queen and a Fishing Boat Parade. See: FESTIVALS.

TARBERT FAIR
In September 1705 an Act was passed by Scottish Parliament in favour of four yearly fairs at the town of East Tarbert. The present Annual Fair is a three-day occasion set up along the Harbour Front on the main street and is one of Scotland's few remaining street fairs. See: FAIRS.

STRATHCLYDE
◆ *Ayrshire* ◆
(INCLUDING ARRAN)

GOD·SCHAW·THE·RICHL·

That sacred hour can I forget
Can I forget the hallowed grove
Where by the winding Ayr we met
To live one day of parting love
ROBERT BURNS

OLD CUSTOMS

JANUARY 25
Burns Night Celebrations:
Ayr.

FESTIVALS

FEBRUARY – 2ND WEEK
Ayrshire One-Act Drama Festival:
Concert Hall, Troon.
MARCH
Ayrshire Music Festival:
Kilmarnock.
JUNE – 3RD WEEK
Robert Burns Festival:
Kilmarnock, Ayr.
JULY – 4TH WEEK
Brisbane Queen Festival:
Largs.
JULY – 4TH WEEK
Ayr Boat Festival:
Ayr.
AUGUST – 2ND WEEK
Scottish Dingy Festival:
Lamlash, Isle of Arran.
AUGUST – 3RD WEEK
Irvine Marymass Festival:
Irvine.

SEPTEMBER – 1ST OR 2ND WEEK
Viking Festival:
Largs.

FAIRS

AUGUST
Beith Carnival Fair:
Beith.
OCTOBER – 2ND WEEK
Troon Boat Fair:
Troon.
JUNE
Colin's Day Fair:
Larg.

GALAS

JULY – 2ND WEEK
Heather Queen Gala:
Lamlash, Isle of Arran.

SHOWS

JUNE – 1ST WEEK
The Prestwick Air Show:
Prestwick.
OCTOBER

Scottish Boat Show:
Troon Marina, The Harbour, Troon.

AGRICULTURAL, HORTICULTURAL & BREED SHOWS

APRIL
Ayr Agricultural Show:
Ayr.
APRIL
Ochiltree Agricultural Show:
Ochiltree.
MAY
Neilston Agricultural Show:
Neilston.
MAY – 3RD WEEK
Dalrymple Agricultural Show:
Dalrymple.
JUNE – 2ND WEEK
Straiton Cattle Show:
Straiton, Maybole.
JUNE – 3RD WEEK
Brodick Sheepdog Trials:
Brodick, Isle of Arran.
AUGUST – 1ST WEEK
Doonvalley Sheepdog Trials:
Dalfarson Park, Loch Doon,
Dalmellington.
AUGUST – 2ND WEEK
Lamlash Horticultural Show:
Lamlash.
AUGUST – 3RD WEEK
Dalrymple Show:
Hollybush, Dalrymple.
JULY – 3RD WEEK

Isle of Arran Sheepdog Trials:
Machrie, Isle of Arran.
AUGUST
Dailly Flower Show:
Dailly.
AUGUST
Ayr Flower Show:
Ayr.
SEPTEMBER
Mauchline Agricultural Show:
Mauchline.

SPORTS

APRIL OR MAY
Lamlash Golf Week:
Lamlash, Isle of Arran.
MAY — EARLY
Brodick Golf Week:
Brodick, Isle of Arran.
MAY — MID
Whiting Bay Golf Week:
Whiting Bay, Isle of Arran.
JUNE — EARLY
Clyde International Dinghy Week:
Largs Sailing Club, Largs.

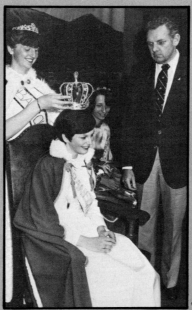

THE HEATHER QUEEN
The Queen, newly crowned and dressed in her ceremonial robes, sits on her throne surrounded by attendants during the summer gala staged in Lamlash on the Isle of Arran. See: GALAS.

◆

JUNE — MID
Arran Open Golf Championships:
Brodick Golf Course, Brodick, Isle of Arran.
JUNE — LATE
West of Scotland Boat Championships:
Saltcoats.

◆

BRISBANE QUEEN FESTIVAL
During July a Queen is elected and crowned who then becomes the figurehead of the festival. She attends various functions which take place including the Decorated Wheels Car Competition and the Crazy Boat Race. See: FESTIVALS.

191

VIKING FESTIVAL
In the 13th century Scotland was beset by Viking invaders but after some fierce fighting at the Battle of Largs, King Haakon and his band were driven off. Today, Largs is a popular Clydeside resort about twenty-five miles from Glasgow, and the Battle of Largs is celebrated by a week of events with mock battles, firework displays, processions, walks, talks, films and fun. See: FESTIVALS.

◆

JULY – EARLY
Stone Golf Trophy:
Routenburn Golf Course, Largs.
JULY – EARLY
Golf Fortnight:
Lamlash Golf Club, Lamlash, Isle of Arran.
JULY – EARLY
Field Day Golf Competition:
Routenburn Golf Course, Largs.
JULY – MID
Fairs Golf Cup:
Corrie Golf Club, Sannox, Isle of Arran.
JULY – MID
Clayburn Golf Trophy:
Brodick Golf Course, Brodick, Isle of

Arran.
JULY – LATE
Arran Riding Club Showjumping and Gymkhana:
Isle of Arran.
JULY
Clyde Sailing Week:
Largs.
AUGUST – MID
Rosa Burn Golf Trophy:
Brodick Golf Course, Brodick, Isle of Arran.
AUGUST – MID
Mainholm Golf Cup:
Westwood Avenue, Ayr.
AUGUST – MID
Boys Golf Internationals:
Kilmarnock Golf Club, Strathclyde.
AUGUST – LATE
Prestwick Golf Foursomes:
St. Cuthbert Golf Course, Prestwick.
SEPTEMBER – EARLY
Largs & Millport Weekly News Golf Trophy:
Routenburn Golf Course, Largs.
SEPTEMBER – MID
European Open Golf Championship:
Ailsa Course, Turnberry.

Highland Games:

JUNE – MID
Ardrossan Highland Games:
Ardrossan.
JUNE – MID
Irvine New Town Highland Games:
Eglinton Park, Irvine Road, Irvine New Town, Kilvinning.
AUGUST – EARLY
Brodick Highland Games:
Brodick, Isle of Arran.

Regattas:

AUGUST
Largs Regatta:
Largs.

MISCELLANEOUS

MAY – MID
Arran Spring Weekend and Goatfell Race:
Isle of Arran.
JUNE – 1ST WEEK
Fiddlers Rally:
Blairquhan Castle, Straiton, Maybole.

STRATHCLYDE

Buteshire ◆

FESTIVALS

AUGUST – 3RD WEEK
Bute Highland Festival:
Bute.

SPORTS

AUGUST – LATE
Bute Highland Games:
Bute.

STRATHCLYDE
Dunbartonshire ◆

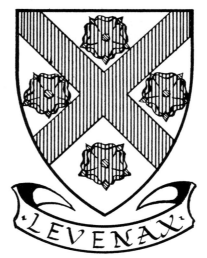

·LEVENAX·

GALAS

JUNE OR JULY
Helensburgh Gala:
Helensburgh.
JUNE OR JULY
Renton Gala:
Renton.
JUNE OR JULY
Alexandria Gala:
Alexandria.

AGRICULTURAL, HORTICULTURAL & BREED SHOWS

MAY
Dunbartonshire Agricultural Show:
Helensburgh.
SEPTEMBER – 2ND WEEK
Milngavie Horticultural Society Flower Show:
Town Hall, Station Road, Milngavie.

SPORTS

JUNE – EARLY
"Gordon Shield" Open Golf Competition:
Dumbarton Golf Course, Dumbarton.
JUNE – MID
Scottish Albacore Sailing Championships:
Helensburgh Sailing Club, Helensburgh.

Highland Games:

JUNE – MID
Bearsden & Milngavie Highland Games:
Kilmardinny Rugby Ground, Bearsden.
JULY – MID
Luss Highland Games:
Games Field, Luss.
JULY – MID
Balloch (Loch Lomond) Highland Games:
Moss o Balloch Park, Balloch.

RENTON GALA
Children indulge in slap-stick fun with a foam machine provided by the local fire brigade. See: GALAS.

ROSMEATH GAMES
Two worthy contestants attempt to unseat one another in the log fight event, a traditional game at Rosmeath. See: SPORTS.

STRATHCLYDE
◆ Lanarkshire ◆

*O*n *Tintock Tap there is a mist,*
And in the mist there is a Kist,
And in the Kist there is a caup,
And in the camp there is a draup,
Tak up the caup; drink off the draup,
And set the caup on Tintock Tap.
LOCAL RHYME

OLD CUSTOMS

MARCH I
Whuppity Scoorie:
Lanark.
This curious custom is thought to be a survival from an ancient pagan ritual for keeping evil winter spirits away. Children circle three times around the church while the bell tolls carrying strings with paper balls attached. Then follows a mock battle which ends in a mass scramble for coins tossed on the ground by town officials.

JUNE – I THURSDAY
Lanimer Day & Riding the Marches:
Lanark.
The elected Lanimer Queen leads various processions through the town decorated with flags and bunting.

AUGUST
Race for the Red Hose:
Carnwath.
The oldest foot-race in Britain run over a one-mile course and part of the local Highland Games. The winner receives a pair of red socks (and a small sum of money).

OCTOBER 31
Hallowe'en Celebrations:
Provand's Lordship, Glasgow.
Traditional activities include dooking for apples, burning sweetheart nuts and entertainment by a group of guisers.

DECEMBER 31 (NEW YEAR'S EVE)
Burning the Old Year Out:
Biggar.

FESTIVALS

FEBRUARY
Pollock Festival of Music, Dancing and Elocution:
Glasgow.
Details: W.M. Pollock, 289 Tantallon Road, Glasgow, G41 3JW.

MARCH
Scottish Co-Operative Musical & Drama Association Festival:
Glasgow.
Details: Mrs. M.C. Gowers, 181 Leithland Road, Glasgow, G53 5AU.

MARCH
Lanarkshire Music Festival:
Details: J. Rarity, 68 Russell Street, Hamilton, ML3 9HY.

APRIL/SEPTEMBER
Motherwell International Festival Fortnight:
Civic Centre, Motherwell.

MAY
Scottish Co-Operative Arts Festival:
Glasgow.
Details: Educational Association, 95 Morrison Street, Glasgow, G5 8LR.

MAY – 4TH WEEK
Eastwood Festival:
Glasgow.

JULY – 2ND WEEK
Glasgow Festival of Folk Music and Dance:
Glasgow.

SEPTEMBER – 3RD WEEK
Festival of Contemporary Music:
University of Glasgow, Glasgow.

OCTOBER/NOVEMBER
Railway Staff Association for Scotland Festival of Music, Speech and Dancing:
Details: John Pendlebury, 58 Port Dundas Road, Glasgow, G4 OHG.

FAIRS

MAY – 4TH WEEK
Glasgow Annual Antiques Fair:
Albany Hotel, Glasgow.

AUGUST – 3RD & 4TH WEEKS
Autumn Gifts Fair:
Kelvin Hall, Glasgow.

CARNIVALS

DECEMBER – IST WEEK, TO JANUARY – 3RD WEEK
Glasgow Carnival:
Kelvin Hall, Glasgow.

CELEBRATIONS

JUNE – 2ND WEEK
Lanimer Celebrations:
Lanark.

GALAS

JUNE – 2ND WEEK
Lanark Gala Day:
Lanark.

HIGHLAND GATHERINGS

MAY – 3RD WEEK
Glasgow Highland Gathering:
Scotstown Showground, Glasgow.

SHOWS

NOVEMBER – 2ND WEEK
Scottish Motor Show:
Kelvin Hall, Glasgow.

AGRICULTURAL, HORTICULTURAL & BREED SHOWS

FEBRUARY
Scottish Dairy Show and National Stallion Show:
Kelvin Hall, Glasgow.
MAY 26
Lesmahagow Cattle Show:
Langside Farm, Lanark.
MAY
Lanarkshire Agricultural Show:
Hamilton.
MAY
Scottish Kennel Club Dog Championship:
Glasgow.
JUNE – 4TH WEEK
Pony Gymkhana & Sheepdog Trials:
Rouken Glen Park, Glasgow.
AUGUST – EARLY
Scottish National Sweet Pea, Rose & Carnation Annual Flower Show:
Motherwell Civic Centre, Airbles Road, Motherwell.
AUGUST – 4TH WEEK
City of Glasgow Horse Show & Country Fair:
Bellahouston Park, Glasgow.
AUGUST – 4TH WEEK
Port Glasgow Horticultural Show:
Port Glasgow.
AUGUST
Biggar Cattle Show:
Biggar.
AUGUST
Carnwath Agricultural Show:
Carnwath.
AUGUST
Abington Cattle Show:
Abington.
AUGUST
Stonehouse Agricultural Show:
Stonehouse.

SEPTEMBER
Crawfordjohn Sheep Trials:
Crawfordjohn.

SPORTS

MAY – EARLY
British National Team Judo Championship:
Kelvin Hall, Glasgow.
MAY – LATE
The Tomatin Cruising Trophy:
Clyde Cruising Club, Glasgow.
MAY – LATE
Morrison Golf Trophy & Lessie Gringean Golf Trophy:
Shotts Golf Club, Shotts.
JUNE – EARLY
Scottish National Aeromodelling Championships:
Lanark Racecourse, Lanark.
JUNE – MID
Tenant Golf Cup:
Glasgow Golf Club, Killermont.
JUNE – MID
Scottish Rifle Championships:
Dechmont Range, Cambuslang.
JUNE – MID
Bishopbriggs Golf Trophy:
Bishopbriggs Golf Club, Brachenbrae and Bishopbriggs.
JUNE – LATE
Biggar Amateur Open Golf Competition:
Municipal Park, Broughton Road, Biggar.
JUNE – LATE
Grand Prix Cycle Race:
Glasgow Green, Glasgow.
JULY – EARLY
Open Golf Championships:
Lanark Golf Course, The Moor, Lanark.
JULY – EARLY
Lanarkshire Golf Open Handicap Mixed Foursomes:
Carnwath Golf Course, Carnwath.
JULY – EARLY
West Region Skateboard Championships:
Kelvingrove Park, Glasgow.
JULY – MID
Lanarkshire Golf Open Scratch Competition (Lockhart de Robeck Trophy):
Carnwath.
JULY – LATE
Shotts Fair Open 18 Golf Handicap:
Shotts Golf Club, Blairhead, Shotts.
AUGUST – EARLY
Dewars Scottish Bowling Championships:
Queens Park Bowling Club, Glasgow.
AUGUST – MID
Blochairn Open Golf Competition

Trophy:
Colville Park Golf Course, Motherwell.
AUGUST – MID
McKee Open Golf Cup:
Shotts Golf Club, Shotts.
AUGUST – MID
Glasgow Boys Golf Championships:
Littlehill Golf Course, Springburn, Glasgow.
AUGUST – MID
Drumpellier Golf Cup:
Drumpellier Golf Club, Coatbridge.
AUGUST – MID/LATE
Robertson Golden Shred Golf Trophy:
Braehead.
AUGUST – LATE
Glasgow District Council Golf Championships:
Pollock Park, Glasgow.
AUGUST – LATE
Scottish Skateboard National Championships:
Kelvingrove Skatepark, Glasgow.
SEPTEMBER – MID
Eastwood Quaiche Golf Tournament:
Eastwood Golf Club, Muirfield Loganswell, Mewton Mearns, Glasgow.
OCTOBER – MID
Glasgow Junior Championships & Open Gymnastics Meeting:
Springburn Sports Centre, Springburn.

Highland Games:

JUNE – EARLY
Airdrie Highland Games:
Rawyards Park, Airdrie.
JUNE
Lesmahagow Highland Games:
Lesmahagow.
JULY – EARLY
Carluke Highland Games:
Scotstown Playing Fields, Carluke.
SEPTEMBER – EARLY
Shotts Highland Games:
Hannah Park, Dykehead, Shotts.

Regattas:
MAY – 2ND WEEK
Strathclyde Park International Regatta:
Glasgow.
JUNE – 2ND WEEK
Scottish Championships Regatta:
Strathclyde Park, Glasgow.

MISCELLANEOUS

JUNE – 2ND WEEK
Pipe Band Contest:
Queens Park, Glasgow.
AUGUST – 2ND WEEK
Strathclyde Police Tattoo:
Kelvin Hall, Glasgow.

STRATHCLYDE
◆ Renfrewshire ◆

FESTIVALS

JANUARY/FEBRUARY
Inverclyde & Renfrew Musical Festival:
Details: Mrs. J.M. Boyd, 15 Moorfield Road, Gourock.
FEBRUARY – 3RD WEEK
Renfrew & Eastwood One-Act Drama Festival:
Eastwood Theatre, Giffnock.
JUNE – 3RD WEEK
British One-Act Drama Final Festival:
Arts Guild Theatre, Greenock.

AGRICULTURAL, HORTICULTURAL & BREED SHOWS

MAY – 2ND WEEK
Kilmacolm & Port Glasgow Agricultural Show:
The Knapps, Kilmacolm.
JUNE
Kilbarchan Cattle Show:
Kilbarchan.

SPORTS

AUGUST – EARLY
Whinhill Golf Trophy:
Greenock Whinhill, Beith Road, Greenoch.
AUGUST – LATE
Krystal Klear Golf Handicap:
Lochwinnoch Golf Club, Burnfoot Road, Lochwinnoch.
AUGUST – LATE
Golden Shred Golf Tournament:
Paisley Golf Course, Braehead, Paisley.
SEPTEMBER – EARLY
Calum Mixed Foursomes Golf Trophy:
Lochwinnoch Golf Club, Burnfoot Road, Lochwinnoch.

Highland Games:

MAY – MID
Gourock Highland Games:
Gourock Park Playing Fields, Gourock.

MISCELLANEOUS

JUNE
Kilbarchan Lilias Celebrations:
Kilbarchan.

◆

GOUROCK HIGHLAND GAMES
Pipe bands march past officials in Gourock Park playing fields during the town's annual Highland Games. See: SPORTS.

LILIAS WEEK
The crowning of the Queen, morris dancing, fancy dress parade, drum majorettes and many other events go to make up Kilbarchan's annual festivities known as Lilias Day. See: MISCELLANEOUS. ▷

◆ Angus ◆

Bonnie Munross will be a moss, Brechin a braw burgh toun,
But Forfar will be Forfar still when Dundee's a' dung doon!
OLD FORFAR TOWN JINGLE

Old Customs

AUGUST – LATE, OR SEPTEMBER – EARLY
Arbroath Abbey Historical Pageant:
Arbroath.
A commemoration of the Declaration of Scottish Independence in 1320.

Festivals

MARCH
Arbroath & District Music Festival:
Webster Theatre, Arbroath.
MAY/JUNE – BIENNIAL (NEXT ONE 1982)
Dundee Schools' Music Festival:
Dundee.
Details: Adviser in Music, Education Offices, Tayside House, 28 Crichton Street, Dundee DD1 3RL.
JULY – EARLY
Dundee Festival Week:
Dundee.
SEPT/OCT
Montrose Festival:
Details: 212 High Street, Montrose.

Agricultural, Horticultural & Breed Shows

JULY – MID
Kirriemuir Agricultural Show:
Kirriemuir.
JULY
Kirriemuir Sheepdog Trials:
Kirriemuir.
JULY
Angus Agricultural Show:
Arbroath.

Sports

MAY EARLY/MID
Spring Golf Tournament:
Medal Golf Club, Montrose.
MAY – LATE
Scottish Ladies Golf Tournament:
Carnoustie.
JULY – EARLY
Northern Counties Ladies Open Golf:
Carnoustie Medal Links Parade, Carnoustie.
JULY – MID
Scottish Rifle Championships:
Barry Range, Carnoustie.
JULY – LATE
Montrose Caledonia Golf Club, Montrose.

JULY – LATE
Open Amateur Mixed Foursomes Golf Tournament:
Edzell Golf Club, Brechin.
JULY LATE
R.B. Cant Carnoustie Medal Challenge Golf Club:
Links Parade, Carnoustie.
AUGUST – EARLY
MacFadyen Golf Cup:
Vaul Golf Club, Scarinish, Isle of Tiree.
AUGUST
Open Amateur Tennis Tournament:
Montrose.
SEPTEMBER – EARLY
Crows Nest Tassie Open Golf Tournament:
Carnoustie.

Highland Games:

JUNE – MID
Forfar Highland Games:
Lochside Park, Forfar.
JULY – EARLY
Dundee Highland Games:
Dundee.

Miscellaneous

JULY – 3RD WEEK
Glamis Vintage Vehicle Rally:
Strathmore Vintage Vehicle Club, Glamis.
SEPTEMBER – 2ND WEEK
Arbroath Highland Dancing:
Arbroath.

ARBROATH ABBEY PAGEANT
The procession prepares to leave the Abbey
headed by King Robert Bruce and the
Abbot. See: OLD CUSTOMS.

ANGUS SHOW
A general view of the Angus Agricultural
Show which is held in Victoria Park,
Arbroath. See: SHOWS

201

TAYSIDE
◆ Kinross-shire ◆

FOR·ALL·TIME

FESTIVALS

APRIL; JULY; SEPTEMBER; OCTOBER;
DECEMBER
Ledlanet Nights:
Ledlanet, Milnathort.
SEPTEMBER — 2ND WEEK
Kinross Folk Festival:
*Details: Publicity Officer, T.M.S.A., 12
Mansfield Road, Scone, Perth.*

SPORT

MAY — LATE
**Milnathort Gents Open Golf
Tournament:**
Milnathort Golf Club, Milnathort.

AGRICULTURAL.
HORTICULTURAL &
BREED SHOWS

AUGUST — 2ND WEEK
Kinross Agricultural Show:
Grounds of Kinross House, Kinross.

KINROSS AGRICULTURAL SHOW
*The County Show is held in the grounds of
historic Kinross House. See: SHOWS.*

TAYSIDE
◆ Perthshire ◆

OLD CUSTOMS

DECEMBER 31 (NEW YEAR'S EVE)
Flambeaux Procession:
Comrie.
This custom was once a pagan rite and is now a fancy dress Hogmany celebration where the townspeople, accompanied by pipes and walking in torch-light procession, march to the market square.

FESTIVALS

FEBRUARY – 3RD WEEK
East Perthshire One-Act Drama Festival:
Town Hall, Blairgowrie.
MARCH
Perthshire Musical (Competition) Festival:
Details: Mrs. O.C. Smith, 46 Strathtay Road, Perth.
MARCH
Arbroath & District Musical Festival:
Details: W.E. Forrester, Bank of Scotland Building, Arbroath.
EASTER
Folk Festival:
Glenfarg.
MAY – 3RD & 4TH WEEKS
Perth Festival Fringe:
Perth.
MAY – 4TH WEEK
Perth Festival of the Arts:
Details: Festival Headquarters, Perth Tourist Association, The Round House, Marshall Place, Perth, PH2 8NS.
MAY
National Accordian Society of Great Britain Festival:
Perth.
MAY/OCTOBER
Pitlochry Festival of Drama, Music and Art:
Pitlochry Festival Theatre, Pitlochry.
JUNE – 2ND WEEK
Perthshire and Angus Provincial Mod:
Aberfeldy.
JUNE – 4TH WEEK
Dunkeld & Birnham Arts Festival:
Dunkeld, Birnam & Murthly.
JUNE
Aberfeldy Pipe Band Festival:
Aberfeldy.

◆

◁ ACCORDIAN & FIDDLE FESTIVAL
Traditional Scottish music comes into its own at this All-Scotland Music Festival devoted to the accordian and fiddle. See: FESTIVALS.

SEPTEMBER – 3RD WEEK
All Scotland Accordian and Fiddle Festival:
City Halls, Perth.
OCTOBER – MID
National Mod:
Perth.

FAIRS

OCTOBER – 1ST WEEK
Perthshire Annual Antiques Fair:
Station Hotel, Perth.

HIGHLAND GATHERINGS

AUGUST – MID
Aberfeldy and Breadalbane Highland Gathering:
Aberfeldy.

PARADES

MAY – 4TH WEEK
Parade of the Atholl Highlanders:
Blair Castle, Blair Atholl.

AGRICULTURAL, HORTICULTURAL & BREED SHOWS

FEBRUARY – 1ST WEEK
Spring Show and Sales of Pedigree Cattle:
Perth.
MARCH
Beef Shorthorn Cattle Society Pedigree Show:
Perth.
JULY – 1ST WEEK
Alyth & District Agricultural Show:
Diamond Jubilee Park, Alyth.
JULY – 1ST WEEK
Doune & Dunblane Agricultural Show:
Keir Mains, Dunblane.
JULY – 4TH WEEK
Ardoch Agricultural Show:
Lodge Park, Braco, Nr. Dunblane.
AUGUST – 1ST WEEK
Perth Agricultural Show:
South Inch.
AUGUST – 2ND WEEK
Aberfeldy Agricultural Show:
Victoria Park, Aberfeldy.

◆

FAIR MAID OF PERTH
The occasion is promoted by the local tourist association and the winning girl is elected to represent Perth for the year at various official functions. See:
MISCELLANEOUS.

AUGUST
Callender Sheepdog Trials:
Callender.
AUGUST
Crieff Sheepdog Trials:
Crieff.
AUGUST
Atholl & Headalbane Agricultural Show:
Aberfeldy.
SEPTEMBER
Blairgowrie Agricultural Show:
Blairgowrie.
OCTOBER – 2ND WEEK
Autumn Show and Pedigree Cattle Sale:
Perth.

SPORTS

MARCH
Tennant Skiing Trophy:
Glenshee, Nr. Devil's Elbow.
APRIL OR MAY
Pitlochry Golf Week:
Pitlochry Golf Course, Pitlochry Estate Office, Pitlochry.
MAY – EARLY
Ram's Head Golf Trophy:
Kenmore.
MAY – MID
The Perth Races:
Scone Racecourse, Perth.
MAY – LATE
The Famous Grouse Scone Palace Carriage Driving Championships:
Scone Palace, Perth.
JUNE – MID
Crieff Ladies' Open Golf Tournament:
Crieff.
JUNE – MID
Scottish Open Hang Gliding Championships:
Cairnwell Mountains, Glenshee.
JUNE – MID/LATE
The Great Kenmore and Aberfeldy Raft Race:
River Tay – Kenmore to Aberfeldy.
JUNE – LATE
Strathearn Open Golf Tournament:
Crieff Golf Club, Crieff.
JULY – EARLY
Mixed Foursomes Open Golf Tournament:
Callender Golf Course, Callender.
JULY – EARLY
Open Gents Golf Tournament:
Dunblane Golf Club, Dunblane.
JULY – MID
Ladies' Highland Amateur Open Golf Tournament:
Pitlochry Golf Course, Pitlochry.
JULY – MID
Calder Golf Cup:

Pitlochry Golf Course, Pitlochry Estate Office, Pitlochry.
JULY – MID
Edinburgh Golf Cup:
Pitlochry Golf Course, Pitlochry.
JULY – LATE
Fiery Cross Open Golf Tournament:
Callender.
JULY – LATE
Jack Scott Punchbowl Open Golf Tournament:
Callender Golf Course, Callender.
AUGUST – EARLY
Harp Lager Amateur Open Golf Tournament:
Dalmunzie Hotel Golf Course, Blairgowrie.
AUGUST – EARLY
Colonel Butler's Golf Foursomes:
Pitlochry Golf Course, Pitlochry Estate Office, Pitlochry.
AUGUST – MID
Annual Bowling Tournament:
Perth.
AUGUST – MID
Men's Amateur Open Golf Tournament:
Pitlochry Golf Course, Pitlochry.
AUGUST – 2ND WEEK
Dunning Open Golf Tournament:
Dunning Golf Course, Rollo Recreation Ground, Dunning.
AUGUST – 2ND WEEK
Motorcycle Trials:
South Inch, Perth.
AUGUST – 3RD WEEK
Scone Palace Polo Tournament:
Perth.
AUGUST – 4TH WEEK
Morton Burnet Golf Trophy:
Crieff Golf Club, Crieff.
AUGUST
Bridge of Allan Athletic Sports Meeting:
Bridge of Allan.
AUGUST
Highland Golf Championship:
Pitlochry.
SEPTEMBER – 1ST WEEK
Targe Golf Trophy:
Kenmore Golf Course, Kenmore.
SEPTEMBER
Highland Tennis Championship:
Pitlochry.

Highland Games:

MAY – LATE
Blackford Highland Games, Blackford.
JULY – EARLY
Kenmore Highland Games:
Playing Field, Aberfeldy, Kenmore.
JULY – MID
Blairgowrie Highland Games:

GLENSHEE SNOW FUN WEEK
A week of winter fun and games in a major ski-ing area, north of Perth; skiers of all ages and expertise are welcome, with ski-ing, tobogganing and snowman-building, while evenings are packed with ceilidhs, folk nights, dinner dances and other entertainment. Families especially welcome. See: MISCELLANEOUS.

◆

Blairgowrie.
JULY – LATE
Balquhidder, Lochearnhead and Strathyre Highland Games:
Lochearnhead.
JULY
Abefoyle Highland Games:
Abefoyle.
AUGUST – MID
Perth Highland Games:
South Inch, Perth.
AUGUST – MID
Crieff Highland Games:
Market Place, Crieff.
AUGUST – MID
Kinloch Rannoch Highland Games:
Kinloch Rannoch.
AUGUST – LATE
Glenisla Highland Games:

Forter Haugh, Alyth.
AUGUST
Birnam Highland Games:
Games Park, Little Dunkeld, Birnam Recreation Ground.
SEPTEMBER – MID
Dunblane Highland Games:
Laighill Parks, Dunblane.
SEPTEMBER – MID
Pitlochry Highland Games:
Pitlochry.

MISCELLANEOUS

MARCH – 4TH WEEK
Glenshee Snow Fun Week:
Glenshee.
MAY – 4TH WEEK
Perth Victorian Week:
Perth.
JUNE – 4TH WEEK
British Hill Climb:
Doune Motor Museum, Doune.
JUNE – 4TH WEEK
Carnoustie Pipe Band Contest:
Carnoustie House Grounds, Carnoustie.
JULY – 2ND WEEK
Perth Veteran & Vintage Rally:
Perth & District Motor Club, Perth.

◆

RAFT RACE
This immensely popular water contest is an extraordinary sight to see when hundreds of competitors take to their rafts for the annual race on the River Tay. See: SPORTS.

· PART THREE ·
WALES

CLWYD
◆ Denbighshire ◆

DUW · A · DIGON

When soft September brings again
To yonder gorse its golden glow,
And Snowdon sends its autumn rain
To bid thy current livelier flow;
Amid that ashen foliage light
When scarlet beads are glistering bright,
While alder boughs unchanged are seen
In summer livery of green;
When clouds before the cooler breeze
Are flying, white and large; with these
Returning, so I may return,
And find thee changeless, Pont-y-wern.

FROM 'PONT-Y-WERN'
BY ARTHUR HUGH CLOUGH

FESTIVALS

MARCH – 4TH WEEK
Wrexham & District Independent One-Act Drama Festival:
Little Theatre, Hill Street, Wrexham.

Details: Secretary, Mrs. R. Jones, Latchford, Stansty Park, Wrexham.
JUNE – (BIENNIAL)
Garthewin Drama Festival:
Georgian Barn Theatre, Garthewin,
Llanfair, Talaiarn.
JULY – 1ST WEEK
Llangollen International Musical Eisteddfod:
Llangollen.
Details: Secretary, Eisteddfod Office, Victoria Square, Clwyd.
North Wales Music Festival:
St. Asaph Cathedral, St. Asaph.
Details: North Wales Music Festival Office, High Street, St. Asaph.

FAIRS

2ND TUESDAY EACH MONTH; 2ND WEDNESDAY IN JULY
Denbigh Fair:
Denbigh.
EVERY MONDAY EXCEPT AUGUST; APRIL 4; OCTOBER 3 & 17
Wrexham Fair:
Wrexham.
JULY
Ruabon Pleasure Fair:
Ruabon.

———AGRICULTURAL,——— ——HORTICULTURAL &—— ———BREED SHOWS———

AUGUST – 4TH WEEK
Denbigh Flower Show:
Denbigh.
AUGUST
Ruthin Sheep Dog Trials:
Ruthin.
AUGUST
Llangollen Sheep Dog Trials:
Llangollen.

Other Shows:

Ruthin Show:
Ruthin.
*Details: Bron-y-Gaer, Castle Street,
Ruthin.*

INTERNATIONAL MUSICAL
EISTEDDFOD
*This popular cultural gathering is a very
important event in the Welsh calendar.
Founded thirty years ago in the ancient
town of Llangollen, the Eisteddfod attracts
as many as ten thousand competitors who
attend from all over the world. Dancers
perform in national costume and there are
many choral and instrumental competitions
with the concluding concert being a major
orchestral and choral performance. See:
FESTIVALS.*

◆

CLWYD
◆ *Flintshire* ◆

GORAU TARIAN CYFLAWNDER

Old Customs

MAY OR JUNE
Rhyl May Day Celebrations:
Rhyl.
MAY
Rhyl Festival:
Rhyl.

Festivals

JUNE – 2ND WEEK
North Wales Craft Festival:
Deeside Leisure Centre, Queensferry.
JUNE – JULY
Holywell Music Festival:
Details: Crnd-y-Gwynt, Holywell.
SEPTEMBER – 4TH WEEK
North Wales Music Festival:
St. Asaph Cathedral, St. Asaph.

Fairs

1ST SATURDAY EACH MONTH
Flint Fair:
Flint.

Carnivals

AUGUST
Mostyn Carnival (and Fair):
Mostyn.
JULY/AUGUST
Prestatyn Carnival:
Prestatyn.

Galas

JULY
Mold Gala:
Mold.

Agricultural, Horticultural & Breed Shows

MARCH
Rhyl Flower Show:
Rhyl.

Sports

MARCH – 1ST WEEK
National Short Course Swimming Championship:
Rhyl Sports Centre, Rhyl.

RHYL MAY DAY CELEBRATIONS
*A festival of pageant and entertainment
with a wide popular appeal makes the
annual May Day celebrations a captivating
occasion. The Parade is the climax in the
week's proceedings which include morris
dancing, drum majorettes and fancy dress.
See: OLD CUSTOMS.*

DYFED

◆ *Cardiganshire* ◆

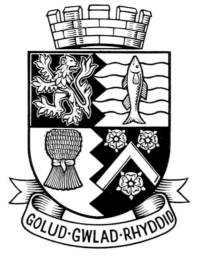

GOLUD·GWLAD·RHYDDID

FESTIVALS

MAY – 1ST WEEK
Aberystwyth Festival:
Aberystwyth.
JUNE
Cardigan Eisteddfod:
Cardigan.
Details: Eisteddfod Office, Cardigan.
AUGUST
Lampeter Eisteddfod:
Lampeter.
Details: Dr. J.L. Williams, Gerltan, Bryn Road, Lampeter.

CARNIVALS

AUGUST
Aberystwyth Carnival:
Aberystwyth.
AUGUST – LATE
Cardigan Civic Week Carnival:
Cardigan.

AGRICULTURAL, HORTICULTURAL & BREED SHOWS

MAY OR JUNE
Aberystwyth & District Agricultural Show:
Aberystwyth.
JULY
Aberystwyth Sheep Dog Trials:
Aberystwyth.
AUGUST
Tivyside Agricultural Show:
Newcastle Emlyn.
SEPTEMBER
Lampeter Agricultural Show:
Lampeter.
SEPTEMBER
Talybont & North Cardigan Agricultural Show:
Talybont.

SPORTS

AUGUST
Aberayron Regatta:
Aberayron.

MISCELLANEOUS

AUGUST – MID
The Coracle Week:
Cilgerran.

◆

CARDIGAN EISTEDDFOD
The delightful presentation of flowers takes place during the chairing ceremony at Cardigan's annual Eisteddfod. See: FESTIVALS.
▽

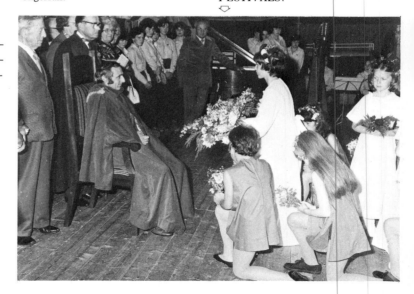

DYFED
Carmarthenshire ◆

RHYDDID · GWERIN · FFYNIANT · GWLAD

The mountains round, unhappy fate!
Sooner or later, of all height,
Withdraw their summits from the skies,
And lessen as the others rise:
Still the prospect wider spreads,
Adds a thousand woods and meads,
Still it widens, widens still,
And sinks the newly-risen hill.

Now I gain the mountain's brow,
What a landscape lies below!
FROM 'GRONGAR HILL' BY JOHN
DYER

OLD CUSTOMS

JANUARY – 1ST WEEK
Mary Lwyd:
Various venues throughout
Carmarthenshire.
A form of hobby-horse which consists of a
horse's skull decked with ribbons is
carried about with jollity during the
Christmas/New Year period.
WHITSUNTIDE
Common Walk:
Laugharne.
The Corporation of Laugharne's traditional
'Beating of the Bounds' in which the Mayor
leads a procession of officials and town folk
on a tour of the corporation boundaries.

CARNIVALS

JULY – 1ST WEEK
Carmarthen Carnival:
Carmarthen.

FAIRS

AUGUST
Llanstephen Fair:
Llanstephen.

AGRICULTURAL, HORTICULTURAL & BREED SHOWS

MAY
Cothi Bridge Agricultural Show:
Nantgaredig.
AUGUST
United Counties Agricultural Society
Show:
The Mount, Carmarthen.

COMMON WALK
Starting from the town the procession of Corporation officials and residents, led by the standard-bearer, make their way across Portreeve Leadink and then circle the Cross Inn on their return. See: OLD CUSTOMS.

DYFED
◆ Pembrokeshire ◆

─── OLD CUSTOMS ───

MARCH 1 (ST. DAVID'S DAY)

St. David's Day:

St. David's Cathedral, St. David's.

A special commemoration service is held every year in the cathedral for St. David, the Patron Saint of Wales. He is thought to have settled in Pembrokeshire during the 6th century where he set up the principal seat of Christianity in the West. Also on this day it is now customary for every member of a Welsh regiment to be ceremonially presented with a leek.

AUGUST 21

Beating the Bounds:

Newport.

AUGUST 29

Beca Mountain Race:

Mynachlogddu area of Presli.

To commemorate the Rebecca riots this race is held in which the first two or three contestants back who have sucessfully run up and down the mountain, jump into women's clothing. The first of the winners so dressed to run through the facsimile tollgate must then chop it down with an axe.

◆

'BECA' MOUNTAIN RACE ⬅

The first of the contestants down the mountains gets ready to chop down the fascimile tollgate at the end of the Beca mountain race. See: OLD CUSTOMS.

BEATING THE BOUNDS

During the annual walk around the parish boundary of Newport the boys are 'beaten' at each boundary to help them remember each one. See: OLD CUSTOMS. ⇨

FESTIVALS

JANUARY – 3RD WEEK
Pembrokeshire Federation of Young Farmers' Clubs Drama Festival:
Milford Haven.
MAY – 4TH WEEK
St. David's Cathedral Bach Festival:
St. David's Cathedral, St. David's.
JULY – 3RD & 4TH WEEKS
Fishguard Music Festival:
Details: Festival Secretary, Festival Office, Summerhill, Fishguard, SA65 9BJ.
AUGUST
St. David's Arts Festival:
St. David's.

CARNIVALS

JUNE
Saundersfoot Carnival:
Saundersfoot.
AUGUST
Haverfordwest Carnival:
Haverfordwest.

FAIRS

2ND TUESDAY EACH MONTH;
SEPTEMBER 20; OCTOBER 5 & 18

Haverfordwest Fair:
Haverfordwest.
LAST MONDAY IN EACH MONTH;
OCTOBER 10
Pembroke Fair:
Pembroke.
JULY 31; AUGUST 1
Tenby Fair:
Tenby.
JULY – 2ND WEEK
St. Margaret's Fair:
Tenby.

AGRICULTURAL, HORTICULTURAL & BREED SHOWS

AUGUST – 3RD WEEK
Haverfordwest Show:
Haverfordwest.

SPORTS

AUGUST – 3RD WEEK
Coracle Races:
River Teifi, Cilgerran.
DECEMBER 26 (BOXING DAY)
Boxing Day Swim:
North Beach, Tenby.

Regattas:

AUGUST – 4TH WEEK
Saundersfoot Regatta: County Regatta: Round the Island Race:
Saundersfoot.
AUGUST (SOMETIMES JUNE)
Milford Haven Regatta:
Milford Haven.

MISCELLANEOUS

MAY
Brawdy Air Day:
R.A.F. Brawdy, Haverfordwest.
JUNE
Bryberian Sheepdog Trials:
Bryberian.
AUGUST
Haverfordwest Sheepdog Trials:
Haverfordwest.

◆

BOXING DAY SWIM
Although this event is only ten years old it is one of the biggest mass swimming gatherings of the winter. Bathers, often in their hundreds, take to the north beach at Tenby and brave the icy waters of the sea. See: SPORTS.
▽

MID, SOUTH & WEST GLAMORGAN
◆ *Glamorganshire* ◆

A · DDIODDEFWS · A · ORFU

OLD CUSTOMS

JANUARY – 1ST WEEK
Mari Lwyd:
Various venues throughout Glamorgan.
A form of hobby-horse which consists of a horse's skull decked with ribbons and carried about with jollity during the Christmas/New Year period.
OCTOBER – LAST THURSDAY
Apple and Candle Night:
Swansea.
A traditional local Halloween celebration.

FESTIVALS

MARCH – 1ST WEEK
St. David's Day Festival:
Merthyr Tydfil.
MARCH – 4TH WEEK
International Theatre Festival For Young People:
Cardiff (& Milford Haven)
MARCH
Chapter March Festival:
Chapter Arts Centre, Market Road, Cardiff.
MARCH
Cardiff Festival of 20th Century Music:
University College, Cardiff.
APRIL – 2ND WEEK
Swansea Bach Week:
Swansea.
MAY – 2ND WEEK
Maytime Festival of Drama:
Bridgend Recreation Centre, Bridgend.
MAY – 4TH WEEK
Cynon Valley 3-Day Festival:
Aberdare.

MAY
Welsh Jazz Festival:
Chapter Arts Centre, Market Street, Canton, Cardiff.
Details: C.R. Hodgins, 7 Sherbourne Avenue, Cyncoed, Cardiff.
MAY
National Accordian Organisation of Great Britain Festival:
Cardiff.
WHITSUN WEEK
Caerphilly Arts Festival:
Caerphilly.
Craig-Y-Nos Opera Festival:
Adelina Pati Theatre, Craig-y-Nos, Castle Neath.
AUGUST – 3RD WEEK
Royal National Eisteddfod of Wales:
Garseinon.
Details: Director, Eisteddfod Office, Midland Bank Chambers, Bute Street, Cardiff.
AUGUST – 3RD & 4TH WEEKS
Vale of Glamorgan Festival:
St. Donat's Castle, Llantwit-Major, South Glamorgan.
AUGUST – 3RD OR 4TH WEEK
Pontardawe Folk Festival:
Pontardawe.
Details: Bob Williams, 11 Bevans Row, Fabian Way, Port Tennant, Swansea, SA1 8PB.
SEPTEMBER
Bridgend Festival:
Bridgend.
Details: Ms. Suzanne Jones, 28 Cefn Coed, Bridgend.
OCTOBER – 3RD & 4TH WEEKS

Rhymney Valley Arts Festival:
Details: Entertainments Officer, Rhymney Valley District Council, Council Offices, Park Road, Hengoed, Mid-Glamorgan.
OCTOBER
Swansea Festival of Music and the Arts:
Swansea.
Details: Festival Director, The Guildhall, Swansea.
OCTOBER
South Wales Miners' Eisteddfod:
Details: National Union of Mineworkers, S. Wales Area, Sardis Road, Pontypridd.
NOVEMBER – 4TH WEEK, TO
DECEMBER – 1ST WEEK
Cardiff Festival of Music:
Cardiff.
Details: Cardiff Festival, Dept. of Music, Univesity College, P.O. Box 78, Cardiff.

FAIRS

APRIL 1 & 16; NOVEMBER 13
Aberdare Fair:
Aberdare.
APRIL 1; NOVEMBER 17
Bridgend Fair:
Bridgend.
WHIT MONDAY; SEPTEMBER 19
Cardiff Fair:
Cardiff.
2ND SUNDAY IN MAY; JULY 2; AUGUST 15; OCTOBER 8
FEBRUARY – 2ND WEEK
South Wales Gift Fair:
Sophia Gardens Pavilion, Cardiff.

⌂
WELSH JAZZ FESTIVAL
*Jazz has a loyal following in South Wales
and fans are privileged with one of the
country's finest jazz festivals which is held in
Cardiff during the Spring. See:
FESTIVALS.*

◆

MARCH
Pontardawe Fair:
Pontardawe.
AUGUST – 3RD WEEK
Lord Mayor's Parade:
Cardiff.

CARNIVALS

JULY – LATE
Barry Carnival:
Barry.

AGRICULTURAL. HORTICULTURAL & BREED SHOWS

AUGUST
Gower Agricultural Society Show:
Penrice Castle Park, Nr. Reynoldston.
AUGUST
Barry Flower Show & Gymkhana:
Barry.
AUGUST
Vale of Glamorgan Agricultural Show:
Penllyn Castle Park, Nr. Cowbridge.
AUGUST
Dyffryn Sheepdog Trials:
Dyffryn.
SEPTEMBER
International Sheepdog Trials:
Cardiff.

SPORTS

FEBRUARY – 1ST WEEK
Indoor Canoe Slalom:
National Sports Centre, Cardiff.
FEBRUARY – 3RD WEEK
Glamorgan Welsh Amateur Fencing

Union Tournament:
National Sports Centre, Cardiff.
FEBRUARY – 4TH WEEK
Welsh Squash Junior Championships:
City Squash Raquets Club, Swansea.
MARCH – 2ND WEEK
South Wales Archery Championships:
National Sports Centre, Cardiff.
MARCH – 2ND WEEK
Basketball Knockout Cup Final:
National Sports Centre, Cardiff.
MARCH – 4TH WEEK
**Welsh International Judo Open
Championships:**
National Sports Centre, Cardiff.
MARCH – LATE, TO APRIL – EARLY
**Welsh Closed Table Tennis
Championships:**
National Sports Centre, Cardiff.
JUNE – 3RD WEEK
**Benson & Hedges International
Showjumping Championships:**
Cardiff Castle, Cardiff.
JULY
Welsh Amateur Golf Championship:
Porthcawl.
SEPTEMBER – 2ND WEEK

Vagliano Golf Trophy:
Royal Porthcawl Golf Club, Porthcawl.

────Miscellaneous────

AUGUST — 1ST & 2ND WEEKS (EVERY
TWO YEARS — NEXT ONE 1983)
Cardiff Searchlight Tattoo:
Cardiff Castle, Cardiff.

LLANDAFF FESTIVAL ⇦
*The cathedral festival of Llandaff was
founded in 1958 and is centred on the
historic Gothic church at Llandaff, one of
the most sacred buildings in Wales.
Emphasis is on a wide range of music with
oratorios, chamber music and orchestral
works forming the basis of the programme
each year. See: FESTIVALS.*

CARDIFF SEARCHLIGHT TATTOO
*The Tattoo is staged in the court of Cardiff
Castle which is dramatically floodlit for the
occasion. Military units and bands perform
with spectacular clockwork precision during
this memorable pageant.
See: MISCELLANEOUS* ⇨

BARRY CARNIVAL
*The Raft Race is one of the fun events to be
enjoyed at Barry's annual carnival. See:
CARNIVALS.*
⇦

GWENT
◆ *Monmouthshire* ◆

UTRIQUE · FIDELIS

Can I forget the sweet days that have been,
When poetry first began to warm my blood;
When from the hills of Gwent I saw the earth
Burned into two by Severn's silver flood.
FROM 'DAYS THAT HAVE BEEN', BY W.H.
DAVIES

FESTIVALS

MARCH – 1ST & 2ND WEEKS
Newport Drama Festival:
Dalman Theatre, Kingsway, Newport,
Gwent.
MAY – 1ST WEEK
Llantilio Crossenny Festival of Music
& Drama:
Details: Llantilio Crossenny Festival, Old
Cottage, Treadam. Abergavenny.
JUNE/JULY
Lower Machen Summer Festival:
Details: 9 The Gardens, Monmouth, NP5
3HF.
North Gwent Festival of the Arts:
Details: Twr Melyn, Monmouth Road,
Raglan, Gwent, NP5 2HG.

CARNIVALS

MAY – 4TH WEEK
Caldicot Carnival:
Caldicot.

FAIRS

2ND MONDAY IN FEBRUARY, MAY,
SEPTEMBER; NOVEMBER 22
Monmouth Fair:
Monmouth.
2ND WEDNESDAY IN AUGUST, APRIL;
WHIT WEDNESDAY; JUNE 23; 2ND
WEDNESDAY IN NOVEMBER
Newport Fair:
Newport.
JUNE
Usk Trinity Fair:
Usk.

AGRICULTURAL, HORTICULTURAL & BREED SHOWS

JUNE – 4TH WEEK
Abergavenny Agricultural Show:
Abergavenny.
AUGUST – 2ND WEEK
Chepstow Agriultural Show:
Chepstow.
AUGUST – 4TH WEEK
Monmouth Show:
Monmouth.
SEPTEMBER – 2ND WEEK
Usk Agricultural Show:
Usk.

SPORTS

FEBRUARY – 2ND WEEK
Welsh Junior Open Squash
Championships:
Newport.
JULY
Welsh Lawn Tennis Championships:
Newport.
AUGUST – 4TH WEEK
Annual Bed Race:
Through the main streets of:
Monmouth.
SEPTEMBER – 1ST WEEK
Raft Race:
River Wye: Monmouth Boat House to
Whitebrook.

MISCELLANEOUS

JUNE – 2ND WEEK
Austin Seven Car Rally:
Caldicot Country Park, Caldicot, Gwent.

◆

MONMOUTH CARNIVAL
Town dignitaries attend the opening of the
annual Monmouth Carnival. See:
CARNIVALS.

ANNUAL BED RACE
This fun event gives the residents of
Monmouth a chance to raise money for
charity and enjoy themselves at the same
time. See: MISCELLANEOUS.

◆ *Caernarvonshire* ◆

(INCLUDING ANGLESEY)

FESTIVALS

EASTER – SUNDAY & MONDAY
Llandudno Easter Hockney Festival:
Llandudno.
APRIL 29 – MAY 5
Menai Music Festival (Gwyl Gerdd Menai):
Details: Director, Music Department, University College of North Wales, Bangor.
MAY MID
University College of North Wales Arts Festival:
Bangor.
Details: Director, U.C.N.W. Arts Festival, Students Union, Deinol Road, Bangor.
JUNE – LATE, TO AUGUST – EARLY
Welsh National Opera Festival:
Llandudno.
JULY – MID
Caernarvon Festival:
Caernarvon.
AUGUST – EARLY
Llandudno Festival:
Llandudno.
OCTOBER/NOVEMBER
Bangor Autumn Festival:
Bangor.
Details: 110 Caernarvon Road, Bangor.
Colwyn Bay Independent Drama Festival:
Details: Entertainments Manager, Civic Centre, Colwyn Bay.

FAIRS

OCTOBER
Llanleechild Fair:
Llanleechild.

CARNIVALS

JULY – LATE
Llaingoch Carnival:
Llaingoch.
SEPTEMBER
Conway Carnival:
Conway.

PARADES

EASTER – MONDAY
Easter Bonnet and Fancy Dress Parade:
Arcadia Theatre, Llandudno.

AGRICULTURAL, HORTICULTURAL & BREED SHOWS

EASTER – MONDAY
Lleyn and District Agricultural Show:
Gefail Bont Field, Nr. Efailnewydd, Pwllheli.
AUGUST – 1ST WEEK
Eglwysbach Agricultural Show:
Conway Valley.
AUGUST
Abersoch Sheep Dog Trials:
Abersoch.
AUGUST
Llanbedrog Sheep Dog Trials:
Llanbedrog.
AUGUST
North Wales Agricultural Show:
Caernarvon.
AUGUST
Anglesey Agricultural Show:
Gwalchmai.

SPORTS

JULY
Irish Sea Yachting Race:
Conway Bay – Cork.

Regattas:

JULY OR AUGUST
Menai Strait Regatta Fortnight:
Menai Strait.
AUGUST
Criccieth Regatta:
Criccieth.

MISCELLANEOUS

MAY
Royal Cambrian Academy of Arts Summer Exhibition:
Conway.

◆

LLAINGOCH CARNIVAL
Small local carnivals abound in rural Wales and the annual celebration at Llaingoch is typical of its kind. Pictures show the Carnival Queen in all her splendour and some of the fancy dress competitors. See: CARNIVALS.

◆ *Merionethshire* ◆

TRA·MÔR·TRA·MEIRION

FESTIVALS

MAY – 1ST WEEK
Barmouth Arts Festival:
Details: Secretary, Manchester House,
Barmouth.
MAY
Dee & Clwyd Festival of Music:
Ardudy, Friddy Gog, Corwen, Clwyd &
Corwen.

FAIRS

APRIL – 1ST WEEK
Spring Antiques Fair:
Portmeirion.
OCTOBER – 4TH WEEK
Autumn Antiques Fair:
Portmeirion.

CARNIVALS

MAY – 4TH WEEK
Barmouth Carnival:
Barmouth.
AUGUST – EARLY
Corwen Carnival:
Corwen.
AUGUST – EARLY
Bala Carnival:
Bala.

AGRICULTURAL, HORTICULTURAL & BREED SHOWS

AUGUST
Bala Horticultural Show:
Bala.
AUGUST
Towyn Sheepdog Trials:
Towyn.
SEPTEMBER
Bala Sheepdog Trials:
Bala.
SEPTEMBER
Harlech Agricultural Show:
Harlech.
SEPTEMBER
Merionethshire Agricultural Show:
Bala.

SPORTS

AUGUST – 2ND WEEK
Seniors Golf Championships:
Royal St. David's Golf Course, Harlech.
AUGUST – 2ND WEEK
Gold Cross Golf Championships:
Royal St. David's Golf Course, Harlech.
SEPTEMBER – 2ND WEEK
Ladies Home Golf Internationals:
Royal St. David's Golf Course, Harlech.

POWYS
◆ *Brecknockshire* ◆

LLIFA'R·DWR·LLEWYRCHA'R·BOBL

Fair, shining mountains of my pilgrimage,
And flow'ry vales, whose flow'rs were stars.
FROM 'THE BRECON BEACONS' BY HENRY
VAUGHAN

Old Customs

ST. DAVID'S DAY
Leek Sergeant Ceremony:
Mountwood, Llanfoist.
Five of the newest recruits at the army camp
are made to eat raw leeks in celebration of
St. David, the patron saint of Wales.
NOVEMBER
The Dunmow Flitch:
Crickhowell.
Four couples compete for a large flitch of
bacon by proving to a drunken judge and
incompetent jury that they have been
happily married for a year and a day.
DECEMBER – CHRISTMAS
Torchlight Procession:
Brymaur.

Festivals

OCTOBER
Cym-du Eisteddfod:
Cym-du.

Agricultural, & Horticultural Shows

JULY – 4TH WEEK
Royal Welsh Agricultural Show:
Llanelwedd Showground, Builth Wells,
Powys.
JULY
Abergavenny & Border Counties
Show:
Abergavenny.
Details: Show Office, Central Chambers,
Lion Street, Abergavenny.
AUGUST
Lanthony Show:
Lanthony.
SUMMER
Welsh National Sheepdog Trials:
Llyswen, Brecon.

SEPTEMBER
Brecknockshire Agricultural Show:
Newton Park, Brecon.
SEPTEMBER
Talybont Agricultural Show:
Talybont.

Sports

DECEMBER & FEBRUARY
International Canoeing Event:
River Usk, Crickhowell.

LEEK SERGEANT CEREMONY
A newly recruited sergeant prepares to eat
five raw leeks during the St. David Day
ceremony. See: OLD CUSTOMS.

225

LANTHONY SHOW
'Tossing the Stook' – a 'stook' being a bale of hay – is a game peculiar to the show at Lanthony. See: SHOWS. ▷

BRYNMAWR TORCHLIGHT PROCESSION
Torchlight processions are unusual in Wales which makes this Christmas occasion of extra interest to the tourist. See: CARNIVALS. ▷

POWYS
◆ *Montgomeryshire* ◆

POWYS · PARADWYS · CYMRU

OLD CUSTOMS

ROGATIONTIDE (5TH SUNDAY AFTER EASTER)
Blessing the Fields:
Castle Caereinion.
A very unusual ceremony in as much as it takes place on board the Llanfair Light Railway between Welshpool and Llanfair Caereinion. The Reverend of St. Mary's Church conducts the service in which prayers are taken each time the train stops at the stations along the route.

FESTIVALS

GOOD FRIDAY; EASTER SATURDAY, SUNDAY & MONDAY
Annual Easter Festival:
Trelydan Hall, Welshpool.
MAY
Newtown Musical Festival:
Newtown.
MAY
Montgomery County Music Festival:
Davies Memorial Gallery, Newtown.

CARNIVALS

SPRING BANK HOLIDAY
Welshpool Carnival:
Welshpool.
JUNE
Newtown Carnival:
Newtown.

AGRICULTURAL, HORTICULTURAL & BREED SHOWS

MAY — 4TH WEEK
Montgomery Agricultural Show:
Welshpool.

SPORTS

MARCH — 1ST WEEK
Welsh School Cross Country Championships:
Newtown.

MONTGOMERY COUNTY SHOW
The Montgomery Show is staged at Welshpool and in keeping with most county shows presents a varied array of events of agricultural and entertainment interest. See: SHOWS.
▽

NEWTOWN CARNIVAL
Newtown is a major town in the county and its carnival equals that of neighbouring Welshpool in regards to entertainment and festive atmosphere. See: CARNIVALS.

POWYS
◆ *Radnorshire* ◆

EWCH·YN·UWCH

FESTIVALS

MAY — 2ND WEEK
**Llandrindod Wells Independent
National Drama Festival:**
The Albert Hall, Llandrindod Wells.

AUGUST — 1ST WEEK
Llandrindod Wells Festival:
*Details: Festival Organisers, Town Hall,
Llandrindod Wells, Powys, LD1 5DW.*

OCTOBER — 4TH WEEK
**Llanidloes Independent National
Drama Festival:**
Community Centre, Llanidloes.

FAIRS

APRIL — 1ST WEEK
Welsh Annual Antiques Fair:
Hotel Metropole, Llandrindod Wells.

CARNIVALS

AUGUST
Llandrindod Wells Carnival:
Llandrindod Wells.

AGRICULTURAL, HORTICULTURAL & BREED SHOWS

JULY
Royal Welsh Show:
Llanelwedd, Nr. Builth Wells.

AUGUST
Old Radnor Flower Show:
Old Radnor.

AUGUST
Llanwrtyd Wells Sheepdog Trials:
Llanwrtyd Wells.

SEPTEMBER
Llangynog Sheepdog Trials:
Llangynog.

SPORTS

MARCH — MID
**Welsh Schools Cross Country Inter
Championships:**
Llandrindod Wells.

◆

ROYAL WELSH SHOW
*A convincing array of beasts on display
during the Parade of Champions at one of
Britain's famous agricultural shows.
Parades, show-jumping, competitions and
agricultural events are held in the show
grounds which are set in some of the most
beautiful countryside in Wales. See:
SHOWS.*
▽

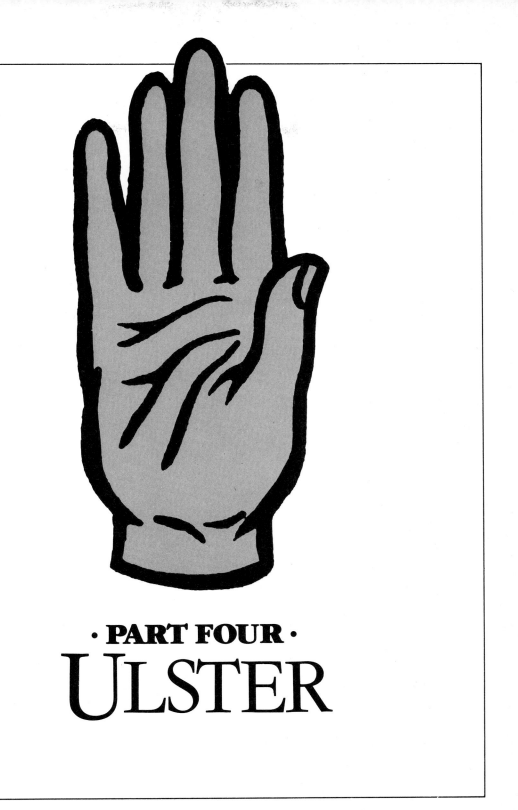

· PART FOUR ·
ULSTER

◆ *County Antrim* ◆

PER·ANGUSTA·AD·AUGUSTA

OLD CUSTOMS

MARCH 17 (ST PATRICK'S DAY)
Ballycastle & District Annual Horse Ploughing Match and Heavy Horse Show:
Magherintemple, near Fair Head, Ballycastle.
This event, which captures the attention of the country lover, takes place annually on St. Patrick's Day. It dates back more than 110 years, and being exclusively horse ploughing (not a tractor in sight!) is thought to be the only one of its kind in the world. There are special competitions for ploughmen and ploughwomen, and the popular 'Style and Appearance' competition is of great interest to visitors.
Details: The Hon. Secretary, 39 North Street, Ballycastle.

JULY – 12TH
Battle of the Boyne Celebrations:
Belfast (and 16 other centres in Northern Ireland)
In 1690, the Protestant King William III (William of Orange) defeated the Roman Catholic King James II at the Battle of the Boyne in defence of the Protestant faith. In 1795 the Orange Order was formed, with members swearing allegiance to the concept of civil liberty. Many Irish Protestants joined the Orange Order, and are now better known as 'Orangemen'.
   The 'twelfth' has become the best-known folk/religious occasion in Northern Ireland, commemorating that historic battle with bands and banners. The 'Orangemen' wear sashes and other regalia, and parade to a field where speeches are made on Protestant themes. There are stalls providing

refreshments. The biggest parade is held in Belfast, starting at Carlisle Circus (north of the city) at 10.00 hrs, taking about 2½ hrs to pass any given point, with the marchers assembling eventually south of the city. On the eve of the holiday (11th July) traditional bonfires are lit around midnight in Protestant areas.
Details: Grand Secretary, Grand Orange Lodge of Ireland, 65 Dublin Road, Belfast, BT2 7HE.

JULY – LATE, TO AUGUST – EARLY
The Lughnasa Medieval Fair:
Carrickfergus.
Lughnasa was one of the quarterly feasts of the old Irish Year. The fair occurred on the first of August and was essentially an agrarian feast associated with the harvest. Lughnasa – 'Lugh' was a God in Irish mythology and 'nasa' games or assembly. In recent years the fair has centred around Carrickfergus Castle, the best preserved Norman castle in the whole of Ireland, and features medieval entertainment as well as the traditional stalls.
Details: Promotions Officer, Carrickfergus Borough Council, Town Hall, Carrickfergus.

AUGUST 15
Ancient Order of Hibernians Annual Processions:
Various venues.

AUGUST – LAST MONDAY & TUESDAY
The Ould Lammas Fair:
Ballycastle, County Antrim.
The principal traditional fair in Northern Ireland, celebrated in song, and probably much older than its 1606 charter. It is not only an important livestock fair, but a great

social occasion for all classes and is marked by the attendance of rural craftsmen selling ladders, ropes, implements, etc. It also has children's amusements and nearly 200 stalls selling everything from jewellery to antiques and the traditional yellowman confection and dulse (edible seaweed). At night there are dances both in halls and in the street.
Details: The clerk, Moyle District Council, Dariada House, Coleraine Road, Ballycastle.

OCTOBER – 1ST WEEK
Mounthill Fair:
Mounthill, 4 miles west of Larne.
Held annually on the first Saturday in October, and is a revival (since 1960) of a 17th century horse fair that had lapsed. It continues to flourish, having more than 50 stallholders as well as horses, cattle, sheep and pigs for sale.
Details: Larne Historical Centre, Town Hall, Larne.

◆

OULD LAMMAS FAIR
The principal traditional fair in Northern Ireland, celebrated in song, and probably much older than its 1606 charter. The practical side of the fair is given over to sales of sheep and ponies while the visitor is drawn and entertained by the street stalls selling 'Dulse', a dried edible seaweed, and 'Yellow Man' a sweet confectionery, ornaments, clothes, bric-a-brac, fruit and many other items. See: OLD CUSTOMS. ⬠

OCTOBER – LAST TUESDAY
Ballycastle Apple Fair:
Ballycastle.
This old tradition, as its name implies, was founded by local apple growers for the vending of their produce after havesting in the autumn. Nowadays, stallholders from all over the province, converge at the Diamond in Ballycastle exclusively selling apples.
Details: The Clerk, Moyle District Council, Dalriada House, Coleraine Road, Ballycastle.

FESTIVALS

FEBRUARY – 1ST WEEK
Belfast One-Act Play Festival:
Group Theatre, Belfast.
FEBRUARY – LATE
Ballymena Musical Society: Music Competitions, Speech and Drama Competition:
Town Hall, Ballymena.
Details: Mrs. R.S. Marshall, 30 Nursery Road, Gracehill, Ballymena BT42 2QA.
MARCH – 2ND WEEK
Ballymoney Drama Festival:
Town Hall, Ballymoney.
MARCH – 2ND WEEK
Ballymena Music Festival: Irish Folk Dancing Competitions:
Town Hall, Ballymena.
MARCH – MID
Belfast Music Festival:
Members Room, Belfast.
Details: R.B. McCandles, 33 Wynchurch Avenue, Belfast BT6 0JP.
MARCH – MID
Larne Competitive Drama Festival:
Victoria Hall, Larne.
EASTER
Ballyclare Music Festival:
Ballyclare.
APRIL
Brass Band Festival:
Ulster Hall, Belfast.
APRIL – MAY
Carrickfergus Musical Festival:
Town Hall, Carrickfergus.
Details: Mrs. E.C. McCullough, 9 Rhanbuoy Park, Carrickfergus BT38 8BS.
MAY – 2ND WEEK
Larne Irish Dancing Festival:
Larne.
MAY – 3RD OR 4TH WEEK
The Ulster Drama Festival:
Grand Opera House, Belfast.
MAY
Ballyclare Civic Festival:
Ballyclare.
MAY
Bundoran Lobster Festival (&

Drama/Sports Events):
Bundoran.
MAY
Belfast Civic Festival:
Various venues. Belfast.
Details: Festival Organiser, City Hall, Belfast 1.
JUNE – 2ND WEEK
East Belfast Community Festival:
Victoria Park and other centres, East Belfast.
JUNE – 2ND WEEK
Festival of Sport:
Antrim Forum, Antrim.
JUNE – 4TH WEEK
Irish Folk Dancing Festival:
Town Hall, Portrush.
JUNE – 4TH WEEK
Larne Civic Week Festival:
Larne, Various Venues.
JUNE
Carnclough Aquatic Festival:
Carnclough.
JUNE – JULY
Antrim Festival:
Antrim.
JULY – 1ST WEEK
Feis na nGleann:
Glenariff.
JULY – LATE
Carrickfergus Civic Festival:
Carrickfergus.
JULY – 3RD WEEK
Bushmills Civic Week Community Festival:
Bushmills.
JUNE
Greenisland Festival:
Greenisland.
JUNE
Whitehead Community Festival:
Whitehead.
JULY –
Lighnasa Medieval Festival:
Carrickfergus.
JULY – LATE
Crumlin Civic Week Festival:
Crumlin.
OCTOBER – LATE, TO NOVEMBER – EARLY
The Royal British Legion Festival of Rembrance:
Ulster Hall, Belfast.
OCTOBER – LATE, OR NOVEMBER – EARLY
Nine Glens Festival of Irish Dancing:
NOVEMBER
Queens University Arts Festival:
Queens University, Belfast.
Details: The Festival Director, 8 Malone Road, Belfast 9.
NOVEMBER – 3RD WEEK
Ballymoney Irish Dancing Festival:
Town Hall, Ballymoney.

NOVEMBER
Belfast Music and Drama Festival:
Queen's University, Belfast.

FAIRS

APRIL – 4TH WEEK
Greenmount Annual Garden Fair:
Greenmount Agricultural and Horticultural College, Muckamore.

CARNIVALS

JULY – 3RD WEEK
Glenariff Community Carnival Week:
The Bay Hall and Sports Field, Glenariff.
JULY
Ballycastle Carnival Week:
Ballycastle.

GALAS

JUNE – 1ST WEEK
Railway Preservation Society & Carrickfergus Lions Club Steam & Vintage Gala:
Whitehead Excursion Station, Carrickfergus.

PARADES

APRIL
St. Georges Day Scouts Parade:
Assembly Hall and Wellington Hall, Belfast.

SHOWS

MAY – 2ND WEEK
The Lord Mayor's Show:
Belfast.
JUNE
Ballymena Summer Show:
Ballymena.

AGRICULTURAL. HORTICULTURAL & BREED SHOWS

JANUARY – 1ST WEEK
Ballymena & District Dog Fanciers Association Show:
Sports Hall, Sentry Hill, Ballymena.
JANUARY – 4TH WEEK
Queen Island Canine Club All Breed Show:
Ballymena Community Centre, Ballymena.
FEBRUARY – 1ST WEEK
Royal Ulster Agricultural Society Spring Show:
R.U.A.S. Showgrounds, Balmoral, Belfast.

FEBRUARY – LATE
Co. Antrim Agricultural Society Spring Show:
Fairhill, Ballymena.
MARCH – 1ST WEEK
Ulster Cocker Spaniel Club: Open Dog Show:
British Legion Hall, Belmont, Belfast.
MARCH – EARLY
Short Brothers and Harland Dog Show:
The Showgrounds, Balmoral, Belfast.
APRIL – 1ST WEEK
German Shepherd Dog Club of N. Ireland Championship Show:
Balmoral Showgrounds, Belfast.
APRIL – 2ND WEEK
Beagle Club of Northern Ireland Championship Show:
Alan McNeil Hall, Larne Harbour.
APRIL – 2ND WEEK
Gilnahirk Horticultural & Civic Society Spring Show:
Tullycarnet Pavilion, Belfast.
APRIL – 3RD WEEK
Ulster Fox Terrier Club All Breed Show:
APRIL – 3RD WEEK
Ulster Fox Terrier Club All Breed Show:
The Showgrounds, Balmoral, Belfast.
EASTER – MONDAY
Easter Monday Dog Show:
The Showgrounds, Balmoral, Belfast.
MAY – 1ST WEEK
Alpine Garden Society's Ulster Show:
Greenmount Agricultural College, Muckamore.
MAY – 1ST WEEK
Beagle Club of Northern Ireland 75 Class Open Show:
Castle Grounds, Antrim.
MAY – 4TH WEEK
The Royal Ulster Agricultural Society's Annual Show.
R.U.A.S. Showgrounds, Balmoral, Belfast.
JUNE – 1ST WEEK
North Antrim Agricultural Association: Ballymoney Show:
The Showgrounds, Ballymoney.
JUNE – MID
Ballymena Show: (Including Benson & Hedges Jumping Competitions):
The Showgrounds, Ballymena.
JULY – 3RD WEEK
Antrim Agricultural Society Annual Show:
Castle Grounds, Antrim.
JULY/SEPTEMBER
City Of Belfast International Rose Trials:
Sir Thomas and Lady Dixon Park, Upper Malone, Belfast.

AUGUST – 1ST WEEK
Ulster Cocker Spaniel Club Open Show:
British Legion Hall, Belmont Church Road, Belfast.
AUGUST – 3RD WEEK
Glenariff Working Sheepdog Trials:
The Bay, Glenariff.
AUGUST – LATE
Carrickfergus and District Garden Society's Autumn Show:
Town Hall, Carrickfergus.
SEPTEMBER – 1ST WEEK
Glencoy Farmers' Committee Sheepdog Trials:
Bay Farm, Carnlough.
SEPTEMBER – MID
Knock Presbyterian Church Flower Show:
Knock Presbyterian Church Hall, Knock Road, Belfast.
SEPTEMBER – 4TH WEEK
Belfast Dog Show Society's Championship Dog Show:
The Showgrounds, Balmoral, Belfast.
SEPTEMBER
N.I.G.F.A.S. Flower Festival:
St. Anne's Cathedral, Belfast.
OCTOBER – 3RD WEEK
Royal Ulster Agricultural Society Autumn Show & Sale:
R.U.A.S. Showground, Balmoral, Belfast.
OCTOBER – 3RD WEEK
Ulster Cocker Spaniel Club: Championship Show:
Alan McNeil Hall, Larne Harbour.
DECEMBER – 1ST WEEK
Ulster Cocker Spaniel Club Open Show:
British Legion Hall, Belmont, Belfast.

───── **SPORTS** ─────

JANUARY – EARLY
Wilkinson Cup Cross Country Race:
Oldpark, Belfast.
JANUARY – EARLY
Coleraine & District Motor Cycle Club Enduro Trial:
Ballycastle.
JANUARY – EARLY
Miskimmon Cup Cross Country Race:
Ballyclare.
JANUARY – LATE, OR FEBRUARY – EARLY
Ulster Women's Squash Racquets Association Ulster Open Championships:
Clarence Place, Belfast.
JANUARY – MID
Bell's Ulster Veterans Open Squash Championships:
Belfast Boat Club, Stranmillis, Belfast.

JANUARY – MID
Northern Ireland Amateur Athletics Association Open Youths and Colts Championships and International Race:
Mullusk.
JANUARY – MID
Mid Antrim Motor Club Icebreaker Rally:
Throughout Co. Antrim.
JANUARY – LATE
Belfast Boat Club Festival of Squash:
Belfast Boat Club, Stranmillis, Belfast.
FEBRUARY – EARLY
Coca Cola Ladies Basketball Tournament:
Antrim Forum.
FEBRUARY – EARLY
Northern Ireland Amateur Athletics Association Crawford Cup Cross Country:
Belvoir Park, Belfast.
FEBRUARY – MID
Louis Herbert Handicap Bridge Pairs:
Jewish Institute, Belfast.
FEBRUARY – MID
Northern Ireland Schools Judo Championships:
Mayfield Leisure Centre, Belfast.
FEBRUARY – MID
Northern Ireland Bridge Union: Belfast Pairs:
Queen's University, Belfast.
FEBRUARY – MID
Mid-Antrim Motor Club Rallysprint:
Craigmore Quarry, Randalstown.
FEBRUARY – MID
Northern Ireland Amateur Athletics Association Islandmagee Races:
Islandmagee.
FEBRUARY – LATE
Irish Open Junior Squash Championship:
Belfast.
FEBRUARY
Mother's Pride Badminton Tournament:
Enniskillen, Coleraine & Belfast.
FEBRUARY – LATE, OR MARCH – EARLY
Methodist College Rowing Club: Lagan Head of the River:
River Lagan, Belfast.
MARCH – EARLY
Ulster Automobile Club Autotest:
Barnett's Park, Belfast.
MARCH – EARLY
Northern Ireland Darts Charity Cup Semi-Finals and Final:
Ulster Hall, Belfast.
MARCH – MID
Northern Ireland Olympic Wrestling Association: Ulster Schoolboys Championships:

Carrickfergus Leisure Centre,
Carrickfergus.
MARCH — EARLY
**Northern Ireland Team Judo
Championships:**
Maysfield Leisure Centre, Belfast.
MARCH — EARLY
**Mid-Antrim Motor Cycle Slemish
Trials:**
Slemish.
MARCH — EARLY
**McCambley Rugby Football Cup
Final:**
Ravenhill, Belfast.
MARCH — EARLY
**Northern Ireland Amateur Athletics
Association: Duncairn Nomads
Relays:**
Woodvale Park, Belfast.
MARCH — EARLY
**County Antrim Open Table Tennis
Championships:**
Town Hall, Ballymena.
MARCH — MID
**Mid-Antrim Motor Club:
Championship Autotest:**
Clinty Quarry, Ballymena.
MARCH — MID
Irish Indoor Bowls Championships:
Antrim Forum.
MARCH — MID
Schools Rugby Football Cup Final:
Ravenhill, Belfast.
MARCH
**Ballymena & District Table Tennis
Association Tournament:**
Town Hall, Ballymena.
MARCH — LATE
Schools Squash Knockout Cup:
Clarence Place, Belfast.
MARCH — late
Yamakwai Judo Club Championships:
Holy Child School, Belfast.
MARCH — late
**Boys' Brigade Cross Country
Championships:**
Ballyclare.
MARCH — LATE
King's Arms Bridge Pairs:
King's Arms Hotel, Larne.
MARCH — LATE
**McCrea Rugby Football Cup Final &
Crawford Rugby Football Cup Final:**
Ravenhill, Belfast.
APRIL — EARLY
**Causeway Coast Board Sailing
Championships:**
Portrush.
APRIL — EARLY
**Bank of Ireland Ulster Graded Squash
Tournament:**
Stranmillis, Belfast.
APRIL — MID
Milk Marketing Board: Schoolboys

International Wrestling Match:
Carrickfergus Leisure Centre,
Carrickfergus.
APRIL — MID
Towns Rugby Football Cup Final:
Ravenhill, Belfast.
APRIL — MID
**Northern Ireland Amateur Athletics
Association Whitehead Road Races:**
Whitehead.
APRIL — MID
**Milk Marketing Board Indoor Hockey
Championships:**
Antrim Forum.
APRIL — MID
Ulster Rugby Football Cup Final:
Ravenhill, Belfast.
APRIL — LATE
Larne Motor Club May Sprint:
Larne.
JULY — LATE
**Carrickfergus & District Motor Cycle
Club Championship Grass Track
Races.**
Carrickfergus.
AUGUST — EARLY
**Carrickfergus Sailing Club Lipton Cup
Series:**
Carrickfergus.
AUGUST — EARLY
**Golden Jubilee Ulster Motorcycling
Grand Prix:**
Dunrod Circuit, Nr. Belfast.
AUGUST — MID
**Larne Motor Club International
Autotest:**
Larne.
AUGUST — MID
Junior Tennis Tournament:
Ballycastle.
AUGUST — MID
**Handicap Tennis Tournament &
Parent/Child Teams:**
Ballycastle.
AUGUST — LATE
**Bannside Rambling Club Annual Moye
Way Walk:**
Ballycastle.
SEPTEMBER — EARLY
I.L.G.U. Nellie Garrett Golf Cup:
Knock Golf Club, Belfast.

———Miscellaneous———

MARCH — 2ND WEEK
**Royal S.P.B.A. Annual Pipe Bank
Solos:**
St. Patrick's, Ballymena.
APRIL
**Irish Transport Trust Annual Bus and
Coach Rally:**
Belfast/Carrickfergus.
MAY — 2ND WEEK

Kirker Kavalcade Vintage Car Run:
Belfast-Armagh.
MAY — 4TH WEEK
Mayor's Sunday:
Carrickfergus.
MAY — 4TH WEEK
**Royal S.P.B.A. Annual Pipe Bank
Contest:**
Ballyclare.
JUNE — EARLY
Senior Citizens' Week:
Portrush.
JUNE — 4TH WEEK
**S.P.B.A. Co. Antrim Pipe Bands
Championships:**
Ahogill.
JUNE — 4TH WEEK
Ulster Vintage Car Club Hill Climb:
Cairncastle, Larne.
JUNE — MID, TO JULY
Ulster Art Exhibition:
Balmoral, Belfast.
JULY — 2ND WEEK
Ulster Vintage Car Club Driving Tests:
Shane's Castle, Antrim.
JULY — 3RD WEEK
**Ulster Traction Engine Club Annual
Rally:**
Shane's Castle, Antrim.
JULY — 4TH WEEK
**Benson & Hedges Historic Motor
Vehicles Run:**
Belfast-Portrush.
AUGUST
Pavement Artist Competitions:
Portrush.
AUGUST/SEPTEMBER
**Belfast Telegraph Ideal Home
Exhibition:**
Kings Hall, Balmoral, Belfast.
OCTOBER
**Royal Ulster Academy of Arts
Exhibition.**
Balmoral, Belfast.
DECEMBER — 1ST WEEK
**Christmas Lights Switching on
Ceremony:**
Belfast City Hall, Belfast.

——————◆

GOLF CHAMPIONSHIPS
*As with Scotland, golf is one of Ireland's
most popular sports and there are many fine
golf courses in Antrim. The picture shows a
game in progress at Ballycastle. See:
SPORTS.*

ULSTER STEAM TRACTION RALLY
*The rally of steam traction engines, with
side shows and associated events, is held in
a large private estate with a permanent
narrow gauge steam railway and a nature
reserve. See: MISCELLANEOUS.*

◆ County Armagh ◆

OLD CUSTOMS

JULY 13
Sham Fight & Historical Pageant:
Scarva.
An historical pageant commemorating the Battle of the Boyne on July 13, 1690.
AUGUST – EARLY WEEKEND
All-Ireland Road Bowls Finals:
Cathedral Road, Armagh city.
A very old custom is the game of 'bullets'. This consists of throwing an iron ball (originally a cannon ball) along a country road to see who can cover two miles of winding road in the smallest number of throws. It is notorious for betting, both country and townsmen alike wagering substantial sums on their favourite 'bullet' thrower. Not strictly legal, but tolerated, it attracts a keen following in County Armagh and County Cork. The sport has its heroes and balladry.
Details: Hon. Secretary, 6 Dares Willows, Armagh.

FESTIVALS

MARCH – MID
Portadown Folk Dancing Festival:
Town Hall, Portadown.
Details: Portadown Festival Association, 14 Charlemont Gardens, Portadown.
MARCH – LATE
Portadown Speech Festival:
Town Hall, Portadown.
APRIL – EARLY
Portadown Ballet Festival:
Town Hall, Portadown.
APRIL – LATE
Portadown Drama Festival:
Town Hall, Portadown.
MAY – EARLY
Portadown Music Festival:
Town Hall, Portadown.

JUNE – LATE, TO JULY – EARLY
South Armagh Festival:
Various centres in South Armagh.
OCTOBER
Armagh Arts Festival:
Armagh City.

AGRICULTURAL, HORTICULTURAL & BREED SHOWS

APRIL – 4TH WEEK
Portadown and District Horticultural Society Spring Show (including Daffodil Championship of Ireland):
Town Hall, Portadown.
JUNE – 1ST WEEK
Co. Armagh Agricultural Society Portadown Show and Show Jumping:
The Showgrounds, Portadown.
JUNE – 2ND WEEK
Armagh Agricultural Show:
Callan Valley Meadows, Armagh.

SPORTS

FEBRUARY – EARLY
N.A.C.A.I. All Ireland Junior Cross Country:
Armagh.
FEBRUARY – LATE
North Armagh Car Club Road Rally:
Craigaron.
APRIL – EARLY
Guinness Lagan Valley Athletic Relay:
Portadown-Belfast.
MAY – MID
North Armagh Motor Cycle Club: Tandragee 100 Road Races:
Tandragee.
MAY – MID
N.A.C.A.I. Armagh Country Track & Field Athletics Championships:

Carrickcruppen, Camlough.
MAY – MID
Open Golf Week:
Armagh Golf Club, Armagh.
JULY – MID
North Armagh Motor Cycle Club Motorcross:
Tandragee.
AUGUST – EARLY
All Ireland Road Bowls Finals:
Cathedral Road, Armagh.

Regattas:

MAY – LATE
Portadown Boat Club Regatta:
River Bann, Portadown.

MISCELLANEOUS

JULY – 1ST WEEK
S.P.B.A. All Ireland Pipe Bands Championships:
Craigavon.
NOVEMBER – 1ST WEEK
International Ploughing Contest:
Castle Dillon.

◆

ULSTER ROAD BOWLS FINALS
A very old custom, which is now seeing a revival, is the game of 'bullets'. This consists of throwing an iron ball (originally a cannon ball) along a country road to see who can cover two miles of winding road in the smallest number of throws. It is notorious for betting, both country and townsmen alike wagering substantial sums on their favourite 'bullet' thrower. See: SPORTS.

PORTADOWN FOLK DANCING FESTIVAL
*Members of the Tara School of Irish
Dancing, from Maghery, with the trophies
they won at the Portadown Folk Festival.
Their teacher Fionnuala McNally is on the
right of the picture. See: FESTIVALS.*

◆ County Down ◆

OLD CUSTOMS

JULY 13
The Sham Fight:
Scarva Demesne, Scarva.
On the site of the Williamite camp before the Battle of the Boyne, which it commemorates. The Sham Fight dates from the 18th century and attracts a gathering of about 30,000 spectators. The main attraction is the colourful parade with bands. The 'fight' is a ritual affair between the two participants, King William II and James II in costume.

SEPTEMBER 23
The Harvest Fair:
Conway Square, Newtonards.
Believed to be more than two centuries old and it is thought that traders from Scotland came over early in the morning of the fair, sold their wares, and travelled back home on the same day. Nowadays, the fair has the customary stallholders, children's amusements, and the traditional dulse and yellowman confection.
Details: Newtonards Borough Council, 2 Church Street, Newtownards.

FESTIVALS

MARCH/MAY & NOVEMBER
Bangor Music Festival:
Hamilton House & Tonic Theatre, Bangor.
Details: Ms. F. Newell, 19 Brunswick Park, Bangor.

APRIL
Bangor Drama Festival:
Little Theatre, Bangor.

APRIL
North Down Choral Festival:
Bangor Girls High School, Bangor.

MAY
Holywood Music Festival:
Holywood.
Details: Ms. G. Marshall, 11 Ballymenoch Place, Holywood.

SPRING BANK HOLIDAY WEEKEND
St. Patrick's Festival:
Downpatrick.

JUNE – 1ST WEEK
Feis an Duin:
St. Patrick's Park, Newcastle.

JUNE – 1ST WEEK
Newtownards Festival:
Newtownards.

JUNE – EARLY
Killough Village Festival:
Killough Village.

JUNE – 4TH WEEK
Comber Civic Week Festival:
Comber.

JUNE – 4TH WEEK
Greyabbey Festival Week:
Greyabbey.

JUNE
Kilreel Prawn Festival:
Kilreel.

JULY – 1ST WEEK
Hilltown Festival:
Hilltown.

JULY – 2ND & 3RD WEEKS
Newcastle Festival: "Loony Moon Fortnight":
Newcastle.

JULY – 2ND & 3RD WEEKS
Yachting Festival:
Strangford Lough.

JULY – 3RD WEEK
Ardglass Festival:
Ardglass.

JULY – MID
Strangford Village Festival:
Strangford Village.

JULY – LATE
Kingdom of Mourne Festival:
Kilkeel & District.

JULY
Strangford Yachting Festival:
Strangford.

AUGUST – 1ST & 2ND WEEKS
Donaghadee Festival:
Donaghadee.

AUGUST
Ballygowan One Day Festival:
Ballygowan.

AUGUST/SEPTEMBER
Percy French Festival:

NOVEMBER – EARLY
Banbridge Speech and Drama Festival:
Belmont Hotel, Banbridge.

FAIRS

JUNE – 4TH WEEK
Game and County Fair:
Clandeboye Estate, Bangor.

JUNE
Ballwalter One Day Fair:
Ballywalter.

FÊTES

SEPTEMBER – 1ST WEEK
Clandeboye Annual Charity Fête (and Gymkhana):
Clandeboye Estate, Bangor.

GALAS

JUNE
Ballyhalbert Gala.
Ballyhalbert.

JUNE
Millisle Gala:
Millisle.

JULY – 3RD WEEK
Portaferry Festival Gala:
Portaferry.

AUGUST – 1ST & 2ND WEEKS
Warrenpoint Gala Week:
Warrenpoint.

PARADES

APRIL
Apprentice Boys Parade:
Ballynahinch.

SHOWS

AUGUST – EARLY
Northern Ireland Boat Show:
Luke's Point, Ballyholme Bay, Bangor.

AGRICULTURAL, HORTICULTURAL & BREED SHOWS

JANUARY – EARLY
Ballycastle & District Engine Club Ploughing Match:
Clandeboye Estate.

JANUARY – 4TH WEEK
Queen's Island Canine Club All Breed Dog Show:
Dufferin Hall, Hamilton Road, Bangor.

FEBRUARY – 3RD WEEK
Northern Ireland Cat Club Second Sanction Show:
Queen's Hall, Holywood.

APRIL – 1ST WEEK
Bangor Horticultural Society Spring Flower Show:
St. Columbanus's Church Halls, Ballyholme, Bangor.

JUNE – 1ST WEEK

⌂
THE SHAM FIGHT
*A triumphant King Billy returning with his
rival and troops after the Sham Fight at
Scarva. See: OLD CUSTOMS*

◆

**Lurgan & District Horse & Cattle
Show:**
The Public Park, Lurgan.
JUNE – 3RD SATURDAY
Saintfield Agricultural Show:
Ballycloughton, Saintfield.
JUNE – 4TH WEEK
**Queen's Island Canine Club All Breed
Dog Show:**
Valentine Playing Fields, Bangor.
JUNE – 4TH WEEK
**Carrowdore and District Society's
Annual Show and Gymkhana:**
Carrowdale Castle Grounds, Carrowdale.
JULY – 1ST WEEK
Greyabbey Horse & Pony Show:
Greyabbey.
JULY – 3RD SATURDAY
Castlewellan Agricultural Show:
Forest Park, Castlewellan.
AUGUST – 4TH WEEK
Newcastle & District Horticultural

Society Annual Show:
Technical College, Newcastle.
AUGUST – 4TH WEEK
**Bangor Horticultural Society Autumn
Flower Show:**
St. Columbanus Church Hall,
Ballyholme, Bangor.

SPORTS

JANUARY – EARLY
**Temple M.C. & A.C. One-Day
Marathon Motorcycling Trial:**
Saintfield.
JANUARY – EARLY
**Reid Trophy Women's Cross Country
Race:**
Warrenpoint.
JANUARY – MID
**Women's Invitation Squash
Tournament:**
Crawfordsburn Country Club.
JANUARY – MID
**Knock Motorcycle Club Kelly Trophy
Trial:**
Bell's Hill, Downpatrick.
JANUARY – MID
East Down Team Bridge Contest:
Downpatrick.

JANUARY – LATE
**Northern Ireland Junior, Boys &
Veterans Cross Country:**
Bangor.
FEBRUARY – MID
**Belfast, Bangor & Newtownards
Motor Club: Tri Sport Rally:**
Newtonwards & East Down.
JUNE – EARLY
**Y.H.A.N.I. Annual Mourne Wall
Walk:**
Annalong.
JUNE – LATE
Dundrum Sports Day and Regatta:
Dundrum.
JUNE – LATE
**Meteor Club: Ulster Close Water
Skiing Competition:**
Lough Henney, Ballynahinch.
JULY – MID
**Belfast, Bangor & Newtownards
Motor Club Croft Hill Climb:**
Croft Road, Holywood.
JULY – LATE
**Ulster Boys Amateur Open Golf
Championship:**
Holywood Golf Club, Holywood.
JULY – LATE
Temple Motor Cycle Club 100 Road

MOURNE WALK

The premier hill-walking event in Northern Ireland, a 22-mile course over the highest peaks of the Mountains of Mourne, County Down. With a total ascent of 10,000 feet, it is a non-competitive event promoted by the Youth Hostel Association of Northern Ireland, and numbers are limited to 2,000. Walkers completing the course within the time limit of 07.00–19.00 hrs. receive a certificate. See: SPORTS.

◆

Race:
Saintfield.
AUGUST – EARLY
Dundrum Regatta and Sports:
Dundrum.
AUGUST – MID
I.L.G.U. Australian Spoons (Golf):
Carnalea Golf Club, Bangor.
AUGUST – LATE
500 Motor Racing Club Meeting:
Kirkistown.
AUGUST – LATE
Guinness Ulster Open Water Skiing Competition:
Lough Henney, Ballynahinch.

AUGUST – 4TH WEEK
Northern Ireland Driving Club Annual Horse and Pony Show:
The Demesne, Moira.
SEPTEMBER – EARLY
North Armagh Motor Cycle Club Race of Aces:
Kirkistown.
SEPTEMBER – MID
500 Motor Racing Club Meeting:
Kirkistown.
SEPTEMBER – MID
Killinchy & District Motor Cycle Club John Donnelly International Moto Cross:
Killinchy.
OCTOBER – EARLY
Belfast, Bangor & Newtownards Motor Club Jack Frost Rally:
County Down.
OCTOBER – LATE
N.A.C.A.I. Sliabh Gullion Mountain Race (Athletics):
Forkhill.
NOVEMBER
500 Motor Racing Club Rallycross:
Kirkistown.

MISCELLANEOUS

MAY – 1ST WEEK
Northern Ireland Folk Dancing Championships:
Hamilton House, Bangor.
JUNE – 3RD WEEK
Waringstown Cavalcade of Vintage Vehicles:
Waringstown.
JUNE – 3RD WEEK
S.P.B.A. County Down Pipe Bands Championships:
Banbridge.
JUNE – 3RD & 4TH WEEKS
Dundonald Arts Club Annual Picture Exhibition:
The Library, Dundonald.
AUGUST – 2ND WEEK
Ulster International Flying Rally:
Newtownards Airport, Newtownards.
AUGUST – 2ND WEEK
Ulster Traction Engine Club Olde Tyme Steam Thrashing Rally:
Clandeboye Estate, Newtownards.
AUGUST – 3RD WEEK
S.P.B.A. Ulster Pipe Bands Championships:
Newcastle.

◆ *County Fermanagh* ◆

——Old Customs——

JULY – LATE
'Lady of the Lake' Festival:
Lower Lough Erne, particularly the area around Irvinestown.
The 12-day Festival was created around a beautiful legend according to which a graceful lady walked through the mists on Lower Lough Erne – particularly the area of that great waterway close to Irvinestown of Killadeas, Lisnarick, Aughinver and Castle Archdale – making her way from island to island, clad in flowing garments, surrounded by light and carrying in her hand a bunch of beautiful wild flowers. The route of this mythical lady is said to have taken in Innismacsaint, Innisgariff, Innisdoney, Innishckare, and she eventually disappeared from view behind Innisgiorraigh.
Many old people, still in the area, firmly believe that the 'Lady' did exist, and her appearance signified to them and the islanders the advent of good weather, good crops and good times ahead.
Details: The Hon. Secretary, The Slates, Shanmullagh, Irvinestown.

——Agricultural,—— ——Horticultural &—— ——Breed Shows——

JULY – OR AUGUST
Enniskillen Horse Show:
Castlecoole, Enniskillen.
AUGUST – 1ST WEEK
West Ulster Hound Show:
Lisbellaw.
AUGUST – 3RD WEEK
Fermanagh Farming Society County Show:
Fairgreen, Enniskillen.
AUGUST – 4TH WEEK
Enniskillen Annual Agricultural Show:
Fairgreen and Technical College, Enniskillen.

——Sports——

JANUARY – MID
Fermanagh Association Open Badminton Championships:
Lakeland Forum, Enniskillen.
JANUARY – MID
Enniskillen Motor Club "Snow Spinner" Rally:
Co. Fermanagh.
FEBRUARY – MID
Northern Ireland Men's Senior Basketball Tournament:
Lakeland Forum, Enniskillen.
FEBRUARY – MID
Co. Fermanagh Open Table Tennis Championships:
Fermanagh Lakeland Forum, Enniskillen.
MARCH – MID
Portora Rowing Club: Portora Head of the River Race:
Enniskillen.
MARCH – LATE
Enniskillen Motor Club Romer Rally:
County Fermanagh.
APRIL – MID
Erne Game Preservation Society Clay Pigeon Shoot:
Lisnaskea.
MAY – EARLY
Western Region Junior Judo Championships:
Fermanagh Lakeland Forum, Enniskillen.
MAY – LATE
Erne Boat Rally:
Enniskillen.
JUNE – MID
Enniskillen Motor Club Erne Trophy Rallysprint:
St. Angelo Airfield, Enniskillen.
JULY – EARLY
Enniskillen Motor Club "Permapost" Special Stage Rally:
County Fermanagh to County Tyrone.
AUGUST – LATE

Enniskillen Horse Show:
Castlecoole, Enniskillen.
OCTOBER – LATE
Enniskillen Motor Club Erne Safari Rally:
Co. Fermanagh to Co. Tyrone.

——Miscellaneous——

MAY – 4TH WEEK
Pipe Band Championships:
Enniskillen.

LADY OF THE LAKE FESTIVAL
Tradition has it that a graceful lady walked through the mist and made her way from island to island on Lower Lough Erne. she was clad in flowing garments, surrounded by light, and carried wild flowers in her hand.
There are parades, bands, sporting events (particularly water sports), song contests and children's events during the Festival.
See: OLD CUSTOMS

PIPE BAND CONTEST
Enniskillen's impressive pipe band contest features traditional entertainment at its best in which many of the top rate bands compete. See: MISCELLANEOUS.

◆ *County Londonderry* ◆

OLD CUSTOMS

AUGUST 12
The Relief of Derry Celebrations:
Londonderry City and St. Columb's
Cathedral.
*The Apprentice Boys of Derry (an adult
organisation so named from the apprentice
boys who closed the city's gates in 1688
against the invading troops of James II
and began the famous 105-day siege of
Derry), walk in procession to a
wreath-laying ceremony at the war
memorial, and then to a thanksgiving
service in St. Columb's Cathedral.*
AUGUST 15
**Ancient Order of Hibernians'
Processions:**
Various centre in Northern Ireland.
*The Catholic equivalent to the Battle of the
Boyne celebrations is Lady Day (15th
August), not celebrating any battle, but
recalling the long devotion of the majority of
the people of Ireland to Roman
Catholicism. Founded early this century, it
is marked by processions and bands of the
Ancient Order of Hibernians with open-air
religious services and Gaelic sports.
Members wear regalia and are accompanied
by Gaelic pipers in saffron kilts. In the past
few years the processions have been very
localised and on a small scale.
Details: The Information Officer, A.O.H.
Office, 23 Foyle Street, Londonderry.*
DECEMBER 19
Closing of the Gates Celebrations:
Londonderry City.
*The effigy of Lundy is still burned (though
no longer on the city's walls) as part of the
'Closing of the Gates' celebrations.
Lieutenant-Colonel Robert Lundy, the
military governor of Londonderry in 1688,
was prepared to admit the troops of the
invading army of James II and for his
disloyalty was branded 'traitor' by the
populace. When the soldiers were only 60
yards away, 13 apprentice boys seized the
keys of the town and slammed the gates
closed.
The Apprentice Boys of Derry (described
under the 12 August entry) have long since
assumed charge of making the effigy of
Lundy and consigning it to flames on the
afternoon of the Saturday nearest 18th
December.*

FESTIVALS

FEBRUARY – 3RD OR 4TH WEEKS
Londonderry Feis:
Union Hall or Guildhall, Londonderry.
APRIL
Feis Dhoire Cholmcille:
Guildhall, St. Columb's Hall and Union
Hall, Londonderry.
MAY – EARLY
Coleraine Music Festival:
Town Hall, Coleraine.
MAY – 4TH WEEK
Foyle Festival:
Londonderry.
MAY/JUNE
Portstewart Musical Festival:
Town Hall, Portstewart.
JUNE – 3RD WEEK
Folk Dancing Festival:
Town Hall, Portrush.

GALAS

JUNE – 1ST & 2ND WEEKS
Newtownards Civic Gala:
Newtownards.
JULY – 3RD WEEK
Portaferry Gala Week:
Portaferry.

AGRICULTURAL, HORTICULTURAL & BREED SHOWS

JUNE – 2ND WEEK
Coleraine Agricultural Show:
The Showground, Ballycastle Road,
Coleraine.

SPORTS

JANUARY – EARLY
**Cutty Sark Junior International Bridge
Championship:**
Coleraine.
JANUARY – MID
**Coleraine & District Motor Club
Snowplough Rally:**
Coleraine.
FEBRUARY – MID
**Maiden City Motor Club Navigation
Rally:**
Londonderry.
FEBRUARY – MID

**Newry & District Motor Club Bann
Rally:**
Banbridge.
MARCH – MID
North Ulster Car Club Sprint:
Aghadowey, Coleraine.
MARCH – LATE
Coleraine Head of the River Race:
River Bann, Coleraine.
MARCH – LATE
**North-West Showjumping Club Horse
and Pony Show:**
Strabane.
APRIL – EARLY
**North Ulster Car Club Forward Trust
Rallycross:**
Aghadowey, Coleraine.
APRIL – MID
**Canoe Association of Ireland Surf
Race:**
Portstewart.
APRIL – MID
**Coleraine Yacht Club Portstewart
Passage Race:**
The Marina, Coleraine.
APRIL – LATE
**Sunblest Coleraine Open Badminton
Championships:**
New University of Ulster, Coleraine.
MAY – EARLY
I.L.G.U. Scratch Golf Cup:
Castlerock Golf Club, Castlerock.
MAY – LATE
**Coleraine & District Motorcycle Club
North West 200 Road Race:**

◆

FEIS DHOIRE CHOLMCILLE
*Fleadh Cheoils (Festivals of Music) are
held annually in Northern Ireland (one in
each county) starting usually in May/June.
Dates and venues are never available until
nearer the time. The fleadh is one of a series
of heats in traditional music competitions
(held in each of the six counties) building up
to the ultimate All-Ireland finals at the end
of August. The All-Ireland Fleadh Cheoil
is always held in the Republic of Ireland.
Tin whistling, fiddling, dancing and singing
(not forgetting the booze!) seem to be the
constituents of these fleadhs. See:
FESTIVALS.*

Triangle Circuit, Portstewart.
MAY — LATE
North Ulster Car Club Rally:
Coleraine District.
JUNE — EARLY
**Remy Martin Causeway Coast
Amateur Golf Tournament:**
Ballycastle, Castlerock, Portstewart and
Royal Portrush courses.
JUNE — MID
Antrim Cup (Golf):
Royal Portrush Golf Club, Portrush.
JUNE — MID OR LATE
Ladies Bowls Tournament:
Recreation Grounds, Portrush.
JUNE — LATE
Coleraine Yacht Club 24 Hour Race:
The Marina, Coleraine.
JUNE — LATE
**Coleraine & District Motor Club Safe
Driving Event:**
Coleraine.
JUNE — LATE
Urney Gymkhana:
Clady, Strabane.
JULY — MID
**North of Ireland Open Amateur Golf
Championship:**
Royal Portrush Golf Club, Portrush.
JULY — MID
**Portstewart Triples Bowls
Tournament:**
The Warren, Portstewart.
JULY — MID
**Coleraine & District Motor Club Hill
Climb:**
Bellarena.
JULY
**North Ulster Car Club Homemakers
Discount Rallysprint:**
Craigahulliar Quarry, Portrush.
JULY
Men's Bowls Tournament:
Recreation Grounds, Portrush.
AUGUST — MID
Open Golf Week:
Royal Portrush Golf Club, Portrush.
AUGUST — MID
**North Ulster Car Club Forward Trust
Rallycross:**
Aghadowey, Coleraine.
AUGUST
Old Bushmills Irish Golf Cup:
Royal Portrush Golf Club, Portrush.
AUGUST
Irish Cup & Shield Golf Finals:
Royal Portrush Golf Club, Portrush.
SEPTEMBER — MID
Open Pairs Mixed Bowls Tournament:
Recreation Grounds, Portrush.
SEPTEMBER — LATE
**Coleraine & District Motorcycle Club
Nutcracker Rally:**
Coleraine.

SEPTEMBER
**North Ulster Car Club Forward Trust
Rallycross:**
Aghadowey, Coleraine.
OCTOBER — EARLY
Gold Cup Lifeboat Golf Trophy:
Royal Portrush Golf Club, Portrush.
OCTOBER — EARLY
Scotts Golf Cup:
Royal Portrush Golf Club, Portrush.
DECEMBER
North Ulster Car Club Rally:
Brown Trout Inn, Aghadowey,
Coleraine.

Regattas:

APRIL — MID
Irish Schools Trials Regatta:
River Bann, Coleraine.
MAY
**Coleraine and Bann Rowing Clubs
Regatta:**
River Bann, Coleraine.

County Tyrone ◆

CONSILIO · ET · PRUDENTIA

OLD CUSTOMS

AUGUST – 1ST SUNDAY
The Auld Lammas Fair:
Ardboe, shores of Lough Neagh, near
Cookstown.
*Relic of an old religious custom when a loaf
was baked from the first corn harvest and
then placed on a church altar for a
celebration Mass. Nowadays the fair is
mainly a social occasion for local people
attracting many stallholders selling
everything from junk and clothes to the
traditional yellowman confection.*

FESTIVALS

MARCH
Dungannon Music & Drama Festival:
Presbyterian Church Hall, Dungannon.
OCTOBER
Cookstown Music Festival:
Cookstown.

AGRICULTURAL, HORTICULTURAL & BREED SHOWS

APRIL – 4TH WEEK
**Omagh & District Horticultural
Society Annual Show:**
Technical College, Omagh.
EASTER
Horse and Pony Show:
Mountcastle, Strabane.
JUNE – 4TH WEEK
Fintona Agricultural Show:
Ecclesville, Fintona.
JULY – 1ST WEEK
Tyrone Farming Society Annual Show:
The Showgrounds, Omagh.
JULY – 4TH WEEK
Clogher Valley Agricultural Show:
Augher.

SEPTEMBER – 2ND WEEK
**Omagh & District Horticultural
Society Autumn Show:**
Technical College, Omagh.
SEPTEMBER – 1ST WEEK
**Dungannon and Castlecaulfield
Horticultural Society's Annual Show:**
Dungannon High School for Girls,
Dungannon.

SPORTS

MAY – MID
**Blackwater Canoe Club Long Distance
Race:**
River Blackwater, Moy.
AUGUST – MID
Killymoon Open Golf Tournament:
Killymoon Golf Club, Cookstown.
SEPTEMBER – EARLY
T.J. Eastwood Golf Cup:
Killymoon Golf Club, Cookstown.
DECEMBER – EARLY
**Blackwater Canoe Club White Water
Race:**
Gortin.

Rallys:

JANUARY – EARLY
**Cookstown & District M.E.C.
Beginners Autotest:**
Cookstown.
JANUARY – LATE
**Cookstown & District Motor Club
"Sizzler" Rally:**
Cookstown.
FEBRUARY – EARLY
Dungannon Motor Club Autotest:
Dungannon.
FEBRUARY – MID
Omagh Motor Club Pre-Circuit Rally:
Omagh.

MARCH – MID
**Dungannon Motor Club Snowdrop
Rally:**
Dungannon.
JULY – 1ST WEEK
**Omagh Motor Club Summer
Autotests:**
Omagh.
JULY
**Cookstown & District M.E.C. Farley
& Reid Rally:**
Moydamlaght, Cookstown.
AUGUST
**Dungannon Motor Club Moonraker
Rally:**
Dungannon.
SEPTEMBER
**Cookstown & District Motorcycle
Club Trial:**
Lough Fea.
SEPTEMBER
**Cookstown & District Motor Club
Northern Bank Autotests:**
Cookstown.
SEPTEMBER – 3RD WEEK
**Omagh Motor Club Bushwhacker
Rally:**
Omagh.
SEPTEMBER
**Dungannon Motor Club Moonraker
Rally:**
Dungannon.

◆

OMAGH AGRICULTURAL SHOW
*Here at the Showgrounds in Omagh the
Tyrone Farming Society present their
annual show. Awards for winning exhibits
are presented by the Ulster Dairy Queen
and the newly elected Dairy Princess. See:
SHOWS.*

TOURIST INFORMATION CENTRES

England:

Abbey Town *Cumbria*
Holm Cultram Abbey
Tel: (09656) 654
Abingdon *Oxfordshire*
8 Market Place
Tel: (0235) 22711
Alfreton *Derbyshire*
Alfreton Library, Seven Square
Tel: (077 383) 3199
Alnwick *Northumberland*
The Shambles, Northumberland Hall
Tel: (0665) 3120
Alston *Cumbria*
The Railway Station
Tel: (049 83) 696
Ambleside *Cumbria*
Old Courthouse, Church Street
Tel: (09663) 2582
Amesbury *Wiltshire*
Redworth House, Amesbury,
Nr Salisbury
Tel: (098 02) 3255
Appleby *Cumbria*
The Moot Hall, Boroughgate
Tel: (0930) 51177
Arundel *West Sussex*
61 High Street
Tel: (0903) 882268/882419
Ashbourne *Derbyshire*
13 Market Place
Tel: (033 55) 3666
Askrigg *North Yorkshire*
The Market Place, Askrigg,
Nr. Leyburn
Tel: Bainbridge (096 95) 441
Aylesbury *Buckinghamshire*
County Hall, Walton Street
Tel: (0296) 5000 Ext 308
Banbury *Oxfordshire*
Borough House, Marlborough Road
Tel (0295) 52535 Ext 250
Barnard Castle *Co. Durham*
43 Galgate
Weekend: Witham Hall,
Market Place
Tel: (083 33) 3481
Barrow-in-Furness *Cumbria*
Civic Hall, Duke Street
Tel: (0229) 25795
Barton-upon-Humber
Humberside
Baysgarth House, Baysgarth Park
Tel (0469) 32333
Bath *Avon*
Abbey Shurchyard
Tel: (0225) 62831 (Enqs.).
60521 (Accom.)
Battle *East Sussex*
Memorial Hall, Langton House,
High Street
Beaulieu *Hampshire*
The National Motor Museum
Tel: (0590) 612345
Bedford *Bedfordshire*
Town Hall, St. Pauls Square
Tel: (0234) 53323
Bellingham *Northumberland*
Council Offices
Tel: (066 02) 238
Berwick upon Tweed
Northumberland
Castlegate Car Park
Tel: (0289) 7187
Beverley *Humberside*
The Hall, Lairgate
Tel: (0482) 882255
Bexhill *East Sussex*
De La Warr Pavilion, Marina
Tel: (0424) 212023

Bideford *Devon*
The Quay
Tel: (02372) 77676
Birkenhead *Merseyside*
Birkenhead Library, Borough Road
Tel: 051-652 6106
Birmingham *West Midlands*
110 Colmore Row
Tel: 021-235 3411/2
Birmingham *West Midlands*
Information Bureau, National
Exhibition Centre
Tel: 021-780 4141
Blackburn *Lancashire*
Tower Block, Town Hall
Tel: (0254) 55201 Ext 214 or 55327
Blackpool *Lancashire*
Central Promenade
Tel: (0253) 21623
Blackpool *Lancashire*
Blackpool Hotel & Guest House
Association Ltd,
87a Coronation Street
Tel: (0523) 21891
Bognor Regis *West Sussex*
Belmont Street
Tel: (024 33) 23140
Bolsover *Derbyshire*
Bolsover Library, Church Street
Tel: Chesterfield (0246) 823179
Bolton *Greater Manchester*
Town Hall
Tel: (0204) 22311 Ext 211/485
Boston *Lincolnshire*
Assembly Rooms
Tel: (0205) 62354
Bournemouth *Dorset*
Westover Road
Tel: (0202) 291715
Bovey Tracey *Devon*
Lower Car Park, Bovey Tracey, Newton
Abbot
Tel: (0626) 832047
Bowness-on-Windermere *Cumbria*
The Globe
Tel: (096 62) 2244 Ext 43
Bracknell *Berkshire*
38 Broadway
Tel: (0344) 50111
Bradford *West Yorkshire*
Central Library, Princes Way
Tel: (0274) 33081
Bradford *West Yorkshire*
City Hall
Tel: (0274) 29577 Ext 425
Brampton *Cumbria*
Allison Pottery & Studio,
32/34 Main Street
Tel: (069 77) 2685
Bridlington *Humberside*
Garrison Street
Tel: (0262) 73474/79626
Winter address: The Spa
Tel: (0262) 78255/6/7
Brigg *Humberside*
Glanford Borough Council,
Bigby Street
Tel: (0652) 52441
Brighton *East Sussex*
Marlborough House,
54 Old Steine
Tel: (0273) 23755; 26450 (weekends)
Brighton *East Sussex*
Seafront, Kings Road
Tel: (0273) 26540 (weekends)
Bristol *Avon*
Colston House, Colston Street
Tel: (0272) 293891
Brixham *Devon*

Brixham Theatre, Market Street
Tel: (08045) 2861
Broadstairs *Kent*
Pierremont Hall
Tel: Thanet (0843) 68399
Bromsgorve *Worcestershire*
47/48 Worcester Road
Tel: (0527) 31809
Bromyard *Herefordshire*
Council Offices, 1 Rowberry Street
Tel: (088 52) 2341
Brough *Cumbria*
The One Stop Shop, Brough,
Nr Kirkby Stephen
Tel: (093 04) 260
Bude *Cornwall*
Old Railway Station
Tel: (039 54) 2311
Budleigh Salterton *Devon*
3 Fore Street
Tel: (039 54) 2311
Burnham-on-Sea *Somerset*
Berrow Road
Tel: (0278) 782377 Ext 43/44
Burnsall *North Yorkshire*
Burnsall Car Park, Burnsall,
Nr Skipton (During winter months open
weekends only)
Tel: (075 672) 295
Burton-upon-Trent *Staffordshire*
Town Hall
Tel: (0283) 45369
Bury St. Edmunds *Suffolk*
Abbey Gardens.
Winter address: Thingoe House,
Northgate Street
Tel: (0284) 64667
Buxton *Derbyshire*
St Ann's Well, The Crescent
Tel: (0298) 5106
Cambridge *Cambridgeshire*
Wheeler Street
Tel: (0223) 58977; 53363
(weekends)
Canterbury *Kent*
22 St Peters Street
Tel (0227) 66567
Carlisle *Cumbria*
Old Town Hall, Green Market
Tel: (0228) 25396/25517
Castle Donington
Derbyshire
East Midlands Airport
Tel: Derby (0332) 810621
Castleton *Isle of Man*
Commissioners' Office,
Parliament Square
Tel: (062 482) 3518
Chard *Somerset*
Taylors Travel, Fore Street
Tel: (046 06) 4414
Cheadle Hulme
Greater Manchester
Oak House, 20 Station Road
Tel: 061-486 0283
Cheddar *Somerset*
The Library, Union Street
Tel: (0934) 742769
Cheltenham Spa
Gloucestershire
Minicipal Offices, Promenade
Tel: (0242) 22878/21333
Chester *Cheshire*
Town Hall
Tel: (0244) 40144 Ext 2111
Chesterfield *Derbyshire*
Central Library, Corporation Street
Tel: (0246) 32047/32661
Chichester *West Sussex*
Council House, North Street

Tel: (0243) 82226
Christchurch *Dorset*
Caravan, Saxon Square
Tel: (020 15) 4321
Church Stretton *Shropshire*
Shropshire Hills, Church Street
Tel: (069 42) 2535
Cirencester *Gloucestershire*
Cotswold Publicity Association,
Corn Hall, Market Place
Tel: (0285) 4180
Clacton on Sea *Essex*
Amenities & Recreation
Department Town Hall
Station Road
Tel: (0255) 25501
Clacton on Sea *Essex*
Central Seafront
Tel: (0255) 23400
Cleethorpes
Humberside
Alexandra Road
Tel: (0472) 67472/66111
Clitheroe *Lancashire*
Church Street
Tel: (0200) 25566
Coalville *Leicestershire*
Coalville Library,
60/62 New Broadway Precinct
Tel: (0530) 32093
Cockermouth *Cumbria*
Riverside Car Park
Tel: (0900) 822634
Colchester *Essex*
4 Trinity Street
Tel: (0206) 46379
Congleton *Cheshire*
Market Square
Tel: (026 02) 71095
Coniston *Cumbria*
Main Car Park
Tel: (096 64) 533
Corbridge *Northumberland*
Vivars Pele Tower
Tel: (043 471) 2815
Coventry *West Midlands*
36 Broadgate
Tel: (0203) 25555/20084/51717
Cranbrook *Kent*
Cranbrook Tourism & Craft
Information Centre, Vestry Hall
Tel: (058 04) 2538
Crewe *Cheshire*
Crewe & Nantwich Borough Council
Delamere House, Delamere Street
Tel: (0270) 583191
Cromer *Norfolk*
North Lodge Park
Tel: (0263) 2497
Danby *North Yorkshire*
Danby Lodge National Park Centre
Lodge Lane, Danby, Whitby
(During winter months open weekends
only)
Tel: Castleton (028 76) 654
Darlington *Co. Durham*
Darlington District Library, Crown
Street
Tel: (0325) 69858/62934
Dartmouth *Devon*
The Quay
Tel: (080 43) 2281
Dawlish *Devon*
The Lawn
Tel: (0626) 863589
Deal *Kent*
Time Ball Tower, Sea Front
Tel: (030 45) 61161 Ext 263
Dedham *Essex*

C.P.R.E. Countryside Centre,
Duchy Barn, Dedham, Colchester
Tel: Colchester (0206) 323447
Derby *Derbyshire*
Reference Library, Central Library, The
Strand
Tel: (0332) 31111 Ext 21856; 48572
(weekdays 17.00-19.00 & Sats)
Doncaster *South Yorkshire*
Doncaster Central Library, Waterdale.
Tel: (0302) 69123
Dover *Kent*
Townall Street
Tel: (0304) 205108
Dover *Kent*
Portakabin, A2 Diversion, Whitfield
(0304) 206941
Douglas *Isle of Man*
13 Victoria Street
Tel: (0264) 4323
Droitwich *Worcestershire*
Norbury House, Friar Street
Tel: (090 57) 2352
Dudley *West Midlands*
39 Churchill Precinct
Tel: (0384) 50333
Dunstable *Bedfordshire*
Queensway Hall, Vernon Place
Tel: (0582) 603326
Durham *Co. Durham*
13 Claypath
Tel: (0385) 3720
Eastbourne *East Sussex*
3 Cornfield Terrace
Tel: (0323) 27474
Eastbourne *East Sussex*
Shopping Precinct, Terminus Road
Tel: (0323) 27474
Eastbourne *East Sussex*
Lower Promenade, Grand Parade
Tel: (0323) 27474
East Grinstead *West Sussex*
East Court, Vollege Lane
Tel: (0342) 23636
Egremont *Cumbria*
Lowes Court Gallery, 12/13 Main Street
Tel: (0946) 820693
Ely *Cambridgeshire*
24 St Mary's Street
Tel (0353) 3311
Exeter *Devon*
Civic Centre, Dix's Field
Tel: (0392) 77888 Ext 2297
Exmouth *Devon*
Alexandra Terrace
Tel: (039 52) 3744
Falmouth *Cornwall*
Town Hall, The Moor
Tel: (0326) 312300
Farnham *Surrey*
Farnham Locality Office, South Street
Tel: Godalming (048 68) 4014 Ext 214/5
Faversham *Kent*
Fleur de lis Heritage Centre, Preston
Street
Tel (079 582) 4542
Felixtowe *Suffolk*
No. 2 Dock Gate, Felixtowe Docks
Tel: (039 42) 78359
Felixtowe *Suffolk*
91 Undercliff Road West
Tel: (039 42) 6129/3303
Filey *North Yorkshire*
John Street
Tel: Scarborough (0723) 512204
Fleetsbridge *Dorset*
Camper Advisory Service, Camping
Reception & Information Centre,
Fleetsbridge, Poole
Tel Poole (020 13) 85436
Fleetwood *Lancashire*
Marine Hall, Esplanade
Tel: (039 17) 71141
Folkestone *Kent*
Harbour Street
Tel: (0303) 58594
*Folkestone *Kent*
The Precinct

Tel: (0303) 53840
Fordingbridge *Hampshire*
Avon Valley Travel Services, 52 High
Street
Tel: (0425) 54410
Fowey *Cornwall*
Toyne Carter & Co Ltd,
1 Albert Quay
Tel: (072 683) 3274)
Gateshead *Tyne & Wear*
Central Library,
Prince Consort Road
Tel: (0632) 773478
Glastonbury *Somerset*
7 Northload Street
Tel: (0458) 32954
Glenridding *Cumbria*
Beckside Car Park,
Glenridding, Penrith
Tel: (085 32) 414
Gloucester *Gloucestershire*
Gloucester Leisure Centre,
Station Road
Tel: (0452) 36498/36788
Grange over Sands
Cumbria
Victoria Hall
Tel: (044 84) 4331
Grasmere *Cumbria*
Broadgate Newsagency
Tel: (096 65) 245
Great Yarmouth *Norfolk*
Dept Of Publicity,
14 Regent Street
Tel: (0493) 4313/4
Great Yarmouth *Norfolk*
Marine Parade
Tel: (0493) 2195
Guildford *Surrey*
Civic Hall
Tel: (0483) 67314
Guiseborough *Cleveland*
Chapel Beck Gallery,
10/12 Fountain Street
Tel: (028 73) 35240
Hailsham *East Sussex*
Hailsham Library Western Road
Tel: (0323) 840604
Halifax *West Yorkshire*
The Piece Hall
Tel: (0422) 68725
Haltwhistle *Northumberland*
Council Offices, Sycamore Street
Tel: (049 82) 351
Harrogate *North Yorkshire*
Royal Baths Assembly Rooms,
Crescent Road
Tel: (0423) 65912
Hartlepool *Cleveland*
Victory Square
Tel: Hartlepool 68366
Winter address: Leisure & Amenities
Department, Civic Centre
Tel: (0429) 66522
Harwich *Essex*
Parkeston Quay
Tel: (025 55) 6139
Hastings *East Sussex*
4 Robertson Terrace
Tel: (0424) 424242
Hawkeshead *Cumbria*
Main Car Park
Tel: (096 66) 525
Haworth *West Yorkshire*
Mill Hey, Nr Keighley
(During winter months open Sats, Suns
& Weds)
Tel: (0535) 42329
Greater Manchester
Hazel Grove
Civic Hall, London Road,
Hazel Grove, Stockport
Tel: 061-456 4195
Hebden Bridge
West Yorkshire
1 Bridge Gate
Tel: (042 284) 3831
Hemel Hempstead
Hertfordshire

Pavilion, Marlowes
Tel: (0442) 64451
Henly-on-Thames
Oxfordshire
West Hill House, 4 West Street
Tel: (049 12) 2626
Hereford *Herefordshire*
Trinity Almshouses Car Park
Tel: (0432) 68430
Herne Bay *Kent*
Council Offices, 1 Richmond Street
Tel: (022 73) 66031
Hertford *Hertfordshire*
Vale House, Cowbridge
Tel: Hertford 54977
Hexham *Northumberland*
Manor Office
Tel: (0434) 5225
High Wycombe
Buckinghamshire
Wycombe District Council,
Queen Victoria Road
Tel: (0494) 26100
Hinckley *Leicestershire*
Hinckley Library, Lancaster Road
Tel: (0455) 35106/30852
Horncastle *Lincolnshire*
Town Hall, Boston Road
Tel: (065 82) 3513
Hornsea *Humberside*
The Floral Hall
Tel: (040 12) 2919
Hove *East Sussex*
Town Hall, Church Road
Tel: (0273) 775400
Hull *Humberside*
Central Library, Albion Street
Tel: (0482) 223344
Hull *Humberside*
Corporation Road, King George Dock,
Hedon Road
Tel (0482) 702118
Hunstanton *Norfolk*
Le Strange Terrace
Tel: (048 53) 2610
Huyton *Merseyside*
Municipal Buildings, Archway Road
Tel: 051-489 6000
Ilfracombe *Devon*
The Promenade
Tel: (0271) 63001
Ilkeston *Derbyshire*
Ilkeston Library, Market Place
Tel (0602) 303361 Ext 289
Ipswich *Suffolk*
Town Hall, Princes Street
Tel: (0473) 55851
Ironbridge *Shropshire*
The Iron Bridge Tollhouse
Tel: Telford (0952) 882753
Jarrow *Tyne & Wear*
Jarrow Hall, Church Bank
Tel: (0632) 892106
Kendal *Cumbria*
Town Hall
Tel: (0539) 23649 Ext 253
Kenilworth *Warwickshire*
The Library, 11 Smalley Place
Tel: (0926) 52595
Keswick *Cumbria*
Moot Hall, Market Square
Tel: (0595) 72645
Winter address: Council Offices, Main
Street
Kettering *Northamptonshire*
Information Centre,
Public Library, Sheep Street
Tel: (0536) 82143/85211
Kingsbridge *Devon*
The Quay
Tel: (0548) 3195
King's Lynn *Norfolk*
Town Hall, Saturday Market Place
Tel: (0553) 61241
Kington *Herefordshire*
Council Offices, 2 Mill Street
Tel: (054 43) 202
Kirkby *Merseyside*
Municipal Buildings, Kirkby, Liverpool

Tel: 051-548 6555
Kirkby Lonsdale *Cumbria*
The Art Stone (Kirkby Lonsdale) Ltd.,
18 Main Street
Tel: (0468) 71603
Knaresborough
North Yorkshire
Market Place.
Knutsford *Cheshire*
Council Offices, Toft Road
Tel: (0565) 2611
Lancaster *Lancashire*
7 Dalton Square
Tel: (0524) 2878
Laxey *Isle of Man*
Commissioners Office, New Road
Tel: (0624) 86241
Leamington Spa
Warwickshire
Southgate Lodge, Jephson Gardens
Tel: (0926) 311470/27072
Ext 216
Ledbury *Herefordshire*
St. Katherines, High Street
Tel: (0531) 2461/3429
Leeds *West Yorkshire*
Central Library, Calverley Street
Tel: (0532) 462453/4
Leek *Staffordshire*
18 St Edward Street
Tel: (0538) 385509/385181
Leicester *Leicestershire*
12 Bishop Street
Tel: (0533) 20644
Leominster *Herefordshire*
Leominster Library, South Street
Tel: (0568) 2384
Lewes *East Sussex*
187 High Street
Tel: (079 16) 6151 Ext 57
Leyburn *North Yorkshire*
Central Garage, Market Place
Tel: (096 92) 3103
Lichfield *Staffordshire*
9 Breadmarket Street
Tel: (054 32) 52109
Lincoln *Lincolnshire*
90 Bailgate
Tel: (0522) 29828
Lincoln *Lincolnshire*
City Hall, Beaumont Fee
Tel: (0522) 32151
Littlehampton *West Sussex*
Council Offices, Church Street
Tel: (090 64) 6133
Liverpool *Merseyside*
187 St Johns Centre, Elliot Street
Tel: 051-709 3631/8681
London *SW1*
London Tourist Board,
26 Grosvenor Gardens
Tel: 01-730 0791
London *SW1*
London Tourist Board
Adjacent Platform 15,
Victoria Station
Tel: 01-730 0791
London *SW1*
British Tourist Authority
Welcome to Britain' Tourist
Information Centre,
64 St James Street
Tel: 01-629 9191
Telex: 21231
London *Tower of London*
London Tourist Board
Tourist Information Centre, Tower of
London
Tel: 01-730 0791
London *Heathrown*
Underground Station
London Tourist Board,
Tourist Information Centre,
Underground Station,
Heathrow Airport
Tel: 01-730 0791
London *Harrods*
London Tourist Board,
Tourist Information Centre,

Harrods, Knightsbridge, SW1
Tel: 01-730 0791
London Selfridges
London Tourist Board,
Oxford Street, W1
Tel: 01-730 0791
London City of London
St. Paul's Churchyard, EC4
Tel: 01-606 3030 Ext 6456/7
London Greenwich
King William Walk, Cutty Sark
Gardens SE10
Tel: 01-858 6376
London Hillingdon
Civic Centre, High Street,
Uxbridge, Middlesex
Tel: Uxbridge 0600
London Richmond
Old Richmond Town Hall,
Hill Street, Richmond, Surrey
Tel: 892 0032
London Thamesmead
Harrow Manor Way, SE2
Tel: 01-310 5223/4
London Tower Hamlets
88 Roman Road, E2
Tel: 980 3749
London Twickenham
58/60 York Street, Twickenham,
Middlesex
Tel: 01-892 0032
Long Eaton Derbyshire
Long Eaton Library.
Tarnworth Road, Long Eaton,
Nottingham
Tel: (060 76) 5426/7
Longtown Cumbria
21 Swan Street, Longtown, Carlisle
Tel: (022 879) 201
Looe Cornwall
The Guildhall, Fore Street,
East Looe
Tel: (050 36) 2072
Loughborough Leicestershire
John Storer House, Wards End
Tel: (0509) 20131
Louth Lincolnshire
East Lindsay District Council,
Area Office, Town Hall, Eastgate
Tel: (0507) 2391
Lowestoft Suffolk
The Esplanade
Tel: (0502) 65989
Lowestoft Suffolk
Town Hall, High Street
Tel: (0502) 62111
Ludlow Shropshire
13 Castle Street
Tel: (0584) 3857
Luton Bedfordshire
25 George Street
Tel: (0582) 413237
Luton Bedfordshire
Central Library, Bridge Street
Tel: (0582) 32629
Lyme Regis Dorset
The Guildhall, Bridge Street
Tel: (029 74) 2138
Lyndhurst Hampshire
Camper Advisory Service,
Main Car Park
Tel: (042 128) 2269
Lynton & Lynmouth Devon
Lee Road
Tel: (059 85) 2225
Lytham St Annes Lancashire
The Square
Tel: (0253) 725610
Mablethorpe Lancashire
Foreshore Office,
Central Promenade
Tel: (052 13) 2496
Macclesfield Cheshire
Town Hall
Tel: (0625) 21955 Ext 114/5
Maidenhead Berkshire
Central Library, St Ives Road
Tel: (0628) 25657
Maidstone Kent

The Gatehouse, Old Palace Gardens
Tel: (0622) 671361
Malvern Worcestershire
Winter Gardens, Grange Road
Tel: (068 45) 4700
Manchester
Greater Manchester
Town Hall
Tel: 061-236 3377 Ext 433
Manchester
Greater Manchester
County Hall Extension,
Piccadilly Gardens
Tel: 061-247 3694
Manchester
Greater Manchester
Manchester International Airport
Tel: 061-437 5233
Margate Kent
Marine Terrace
Tel: Thanet (0843) 20241/2
Teletourist: (0843) 291540
Market Harborough
Leicestershire
Market Harborough Librarry,
53 The Square, Market Harborough,
Leicester
Tel: (0858) 2649
Maryport Cumbria
Maryport Maritime Museum,
1 Senhouse Street
Tel: (090 081) 3738
Matlock Bath Derbyshire
The Pavilion
Tel: (0629) 55082
Melton Mowbray
Leicestershire
Melton Carnegie Museum,
Thorpe End
Tel: (0664) 69946
Mere Wiltshire
The Square, Mere, Warminster
Tel: (074 786) 341
Middlesbrough Cleveland
125 Albert Road
Tel: (0642) 245750/245432
Ext 3580
Millom Cumbria
The Folk MUseum,
St Georges Road
Tel: (0908) 76311
Milton Keynes
Buckinghamshire
Milton Keynes Development
Corporation, Wavendon Tower,
Wavendon
Tel: (0908) 74000
Milton Keynes
Buckinghamshire
6 Church Street, Wolverton
Tel: (0908) 312581
Minehead Somerset
Market House, The Parade
Tel: (0643) 2624
Morecambe Lancashire
Marine Road Central
Tel: (0524) 414110/417120 Ext 249
Moreton-in-Marsh
Gloucestershire
Council Offices
Tel: (0608) 50881
Morley West Yorkshire
Leeds City Council, Town Hall, Morely,
Leeds
Tel: (0532) 535541
Nantwich Cheshire
Crewe & Nantwich Borough Council,
Beam Street
Tel: (0270) 63914
Nelson Lancashire
19/23 Leeds Road
Tel: (0282) 692890
Newark-on-Trent
Nottinghamshire
The Ossington, Beast Market Hill
Winter address:
The Palace, Appletongate
Tel: (0636) 71156
New Brighton Merseyside

The Pier
Tel: 051-639 3929
Newbury Berkshire
Newbury District Council,
Wharf Road
Tel: (0635) 42400/44000
Newcastle upon Tyne
Tyne & Wear
Central Library, Princess Square
Tel: (0632) 610691
Newhaven East Sussex
Car Ferry Terminal Car Park
Tel: (079 12) 4970
Newport Isle of Wight
21 High Street
Tel: (098 381) 4343
Newquay Cornwall
Cliff Road
Tel: (063 73) 4558/2119/2716/2822
Northampton
Northamptonshire
21 St Giles Street
Tel: (0604) 34881 Ext 404/537; 32054
(Sats 10.00-12.30)
Norwich Norfolk
14 Tombland
Tel: (0603) 20679/23445
Nottingham
Nottinghamshire
18 Milton Street
Tel: (0602) 40661
Nuneaton Warwickshire
Nuneaton Library, Church Street
Tel: (0682) 384027/8
Oakham Leicestershire
Oakham Library, Catmos Street
Tel: (0572) 2918
Oldham Greater Manchester
Greaves Street
Tel: 061-620 8930
Onchan Isle of Man
Onchan Village Commissioners Office,
79 Main Road
Tel: Douglas (0624) 22311/5564
Oswestry Shropshire
Caravan, Babbinswood, Nr Whittington
Tel: Whittington Castle (069 187) 488
Otley West Yorkshire
Council Offices, 8 Boroughgate
Tel: (094 34) 2241/2
Oxford Oxfordshire
St Aldates
Tel: (0865) 48707/49811
Paignton Devon
Festival Hall, Esplanade Road
Tel: (0803) 558383
Peel Isle of Man
Town Hall, Derby Road
Tel: (062 484) 842341
Penrith Cumbria
Robinsons School, Middlegate
Tel: (0768) 4671 Ext 33
Penzance Cornwall
Alverton Street
Tel: (0736) 2341
Pershore Worcestershire
37 High Street, Pershore, Worcester
Tel: (038 65) 2442
Peterborough
Cambridgeshire
Town Hall, Bridge Street
Tel: (0733) 63141
Peterborough
Cambridgeshire
Central Library, Broadway
Tel: (0733) 69105
Peterleee Co. Durham
Arts & Information Centre,
The Upper Chare
Tel: (0783) 864450
Pickering Yorkshire
North York Moors Hallway,
The Station
Tel: (0751) 72508
Plymouth Devon
Civic Centre
Tel: (0752) 68000
Plymouth Devon
Ferry Terminal, Millbay Docks

Tel: (0752) 68000
Poole Dorset
Arndale Centre
Tel: (020 13) 3322
Poole Dorset
Civic Centre
Tel (020 13) 5151
Pooley Bridge Cumbria
Eusemere Lodge Car Park,
Pooley Bridge, Penrith
Tel: 085 36) 530
Portbury Avon
Gordano Services, M5 Motorway,
Bristol
Tel: Pill (027 581) 3382
Port Erin Isle of Man
Commissioners Office, Station Road
Tel: 062 483) 2298
Port St Mary Isle of Man
Town Hall, Promenade
Tel: (0624) 832101
Portsmouth & Southsea
Hampshire
Continental Ferry Terminal,
Mile End Quay
Tel: (0705) 819688
Portsmouth & Southsea
Hampshire
Castle Buildings, Southsea
Tel: (0705) 26722
Portsmouth & Southsea
Hampshire
Civic Information Centre, Civic Offices,
Guildhall Square
Tel: (0705) 834092/3
Preston Lancashire
Town Hall, Lancaster Road
Tel: (0772) 53731
Prudhoe Northumberland
Council Offices, South Road
Tel: (0661) 32281
Ramsey Isle of Man
Town Hall, Parliament Square
Tel: (0624) 812228
Ramsgate Kent
The Ramsgate District Office,
Queen Street
Tel: Thanet (0843) 581261
Ramsgate Kent
South East England Tourist Board,
International Hoverport
Tel: Thanet (0843) 57115
Ravenglass Cumbria
Car Park, Ravenglass & Eskdale
Railway Station
Tel: (065 77) 278
Reading Berkshire
Civic Offices
Tel: (0734) 55911
Redcar Cleveland
Zetland Shipping Museum,
Esplanade
Tel: (064 93) 71921
Redditch Worcestershire
Kingfisher House
Tel: (0527) 60806
Reeth North Yorkshire
Swaledale Folk Museum
Richmond North Yorkshire
Friary Gardens, Queens Road
Tel: (0748) 3525
Winter address: Swale House,
Frenchgate
Tel: (0748) 4221
Rickmansworth Hertfordshire
17/23 High Street
Tel: Rickmansworth 76611
Ripon North Yorkshire
Market Place
Tel: (0765) 4625
Rochester Kent
85 High Street
Tel: Medway (0634) 43666
Ross-on-Wye Herefordshire
20 Broad Street
Tel: (0989) 2768
Rothbury Northumberland
United Auto Services Ltd., Malting
Yard, High Street, Rothbury, Morpeth

Tel: (0669) 20358
Rugby *Warwickshire*
Rugby Divisional Library,
St Matthews Street
Tel: (0788) 2687/71813
Runcorn *Cheshire*
57 Church Street
Tel: (092 85) 76776/69656
Ryde *Isle of Wight*
0983) 62905
Rye *East Sussex*
Council Offices, Ferry Road
Tel: (079 73) 2293/4
St Albans *Hertfordshire*
37 Chequer Street
Tel: (56) 64511
St Ives *Cornwall*
The Guildhall, Street an Pol
Tel: (073 670) 6297
Salcombe *Devon*
Salcombe Town Association,
Shadycombe Road
Tel: (054 884) 2736
Salisbury *Wiltshire*
Fisherton Street
Tel: (0722)) 27676/4432
Sandown *Isle of Wight*
The Esplanade
Tel: (098 384) 3886/4641
Scarborough *North Yorkshire*
St Nicholas Cliff
Tel: (0723) 72261
Scilly, Isles of
Town Hall, St Mary's
Tel: Scillonia (072 04) 536
Scunthorpe *Humberside*
Scunthorpe Central Library, Carlton
Street
Tel: (0724) 60161
Seaford *East Sussex*
The Downs, Sutton Road
Tel: (0323) 892224
Seahouses *Northumberland*
Main Car Park, Seafield Road
Tel: (0665) 720774
Seaton *Devon*
The Esplanade
Tel: (0297) 21660
Settle *North Yorkshire*
Town Hall, Market Place
Tel: (072 92) 3617
Shanklin *Isle of Wight*
67 High Street
Tel: (098 386) 2942/4334
Sheerness *Kent*
Bridge Street Car Park
Nr. Sheerness Docks, Sheppey
Tel: (079 56) 5324
Sheerness *Kent*
Swale District Council, Sea Front
Tel: (079 56) 2395
Sheffield *South Yorkshire*
Civic Information Office,
Surrey Street
Tel: (0742) 734760
Sheringham *Norfolk*
Station Car Park, Station Road
Tel: (026 382) 4329
Shrewsbury *Shropshire*
The Square
Tel: (0743) 52019
Sidmouth *Devon*
Esplanade
Tel: (039 55) 6441
Silloth *Cumbria*
Central Garage, Waver Street
Tel: (0965) 31276
Skegness *Lincolnshire*
Tower Esplanade
Tel: (0754) 4821 (summer)
4761 (winter)
Skegness *Lincolnshire*
Council Offices, North Parade
Tel (0754) 5441
Solihull *West Midlands*
Library Theatre Box Office Homer Road
Tel: 021-705 0060
Southampton *Hampshire*
Above Bar Shopping Precinct

Tel: (0703) 23855 Ext 615
Southport *Lancashire*
Cambridge Arcade
Tel: (0704) 33133/40404
South Shields *Tyne & Wear*
South Foreshore
Tel: (0632) 557411
Southwaite *Cumbria*
M6 Service Area,
Southwaite, Carlisle
Tel: (069 93) 445
Southwold *Suffolk*
Waveney District Council,
Town Hall
Tel: (0502) 722366
Spalding *Lincolnshire*
Ayscoughfee Hall,
Churchgate
Tel: (0775) 5468
Spilsby *Lincolnshire*
Council Offices, 41b High Street
Tel: (079 02) 2301
Stafford *Staffordshire*
Borough Hall, Eastgate Street
Tel: (0785) 3181 Ext 244
Stamford *Lincolnshire*
Council Offices, St Mary's Hill
Tel: (0780) 4444
Stockport *Greater Manchester*
9 Princes Street
Tel: 061-480 0315
Stoke-on-Trent *Staffordshire*
Central Library,
Bethesda Street, Hanley
Tel: (0782) 21242/25108/23122/263568
Stratford upon Avon
Warwickshire
Judith Shakespeare's House, 1 High
Street
Tel: (0789) 3127/66175/66185
Stroud *Gloucestershire*
Council Offices, High Street
Tel: (045 36) 4252
Sudbury *Suffolk*
Sudbury Library, Market Hill
Tel: (078 73) 72092/76029
Sutton Bank *North Yorkshire*
National Park Centre,
Sutton Bank, Sutton,
Nr Helmsley
Tel: (084 56) 426
Swadlincote *Derbyshire*
Swadlincote Library, Civic Way,
Swadlincote, Burton-upon-Trent
Tel: Burton-upon-Trent (0283) 217701
Swanage *Dorset*
The White House, Shore Road
Tel: (092 92) 2885
Swindon, *Wiltshire*
32 The Arcade,
David Murray, John Building,
Brunel Centre
Tel: (0793) 30328/26161 Ext 518
Tamworth *Staffordshire*
Minicipal Offices, Church Street
Tel: (0827) 3561
Taunton *Somerset*
Taunton Area Library,
Corporation Street
Tel: (0823) 84077/53424
Torquay *Devon*
Vaughan Parade
Tel: (0803) 27428
Totnes *Devon*
Totnes Publicity Association
The Plains
Tel: (0803) 863168
Truro *Cornwall*
Municipal Buildings,
Boscawen Street
Tel: (0872) 4555
Tunbridge Wells *Kent*
Information Bureau, Town Hall
Tel: (0892) 26121 Ext 163
Tynemouth *Tyne & Wear*
Grand Parade
North Shields (089 45) 70251
Ulverston *Cumbria*

The Centre, 17 Fountain Street
Tel: (0229) 52299
Upton upon Severn
Worcestershire
69 Old Street
Tel: (068 46) 2318
Ventnor *Isle of Wight*
34 High Street
Tel: (0983) 853625
Walsingham *Norfolk*
Shirehall Museum, Common Place
Tel: (032 872) 510
Walton-on-Thames *Surrey*
Elmbridge Borough Council
Town Hall, New Zealand Avenue
Tel: Walton-on-Thames 25141
Walton on the Naze *Essex*
Mill Lane
Tel: Frinton-on-Sea (066 478) 5542
Warrington *Lancashire*
80 Sankey Street
Tel: (0925) 36501
Warwick *Warwickshire*
Court House, Jury Street
Tel: (0926) 42212
Wellington *Somerset*
Bowermans Travel Agency Ltd.,
6 South Street
Tel: (082 347) 2716
Wells *Somerset*
Town Hall, Market Place
Tel: (0749) 72552
Weymouth *Dorset*
Publicity Office,
12 The Esplanade
Tel: (030 57) 72444
Whitby *North Yorkshire*
New Quay Road
Tel: (0947) 2674
Whitehaven *Cumbria*
Market Place
Tel: (0946) 5678
Whitely Bay *Tyne & Wear*
Promenade
Tel: (0632) 524494
Whitstable *Kent*
1 Tankerton Road
Tel: (0227) 272233
Widnes *Cheshire*
Municipal Buildings. Kingsway
Tel: 051-424 2061
Wigston Magna *Leicestershire*
Wigston Magna Library, Bull Head
Street
Tel: Leicester (0533) 887381
Wincanton *Somerset*
The Library, 7 Carrington Way
Tel: (0963) 32173
Winchester *Hampshire*
The Guildhall
Tel: (0962) 68166, 65408 (Sats.)
Windermere *Cumbria*
Victoria Street
Tel: (096 62) 4561
Windsor *Berkshire*
Windsor Central Station
Tel: Windsor 52010
Woodhall Spa *Lincolnshire*
Caravan Site Office, Jubilee Park,
Stixwould Road
Tel: (0526) 52448
Woolacombe & Morthoe
North Devon
Hall '70 Beach Road
Tel: (027 187) 553
Wooler *Northumberland*
Padgepool Place Car Park
Tel: (066 82) 602
Worcester *Worcestershire*
Guildhall
Tel: (0905) 23471
Workington *Cumbria*
Carnegie Theatre & Arts Centre, Finkle
Street
Tel: (0900) 2122
Worthing *West Sussex*
Town Hall, Chapel Road
Tel: (0903) 204226
Yarmouth *Isle of Wight*

The Quay
Tel: (0983) 760015
York *North Yorkshire*
De Grey Rooms, Exhibition Square
Tel: (0904) 21756

Scotland:
BORDERS
Coldstream
Information Centre,
Henderson Park
Tel: (0890) 2607
Hawick
Volunteer Park
Tel: (0450) 2547
Jedburgh
Scottish Tourist Board
Information Centre, Murray's Green
Tel: (083 56) 3435
Kelso
Turret House
Tel: (057 32) 3464
Melrose
(Joint with NTS)
Priorwood Near Abbey
Tel: (089 682) 2555
Peebles
High Street
Tel: (0721) 20138
Selkirk
Sir Walter Scott Courtroom
Market Price
Tel: (7050) 20054
DUMFRIES AND GALLOWAY
Castle Douglas
Information Centre, Markethill
Tel: (0556) 2611
Dumfries
Information Centre, Whitsands
Tel: (0387) 3862
Gatehouse of Fleet
Information Centre, Car Park
Tel: (055 74) 212
Gretna
Information Centre, Annan Road
Tel: (046 13) 834
Kirkcudbright
Information Centre, Harbour Square
Tel: (0557) 30494
Moffat
Information Centre, Church Gate
Tel: (0683) 20620
Newton Stewart
Dumfries and Galloway Tourist
Association,
Douglas House, Newton Stewart
Tel: (0671) 2549
Newton Stewart
Information Centre,
Dashwood SquareTel: (0671) 2431
Stranraer
Information Bureau, Port Rodie
Tel: (0776) 2595

LOTHIAN
Dunbar
Information Centre,
Town House, High Street
Tel: (0368) 63353
Edinburgh
Scottish Tourist Board,
5 Waverley Bridge, Edinburgh
Tel: 031-332 2433
Telex: 72272
Linlithgow
The Vennel Car Park
Tel: (050 684) 4600
Middleton
Tourist Information Caravan, A7 by
Middleton Mains Farm
Tel: Heriot (087 535) 262
North Berwick
Information Centre, Quality Street
Tel: (0620) 2197
Pathhead
Tourist Information Caravan,
Hope Cottage
Tel: Ford (0875) 320525